ENDORSEMENTS

We live in a world where widespread assertions foster misunderstanding and confusion about the Bible and human sexuality. These assertions are often hard to refute because we lack the resources to put them to the test. This is where this excellent work by Rubel Shelly can be such a blessing. Rubel approaches this discussion of LBGTQ claims with both a love for people and for truth. With scholarly research and sharp analysis, Rubel addresses many of the assertions and assumptions that create this confusion. If you have questions, are open to examining the evidence, and want to be better informed on this topic, this book is for you.

Jimmy Adcox
Minister at Southwest Church of Christ, Jonesboro, AR
Associate Director of Learning Communities with Renew

There is no fiercer spiritual battleground than the cultural malaise of sexuality. Shelly's tour-de-force of the Bible's view on sexuality is foundational for our church's traditional stance on sexuality. He helps us interact with both Scripture and culture with quotes as wide-ranging as Richard Dawkins, J.K. Rowling, Psychology Today, and the Mishnah. It is both well documented and well written.

Dr. Mark E. Moore
Teaching Pastor at Christ's Church of the Valley, Phoenix

Every era of Christian history has its issue—a dominant cultural objection to Biblical truth—and in our time, the LGBTQ+ claims are that issue. In this book, Dr. Rubel Shelly serves God's purpose in our own generation by speaking ably to those claims. With the research of a scholar, the wisdom of an apologist and the compassion of a pastor, he guides us in answering our LGBTQ+ neighbors, friends, and family members with grace and truth. Though "the ink has been dry on this topic for several centuries now," Dr. Shelly helps us articulate those written-long-ago words—God's Word—in relevant ways. This book will be an invaluable resource for every Christian.

Matt Proctor
President of Ozark Christian College

Some are hearing that we must now choose between loving people well or taking scripture seriously. Dr. Rubel Shelly offers an insightful way forward from that false dichotomy. With the mind of an accomplished academic and the heart of a church servant, Rubel dives deep to make accessible the theological and historical data that has been overlooked or mis-construed by recent revisionists. Claims that the biblical texts could not have applied, and therefore do not now apply, to loving and committed same-sex relationships are thoroughly considered with strong historical, literary, artistic and biblical testimony. This book emphasizes the "grace and truth" of our Lord as followers of Jesus are sensitively encouraged toward holiness.

Dr. Doug Peters
Senior Minister, Grace Crossing
A Community Church of Christ, Conroe, TX

With both theological acumen and the heart of a caring pastor, Dr. Shelly joins what is perhaps the most important—and challenging—conversation in the current moment of the life of the church. He neither fears nor ignores the prevailing arguments of contemporary culture, but engages them with requisite consideration. His approach is openly and diligently biblical theological, and his main concern is the faithfulness of those who follow Jesus, for whom he writes this book. Dr. Shelly goes to great lengths to avoid simplistic moralizing and politicizing of the issues; he seeks, instead, to promote a biblical way of life that is God-honoring. Every Jesus follower would do well to read this book carefully; it is an especially important read for Christian pastors, preachers, evangelists, and teachers.

James D. Dvorak, PhD
Vice President Academic,
Professor of New Testament
McMaster Divinity College

I needed this book. It provides a comprehensive, scholarly resource that reinforces my simplistic position that God created just two genders. More importantly, I need Dr. Shelly's frequent reminder to "speak the truth in love" regardless of how outrageous the challenges of our culture seem to be. Every church leader would be wise to have several copies of this book available to share with those who have family members struggling with gender dysphoria.

Bob Russell
Retired Sr. Minister, Southeast Christian Church, Louisville, Kentucky

Americans are having important, sometimes volatile, conversations about the role of the Christian faith as it relates to LGBTQIAA persons. Dr. Shelly's new book is a must-read for any pastor or church leader desiring a clear understanding of the best of the traditional Jewish-Christian approach to this tender topic. *Male and Female God Created Them* will be part of many Protestant congregations for years to come because Shelly seeks to enter the current "culture wars" as a voice of charity and clarity.

Dr. Joshua Graves
Lead Minister Otter Creek Church,
author of The Simple Secret *(2023)*

If anyone wants to explore a credible and sensitive case for a traditional Christian sexual ethic in the context of the Bible's narrative, this book offers a competent, comprehensive, and compassionate case. Rubel writes from his own principled understanding of the biblical text without irate defensiveness or mere dismissal of other viewpoints. He fairly engages leading influencers within the church. While this work has many beneficial aspects (including a Q&A in the last chapter that provides brief responses to questions addressed in depth in the previous chapters), some of the more helpful are his analysis of Genesis 1-2, the Greco-Roman background, and the theology of marriage. Perhaps most importantly, Rubel draws on his years of pastoral experience as a minister and professor to navigate difficult circumstances with sincerity, grace, and conviction. As the church attentively listens to the

LGBTQ+ community and welcomes dialogue, it would be a mistake to ignore or neglect this significant offering by a seasoned pastor and scholar.

John Mark Hicks
Professor of Theology
Lipscomb University

I wish I could put a copy of *Male and Female God Created Them* in the hands of every Christian pastor, minister, teacher, and counselor! As many Christian leaders have come to realize, the LGBTQ+ challenge is the question of our age. We must meet this challenge! And *Male and Female God Created Them* is the book for just such a time as this. Brilliant! Penetrating! Courageous! Yet… fair, measured, and compassionate. Shelly's analysis and critique of the "affirming" position blows away the rhetorical dust and smoke of the biblical revisionists and gets to the heart of the matter. His positive explanation and defense of the "traditional" (that is, biblical) view of marriage and sex is the best I've read in a long time. If you have time to read only one book on this subject, read this one! Then read it again!

Ron Highfield
Professor, Religion & Philosophy Division
Seaver College, Pepperdine University

With concern, compassion, and knowledge of Scripture and the LGBTQ+ community, Dr. Rubel Shelly presents the concerns that are central to LGBTQ+ conversation. This one volume not only provides explanations of the major, relevant, biblical texts, but also practical suggestions for individuals and churches as they navigate this topic. The book will continue to serve as a valuable resource in years to come for those who seek answers to difficult questions.

Dr. Jerry Jones, ThD
Leader of Marriage Matters

In our age, a book on the hot button issues of sexuality that tries assiduously hard to be biblically based, while also being loving and sensitive to those living through such issues is hard to find. Rubel Shelly has produced that book. It deserves careful reading and loving discussions.

Mark Lanier
Author, Lawyer, and Minister
Founder, Lanier Law Firm

Rubel Shelly is an absolute treasure to the cause of Christ. In this timely book, Rubel brings a winning combination of scholarly rigor, discernment, and a redemptive aim. God continues to use Rubel in calling His people to the noble journey of being light in the darkness. Absorb this invaluable book, share it, and prepare to be encouraged, challenged, and equipped.

Ronnie Norman
Senior Minister at First Colony Church of Christ

In our world today, there is so much confusion and pain associated with the tender matters of our bodies and sexuality. There's also no shortage of complexity and nuance which makes such things all the more daunting to address today in communities of faith, not to mention the public arena in general.

We're in desperate need of trustworthy conversation-partners when it comes to processing the teachings of Jesus and the rest of Scripture in regard to these matters. In more than 30 years of full-time ministry, I've not found a resource more helpful in these matters than Dr. Rubel Shelly's book.

It's stunning in its thorough assessment of the pertinent Scriptures in their context. It's insightful in its assessment of the various cultural narratives in which all of us are swimming today. It's preeminently gracious and practical when it comes to suggesting ways to move forward. I'm so thankful to have it as a resource. I believe you will be, too.

Chris Seidman
Lead Minister at The Branch Church, Dallas, Texas

Rubel Shelly is the rarest of scholars: biblically sound, humble, and compassionate. *Male and Female God Created Them* is a must read for any seminarian, pastor, youth worker, teacher, or counselor searching for a well-researched historical and biblical context for understanding today's gender issues.

Matthew Sleeth, MD
Author of Hope Always, 24/6, *and* Reforesting Faith

Highlighters and stones. When (not if) you read Dr. Shelly's comprehensive work on gender specificity and biblical sexuality you will need highlighters, and you will think of stones. You will need a highlighter to underscore important ideas (and don't be surprised if many of the pages are almost all highlighted). You will also realize that there is no stone unturned on this subject. The book unpacks the specific passages in the Bible that touch on this subject, but the work is much larger than that. The work is exegetically keen, theologically astute, scientifically accurate, logically impeccable, culturally aware and agile, clearly written, and compassionately sensitive. So many works that argue the "other side" have allowed some nuance of the historical background to override the straightforward exegetical foreground. Dr. Shelly does not fall prey to such erroneous hermeneutical fallacies. The book deals with the macro issues of God's created order all the way to answering cultural objections today to biblical sexuality. Keep your highlighter close and be ready to turn over all the stones.

Dr. Mark Scott
Lead Minister at Park Plaza Christian Church
Online and Graduate Studies Professor at Ozark Christian College

In Loving Memory of My Wife

Myra

(died August 13, 2023)

Always the first editor of my writings

Always my faithful partner in ministry

Always the love of my life

MALE & FEMALE GOD CREATED THEM

Joplin, Missouri

MALE AND FEMALE GOD CREATED THEM:
A Biblical Review of LGBTQ+ Claims

Copyright © 2023

Rubel Shelly

Author Photo Credit: Lily Arms Studio

ISBN: 978-0-89900-052-7 (hardcover)
ISBN: 978-0-89900-051-0 (paperback)
ISBN: 978-0-89900-053-4 (ebook)

On the web at www.collegepress.com

All Scripture quotations, unless otherwise indicated, are taken from the Holy Bible, New International Version®, NIV®. Copyright ©1973, 1978, 1984, 2011 by Biblica, Inc.™ Used by permission of Zondervan. All rights reserved worldwide. www.zondervan.com The "NIV" and "New International Version" are trademarks registered in the United States Patent and Trademark Office by Biblica, Inc.™

TABLE OF CONTENTS

Preface _____ 5

1. The Goal of This Book: Grace and Truth _____ 9
2. Is It Possible to Think Someone Is Morally Wrong Without Being a Bigot? _____ 37
3. Putting Sex in Its Proper Place _____ 57
4. Look What We've Done to Marriage! _____ 67
   Excursus: Our Sin Against Singles _____ 77
5. How Important Is the Genesis Creation Story? _____ 91
6. Have We Missed the Point of All Those Old Testament Texts for All These Centuries? _____ 125
7. Why Didn't Jesus Talk About Same-Sex Issues? _____ 151
   Excursus: Sex(es) and Gender(s): The Other 72 Genders? _____ 167
8. The Greco-Roman World of Corrupted Sexuality _____ 183
9. Committed Same-Sex Relationships in Greek Culture _____ 201
10. Committed Same-Sex Relationships in Roman Culture _____ 223
    Excursus: The Book of Acts: A Method for "Changing the Rules"? _____ 245
11. The Pauline Texts (Part 1): Romans 1:18-32 _____ 257
12. The Pauline Texts (Part 2): 1 Corinthians 6:9-11 and 1 Timothy 1:9-11 _____ 281
13. Inner Strength from the Holy Spirit _____ 301
14. The Value of Christian Community _____ 317
15. Questions People Ask _____ 337

Appendices
   Appendix A: Single to God's Glory _____ 373
   Appendix B: Married to God's Glory _____ 383
   Appendix C: Sexually Purity and the People of God _____ 393
   Appendix D: Review of "1946" _____ 397

Special Notes in Chapters _____ 405
Scripture Index _____ 413
Index of Persons & Subjects _____ 417
Index of Authors _____ 425
Acknowledgments _____ 427

A word about terminology . . .

I have tried to be consistent in making the contemporary distinction between the nouns *homosexual* and *homosexuality* on the one hand and terms such as *same-sex behaviors, same-sex intercourse,* or *gay/lesbian lifestyle* on the other. Consistent with contemporary usage, I understand the former to be an orientation or preference – without presuming actual involvement; thus, for example, one can be a "celibate homosexual" or "sexually active homosexual" in the same way another may be a "celibate heterosexual" or "sexually active heterosexual." Used as an adjective, references to *homosexual acts* or *homosexual relationships* and *same-sex acts/ relationships* are taken to be equivalent.

Different ways of referring to one's primary sexual attraction versus actual lived experience creates confusion at several levels. The confused discussions around the use of the word "homosexual" in the 1946 edition of the Revised Standard Version is a case in point. (See Appendix D of this book for more information.)

There is an even greater terminology problem in daring to use words such as "straight," "gay," "civil union," "same-sex marriage," "sex," "gender" – whatever terms of reference are current when you pick up this book. The language in this discussion changes rapidly, and my failure to use your preferred term should not be taken as an insult to you or a rejection of your value as a person. Please know that I will not use a particular term with the intent of being offensive to anyone who chooses to read the book. Even if I am successful in avoiding what I regard as disrespectful terms of reference, I still may not use the term(s) you prefer in the ways you would have chosen. A word I use in a given sentence may be standard language in these discussions but offensive to you. Please know that it was not chosen with that intent. Please don't let that keep you from reading.

Preface

When she asked me what I believed about same-sex relationships, my quick answer was to say, "The ink has been dry on that topic for several centuries now!"

As it turned out, the question was anything but theoretical. Someone she loves deeply had started down a path that had her frightened for his spiritual welfare. She was frantic to help – without frightening, closing off the door of communication, appearing "judgmental," etc. What to do?

Wanting to be helpful, I did a terribly *un*-helpful thing. I recommended that she refer the friend in question to a Christian counselor I knew from both academic and church settings. He is a good man with a gentle spirit. I was confident he would show the compassion and kindness too often lacking in believers when dealing with persons struggling with sexual issues. He was certainly in a field that should know more about gender dysphoria than I did. But I mistakenly assumed far too much. I assumed our similar backgrounds meant we shared similar biblical-ethical beliefs. *We don't.*

I feel betrayed and angry by that counselor's handling of the situation. He has felt obligated by his training to affirm the "authentic personhood" of his counselee. So, he uses the opposite-sex name the person has chosen. Uses opposite-sex pronouns. Encourages the individual to be true to the chosen new sex-gender identity. *Very Postmodern. Very consistent with majority views in psychology, psychiatry, and counseling. Very wrong in terms of biblical ethics.*

As I told the counselor in a subsequent meeting, I understand the term "Christian counseling" to elevate Scripture, biblical ethics, and the person of Christ above all other considerations. Not to be coercive, for faith is a choice. Not to be "mean" to a client, for that is not Christlike. But to point anyone who is consulting a "Christian" counselor to weigh what the Bible says on a subject against his or her own experience, leanings, preferences, desires, relationships, etc. But he explained that it would be unethical for him ever to be "directive" in his therapy sessions. I asked what that would mean for a client involved in adultery against a mate, fraud in a business, or drug addiction. The awkward answer – which seemed more of an evasion than an answer – wasn't reassuring at all.

Another time and place will have to do for the discussion of ethical practice in Christian counseling. My sense is, however, that Moses or Paul would have made terrible counselors – if my friend's view is correct. Even worse, Jesus surely could never have been licensed to open a practice. Moses, Paul, and Jesus all believed that faith was a commitment to righteousness. It cannot be separated from one's moral life and influence on others. They taught that the commands of God were given to be taught and obeyed. Does anyone seriously think they would have adopted a different take on things in a one-on-one counseling session from what they said publicly in the Torah, the epistles, or the Sermon on the Mount? For that matter, we will look in on a one-on-one session Jesus had with someone about sexual ethics a bit later in this book. We will see him as the very personification of *both* grace and truth.

I failed that sister. Failed her miserably. And I cannot think about my failure without feeling terribly, miserably guilty – even though I have admitted my mistake to her, asked forgiveness, and received it. No, I will never refer anyone seeking help on an ethical issue to that counselor again. Neither will I refer anyone to a psychiatrist, therapist, clinical psychologist, counselor, life coach, or anyone else for help on an issue of this sort without doing my personal due diligence to know which comes first for that person – the professional standards of his discipline or the ethical teaching of the Bible, the culture of her occupation or the Christ of her confession.

So I set out to learn enough about same-sex issues to try to be more helpful than I was in that sad instance. The result is *Male and Female God Created Them: A Biblical Review of LGBTQ+ Claims*. The original plan was to do a book of perhaps

120 pages to address the swirl of questions being raised in churches of all Christian tribes about how churches should view and treat gay, lesbian, transgender, and other persons who identify with the LGBTQ+ community. As the research became more serious, the number of pages grew into this book of well over my intended limit.

Yes, there is a lot of history, linguistic material, and theology in this book. And there are lots of footnotes for those readers who want to get into the material even more deeply. But it was important for me to spend the time and track down the information. If there was something deficient or malicious in the traditional view of the church, I wanted to know that for myself. I can change my mind on a subject in the face of better information than I have had. That information and the conclusions I believe to be established by it are here for you to explore and test for yourself.

More than anything, I want this book to help people who are confused or wavering in their own behavior choices or who are already involved in a same-sex relationship. I want to help people read the dried ink (i.e., fixed teaching) of the various biblical statements about same-sex behaviors without having that ink dismissed, erased, or smudged on the page by the things being said lately in an effort to minimize and avoid them.

The most authentic life ever lived was that of Jesus Christ. He situated himself firmly within the will of the one to whom he prayed as his Father in Heaven. He said the moral instruction of the Torah was not being abolished but fulfilled in his life – and warned against setting those commandments aside or teaching others to do so. That is the life toward which university professors, parents, Sunday School teachers, coaches, therapists, and anyone else who is a disciple of Jesus Christ should be pointing others – and modeling for them.

The ink really is dry – both literally and metaphorically – on this subject. With respect, kindness, love, and gentleness, I want to make a case here for a "traditional view" – as opposed to what has come to be called the "affirming view" or "revisionist view" – of Christian sexual ethics. Oh, I know how loaded both those adjectives are!

I am anything but "traditional" to some beliefs, attitudes, and behaviors within my own faith group. All conservative churches have gone through the so-called "worship wars" and are working through the issues around female leadership. These have been controversial topics across the centuries and have pro and con "prooftexts" people pull from the Bible. The difference with this topic is that *every mention of same-sex intercourse in both Old and New Testaments is prohibitive.* That fact alone makes it strikingly different.

As to the other adjective, I am altogether "affirming" toward the personhood, dignity, and protection of every LGBTQ+ person in the world. The range of treatment from mockery to violence against gay, lesbian, transgender, or other persons in that community by men and women who self-identify as Christians is deplorable. If those people are "dead right" about their interpretation of Scripture, they are "dead wrong" to dehumanize and abuse their fellow human beings.

Finally, this book is not a rant against the courts and legislatures for their actions over the past several years. It is not part of a strategy some advocate for getting laws struck down or changed that give protections and rights to persons in same-sex relationships. How could we misunderstand what Paul said about that in 1 Corinthians 5:9-13? It is not the business of churches to write laws, punish offenders, or otherwise regulate the larger communities in which we exist and function. The Kingdom of God is neither America nor Sweden nor Russia, and the salvation of our own country is neither the Republican Party nor the Democratic Party nor the Independents. As the apostle taught the Christians living in Corinth's libertine culture, we are not commissioned to judge sexually immoral, greedy, or people with unorthodox beliefs *outside* the church's membership. But we are honor bound to God and one another to teach and enforce orthodoxy *inside* the fellowship. I like the way his words are translated by the late Eugene Peterson: "I'm not responsible for what the *outsiders* do, but don't we have some responsibility for those within our community of believers?" (v.12).

So I ask your patient reading and thoughtful analysis of what follows. I hope it will help clarify your own views and equip you in helping others.

Holy Triune God, as we begin this study, guide us. Father, help us to believe that your love for us is real – that it is the compassionate love that led you to create us in your very own image and likeness. Lord Jesus, be the Way, Truth, and Life for us by helping us hear what will guide us to walk in the way of truth that leads to eternal life on the merit of your sacrifice for us. Holy Spirit, be the living presence in God's people that will give us the strength we need to model both grace and truth in this confused time. Amen.

"The only effect I ardently long to produce by my writings, is that those who read them should be better able to imagine and to feel the pains and the joys of those who differ from them in everything but the broad fact of being struggling, erring human creatures."
– Mary Ann Evans (aka George Eliot)

CHAPTER 1

The Goal of This Book: Grace and Truth

This book attempts something quite audacious by modern standards. *It proposes that love requires truth, while conceding that truth sometimes makes stringent demands.* It dares to say that some things we see as "loving" and "caring" are in fact morally impermissible to Christian ethics. Is it possible for love to be something other than a soft sentimentality that approves and defends whatever a beloved person does? Can truth be embraced as something other than a bludgeon with which to vilify and intimidate those believed to be mistaken?

This book attempts to use the Bible responsibly in making a case for marriage as the one-flesh covenant between one male and one female that God has authorized. Sexual intercourse outside such a marriage is morally wrong. It is an *irresponsible* use of the Bible for those who say they believe and follow it to write some version of its prohibition of same-sex activities into our civil statutes. When church and state were a single entity in Old Testament times, Moses and his successors exercised authority over everything from an Israelite's worship of false gods to that person's sexual behavior to his or her diet. Thus, laws found in the Torah not only outlawed the worship of Baal but also sexual intercourse between two males and eating shrimp.

In the New Testament, a great deal is made of the fact that the dietary laws of the Old Testament are no longer binding. The same can be said of a number of ceremonial laws about sacrificing animals or observing certain fasts and festivals. What is even more fundamental to some of the wrong-headed uses of the Bible by modern-day Christians and unbelievers alike is that the New Testament envisions the separation of powers between church and state. For example, the apostle Paul called out a particularly immoral situation in the church at Corinth where a man was having sex with the wife of a family member – apparently his own stepmother (1 Cor 5:1). Whereas the Torah called for the extreme civil penalty of death in such cases (cf. Lev 20:11), Paul called for the church to "Expel the wicked person from among you" (1 Cor 5:13b).

In dealing with this situation by calling for a man's rebuke and dismissal from participation in the church's life, the apostle applied the church's internal standard of moral behavior to church members and proceeded to acknowledge that "outsiders" – persons who had no covenant commitment to Christ and the gospel – do not fall within the purview of accountability to distinctively Christian codes of behavior. Yes, Christians and non-Christians are equally responsible to civil laws about murder and mayhem, federal and state taxes. No, non-Christians cannot be put in the stocks or jailed – as in colonial times in Puritan New England! – for failing to attend worship or withholding tithes.

Any number of behaviors that are morally wrong may not be criminal acts under either state or federal statutes. In fact, certain behaviors that are authorized by civil law (e.g., same-sex marriage) are still immoral under the historic teaching of both Scripture and the church – Catholic, Orthodox, and Protestant for two millennia. Only within the past half century has that position been challenged seriously from within those traditions.

The relationship between church and state on these issues will be explored in some detail later in this book. For now, however, I think it is important from the start to call out misuses of the Bible that are common to discussing same-sex relationships.

From the most conservative of Christian groups, there is an unambiguous call for making same-sex behaviors into criminal offenses. Therefore, some have applauded the harsh Ugandan law that its president, Yoweri Museveni, signed that not only makes homosexual acts illegal but mandates "treatment" on the model of conversion-therapy for arrested gay and lesbian persons and can impose the death penalty for what the law terms "aggravated homosexuality."[1] The Anti-Homosexuality Act 2023 imposes life in prison for anyone found guilty of sexual intercourse with someone of the same sex and up to seven years in prison for any attempt to commit an act of same-sex intercourse.

Going back to the situation Paul addressed in the church at Corinth, he used unambiguous language to name one of the several types of sexual sin for which Leviticus 20 calls for the death penalty (i.e., incest). But expulsion from the Christian community was his specified penalty for the church – not capital punishment.

> **Criminalizing Same-Sex Acts?**
> Not everything that's a sin is a crime. To equate all sin with crime, without the authority to do so, is itself a sin against God – to take the name of the Lord our God in vain. If the historic Christian vision of marriage and family is true and good and beautiful, as I believe it is, then we demonstrate that truth, goodness, and beauty to our unbelieving neighbors through our witness – not by threatening to kill them.
> Unleashing the violence of state-ordained execution, imprisonment, and surveillance on gay and lesbian Ugandans is a condemnable act of authoritarianism and a violation of the self-evident and unalienable rights to life, liberty, and the pursuit of happiness. To do such a thing is a matter of power, not of conviction. It demonstrates not a commitment to the Bible's authority but a rejection of it.
> — Russell Moore

From times well before his own, the right to apply the death penalty has been reserved to the civil state. The power of the sword is not within the right of the church to wield (Rom 13:1-7; cf. Matt 26:52).

This one clarification simultaneously silences both the reactionary homophobic comment (e.g., "They should all be locked up – or hung!") and the dismissive non-Christian quibble (e.g., "If you're going to use the Bible, you can't eat lobster or have sex during your wife's period!). In a word, the New Testament church is not a *theocracy* (i.e., a form of government in which priests govern society by religious canons) on the model of Old Testament Israel. Until this point is clear in our minds, confusion reigns and all parties involved are liable to be guilty of taking the Bible out of context.

The Fourth Gospel affirms that *both* "grace and truth came through Jesus Christ" (John 1:17). His followers should also try to exhibit both – not choose between them.

Male and Female God Created Them: A Biblical Review of LGBTQ+ Claims is my response to the current wave of anxiety and uncertainty among Christians about same-sex relationships. I want to present – with respect, love, and *grace* – what I believe to be the dry-ink *truth* of Holy Scripture on a most controversial subject. My initial concern in that attempt is threefold.

Three Concerns to Address

First, I am horrified by the degree of vitriolic speech and aggressive behavior from "conservative" and "Christian" people toward gay, lesbian, and transgender persons.

In the single instance in the Gospels where Jesus might have been drawn into an aggressive action against a woman who had violated the Bible's Holiness Code by committing adultery, he calmed a mob. She had done something classified "detestable" (NIV) or "abominable" (NRSVue) – in Hebrew, *toevah* – in Leviticus 18. Exposing her accusers for their hypocrisy and deceit,[2] Jesus used the Torah they professed to honor and protect to show grace to her.

> **Homophobia**
>
> Yes, homosexuality is a sin, but so is homophobia. Homophobia is the irrational fear of a whole people group, failing to see in that group God's image diminished but not extinguished by sin, and that God's elect people linger there, snared by their own sin and awaiting gospel grace. It is an act of homophobia to believe that people in the LGBT community are either too sinful to respond to God's call on their life, or to believe that people in the LGBT community have a fixed nature that will never, according to the blustering, unfounded, and uncharitable declarations of secular psychology, change by the power of God's command.
>
> What does God change? Our heart. That is where it all starts.
>
> — Rosaria Butterfield

When the angry crowd melted away, Jesus did not tell her "The rules have been changed" or "They were misinterpreting the Bible when they judged you." Having intervened on her behalf and acting lovingly toward the woman, he challenged her, "Go now and leave your life of sin" (John 8:1-11). If Jesus could honor the inflexible demand of moral uprightness and simultaneously be loving and restorative with someone who had done something Scripture says is detestable, can we not learn to imitate his example?

Second, I am concerned to help teens and young adults – along with their anxious parents and Christian leaders – sort out information they are being given about sexuality.

I don't expect a widespread interest in reading this book. Its target audience is pastors and ministers, teachers of high school and college students, church leaders, administrators of Christian schools, and adults with a high motivation to study the subject of same-sex relations (and relationships) from a biblical frame of reference. There is a much shorter and simpler version of this material in the works for what

CHAPTER 1: GRACE AND TRUTH

I hope will be a wider audience. Whereas this volume is heavy with footnotes and goes into details of the sort most people don't care to explore (i.e., linguistics, ancient history, hermeneutics), the "shorter and simpler version" is designed to be read by students and parents who are perplexed about the topic, teens and college students whose friends are involved in same-sex activity, and study groups in churches. Some of these study groups may be tailored to a church's Youth Ministry, Parents of Students, or even a church's teaching staff. *It is strongly recommended that persons leading any of these study groups from the smaller book have this volume as a resource.*

Not many 15-year-olds or university students have parents who are Bible scholars capable of helping them weigh what their friends, teachers, and media are telling them about sexuality. Sadly, many of them have pastors who are unequipped to help, for one can graduate with honors from a seminary these days by focusing on some area of "ministerial competence" that requires little to nothing in terms of textual or theological studies. Competence in church administration or counseling does not equate to competence in biblical studies.

Did ancient cultures simply know nothing about homosexuality beyond child molestation and anal rape of conquered soldiers? Is it true that the biblical languages of Hebrew and Greek do not even have the vocabulary for naming gay and lesbian behaviors? Was same-sex marriage an unimagined possibility for persons who lived in ancient Greece or Rome? Aren't we dealing with social-legal options and psychological understandings today that biblical writers never would have considered – much less actually encountered? I think we sell short both non-scholars (whether young people or their parents) and biblical writers by such condescending claims. My goal is to write accurately, clearly, and informatively – and with respect for your intelligence as a reader. For academics and anyone wishing to delve more deeply into linguistic details and historical sources, the otherwise-cumbersome endnotes are for your benefit.

Third, I am determined to mark a path that follows Jesus' ideal example of loving everyone in his world within the context of both being *and* teaching *the T/truth that sets humans free.* As in the distressing case of the woman in John 8, Jesus did not retreat from the high moral requirements of the Word of God. On the other hand, neither would he rant in some "self-righteous preacher style" to prove he would not compromise

> **Love and Truth**
>
> Love without truth is sentimentality; it supports and affirms us but keeps us in denial about our flaws. Truth without love is harshness; it gives us information but in such a way that we cannot really hear it. God's saving love in Christ, however, is marked by both radical truthfulness about who we are and yet also radical, unconditional commitment to us. The merciful commitment strengthens us to see the truth about ourselves and repent. The conviction and repentance moves us to cling to and rest in God's mercy and grace.
>
> — Tim Keller

the truth and then leave her at the mercy of a wrong-headed pack of theological wolves.

Along the way in this book, I will share occasional stories of people who have trusted me as their dialogue partner and supportive friend as they wrestled with these very personal challenges. I will not, of course, use their real names or give details adequate to identify them. I have surely mishandled some of those relationships by leaning either too far to the love-and-gentleness side that someone did not hear the truth as clearly as it needed to be stated or in other settings so far to the truth-and-repentance side that someone took me to be uncaring or lacking in the Christian virtue of compassion.

My goal is to write clearly enough to be understood, faithfully to the Bible so God will be pleased, and kindly enough that the person who rejects my view will not see me as an enemy.

The Argument Here: A Positive Negative

The methodology of this book will *not* be to begin by exploring the negative statements of the Bible to the matter of same-sex intercourse, reflecting on what we have come to call "the LGBTQ+ community," or replying to efforts of some to legitimize "loving, covenanted, monogamous" same sex relationships. I think the best place to start is with the Bible's positive case for marriage.

> **Why Male-Female Monogamy?**
>
> Marriage is the fundamental, cross-cultural institution for bridging the male-female divide so that children have loving, committed fathers and mothers. Marriage is inherently normative: It is about holding out a certain kind of relationship as a social ideal, especially when there are children involved. . . .
>
> The marriage idea is that children need mothers and fathers, that adults have an obligation to shape their sexual behavior so as to give their children stable families in which to grow up.
>
> — Maggie Gallagher

In Scripture, marriage is always and only a covenant pledge between opposite-sex partners.

And it is only within heterosexual marriage that sexual intercourse is sanctioned and honored, declared pure and given ethical protection. "Marriage should be honored by all, and the marriage bed kept pure, for God will judge the adulterer and all the sexually immoral" (Heb 13:4). Eugene Peterson paraphrases this verse as follows in *The Message*: "Honor marriage, and guard the sacredness of sexual intimacy between wife and husband. God draws a firm line against casual and illicit sex." If there is a theme verse for this book, this is it. No, I do not believe a single Bible verse should be used to build a theology of sexual purity. But, yes, I do believe Hebrews 13:4 is a summary statement of what the Bible teaches about the importance and sanctity of marriage. Part of affirming the significance of marriage is putting up markers to warn against attitudes and behaviors that compromise it – things such as adultery and sexual immorality.

The unnamed writer of this canonical text has marked the path I intend to pursue. If there is something uniquely honorable about heterosexual marriage, there is good reason to think that any distortion of it would be *dis*-honorable. Now, it does not follow that all other sexual acts and relationships are disallowed simply from the fact that the male-female marriage bed (Gk, *koitē*) is "pure" (NIV) or "sacred" (MSG). There will need to be clear prescriptive language that prohibits any other form of sexual act or relationship for us to claim as much.

In fact, the latter part of Hebrews 13:4 does prohibit other types of sexual intimacy. God will judge anyone who abandons the exclusivity of the marriage bed to have sex with another person as an adulterer (Gk, *moichos* = one who breaks a vow) or a sexually immoral person (Gk, *pornos* = one who engages in any form of prohibited sexual intercourse).

Hebrews 13:4 is not an isolated text in your Bible. It is not debated as to its textual authenticity. It most certainly is not an outlier verse that needs to be explained for being out of step with the central texts of the Bible about marriage and honorable sexual behavior or, from the opposite point of view, sexual actions and relationships that offend God. It is, instead, *a summary statement of everything the Bible affirms about the place of sex in human relationships.* Sex between one man and one woman who have covenanted in good faith to live as husband and wife is ethical, honorable, and pure. All other sexual acts (i.e., consensual premarital sex, rape, prostitution, loving twosomes, non-exploitative couples – whether with a person of the same

15

or opposite sex) come under divine judgment as disapproved behaviors. They are outside the will of God and sinful.

I call this a *positive-negative argument* for the simple reason that by affirming one thing (i.e., covenanted heterosexual intimacy) and simultaneously excluding all other categories of sexual intimacy (i.e., whether voluntary or coerced, casual or devoted, promiscuous or exclusive) it addresses the matter comprehensively. From this summation of biblical teaching, we are left without ambiguity on a topic where so many claim to be hopelessly uncertain. With no intention of being needlessly offensive, the uncertainty is not about what the text says or means but about the degree of authority one grants to the Bible.

The Historic Case for Jews and Christians

By contrast, there is no positive case that can be offered from Scripture to support same-sex acts or relationships. The only biblical argument for the acceptance of same-sex behavior in any context is to claim that the clear denunciations of such actions has been misinterpreted for 3,500 years by Jewish and Christian interpreters – the negation of Scripture's negatives. The Bible's disapproval of same-sex intercourse is uniform in both the Old and New Testaments – absolute, unqualified, unyielding, and counter-cultural. As David Gushee is honest enough to admit in a book written to make an affirming case for same-sex marriage: "I grant the historical claim that the Church has believed that same-sex acts and relationships are always wrong, and I acknowledge that many millions of Christians still believe this."[3]

How, then, does Gushee propose to make an affirmative case for same-sex relationships? He argues (1) that readers have misinterpreted certain texts as negative to same-sex relationships that in fact are not, and (2) those texts that are in fact negative statements apply to acts and relationships altogether different from the loving, committed, and monogamous same-sex partnerships that are possible in our time. In the course of this book, various forms of both these arguments will be examined from his and similar writings that challenge the historic position of the Christian church.

A sub-theme to all these arguments is that Christians in modern times have changed our views on such subjects as slavery and female leadership in the church.

So why should we be threatened by having to admit the church has been wrong on at least some elements of the same-sex issue? Isn't there a "biblical trajectory" of inclusion through love that Christ modeled for us that allows us to change our minds about loving commitments between persons of the same sex? The issue for debate is not exploitation, sexual abuse, casual sex, and the like. All Christian parties acknowledge those to be sinful behaviors.

Might Adam Hamilton be right in claiming that everything negative in Scripture about same-sex behaviors is about pedophilia or pederasty, temple prostitution by male and female prostitutes, and people who were simply given over to unrestrained sexuality? Thus, Hamilton claims, the Bible doesn't really speak negatively about what he is endorsing:

> Paul had no conception of the kinds of things some of us are just beginning to understand . . . It's clear that Paul couldn't see two people of the same sex living as a family together for the rest of their lives, the way he couldn't see that slavery was wrong or that women could speak in church.[4]

Marriage: Shifting Without Compromise?

Then there is the work of Karen Keen who proposes "a shift to the acceptance of same-sex relationships" that "does not require compromising Scripture" and what it teaches about marriage.[5] She repeats the discredited claim of Robin Scroggs and others that the biblical writers were reacting to male prostitution, pederasty, and other forms of exploitation in their condemnations of same-sex relationships. "But the biblical authors don't write about the morality of consensual same-sex relationships as we know them today."[6] The inaccuracy of that claim will be spelled out in Chapter 9 of this book. She also pushes back on Paul's use of the term "unnatural" in Romans 1. A careful analysis of that claim will come in Chapter 11. Both of these arguments are in the vein of what I insist is an attempt to make a case for same-sex relationships by claiming we have misunderstood the explicit prohibitions of the Old Testament for 3,500 years and – without Jesus or the apostles bothering to correct those misinterpretations – the negative New Testament statements from Paul until the mid-twentieth century. There is nothing new in making a *negative* assessment of the traditional readings of the Bible.

What, then, is Keen's *positive* case for a "shift" to affirming same-sex relationships that "does not require compromising Scripture"? She announces her positive rationale in the opening sentence of her book: "When it comes to same-sex relationships, there's one thing we cannot forget: *people*."[7] Even though I disagree with landing site for her thesis (i.e., affirming same-sex coupling), I respect her for naming the launch site that justifies it: her appeal is *not* to the imitation of Christ, honoring our humanity by embracing the biblical standard for ethical behavior, or crucifying the flesh for the sake of the Kingdom of God but to personal fulfillment and happiness. In summary, *her argument is anthropocentric rather than theocentric or Christocentric.*

The great temptation of humanity across the centuries is to interpret God and his will for us in terms of our felt needs and natural desires. Thus, the prophet reminds us that "people's lives are not their own; it is not for them to direct their steps" (Jer 10:23). Indeed, an ancient proverb holds: "There is a way that appears to be right, but in the end it leads to death" (Prov 14:12). It is this common mistake of fixing the standard of right and wrong by human sentiment rather than divine guidance that sabotages Keen's thesis.

It is unquestionably correct that people – all males and females of the human race – are worthy of respect and are to be affirmed for their dignity and worth as God's image-bearers. Without forgetting Keen's opening-line concern for "people," believers must grant that the God who created us knows what serves our best interest better than we do. Yes, "the conversation affects the lives of real people."[8] From this concern, Keen derives what she labels her "key interpretive principle" of human need. "The interpretive key," she alleges, "is attention to human need."[9] In summing up her methodology for reading the biblical text, she writes:

> According to the biblical authors, a creation ordinance in and of itself does not mean we can neglect the deliberative process in applying biblical mandates today. . . . Mandates are applied with attention to human need and suffering. This means that when we are confronted with an ethical question, we must prayerfully consider the needs of those involved. In the case of same-sex relationships, we might consider how the needs of gay and lesbian people nuance application of the biblical prohibition, particularly concerning the expectation of lifelong celibacy.[10]

By this "interpretive key," it seems altogether possible to so "nuance" any biblical prohibition – adultery, lying, theft, even murder – that the biblical mandate of repentance can be removed from human experience. Do we not all plead "special circumstances" in attempting to justify our nonconforming behaviors? Perhaps there is a way to nuance Jesus' call to discipleship so that people really do not have to "deny themselves and take up their cross" to follow him (Mark 8:34-35). Perhaps Jesus was too harsh with the rich young ruler by demanding that he "sell everything" in order to follow him (Luke 18:18-23). Nuancing the demand to a double tithe or perhaps even half his possessions would have made the difference in keeping the man from walking away and being "very sad" in doing so.

Keen's thesis and what are offered as arguments are given their credibility by her setting all that follows by opening her book with accounts of how gay and lesbian persons have been abused so frequently. Her concern for "people" on the first page is immediately contrasted with accounts of how persons with same-sex attraction have been deemed "spiritually corrupt," guilty of "monstrous insanity" (John Chrysostom), "spiritual depravity" (Martin Luther), or "not to be mentioned without horror" (Matthew Henry). These demeaning descriptors that cause twenty-first century persons to wince are less than half the list she offers by the end of page 2. This rhetorical device makes a reader reluctant to acknowledge or hear a case that is negative to same-sex relationships for fear that one be deemed a bigoted homophobe. The compassion one

---

Changed Views of Same-Sex Marriage

From a Pew Research survey fielded in October 2022, findings showed . . .

About six-in-ten adults (61%) express a positive view of the impact of same-sex marriage being legal, including 36% who say it is very good for society. Roughly four-in-ten have a negative view (37%), with 19% saying it is very bad. . . .

There has been a dramatic increase in public support for same-sex marriage over the past two decades. As recently as 2004, nearly twice as many Americans opposed than favored allowing gay and lesbian people to marry legally; by 2019, public opinion had reversed, with 61% in favor and 31% opposed. . . .

Opinions about the effect of same-sex marriage vary widely among religious groups. While 71% of White evangelical Protestants say the legalization of marriage between same-sex couples is bad for society, 62% of White non-evangelical Protestants say it is good. So too do about two-thirds of Catholics (66%) and a much larger majority of religiously unaffiliated adults (82%). In contrast, Black Protestants are closely divided on same-sex marriage: 49% say it is good, while 46% say it is bad.

— Gabriel Borelli

feels for gay persons from the opening lines of the book inclines a reader to give their self-reported experience greater weight than the biblical text.

It is this groundwork that allows Keen to nuance what I will argue is *the creation norm for male-female marriage found in Genesis 1 and 2*. With a priority concern for reading the text through an anthropocentric rather than theocentric lens, she is able to discern that commonality, similarity, companionship, and covenant loyalty are the real issues rather than the text's "male and female he created them" (1:27), "she shall be called 'woman' (Heb, *ishah*) for she was taken out of man (Heb, *ish*)" (2:23b), and "a *man* . . . is united to his *wife*, and they become one flesh" (2:24). I seriously question that this is a "shift to the acceptance of same-sex relationships" that "does not require compromising Scripture" to get to this and other conclusions in her book.

This book will offer a *theocentric* reading of Scripture. Stated simply, this will involve reading Scripture with the confidence that it is not the evolving understanding of God by fallible human beings but the end product of speakers and writers who, "though human, spoke from God as they were carried along by the Holy Spirit" (2 Pet 1:21). This theocentric reading is ultimately also *Christocentric* by calling for us to read Scripture as Jesus himself read it. His mercy to a woman taken in the very act of adultery was for the sake of calling her back to the authority of the Torah and exhorting her to "leave your life of sin" (John 8:11b). His concept of love was not that it eclipsed and cancelled commands but was the truest motivation for obeying them. So he did *not* teach his disciples and say, "If you love me, your authentic personhood just might overshadow the old moral demands of Scripture." The correct quotation from Jesus is this: "If you love me, keep my commands" (John 14:15). He not only authenticated what the Law, Prophets, and Psalms of our Old Testament contains (Matt 5:17-19) but also spoke with authority that his hearers acknowledged (Matt 7:28-29) and promised the same guidance of the Holy Spirit to the apostles, evangelists, and prophets of the earliest church that their Old Testament forebears had experienced (John 16:12-13).

Keen and others argue the sexual ethics of the Bible evolved as "prompted by social-cultural dynamics" of the Jewish and Greco-Roman world rather than being received through Spirit-given instruction.[11] Thus the move toward monogamy as opposed to polygamy, polygyny, concubinage, or the sexual exploitation of slaves, low-born persons, and children (both female and male) are non-definitive? Or are they definitive now but not when originally recorded? Were they serious in relation to idolatry and cult prostitution but not within committed, loving, and monogamous relationships within ancient Israel or the earliest church? Serious for both ancient Israel and the earliest church but able to be jettisoned today because of what modern psychology says about same-sex coupling? Keen feels confident to write: "It was not the result of special divine revelation unique to early Jews and Christians."[12]

I do *not* have that confidence. To the contrary, I believe the infinite wisdom of Creator God (Psa 147:5) and the deposit of "all authority in heaven and on earth" (Matt 28:18) in Jesus establishes an obligation upon all who profess a biblical faith to submit to a biblical standard of ethical behavior. Keen's claim that her view "does not require compromising Scripture" is contradicted by her own explicit statements that link the Bible's sexual ethics to "social-cultural dynamics" in the ancient world as opposed to "special divine revelation." It allows cultural dependence to count for more than Spirit-guided instruction.

The Existential Concern for Loved Ones

Then come the real-life situations that either offend or break the hearts of all of us who are concerned to follow Jesus' example of loving our neighbors as ourselves and treating people as we want to be treated. Those of us who have work colleagues, relatives, friends in the community, or Christian brothers and sisters who are gay don't want to hear others bashing them. We do not want them mistreated. And we take it as an offense to our shared humanity in God's image when that sort of mistreatment occurs. We are willing to put ourselves at risk for them.

I have been criticized harshly by people from both sides of this controversy. Some who know my view that same-sex intercourse is against God's will regard me as a hateful bigot. On the other hand, some who agree with my view nevertheless think I compromise the Word of God by maintaining personal friendships with gay persons and defending their civil rights. I fully expect this book to receive similar mixed reviews.

Mark Achtemeier frames his book that affirms same-sex marriage around "Kristi" – a fictitious name for a person from his experience whose story parallels

> **Biblical Consistency**
>
> The primary biblical case against homosexual practice is not the few texts that explicitly mention it. Rather, it is the fact that again and again the Bible affirms the goodness and beauty of sexual intercourse – and everywhere, without exception, the norm is sexual intercourse between a man and a woman committed to each other for life. Although this is familiar ground, and less and less contested even by those who advocate for a revision of Christian ethics, it is important to state just how strongly and consistently the Bible speaks to the goodness of marriage between a man and a woman, and equally consistently to the immorality of sexual acts (heterosexual and homosexual) that do not honor that bond. . . .
>
> This widespread biblical affirmation of the goodness of sexual intercourse when it occurs within the life-long commitment of a man and a woman provides the context for understanding the few biblical texts that explicitly mention same-sex intercourse. Notably, none of these texts address motives or specific types of homosexual acts. Instead, they pronounce a sweeping condemnation of same-sex intercourse – whether female with female or male with male.
>
> — Ron Sider

that of people in my own. Kristi self-describes as a woman from conservative Christian roots, committed to Christ, called into ministry, and ready to begin seminary work. Kristi also confides that she has struggled with same-sex attraction since she was a young teen without ever acting on her feelings. Why had God not heard her prayers to take away those feelings? Should she give up her faith and her sense of call to serve Christ and the church? She had even been thinking about suicide.

From that beginning, Achtemeier moves to discover that Kristi's feelings have the right to be expressed in "committed, covenanted partnerships or marriages" that are within the will of God. He finds security in his discovery because Kristi's new perspective he helped her find reveals a spiritual life that "flourishes" and proves to him that God is blessing her.

> Seeing Kristi's vibrant faith and strong commitment reemerge as a result of her newfound openness made as deep an impression on me as her former despair. I couldn't help wondering if this really was the path God intended for her. I could see nothing in Kristi's life that looked like the spiritual withering one would expect to find in a person whose life had moved away from abiding in Christ.[13]

As one struggler among others, does compassion remove obligation? Does "flourishing" in specific elements of life and ministry validate a lifestyle? The choice in Achtemeier's book is the one many seem to think is necessary – either to be a hard-edged soul who is mean or have a sweet spirit that can bathe others with Christlike love.

Over the several chapters to follow, we will examine the textual, theological, and existential cases just outlined. From these and other writers whose work they use, I will present and examine arguments and their underpinnings. I promise to be fair and reasonable. I will not castigate and slander persons with whom I take issue. At the end, the case I make will be yours to weigh. As I have told students in classrooms over the years: *My task is not to do your thinking and draw your conclusions, but I do accept the responsibility of challenging you to think by giving you good information.* That is what I propose to do in these pages.

Love and Truth: Are They Compatible?

The gospel of Jesus Christ requires an emphatic "Yes!" to both truth and love. Modeled on Jesus' example, the revealed truth of the Bible – however contrary it may be to one's inclinations or desires – exists to be heard, obeyed, and shared. By that same standard, men and women – all of whom bear the image and likeness of God, however defaced that image is in some of us – must be treated with respect and compassion. We will not be saved because we maintain this balance, but saved people strive to achieve it for the sake of honoring the Holy and Loving God in whom we believe.

The conviction I carry in writing this book is that God's love for all his creation – and for humans in a unique way via the enfleshment of the Eternal Logos – is real. With whatever defects of physical form, mental ability, or spiritual life any one of us manifests, we are loved for the

---

The Highest Human Welfare

On several different occasions a married man has told me that he has fallen in love with another woman. When I have gently remonstrated with him, he has responded in words like these: "Yes, I agree, I already have a wife and family. But this new relationship is the real thing. We were made for each other. Our love for each other has a quality and a depth we have never known before. It must be right." But no, it is not right. No man is justified in breaking his marriage covenant with his wife on the ground of the quality of his love for another woman. Quality of love is not the only yardstick by which to measure what is good or right.

Similarly, I do not deny the claim that homosexual relationships can be loving (although a priori I do not see how they can attain the same richness as the heterosexual mutuality God has ordained). But their love quality is not sufficient to justify them. Indeed, I have to add that they are incompatible with true love because they are incompatible with God's law. Love is concerned for the highest welfare of the beloved. And our highest human welfare is found in obedience to God's law and purpose, not in revolt against them.

— John R.W. Stott

simple reason that we are in our Creator's likeness and image. That is the *why* of God's love for gays and straights, prophets and prostitutes, atheists and saints. But the fact that we are all loved by God is not equivalent to saying that God nods divine approval of everything we do. And that takes us to the other element of the book's intent.

How God demonstrates his love is very much in the same way a loving mother or father loves a child. The divine purpose in relation to you and me is not to make "gods" of us but to aid us in the task of being fully and authentically human. Therefore, God has made known to us what we could not have discovered fully for ourselves. In the form of instruction, coaching, and directives, God has told us what is right and wrong – and indicated something of the consequences of choosing one path over the other. Echoing the language of Hebrews 1:1-4, God spoke in various ways through prophets across the centuries to teach us about our true identity and purpose as his human offspring. That instruction reached its apex in Jesus – who both taught and modeled the lifestyle his disciples were to follow. This "how" element of following Jesus often involves a change from the course of action one has been following – a change called repentance.

Repentance is never about giving up what is good for what is bad. But it is difficult for us to grasp that in the context of our fallen humanity. Living with a degree of wealth and comfort is a good thing – unless that wealth and comfort exhibit themselves in unethical or even criminal behavior. Suppose, for example, that one is living well because of being dishonest in business or outright theft of another's property. "Anyone who has been stealing must steal no longer, but must work, doing something useful with their own hands, that they may have something to share with those in need" (Eph 4:28). Does God love someone who has been dishonest? Yes, because she is God's beloved creation who bears his own image and likeness. In this case, that love calls her to stop one set of behaviors and to adopt another in their place – at the loss (at least temporarily) of personal comfort. The same principle can be illustrated in countless ways.

First, my gay or lesbian or trans neighbor is a *person* – not a project, pervert, or problem. Second, that same neighbor is *loved* by virtue of nothing more than existence – a recipient of God's daily sustaining grace of life on Planet Earth. Third, one element of God's love for gays and straights is the Bible's righteous instruction about sexuality – asserting the holiness of some behaviors and marking others as prohibited. Fourth, God's love for and instructions to us are not negated by the fact that we may want to behave differently or have found pleasure in doing so – making a choice between "*your will* be done" and "but this is *what I want*" inevitable.

Idolatry: Ancient and Modern

Specifically, I will claim that loving the God who loves us requires one's abandonment of the various distractions – the Bible calls them *idolatries* – that lie at the root of all sin. From a biblical point of view, it is not that idolatry is simply one among many sins. It is the fundamental disorientation of a human life that lies at the root of all sin.

Whether we point to the experience of Israel at Mount Sinai or Paul's indictment of the first-century pagan world, turning from the worship of the One True God has consequences. Contrary to the way we usually express that move, such people do not become bona fide atheists (i.e., people without devotion to a god). Instead, they find a substitute deity and worship it. They embrace an idol that displaces God – or, in most instances, multiple idols.

That substitute deity may be some variety of materialism that thinks it is repudiating theism by renouncing faith in an invisible Spirit Being. But it simply displaces the invisible with the visible. Thus some people venerate or otherwise give ultimate value to Planet Earth itself and worship Gaia. More commonly, those who deny the existence of the God of Judeo-Christian Scripture worship some variation of an unholy trinity of money, sex, and power – all of which are tangible deities we may choose to embrace as alternatives when we "exchange the glory of the immortal God" for various elements of his good creation (Rom 1:18-23, esp. v.23).

An idol need not have a carved or molded shape such as the ancients gave to Zeus, Athena, Artemis, or Dionysus. Neither is a geographically located temple required. One of the standard definitions of the word "god" is that it identifies the person or thing to which a person attaches supreme importance and gives ultimate allegiance. In Christian terms, to worship and serve anything with devotion greater than one has for the One True God is idolatry. Thus, Paul could say that greed is idolatry (Col 3:5) – without any reference to Plutus, the Greek god of wealth.

If we understand Paul's claim about greed to refer to money, he was echoing Jesus himself. In the Sermon on the Mount, he said, "You cannot serve God and wealth" (Matt 6:24; cf. Luke 16:13). The word for wealth (Gk, *mamōnas*) appears to be borrowed from an Aramaic word meaning wealth, possessions, or property. It is not a sinister term *per se*. When personified in Jesus' warning, however, it functions as the equivalent of someone's "god." In fact, the King James Version translates his statement this way: "Ye cannot serve God and Mammon."

One hardly needs proof to say that the unbounded yearning for wealth still drives many a devotee. The countless shrines to Mammon – money, houses, luxury cars, what many would call "the good life" – have made room for countless worshippers who prostrate themselves to seek its favor. It is not that money is evil or that anyone with wealth is an idolator. It is not wealth but one's attitude toward it that is problematic. Any good thing under my power – bank account, business, jewelry, land, title, perks – becomes a bad thing if and when it becomes my identity, the defining focus of my life. As one or all of those things become more important than honoring God *with* those things, they have displaced him as the matter of Ultimate Worth in my life. Put simply, to follow that path is to abandon stewardship for slavery. Sought for its own sake, wealth becomes a life-draining, corrupting master.

The same is true of human sexuality.[14] It is possible to make one's sexuality the center of gravity for a person's identity, life energy, and fantasies. And that is true not only for the stereotypical "Hollywood personality" but also for the "average Joe/Jane" who believes the mantra tied to so much of today's entertainment that good sex – or perhaps just sex in whatever setting or manner – is the *summum bonum* of life.

> **Why "Consent" Is Not Enough**
>
> In our post-sexual-revolution culture, there seems to be wide agreement among young adults that sex is good and the more of it we have, the better. That assumption includes the idea that we don't need to be tied to a relationship or marriage; that our proclivities are personal and that they are not to be judged by others — not even by participants. In this landscape, there is only one rule: Get consent from your partner beforehand.
>
> But the outcome is a world in which young people are both liberated and miserable. While college scandals and the #MeToo moment may have cemented a baseline rule for how to get into bed with someone without crossing legal lines, that hasn't made the experience of dating and finding a partner simple or satisfying. Instead, the experience is often sad, unsettling, even traumatic.
>
> — Christine Emba

Obsession with sex was a major focus of worship – both formally and practically – in the ancient world. Not only was Aphrodite known and worshipped as the Greek goddess of beauty and sexuality, but her son, Eros, carried on the family tradition of sensuality. We even preserve these ancient names with modern terms such as aphrodisiac (i.e., food or drink thought to make sex more attainable and/or pleasurable). Or perhaps you know Aphrodite better by her Latin name, Venus, from which we derive the word venereal (i.e., pertaining to sexual desire and/or intercourse). Then, of course, the English derivations from Eros are in even more widespread usage – erotic, erotica, heteroerotic, homoerotic, autoerotic, eroticism, and several others.

The modern versions of idolized sexuality come in such varied forms as pornography, sexual experimentation, sexualized clothing, premarital sex, extramarital affairs, open marriage, lesbianism, same-sex coupling, "friends with benefits," polyamory, and fetishism of all sorts. These behaviors are of such supreme importance to many people that they self-define by them. They find their identity in them. I know people who define themselves by and give their ultimate allegiance to them. Even within traditional long-term heterosexual monogamy, it is altogether possible for sexual experiences and/or one's sexual partner to become nothing less than her/his object of worship.

To make sexual experience the defining feature of one's life is – to use Paul's language to which we return in detail in Chapter 11 – to have "worshiped and served the creature rather than the Creator, who is blessed forever" (Rom 1:25b). For himself, Paul had found a center for his life that was other than himself and his sexual experience. "I have been crucified with Christ and I no longer live, but Christ lives in me. The life I now live in the body, I live by faith in the Son of God, who loved me and gave himself for me" (Gal 2:20). He seems neither to feel repressed as a person nor bound up in theological legalism to make such a concession.

Christian Ethical Distinctives and Civil Law

Finally, for my explanation of the nature of this book, let me state a conviction that will surface at various times as it expands. My intention here is to locate in Scripture, explain in clear fashion, and defend against recent criticisms a view of same-sex behaviors that I believe is *normative to Christian faith*. Many people who are not Christians inevitably will hear the argument of this book as a judgment and condemnation of their beliefs and life choices. That Christians have a standard of distinctive ethics to which non-Christians do not subscribe and which *Christians should not attempt to legislate outside the church* has always been problematic.

This seems to be a minority opinion among many Christians who might otherwise be inclined to agree with the larger view advanced in this book. Yes, there are implications for church-state separation at stake here. And, no, Christians need not be silent on any public issue for which they can argue a reasonable case that does not depend exclusively on the authority of the Bible. It simply isn't right to bind distinctive Christian values on our non-Christian neighbors. In fact, attempting to do so will be so offensive and off-putting to them that they are likely to be less inclined to hear the gospel favorably.

Would you want your child to be required to pray to Allah? Or, if you are Protestant, required to offer a Catholic prayer through the mediation of Mary? If not, you might want to reconsider the view so many conservative Christians voice that we need to "bring prayer back to our public schools." The argument is simple: *If we would not want contrary values bound on us through law or institutional rules, we should not attempt to bind our distinguishing moral values on others.*

C.S. Lewis staked out his view on the matter in a discussion of divorce laws in his native England.

> Before leaving the question of divorce, I should like to distinguish two things which are very often confused. The Christian conception of marriage is one: the other is the quite different question — how far Christians, if they are voters or Members of Parliament, ought to try to force their views of marriage on the rest of the community by embodying them in the divorce laws. A great many people seem to think that if you are a Christian yourself you should try to make divorce difficult for every one. I do not think that. At least I know I should be very angry if the [Muslims] tried to prevent the rest of us from drinking wine. My own view is that the Churches should frankly recognize that the majority of the British people are not Christians and, therefore, cannot be expected to live Christian lives. There ought to be two distinct kinds of marriage: one governed by the State with rules enforced on all citizens, the other governed by the Church with rules enforced by her on her own members. The distinction ought to be quite sharp, so that a man knows which couples are married in a Christian sense and which are not.[15]

A version of what Lewis was proposing for British efforts to write Christian limitations on divorce into civil statutes is consistent with my view about same-sex unions.[16] While I am convinced the New Testament teaches that all sexual intercourse is to be reserved as a privilege for married heterosexual persons, I would not argue for consensual premarital sex – whether between persons of the same or opposite sex – to be criminalized. Rather than Lewis' "two distinct kinds of (heterosexual) marriage," I would prefer civil unions for same-sex couples and marriage for heterosexual couples. But that is a legislative decision already made and not one where the church will have a decisive voice. In cases of premarital sex, adultery, or same-sex unions, impenitent parties should be subject to church discipline,[17] but not civil punishment. Whether the consenting adults are same-sex partners or opposite-sex partners, *their civil rights in a free society are different from their ethical rights as Christians*. But this is true of a wide range of behaviors and is hardly unique to this one.

The New Testament confronts this issue in a letter Paul wrote to the church in Corinth. Not surprisingly in that culture, the issue involved a breach of marital fidelity. After drawing a clear and definitive line against the behavior of a man who was having a sexual affair with his own stepmother, Paul was adamant that no Christian community could tolerate such immoral behavior. He called the church to act in concert to hold the man responsible for what he was doing. (Apparently the woman was not a member of the Jesus followers in Corinth.) Behavior so public and flagrant as this simply could not be ignored. As you read the paragraph below, notice the distinction between "the immoral of this world" and "anyone who bears the name of brother or sister" – that is, between members and non-members of the Christian community.

> I wrote to you in my letter not to associate with sexually immoral persons – not at all meaning the immoral of this world, or the greedy and robbers, or idolaters, since you would then need to go out of the world. But now I am writing to you not to associate with anyone who bears the name of brother or sister who is sexually immoral or greedy, or is an idolater, reviler, drunkard, or robber. Do not even eat with such a one. For what have I to do with judging those outside? Is it not those who are inside that you are to judge? God will judge those outside. "Drive out the wicked person from among you" (1 Cor 5:9-13).

The instruction of an apostle to a church he had planted in a city notorious for its wide-open, libertine culture was not that they should lobby the city fathers to write Christian standards about sex, idol worship, and alcohol abuse into their civil statutes. His counsel to the church was about its obligation to be an alternate community to Corinth's low standards of moral conduct. Specifically, he made it clear that the church's obligation was to judge the appropriateness of those "inside" their number, not "with judging those outside."

> Neither [Paul] nor [Christians in Corinth] are to pass sentence on the people of the world in their present existence. The reason for that is simple: "God will judge those outside"; and God's judgment is still future, a judgment in which the church will also participate (6:2). But for now, the church takes the world as they find it. As God's temple in the "world," they are to offer a striking alternative to the world, and in that sense the church must always be "judging" the world. But it is not ours to bring sentence on those who belong to another worldview, to another age altogether. The time for that judgment is coming.[18]

The right of Christians to speak our convictions for the common good versus pressuring legislators to write laws that make specific Christian values compulsory is a larger topic than can be addressed here.[19] For my purpose in this book, it must be enough to say that I am convinced I have seen Christians make our witness to the gospel obnoxious by using language and tactics in public forums that confused their church duties with their civic rights. What has come to be known as "Christian nationalism"[20] is a misguided belief that the United States is a "Christian nation" that must preserve a privileged position for Christian beliefs in the public square.

In the first few centuries of the church's existence, its influence for righteousness was exerted from the margins of Roman culture. When a post-Constantine church received privilege from the state and began to impose its doctrines by edict rather than through persuasion in love, the results were disastrous for the gospel. Instead of teaching potential converts about a distinctive way of life to which their baptism would commit them, a cultural version of the Christian faith – most use the term "Christendom" for it – replaced and watered down what had once been clear moral distinctions between the two groups Paul identified at Corinth. The meaning of "conversion" changed from the adoption of new beliefs and behaviors to nominal inclusion within a group culture.[21]

This book does not seek to define what courts and legislatures may do to (re)define marriage or permit sexual behaviors the Bible prohibits. Instead, it is an explanation of a Christian posture on same-sex intimacies. It is a call for church leaders to maintain a biblical standard of conduct for themselves and the souls under their care. It is – even if it must be in the face of failed church leadership – a call for believers to hold ourselves accountable to the norms given in Holy Scripture. In a modern, non-privileged, post-Christendom culture, one missiologist has reminded us that "God has not called the church to govern the world but to witness to God's plan to renew the world based on the justice/righteousness of God."[22] That witness must be not only with words but also with daily demonstration of "righteousness, peace, and joy in the Holy Spirit" (Rom 14:17). That is a true "missionary task" for the church.

> **"No" to Cultural Accommodation**
>
> Accommodation to the broader culture should not be part of the Christian project. . . .
>
> If Christian identity matters, then difference must matter as well. In the most general sense, get rid of difference and what remains will be nothing – you yourself, along with everything else, will be drowned in the sea of undifferentiated "stuff." To erase difference is to undo the creation, that intricate pattern of separations and interdependencies that God established when the universe was formed out of no-thing. Literally, every-thing depends on difference. Now apply this insight to the relation between gospel and culture. Here too everything depends on difference.
>
> If you have difference, you have the gospel. If you don't you will either have just plain old culture or the universal reign of God, but you won't have the gospel. The gospel is always also about difference; after all, it means the good news – something good, something new, and therefore something different! . . .
>
> Christian identity is established not primarily by denying and combating what is outside but by embracing and highlighting the center of what is inside – Jesus Christ as the Word who took on flesh and became the Lamb of God bearing the sin of the world. . . . Put slightly differently, properly understood Christian identity is not reactive but positive; the center defines the difference, not fear of others, either of their uncomfortable proximity or their dangerous aggressiveness.
>
> — Miroslav Volf

To Christians living as "exiles" in the Roman Empire in the first century, Peter gave counsel that Christians should heed today. As we realize that the culture has changed and that we are living at the margins of our global society, we are not called to be self-righteous and arrogant. We would be wise not to be the screaming and angry faces on evening news broadcasts or in online tirades. Instead, we will do better and have more influence that is positive by living as God's alternative community and not by lobbing spiritual grenades into our neighbors' world.

> But you are a chosen race, a royal priesthood, a holy nation, God's own people, in order that you may proclaim the mighty acts of him who called you out of darkness into his marvelous light.
> Once you were not a people,
> but now you are God's people;
> once you had not received mercy,
> but now you have received mercy.
> Beloved, I urge you as aliens and exiles to abstain from the desires of the flesh that wage war against the soul. Conduct yourselves honorably among the Gentiles, so that, though they malign you as evildoers, they may see your honorable deeds and glorify God when he comes to judge (1 Peter 2:9-12).

Exploring Contrary Views

I cannot, of course, grapple with every significant person, book, or article that has advanced some element of an affirmative case for Christian acceptance of homosexuality. While a variety of them will be quoted to represent one point or another because of their significance to some element of the case opposite my own, a book of this size cannot offer a critique of every writer and every publication. But representative arguments from serious proponents of the affirmative case will be examined. Endnotes will identify the sources.

At every level of discussing this issue, Christians should be both respectful toward those who argue a different case and those persons who are part of what we now call the LGBTQ+ community. I cannot put it better than this: "We must love homosexual persons while remaining clear in our convictions about God's intentions for human sexuality – and equally clear that all of us stand guilty and in need of redemption."[23] Incidentally, this quotation is from a book on ethics that was written by two men – one of whom later changed his view toward committed same-sex partnerships.

Therefore, I offer this book and its thesis to you with "fear and trembling." When Paul thought back to his initial visit to Corinth and his first interactions with people there, he recalled this: "I came to you in weakness with great fear and trembling" (1 Cor 2:3). Was he sick? Was he discouraged from just-completed experiences in Athens? Was he simply feeling the weight of his missionary task? Without knowing the answer to those questions, I confess to the "fear and trembling" of personal insecurity I have always felt as a teacher.

CHAPTER 1: GRACE AND TRUTH

I don't pretend to have all the answers. It is not my intention to cause needless offense to those who will disagree. Above all, however, I don't want to fail The One who called me to the task of being one of his followers and students who, in turn, is also called to teach others. Attempting to teach the Word of God accurately and faithfully is a high calling that must be taken on with urgent prayer and deep humility. I will argue my case as clearly as possible and with charity and respect for those who disagee.

At a time in history when the word *truth* has been redefined to mean subjectivity or general consent, I still use the word to refer to knowledge that is faithful to reality, attainable by the human mind, and able to be shared. Feelings are significant and often outdo unwelcome facts in making our decisions. My hope is that the content of this book will shine helpful light on your search for factual truth that will assist you in following Jesus of Nazareth – the person who claimed to be the very personification of the way, the truth, and the life.

> **"Feelings" Are Less Than Moral Justification**
>
> It has become an unquestioned moral assumption of most Western cultures, and certainly of North American ones, that people should be free. What that means in the popular mind and popular culture is that people should be permitted, if not actually enabled, to do what they want. This is almost always joined with the assumption that what people do want is to enjoy pleasure. Sometimes they speak of "happiness," but that term has little meaning to most folks other than feeling good.
>
> So it is now generally thought that desiring to do something is a sufficient or at least a weighty reason for doing it. From this we get our overall culture of sensuality, in which people are almost totally governed by their feelings . . . [Thus we have] a culture that finds the saying "If it feels good, do it" humorous instead of morally ridiculous of shameful.
>
> — Dallas Willard

ENDNOTES

1. Leo Sands and Rael Ombuor, "Uganda imposes death penalty for 'aggravated homosexuality,'" *Washington Post* (May 29, 2023), accessed at https://www.washingtonpost.com/world/2023/05/29/uganda-anti-homosexuality-law-lgbtq.

2. Jesus neither set aside nor relaxed the Old Testament's condemnation of extra-marital sex in this episode. The woman's sin was so serious that it could have invoked the death penalty in the days of Israel as a theocracy. (In Jesus' time, Jewish authorities did not have the right of executing anyone. This comes into play later in the Gospels when the Sanhedrin is forced to deliver Jesus to the Roman authorities for the possibility of crucifying him – not for blasphemy in claiming to be the Son of God, but for treason in making himself a rival king to Caesar.) In the John 8 episode, Jesus proved more astute than the woman's accusers who were trying to trap him. For one thing, adultery would have required a second party. Where was the partner to her forbidden act? Had the woman been "set up" and the man allowed to escape? More significantly, Torah provided that anyone shown to be a "malicious witness" by giving false testimony was to suffer the punishment his testimony would have brought on the accused (cf. Deut 19:15-19). Cf. J.D.M. Derrett, "Law in the New Testament: The Story of

the Woman Taken in Adultery,"*New Testament Studies* 10, no. 1 (Oct 1963): 1–26.

3. David P. Gushee, *Changing Our Mind* (Canton, MI: Read the Spirit Books, 2017), 10.

4. Adam Hamilton, *When Christians Get It Wrong*, updated and revised (Nashville: Abingdon Press, 2013), 90.

5. Karen R. Keen, *Scripture, Ethics, and the Possibility of Same-Sex Relationships* (Grand Rapids: Eerdmans, 2018), 102-103.

6. Ibid., 20.

7. Ibid., 1.

8. Ibid., 14.

9. Ibid., 63.

10. Ibid., 66-67.

11. Karen R. Keen, *The Bible and Sexuality* (Durham, NC: Contemplatio Publishing, 2020), 17.

12. Ibid.

13. Mark Achtemeier, *The Bible's Yes to Same-Sex Marriage*, new edition (Louisville: Westminster John Knox Press, 2015), 6.

14. One can even make the case that the "greed" (Gk, πλεονεξία = unrestrained desire for more, always craving more) named at Colossians 3:5 is as directly linked to the passion for more and novel sexual experience as for money. The first four vices Paul specifies all relate to sexual attitudes and actions (i.e., "sexual immorality, impurity, lust, evil desires"), so it is not impossible that the fifth (i.e., "greed" NIV) does so as well.

15. C.S. Lewis, *Mere Christianity* (New York: HarperCollins, 1980), 112. Lewis' notion of "two distinct kinds of marriage" – one governed by civil and another, if desired, blessed by and accountable to religious standards – seems to be consistent with what a noted American professor of law has advocated. Cf. Alan M. Dershowitz, "To Fix Gay Dilemma, Government Should Quit the Marriage Business," *Los Angeles Times*, Dec 3, 2003. Accessed at https://www.latimes.com/archives/la-xpm-2003-dec-03-oe-dersh3-story.html.

16. Lewis' view on divorce led to a sharp response from his friend, J.R.R. Tolkien, and many have taken the Tolkien path to argue that Lewis has (even if unintentionally) reduced Christian ethical standards to nothing more than "private devotional beliefs" with his view. Cf. Jake Meador, "Why C.S. Lewis Was Wrong on Marriage (and J.R.R. Tolkien Was Right)," *Christianity Today* (Dec 5, 2012). I believe this misses the central point of what Lewis and Paul both believed – viz., that Christians are answerable to a higher standard than is society at large. The moral prohibitions against a variety of sexual acts (e.g., lust, fornication, adultery, incest, same-sex intercourse) apply to all. But it is not the task of the church either to manipulate civil law to incorporate these bans or to punish persons who violate them. As with the overlapping area of a Venn Diagram, some items may be proscribed in both civil and biblical rulings (e.g., incest). But there well may be others (e.g., lust) that are distinctive to the church.

17. Perhaps I should clarify that by "church discipline" I do not mean excommunication, disfellowship, or some other form of punishment. To bring a Christian under discipline is to offer that person teaching, counsel, and encouragement designed to bring his or her life into conformity to the teaching and example of Jesus. Only at the end of a time of loving instruction and nurture do such actions as removing a person from the life of the larger church community for the sake of protecting the body become appropriate (cf. Matt 18:15-17).

18. Gordon D. Fee, *The First Epistle to the Corinthians*, rev. ed., The New International Commentary in the New Testament (Grand Rapids, MI: William B. Eerdmans Publishing Company, 2014), 248.

19. Someone wishing to pursue this topic might begin with Miroslav Volf, *A Public Faith: How Followers of Christ Should Serve the Common Good* (Grand Rapids, MI: Brazos Press, 2011).

20. Cf. Paul D. Miller, "What Is Christian Nationalism?", *Christianity Today* (Feb 3, 2021), https://www.christianitytoday.com/ct/2021/february-web-only/what-is-christian-nationalism.html?utm_medium=widgetsocial. Accessed April 2, 2022.

21. For helpful insights into this process and its ramifications, see Alan Kreider, *The Change of Conversion and the Origin of Christendom* (Eugene, OR: Wipf & Stock Publishers, 1999).

22. Wilbert Shenk, "New Wineskins for New Wine: Towards a Post-Christendom Ecclesiology," *International Bulletin of Missionary Research* 29 (April 2005): 77.

23. Glen H. Stassen and David P. Gushee, *Kingdom Ethics: Following Jesus in Contemporary Context* (Downers Grove, IL: InterVarsity Press, 2003). In this book, the authors present a traditional (i.e., non-affirming) view of homosexual behaviors in their Chapter 14 on Sexuality. Regarding same-sex behavior, they write: "Homosexual conduct is one form of sexual expression that falls outside the will of God, one manifestation of what Hays calls 'the disordered human condition' under the impact of sin" (311). Gushee's changed view of committed same-sex relationships (cf. fn2 above) will be examined in some detail later in this book.

> *"A person who is obstinately or intolerantly devoted to his or her own opinions and prejudices; especially: one who regards or treats the members of a group . . . with hatred and intolerance."*
> – Merriam-Webster, s.v. "bigot"

CHAPTER 2

Is It Possible to Think Someone Is Morally Wrong Without Being a Bigot?

The current and generally assumed correct answer to the title question for this chapter seems clear and emphatic. *No!*

But is that correct? Even if we grant – as I believe we must – that some of the views of some people we know *are* bigoted, is everyone who holds that a given behavior is morally wrong a bigot for taking a negative position on the topic? For example, Roman Catholics have always been a minority population in the United States and often have been the targets of religious bigotry. Perhaps it was the election of John F. Kennedy, the nation's first Catholic president, that turned back some (but not all) of that sentiment.

Most Americans have decided that Catholicism is not a subversive declaration of allegiance to a foreign political power (i.e., the Vatican) but a particular version of Christian belief and practice. Most non-Catholics now believe that the massive waves of Catholic immigrants who came to this country in the 1800s arrived in search of freedom, economic opportunity, and a better future for their children and not as members of a conspiracy to subvert the country's democratic institutions.

If that is granted about Roman Catholic beliefs and the presence of Catholics in the United States, then can a Presbyterian hold a different view on contraception from that of her Catholic friend next door without being a bigot? Could two men who are business partners – one a deacon in the United Methodist Church and the other a deacon in the Roman Catholic Church – hold opposing views about abortion in any and all situations without a charge of bigotry? (And would it be the Catholic or the Methodist who is a bigot for his view?)

Intelligent people can and often do disagree on significant topics in ethics. Our behaviors – behaviors that some defend as moral and others consider immoral – vary among neighbors, business associates, and church members. They are sometimes different even among members within the same Catholic or Protestant church – or in nuclear families within those traditions.

Then there are differences of sincere conviction and accepted practice among Christians and Jews, Jews and Muslims, Muslims and Christians. Must everyone with whom you or I disagree on some moral issue be labeled a bigot for thinking differently? Am I a bigot for believing abortion for sex selection is wrong? Must I think the person who believes abortion is sinful even in a case of rape to be a bigot for holding and arguing for that position?

In the hyperpolarized socio-political atmosphere of our time, people tend to demonize rather than debate. We are quick to assume the worst about one another and to presume that our opponents have bad motives for their views. Do we need a clearer example right now than immigrants coming to the United States via Mexico? A racist may argue that immigrants are displacing American workers by taking jobs for lower pay. One is not by definition racist, however, who argues that illegal immigration through Mexico should be controlled and regulated. In the same way, since there have been terrorist acts in the United States, as well as in France, Great Britain, and other countries, is it incontrovertibly racist and bigoted to argue that immigrants should be scrutinized with a reasonable degree of diligence?

Xenophobia, racism, bigotry, emotional judgments – all these exist. But not everyone who holds a negative view toward open-border immigration is either racist, prejudiced, or bigoted. Such judgments may disadvantage, mistreat, or demean a thoughtful and caring human being whose friendship would be a delight. One who crosses one of these lines for respectful dialogue might or might not change her mind on abortion, immigration, or same-sex marriage. She just might, however, learn things she did not know and learn that labeling and name-calling is counter-productive to civility, peace, and decency.

We might even say that handling our differences in moral decision-making in such a manner is a sign of intellectual, emotional, and spiritual maturity.

Assuming (and Saying) the Worst

Remember the childish arguments we used to have with our playmates around the sandbox or when playing dodgeball?

"I hit you," he yells. "You're out!"
"Did not!" he shouts back. "You missed me."
"No, I saw it. I hit you, so you're out!"
"You're trying to cheat. Cheater! Cheater!"
"You're the cheater! You're trying to stay in the game after you got hit!"
"I'm not the cheater. You are!"

Okay, enough of the childish spat. No matter which child is correct, the issue has become name-calling and perhaps squaring off to throw a punch or two. That's why we call arguments like those "childish" or "immature" – even when they happen years later between attorneys in a courtroom or professional athletes on the field, politicians during their campaigns or scholars pressing their theories at annual conferences. (That's when somebody mutters, "We could use an adult in the room about now!") We've all seen it happen. And it sometimes results in lifelong alienation of friends, the dissolution of business partnerships, or violence. It is never "pretty" – even when onlookers laugh because of the pettiness on display and extremes of rhetoric overheard.

One of the paralyzing, event-stopping words in conversations about human behavior in those settings is our English word *bigot*. People who study words aren't quite sure where the term originated, but it gets thrown around a lot these days in politics, sociology, ethics, and religion. It could use a bit more clarity.

One of the conversations in which the word finds frequent use these days is when same-sex behaviors are referenced by religious people who dare to challenge them. Their legitimation and normalization to the larger culture is such an agenda item for American media that anyone who questions them is subjected to the sort of name-calling that wouldn't be tolerated on most playgrounds. One becomes a bigot for supporting

> **"Judge Not..."**
>
> I know. I know. Nobody is supposed to be "judgmental." It is the cardinal sin of our time – and certainly far worse than pornography, drug addiction, or same-sex unions. Other than the obvious logical contradiction in saying "Judging is wrong" – which is a moral judgment itself – it simply makes no sense to make an unqualified statement of that sort.
>
> "But didn't Jesus himself tell us 'Judge not that you be not judged'?" somebody asks. Of course, he did. But it was hardly an unqualified statement. He certainly made judgments about behaviors and people. He called some people "snakes" and others "children of the devil." Sounds "judgmental" to me.
>
> A fuller statement from Jesus on the matter of judging is this one: "Look beneath the surface so you can judge correctly" (NLT). Or, in the traditional versions: "Do not judge by appearances, but judge with right judgment." The verse is John 7:24, and it does not contradict the one quoted above. It says the same thing in different words: You must make judgments. Just try to make good ones.
>
> I fear "You're being judgmental!" too often means "I've been caught doing something I know I really shouldn't be doing!"

the tenets of her or his faith – and what Western civilization has thought about sexual morality for a very long time.

Take, for example, an article in the *Asheville (North Carolina) Citizen-Times* that addressed the question "Does my Bible belief make me a 'bigot'?"[1] I ran across it doing a Google search of the title for this chapter. In a question-and-answer column that ran in the paper for a time, this was the issue addressed.

> Because I am a Bible-believing Christian, I have no choice but to believe that homosexuality is a sin. I know that opinion wouldn't make me popular in certain circles, and I'm OK with that. But here's the thing: I've been told, twice now, just for believing what I do about gays and gay marriage, that I am a bigot. A bigot! That's so crazy and wrong. Do you have any advice for how I should respond the next time someone calls me a bigot just because I choose to believe the word of God?

The answer given by the newspaper columnist illustrates one take on the opening sentence of this chapter. Beginning with an appeal for "the civility of our public discourse" and a plea for disputants to avoid "self-serving exercises in histrionic accusations and inflammatory hyperbole," the writer seemed determined to violate his own canons.

> Here's to equal parts passion and compassion returning to fashion.
> That said, I'm constrained to say that you are most definitely a bigot. Which I hate to say! But you've stated that you believe gay people are morally inferior (for to say "homosexuality is a sin" is to say exactly that), and that gay people should be denied the same civil rights enjoyed by all other Americans.
> By definition those opinions make you, my friend, a bigot.

Did the questioner say or imply that he believed gay people were "morally inferior"? Did he suggest they should be denied their civil rights? Does the question make "homosexuality is a sin" linguistically or logically equivalent to "gay people are morally inferior"? Think it through.

Good People Sometimes Do Bad Things

One can believe and say "X is a sin" without any implication that the person who does X is morally inferior. One of my dearest friends is an alcoholic. He is *not* morally inferior to me or anyone else in our shared circle of association. In fact, he is one of the most compassionate and generous people I know. He recently helped a person he knew only slightly get the legal help she needed to be protected from a sexual predator. He put himself at personal risk in a way that many would not – and paid the woman's legal fees. Morally inferior? Hardly. But with an ongoing weakness – probably rooted in genetics and reinforced by childhood experiences he did not choose – for alcohol.

People sometimes lie because they are frightened. They steal because they or their children are hungry. A teenager gets hooked on cocaine or pornography because "everybody's fooling around with it." Lying, stealing, addiction – these behaviors are called "sin" in Holy Scripture, but there is no warrant there for either considering people caught up in these behaviors "inferior" or unworthy of compassion.

Do you remember the Gospel account of Jesus and a woman of Samaria? She had been married five times and was living with a man to whom she was not married when Jesus met her beside Jacob's Well (John 4:1ff, cf. esp. vs.16-18). We don't know whether she was a libertine of some sort or a truly good person trapped in cycles of patriarchal power and abuse. Perhaps she was one of many Jewish women – both ancient and modern – who was trapped by her last husband's refusal to certify the termination of their marriage with a certificate of divorce.[2] Regardless of the details about which we can only speculate, she had no moral justification for living with a man who was not her husband. But notice how Jesus treated her with kindness. Israel's Messiah affirmed her personal dignity, related to her across the chasm of their ethnic backgrounds and sharp religious differences, and wound up sharing his message of the Kingdom of God with many from the woman's village because of her

> **How Christian Values Became Bigotry**
>
> [Court decisions and legislative action have] affirmed the validity of gay marriage, and I believe this creates a tipping point in American public discourse. The silencing of any privileged voice that biblical belief once had in our public square is just about complete.
>
> This trend has been building for a long time. Gay marriage is only one of the many issues that have transformed our culture. But given the intimate and embodied nature of the relationship in every genuine marriage, and the traditional procreative implications it has for making or closing off a nation's future, gay marriage has a uniquely powerful sign value.
>
> The most disturbing thing about the debate around gay marriage is the destruction of public reason that it accomplished. Emotion and sloganeering drove the argument, and the hatred that infected the conversation came far less from so-called "homophobes" than from many gay-issue activists themselves. People who uphold a traditional moral architecture for sexuality, marriage, and family have gone, in the space of just twenty years, from mainstream conviction to the equivalent of racists and bigots.
>
> — Charles J. Chaput

positive impression of him. That is the Christian model for dealing with marginalized people – a model not always imitated by his followers. Often, however, it is.

In fairness, I would agree with the columnist's answer if someone really did try to take away someone's civil rights because he or she is gay. No person's right to vote, live in public housing, buy property in a good neighborhood, attend high school or college, find employment, and the like should be denied for no other reason than being gay or lesbian. Yes, the Bible says homosexual *behavior* is outside God's will. It also says that about premarital and extramarital sexual behavior among heterosexuals. Does believing those behaviors are sinful mean a pregnant teenager, fornicating football player, philandering store manager, or cheating wife should be denied basic civil rights? Surely there are very few people who would argue for that.

That sort of unfair treatment is what happened to African Americans before civil rights legislation gave them legal protection from racism and bigotry. No one should be denied the basic civil right to get an education or live in decent housing because of skin color. Similar laws justly protect people of the LGBTQ+ community. No one should be denied her basic civil right to work for Walmart or to receive due process because she is lesbian. I trust that was made clear in the opening chapter of this book. The laws that protect minority populations are *good* laws that I support. They are rooted in the Christian ideal of love for our neighbors – even the neighbors with whom we have serious moral disagreements.

CHAPTER 2: IS BIBLICAL MORALITY MERE BIGOTRY?

By anyone's definition, the man Paul was a Christian. He clearly believed that people involved in sexual immorality (Gk, *porneia*) – including, specifically, "adulterers" (Gk, *moikoi*) and "men who have sex with men" (Gk, *oute malakoi oute arsenokoitai*) were guilty of sin and involved in behavior incompatible with the kingdom of God (1 Cor 6:9-10). At the same time, that same Christian apostle-evangelist believed it was not the business of Christian communities to denounce and treat with contempt persons outside their churches. "What business is it of mine to judge those outside the church?" he asked. "Are you not to judge those inside?" (1 Cor 5:12).

Paul functioned as a member of an alternative community that was situated within the Roman Empire and its low standards of moral behavior. In a world where violence was the norm, brothels were commonplace, and committed same-sex partnerships were a known and public part of the culture, he insisted that Jesus' followers must live by contrasting values of peace and reconciliation of conflict, abstinence from premarital sex, and fidelity within traditional opposite-sex marriages. There is no evidence that he lobbied the city fathers of Ephesus or Corinth to write his Christian convictions into public law. To the contrary, Christians of the first few centuries of the common era knew that their values were different from those of the general population. They believed that their moral values lived faithfully before a pagan world could turn heads to consider the claims of Jesus and choose to follow him.

For the sake of clarity, let me summarize and repeat. Our socio-political system is quite different from that of imperial Rome. In a democratic republic, people from all points of view are permitted to express and argue for the things they believe will serve the common good. Unfortunately, the American experiment generated what we now recognize to be a type of civil religion that allowed people to write and enforce laws that reflected their interpretations of Scripture. Should distinctive features of the Jewish, Christian, or Islamic religions be written into law codes that are meant for the common good? Or should those distinctive features (e.g., Muslim dress, Jewish Sabbath, Christian marriage) be written into the public duties of people who do not subscribe to those religions?[3] I am opposed to writing the distinctive features of any religion into civic statutes.

Respectful Disagreement

Perhaps to the chagrin of some, the path of civil religion is not the route I take in this book. Whether you agree with or reject the view I offer, I want you to know where I'm coming from in daring to go on record with my views about same-sex behavior, straights and gays, civil unions, same-sex marriage, sex and gender, and a host of interrelated subjects.

For the sake of identifying the landscape, let's just say this book is one attempt at exploring a range of topics about the world of LGBTQ+ "issues" from one Christian's point of view. I put the word "issues" in scare quotes for the simple reason that I prefer to think in terms of people rather than topics. But words such as topics and issues allow us to collect our thoughts around general ideas, patterns of action, or personal behaviors that play out with infinite variety among the billions of us who share Planet Earth.

That is also the reason for conceding that I am writing about these "concerns" – another of those collective terms – from "*one* Christian's point of view." When I have finished, I believe I will have represented a view shared by a reasonably large (but apparently diminishing!) group of people who self-identify as

> **Some Historical Perspective**
>
> Most striking is the view of "religion" in the abstract as the source of violent conflict, given the actual historical experience of most European societies in the twentieth century. . . . None of the horrible massacres – neither the senseless slaughter of millions of young Europeans in the trenches of World War I; nor the countless millions of victims of Bolshevik and communist terror through the Russian Revolution, Civil War, collectivizations campaigns, the Great Famine in Ukraine, the repeated cycles of Stalinist terror and the Gulag; nor the most unfathomable of all, the Nazi Holocaust and the global conflagration of World War II, culminating in the nuclear bombing of Hiroshima and Nagasaki – none of these terrible conflicts can be said to have been caused by religious fanaticism and intolerance. All of them were rather the product of modern secular ideologies.
>
> Yet contemporary Europeans obviously prefer to selectively forget the more inconvenient recent memories of secular ideological conflict and retrieve instead the long forgotten memories of the religious wars of early modern Europe to make sense of the religious conflicts they see today proliferating around the world and increasingly threatening them. . . . One may suspect that the function of such a selective historical memory is to safeguard the perception of the progressive achievements of Western secular modernity, offering a self-validating justification of the secular separation of religion and politics as the condition for modern liberal democratic politics, for global peace, and for the protection of individual privatized religious freedom.
>
> — José Casanova

Christians. Furthermore, I think the view I will offer is an orthodox (i.e., historically approved and regarded as doctrinally correct) view of both Jewish and Christian interpreters. It is not only what I was taught in my formative years – both by family and church mentors and in academic settings – but what "outsiders" to Judaism and Christianity would have known as their common shared view of same-sex relationships until only recently.

The fact that Judaism and Christianity have regarded a variety of same-sex activities as sinful behaviors is a matter of record. In the Tanakh (i.e., the Jewish term for what Christians call the Old Testament or Hebrew Scripture), the Holiness Code of Israel forbids male-with-male sexual coupling. Christian Scripture honors and repeats that prohibition. In successive chapters of this book, we will identify and explore the setting, intent, and application of the key texts from both testaments. I'm not sure those texts speak to every specific situation that can be identified. In fact, I'm quite sure they do *not* address those rare instances of what are termed intersex bodies that present with atypical chromosomes, hormones, or genitalia. But they establish moral boundaries within which biblical revelation expects believers to live.

Some argue we have reached the point in our cultural evolution that ethical categories and our attendant moral judgments are no longer appropriate. Yet not one of those people believes that argument holds, however, when she is robbed, he is raped, or their home is burgled and vandalized. Whether one believes in God or not and however that person views the Bible, *everyone* regards some things to be wrong and others to be right. For example, I have never had personal experience with anyone – even those who deny there are legitimate moral categories for human behaviors – who regarded the act of torturing human infants as acceptable (although there may be some) or thought the Holocaust was a good thing (although there definitely are such persons).

As already conceded, the words "bigot" and "bigotry" are tossed about freely these days – usually without clear definitions. What do the words mean? Once defined correctly, is one in fact a bigot who embraces Islamic, Jewish, or Christian religious beliefs? Is it a form of bigotry to hold that same-sex intercourse is outside the will of God? Is it bigotry to argue that heterosexual intercourse outside marriage is sinful? For that matter, is a Muslim or Jew guilty of bigotry for believing that

Trinitarian Christians are not monotheists? Is a Christian a bigot who believes that non-Christians are in spiritual jeopardy apart from knowing the gospel and being born from above?

What, then, does all this mean? It means we need clear definitions for the terms we use. Otherwise, we are still playing what I called a "playground argument" that amounts to nothing more than childish name-calling. So let me make a case for what these words mean.

A Clarification of Terms: Bigot, Bigotry, Bigoted

For some, the word bigot means little more than their dislike for those who hold opinions different from their own. But it seems to sell the word short to say that anyone who has ever voted for a Demopublican candidate is a bigot or, for that matter, anyone who wouldn't vote for a Republicrat is. Is a Roman Catholic a bigot because she has never attended a Protestant church or believes all Protestants are outside the true church and in spiritual jeopardy? Most of us don't use the word that way. Even when we believe someone is wrong – even seriously wrong about something – we don't treat the words "bigoted" and "mistaken" as synonyms.

Generally, the word "bigot" is reserved for someone deemed obsessively intolerant toward a particular ideology or group of people. Either a Protestant or Catholic could be a bigot for using religious dogma and scruples to deny housing, employment, or basic civil rights to someone who is not a member one's own group. Oh, it happens! Things are better now in Northern Ireland, but does no one remember the sharp religious division between the rival Protestant and Catholic groups there? The rhetoric and violence, the bombs and murders? The Protestant Reformation was itself not simply a shift in biblical interpretations and sacramental practices. It was the trigger to a series of wars across Europe – among them the famous Thirty Years War of 1618-1648 – that spread across the continent for parts of three decades.

Then, of course, there is the proper use of the term in modern times for the racist attitudes and behaviors of Adolf Hitler. The world was plunged into conflict because of the frenzied bigotry of the little corporal against the imaginary non-Aryans of the word – with Jewish people the most direct and extensive objects of his campaign of extermination. Lest we be dishonest with history, the historic and still-pervasive racism in America has spawned bigots and bigoted behaviors of unjust discrimination, economic oppression, sexual violence, and murder. The Ku Klux Klan and numerous varieties of skinheads revere Hitler, despise minorities generally, and hate Black people in particular with unwavering and unreasonable animus. But these are *descriptions* of bigoted ideologies and some examples of their notable advocates. We still need a definition.

Negatively, one is not a bigot who is wrong about something. Neither is it bigoted behavior to be wrong with passion and zeal. It does not make one a bigot to be so committed to an idea or person that he or she can't "listen to reason" in certain settings or during heated confrontation. But we are getting closer now to the line where bigotry begins.

Positively and for the purposes of this book, let me offer a working definition of the two words in question. I will use the term *bigotry* to mean "such intolerant devotion to one's own beliefs, prejudgments, or group that one is willing for outsiders to those views and associations to be denied basic rights, physically abused, or otherwise harmed." By this definition, a *bigot* is "one who is so intractably committed to his or her beliefs that persons of other views and groups are viewed as unworthy of respect or toleration and may be legitimate objects of hatred and abuse."

This definition of bigot is consistent with what I would call the well-established common usage of the word to mean "a person who is obstinately or intolerantly devoted to his or her own opinions and prejudices; *especially*: one who regards or treats the members of a group (as a racial or ethnic group) with hatred and intolerance."[4]

More about Words: "Homosexual" and "Homosexuality"

I will do my best to avoid using the words "homosexual" and "homosexuality" as *nouns* in this book. (That does not mean, of course, that other writers I may choose to quote employ them according to my preference and usage.) Instead, I choose to use them as *adjectives* and will write the slightly more cumbersome "homosexual activity" or "homosexual relationships." (Far more frequently, however, I will speak of "same-sex relationships" or "same-sex intercourse.") This is more than a semantic decision for me. For those who are new to any nuanced discussion of this subject matter, let me explain.

The *noun* "homosexual" may refer to a person whose inclination, natural desire, or orientation is to persons of the same sex. It may even capture elements of the life history of a person. But the noun versions do not require that we presume someone to be active in a same-sex relationship or to be acting out her or his inclination. That is, same-sex desire is not the same thing as same-sex activity. I have a Christian friend who is homosexual. That is his own *self*-description. You should also know that he has been chaste (i.e., celibate) for over a quarter of a century. But I will not use the term "homosexual" of anyone here because of the connotation of ongoing same-sex activity that so many attach to it.

Similarly, "homosexuality" is an abstract term similar to words such as "personality" or "machinery." To speak of Jane's personality tells you nothing about her state as a cheerful, gloomy, pleasant, or irritating woman. To say a railroad car is loaded with machinery indicates nothing to help you distinguish tractors from coffee makers as the cargo in shipment. So, too, if you tell me Bill is "dealing with homosexuality" or "struggling with homosexuality" you have not distinguished among his personal relationships, academic research, sexual actions, or most recent Bible study.

In attempting to reflect what I understand the Bible to teach, it is the use of the word "homosexual" as an *adjective* to name a function or activity – homosexual practice, homosexual activity, homosexual intercourse – that matters. In short, biblical language does not describe persons in terms of what we refer to as their sexual orientation so much as actions (i.e., lay with his wife, a man

> **Orientation or Conduct?**
>
> "Homosexuality" can refer to a condition or inclination apart from the acting-out of sexual relations, whereas the Bible does not recognize this distinction but normally speaks rather in terms of actual same-sex sexual relations.
>
> In view of the danger to which the church has often succumbed, that of showing insensitivity towards chaste persons of homosexual orientation, it is important to clarify that the issue for the Christian is not whether persons with homosexual orientation should be welcomed into the fellowship of the church – let us never forget that Christ died for all – but whether sexual relations between homosexuals are ever appropriate and, if so, on what terms.
>
> Because conduct and not orientation is the real issue, the purpose in this [study] is to ask whether the Bible considers homosexual relations to be sinful. If the answer suggested by biblical reflection is "yes," even when the case of covenanted Christians of homosexual orientation is considered, then the homosexual person accepted by God in Christ could no more engage in this activity than any other faithful Christian could in other forms of sin.
>
> — J. Glen Taylor

has sexual relations with a woman, a man has sexual relations with a man as one does with a woman) when addressing sexual norms or behaviors. Just as the word "heterosexual" tells you nothing about the celibate or promiscuous behavior of a man or the single versus married status of a woman, we should not presume to use the word "homosexual" of someone to say that person is engaged in sinful behavior.[5]

Sexual conduct, not orientation or inclination, is the issue to be explored in this book. Persons who experience "same-sex attraction" or who believe they have an inborn "homosexual orientation" should be welcomed by churches for the support in community we can give one another to deal with our divergent "issues" of weakness or liability to err. We are *all* sinners. Christ died for *all* of us. The Holy Spirit indwells *all* baptized believers to provide strength for renewal and holiness. The focus of this book is to determine if the Bible teaches that homosexual activity or same-sex intercourse is contrary to God's will.

Bigotry vs. *Agapē*

There is no honorable way to defend the church's[6] bigoted mistreatment of men and women of the LGBTQ+ community across the centuries.

I look back over my own life experience and confess my personal guilt for holding and expressing this sort of contempt and hypocrisy. Not only have I heard but also have told "gay jokes" and used language that I now regard as demeaning to others. I have been thoughtless and judgmental. Some of the times and situations were essentially private; others have been public and likely served to foster the same attitudes and behaviors in others.

I was wrong to hold those views, use those descriptors, laugh at or tell those jokes, or otherwise mistreat anyone from the LGBTQ+ community.

That statement of apology grows out of experiences going back to the late 1960s. While preaching for what is surely the most conservative church I ever served, a long-time member – who had grown up in that same body of people – wanted to meet and talk. Known to practically everyone in the church by first name and respected for being helpful in everything the church did from VBS to community service to periodic work on building and grounds, I was more than happy to make the time. In my office, that adult male Christian revealed a secret to me that no one in the church knew. He confided that he was same-sex attracted and had experienced occasional same-sex involvement with someone for whom he cared deeply. My sense of confusion and uncertainty was equal to the trepidation of my conversation partner in sharing a secret he had never disclosed to anyone else.

Did I not have a fixed, negative view of homosexuality? Had I not thought that persons caught up in such behavior were revolting? Had I not sneered at and judged them? Thought my narrow world had no such persons in it? That our church was a haven of the morally upright who were faithful to biblical teaching? Yet here was one of the kindest and most respected adult members of our church revealing what I never would have expected.

I no longer minister at that church. I have not been on their property or had meaningful contact with that church for more than 50 years – except for occasional contacts with the person who challenged me to rethink (and change!) my bigoted opinions about and reaction to members of what has since come to be known as the LGBTQ+ community. Until his death only a few years back, we had occasional contact as lifelong friends.

The struggle was always there for him. Just as I have other Christian friends who have had lifelong struggles with greed or heterosexual actions, diabetes or high blood pressure, there was no way for him to avoid the reality of certain inclinations, triggers, or desires. Choosing to live by an understanding of Holy Scripture that requires those impulses to be brought under the control of God's Spirit, his life was neither burdensome nor lived under a dark cloud of resentment. (We will come back to the topics of genetics, social conditioning, and orientation in later chapters.)

Culture tells us that inclinations and desires – wherever they come from – have the right to be satisfied and that neither God nor humans can tell us otherwise. But can that be correct? Anger, wanting something you cannot afford, meeting a person of the opposite sex to whom you feel attracted – those feelings do not justify violence, stealing, or fornication/adultery. Of all the false gods our culture prostrates itself to worship, Eros – the god of romantic passion and sensual love – seems to have primacy. Entertainment and art tell us that sexual ecstasy is the most desirable of all things. Indeed, we are told that life is empty and unrewarding apart from romantic love and erotic satisfaction.

Life's Greatest Good

Without denying for a moment the important place romantic love has played in my own life with a devoted wife of more than half a century, I have friends who have chosen not to marry. Most are Christians, and a few are not. I think of one of them in particular whose adult life has been lived as a single and celibate adult. Yet that dear friend would be the first to tell you that church has not always made that choice easy. Church leaders promote various family seminars, sponsor family-friendly events for our churches, and teach our teens how to choose godly mates for life.

Without intending harm, we have marginalized the single life. We have even made it appear disordered and distressing for anyone to be unmarried and/or without children. It could appear that unmarried people are somehow abnormal. Really? Do we really think Paul was unfulfilled? That Jesus was somehow less than he could have been as a married father of three?

Foreign as it may sound to modern ears, great sex is not the epitome of human life. Romantic love is an impulse created by God to assure the reproduction of the race. More than that, it is an instrumental good to enhance marital commitment and to provide a nonverbal means for expressing intimate delight in another. But sensual delight in another person is not the essence of being human. It is not the goal or highest ideal of human life. It can, in fact, be frustrating, confusing, ugly, and painful. Holy in its God-ordained proper context, the power of sensual attraction can stir passions that have the ability to blind people to what is true, pure, and holy.

Against the hold of Eros on devotees ancient or modern, the distinctive God of Christian Orthodoxy makes himself known as *agapē*. This Greek word that lacked a clear and consistent meaning in its use was taken into the earliest Christian vocabulary and increasingly used in a distinctive way to describe a type of love that is beyond erotic feelings that can come and go quite independently of one's will. *Agapē* is the love one wills toward another. As an action undertaken by one's choice and with deep resolve, *agapē* is love that seeks another's wellbeing and happiness. It is a love that can waive its rights, show great patience, refuse to take advantage, and find joy in doing right things that honor God's will. This is the type of love that can lay down its life for another.

It is a shame that our single English word "love" runs the gamut to cover actions ranging from pedophilia to parental sacrifice, from forbidden passions to the willing sacrifice of his life by Jesus, from grooming and exploitation to lifelong commitment and enhancement of another's welfare. Christian belief is that the God who created human males and females in his likeness and for the sake of bearing his image to one another is the one best qualified to teach us what love is and to define the parameters for its holy expression.

In biblical literature, it is not simply that God knows about love or does loving things. According to Scripture, God *is* love (1 John 4:8). This is not to say that God is a mere abstraction or disembodied principle of human behavior. To the contrary, it is to affirm that love is defined by and given its ideal personification by the God who made himself known to Abraham, rescued Abraham's enslaved descendants through Moses, appeared in space-time history as Jesus of Nazareth, and invites all who believe in him to share in life as it was meant to be lived. This is what the Bible calls "eternal life" – not meaning merely life that can extend endlessly, but more especially a life with the beautifully distinct quality of reflecting God's holiness into his creation.

The God whose essential nature is self-giving love is not driven by hatred and intolerance. Even when his intrinsic holiness is offended and grieved by something false, unholy, or impure, he pleads with (but does not coerce!) his human offspring. Even when he threatens by warning of the consequences of sin, that very threat is more correctly heard as an invitation to repent, be healed, and accept restoration to life as it is meant to be lived.

We should not be surprised, then, that the Bible calls the people of this God to embrace holiness and upright behavior. With other value systems dominant in the Ancient Near East, Israel was called to "Be holy, for I am holy" (Lev 11:44-45). With pagan philosophies and polytheistic religions dominant in the Roman Empire, Christians likewise were called to "abstain from sinful desires" that were catered to in that culture. To the contrary, this was the Christian challenge: "Live such good lives among the pagans that, though they accuse you of doing wrong, they may see your good deeds and glorify God on the day he visits us" (1 Pet 2:11-12).

Given that the earliest Christians could not escape charges of *atheism* (because they would not worship the gods of Rome), *cannibalism* (because they took the bread and wine of Communion as the body and blood of Jesus), and *incest* (because these brothers and sisters met in secret and greeted each other with a holy kiss), I cannot hope to escape the charge of bigotry from some quarters. That will be inevitable. So I confess appreciation for David Gushee's response to those who have disagreed with his switch from a traditional, non-affirming view of this matter to a revisionist, affirming posture: "Let me clarify here that I am not saying that simply holding traditionalist beliefs on LGBTQ sexual relationships is bigoted and hateful."[7] He and I – for all the things on which we may disagree – are united in our renunciation of demeaning rhetoric about or hateful language to gay and lesbian persons. The label "Christian love" or "doctrinal soundness" does not attach to mean-spirited verbal grenades tossed toward those with whom we disagree on any topic.

> **The Bible and Human Dignity**
> "There is no graded scale of essential worth," [Dr. Martin Luther] King had written a year before his assassination. "Every human being has etched in his personality the indelible stamp of the Creator. Every man must be respected because God loves him." Every woman too, a feminist might have added. Yet King's words, while certainly bearing witness to an instinctive strain of patriarchy within Christianity, bore witness as well to why, across the Western world, this was coming to seem a problem. That every human being possessed an equal dignity was not remotely self-evident a truth. A Roman would have laughed at it. To campaign against discrimination on the grounds of gender or sexuality, however, was to depend on large numbers of people sharing in a common assumption: that everyone possessed an inherent worth. The origins of this principle – as Nietzsche had so contemptuously pointed out – lay not in the French Revolution, nor in the Declaration of Independence, nor in the Enlightenment, but in the Bible.
> — Tom Holland

What Makes Relationships "Legitimate"

"So, it's just that you don't believe gay people can be devoted to one another, faithful to one another, and truly loving in their relationship? Is that what you think? Is that where you are going in this book?"

That is most definitely *not* what I believe. To the contrary, I am quite sure there are males and females who are as content and happy in their same-sex relationships as their heterosexual neighbors are in theirs. Neither do I feel compelled to argue that the percentage of happy relationships of the latter kind is higher. For the ethical question this book is raising, the degree of happiness in a relationship is not relevant. For psychologists, maybe. For sociologists, perhaps.

That love makes a relationship legitimate is one of the great misunderstandings of our time. It is why novels, TV series, and movies can make the sexual relationship of a 45-year-old married woman to her husband's 32-year-old neighbor appear both desirable and noble. Especially if her 45-year-old husband is neglecting her to play golf constantly. It is why many people would be unable to find fault with that 30-something man who has found his soulmate in his best friend's wife. They simply "fell in love" – and could not help it. And, increasingly, people might be unable to find fault if that same man were to find his soulmate and sexual fulfillment in that couple's college-age son. We live in a culture that celebrates romantic love as the ultimate good and revels in sexual intimacy with very few boundaries.

Attraction, great sex, devotion, romance – not one of these nor all of them together can make a relationship legitimate for people who call themselves disciples of Jesus. His call to his people is not "Find your authentic selves!" or even "Don't worry; be happy!" His challenge to his people is that we should seek the reign of God over all things in our lives (Matt 6:33). Love him more than any other person (Matt 10:37-38; cf. Luke 14:26-27). Deny yourself, take up your cross, and follow Jesus (Mark 8:34). And keep the commandments he and the Father have given (John 14:21).

It will be the task of this book to demonstrate that rabbis, apostles, and evangelists have not missed the meaning of the Bible's consistent censure of the lifestyle practiced and defended by the LGBTQ+ community and

---

> **"A Whole Forest of Possibilities"**
>
> In her book *Can't We Make Moral Judgments?* [British philosopher Mary] Midgley notes our contemporary search for a nonjudgmental politics and quotes all those who cry, in effect, "But surely it's always wrong to make moral judgments." We are not permitted to make anyone uncomfortable, to be "insensitive." Yet moral judgment of "some kind," says Midgley, "is a necessary element to our thinking. . . . Judging makes it possible for us to "find our way through a whole forest of possibilities."
>
> Midgley argues that Jesus was taking aim at sweeping condemnations and vindictiveness: he was not trashing the "whole faculty of judgment." Indeed, Jesus is making the "subtle point that while we cannot possibly avoid judging, we can see to it that we judge fairly, as we would expect others to do to us." . . . Subjectivism in such matters – of the "I'm okay, you're okay," variety – is a copout, a way to stop forming and expressing moral judgments altogether. This strange suspension of specific moments of judgment goes hand-in-glove, of course, with an often violent rhetoric of condemnation of whole categories of persons, past and present – that all-purpose villain, the Dead White European Male, comes to mind.
>
> — Jean Bethke Eishtain

its sympathizers. From both Old and New Testaments, it will be demonstrated that the clash between erotic love outside monogamous heterosexual marriage falls short of the divine will.

At the same time, it will be my task to demonstrate that the love of God for anyone caught up in various aspects of what the New Testament calls *porneia* is both real and meaningful. God is not unfair or unloving to call believers to a distinctive way of life that is more challenging to some than others because of their strong inclinations – whether from genetic or cultural factors, or both.

So, regardless of where your sympathies lie at the moment, please read on with a view to exploring the biblical text as the definitive word on this issue. I hope you will find some helpful clarification and insight as you do so.

ENDNOTES

1. N. John Shore Jr., "Ask John: Does my Bible belief make me a 'bigot'?" *Asheville Citizen-Times (Online)*, Oct 17, 2017, https://www.citizen-times.com/story/entertainment/2017/10/17/ask-john-does-my-bible-belief-make-me-bigot/769978001. Accessed Mar 12, 2022.

2. Cf. Caren Chesler, "'Unchain Your Wife': the Orthodox women shining a light on 'get' refusal," *The Guardian*, June 4, 2021. Accessed at https://www.theguardian.com/world/2021/jun/04/jewish-orthodox-women-divorce-get-refusal.

3. Murder, stealing, lying, and other basic ethical tenets are shared among both religious and non-religious groups. There are no cultures, however primitive, that do not have such rules. The distinctive features of various cultures have to do with behaviors such as family structure, sexual mores, and religious rituals. What we variously call civil religion or civic religion is the imposition of some group's theistic beliefs and religious dogmas to be imposed on a culture through public sentiment and law. While I would argue that America has been blessed by God (as have other nations), I do not believe the United States is a modern "God's Chosen People" or that Christians should be allowed to impose our faith on non-Christians through civil statutes. Old Testament Israel functioned as a theocracy in which religious and civil authority were often united. The early church operated at the edges of the Roman Empire – until the fateful events of Constantine and the fourth century that created something that came to be known as Christendom.

4. "Bigot," *Merriam-Webster.com Dictionary*, Merriam-Webster, https://www.merriam-webster.com/dictionary/bigot.

5. A failure to make this distinction has created a "translation furor" that some are attempting to exploit in the recent documentary "1946: The Mistranslation That Shifted Culture." See Appendix D for more information on the film, its claims, and an evaluation of those claims.

6. The word "church" in this sentence is used to mean all those Christian associations – whether Roman Catholic, Orthodox, Protestant, Free Church, non-denominational, or others – of modern "Christendom." It is certainly not meant to include every single member of all these groups but to say that self-described Christians from all tribes have been guilty of prejudice, intolerance, racism, bigotry against gay people across time. Unless a given denomination is specified in this book (e.g., Roman Catholic Church, Baptist Church, Churches of Christ, etc.), the word should be understood in the sense of this big-tent perspective.

7. Gushee, *Changing Our Mind*, 169.

> *"Haven't you read that at the beginning the Creator 'made them male and female,' and said, 'For this reason a man will leave his father and mother and be united to his wife, and the two will become one flesh'?"*
>
> — Jesus of Nazareth

CHAPTER 3

Putting Sex in Its Proper Place

The argument of this chapter – of the entire book, in fact – is that the ethically appropriate and healthiest personal view of human sexuality is the one found in the Bible's teaching about the nature, purpose, and outcomes of marriage and family life within the will of God. So let me be clear: I am not writing to bash the LGBTQ+ community or any individual in it. I am writing to affirm what I believe to be a biblical view of sex in the lives of people in God's image. From the point of view of orthodox Christian faith, monogamous male-female marriage is the starting place for discussing all things sexual. It is marriage that puts sex in its proper place.

The chaste single life is equally honorable to a faithful, loving married life between one man and one woman. A good deal will be said on the subject of being single to God's glory later in the book, but the purpose of this chapter is to define the biblically authorized (though not commanded) possibilities for marriage. Specifically, this chapter will argue that genital sexual activity has ethical approval in Holy Scripture within one-woman, one-man marriage.

"Marriage should be honored by all, and the marriage bed kept

> **God Created Marriage . . .**
> According to the Bible, God devised marriage to reflect his saving love for us in Christ, to refine our character, to create stable human community for the birth and nurture of children, and to accomplish all this by bringing the complementary sexes into an enduring whole-life union. It needs to be said, therefore, that this Christian vision for marriage is not something that can be realized by two people of the same sex. That is the unanimous view of the Biblical authors . . .
>
> — Tim Keller

pure, for God will judge the adulterer and all the sexually immoral" (Heb 13:4). This is the text introduced back in Chapter 1, where I described it as "a summary statement of everything the Bible affirms about the place of sex in human relationships." Much that will follow in the next several chapters is explanation and defense of what earlier was called its "positive-negative argument" about sexuality.

No theology can be built on a solitary verse from the Bible. Brief though it is, this one very specific statement about sexual ethics identifies the context within which sexual intercourse is virtuous and affirms divine judgment against its misplacement and misuse.

The affirmation of *marriage* as worthy of being "honored by all" in this text can be taken to be nothing other than covenanted male-female union. The word has always and only been understood to mean that until just recently. As will be documented directly, when Greeks, Romans, or others in biblical times referred to same-sex relationships as "marriages," they did so in some form similar to this sentence. They used the social and linguistic equivalent to scare quotes to identify it as a parody of a real marriage. On the other hand, the denunciation of an *adulterer* (Gk, *moichos*) or *sexually immoral* (Gk, *pornos*) person leaves no doubt about the moral status of behaviors ranging from premarital heterosexual intercourse to marital infidelity, from one-night stands to long-term relationships outside marriage, from male prostitution to covenanted same-sex relationships proffered as marriages. They all lie outside the will of God and are, by definition, sinful.

> In saying that the marriage relationship should be "undefiled" the writer reverts to the cultic language so pervasive in Hebrews. By so doing, the author brings marriage into the circle of sanctification essential to worship that is acceptable to God (12:28). This directive about marriage is given support by a reminder that God judges fornicators (a general reference to sexual immorality) as well as adulterers (a specific reference to a breach of marriage vows).[1]

Later in this book, I will provide the linguistic data that establishes *pornos* as a generic term that names any person engaging in sexual intercourse other than as a husband and wife in their heterosexual marriage. *Moichos* extends the category of moral offense beyond merely sex outside marriage to name the specific sin of faithlessness to one's covenant of marriage in having sex with anyone other than his or her lawful mate. The essential difference in the Greek terms *pornos* – one who is "sexually immoral" (NIV, NRSVue) or a "fornicator" (KJV) – and *moichos* is that the latter person is not only guilty of a sexual offense but also adds to it the additional transgression of the covenant promise someone has made to a marriage partner. The latter is an even more serious moral infraction precisely because of the breach of faith involved. Again, the linguistic and textual details to this come later.

For now, my responsibility is to trace the biblical narrative about marriage sufficiently to show that the Hebrews 13:4 statement is what I have claimed – a summary statement of the Christian code of sexual ethics that affirms the honor and purity of traditional marriage and simultaneously rejects the ethical legitimacy of sexual intercourse in all other settings. Even though Greek culture legitimated pederasty, Roman statutes recognized a man's right to sex with his male or female slaves, or American law declares same-sex marriage to be legally equivalent to heterosexual marriage, Christians are accountable to God's higher authority.

So we begin with the Genesis account of creation to find the biblical explanation of how to put sex in its God-intended, God-approved place in human relationships.

> **But Have We Thought about Sex?**
>
> We live in a sexualized culture. But that fact is increasingly difficult for us to recognize. We are becoming like the baby fish who said to its mother, "Where's all this water everyone's talking about?" A distorted sexuality is the water we swim in. . . . When I say our culture is "sexualized," I mean we talk a lot about sex. We joke about it and write in bathroom stalls about it, but we rarely stop to think about sex.
>
> Frank Sheed, the Australian apologist, explains: "The typical modern man practically never thinks about sex. He dreams of it, of course, by day and by night; he craves for it; he pictures it, is stimulated or depressed by it, slavers over it. But this frothing, steaming activity is not thinking. Slavering is not thinking, picturing is not thinking, craving is not thinking, dreaming is not thinking. Thinking means bringing the power of the mind to bear: thinking about sex means striving to see sex in its innermost reality and in the function it is meant to serve."
>
> Since this is our situation, chastity has no interest in our not thinking about sex; it would really like for us to think well about sex. The place to start is with the telos for which God created us, and why God made the other creatures and us sexual beings: "Be fruitful and multiply" (Genesis 1:22, 28). This tells us that sex, sexual desire, and orgasms are good. Chastity wants us to think about what good it is that they were created for. How do they fit within God's plan for us to love one another and honor God?
>
> The virtue of chastity calls us, as sexual beings, to revere ourselves as creatures made in the image of God and made to honor God through our actions – through how we do have sex and do not have sex.
>
> — Matt Fradd

The Biblical Narrative: Marriage

In Genesis, the male-female relationship that has been called marriage ever since is defined in unmistakable language and set forth as the divine ideal. When Adam received Eve as "bone of my bone and flesh of my flesh," the text immediately explains the significance of the event: "That is why a man leaves his father and mother and is united to his wife, and they become one flesh" (Gen 2:24). The one-flesh union of male and female in marriage is not euphemistic jargon that allows the biblical writer to avoid saying Eve had sexual intercourse with Adam. To the contrary, it is an indication of the theological placement of sex's dynamic power within a gendered, covenanted, and exclusive relationship. Genesis also contains histories of conflict and chaos that result when that ideal is not maintained. The prime example would be the Abraham and Sarah story that begins going sideways when Sarah's handmaid becomes Abraham's sexual partner – consistent with custom and law in the Ancient Near East – as they try to solve the mystery of a promised child on their human initiative.

In Exodus, the creational intent for marriage is affirmed in the Ten Commandments. Among the central elements required of Yahweh's covenant people is that they were to honor covenant commitments within the community. "You shall not commit adultery" (Ex 20:14) speaks directly to the positive and exclusive place of sexuality within marital covenants. The Torah sees the violation of one's own or another's marital covenant by a breach of covenant fidelity as not only a sin against human good faith but also a sin against God himself (cf. Gen 39:9). In fact, the nurturing of a concept of integrity within one's commitments is emphasized by the use of adultery language in various writings of the prophets to describe Israel's betrayal of Yahweh (cf. Book of Hosea). The standard against which individuals or a nation could be faulted was always the divinely mandated ideal of covenant fidelity as expressed in the positive function of sexual loyalty in marriage.

In the later sections of Exodus and particularly in the Holiness Code of Leviticus (chs 17-26), the prohibitions of incest, same-sex intercourse, bestiality, and other sexual acts are hardly to be thought of as free-standing bits of legislation. They are protections of marriage and family. It is a mistake of the first order to characterize marriage as "an institution that was born, formed, and structured for and by patriarchy."[2] Torah presents *both* females and males as being created "in the image of God" (Gen 1:27), with *both* mothers and fathers to be honored by their children (Ex 20:12), and *women* given special protection under its provisions for divorce[3] (Deut 24:1-4).

In the New Testament, both the Gospels and Epistles follow the precedent established in the Hebrew Scriptures. Interestingly, when Jesus was asked about an ongoing dispute among the rabbis about divorce, he appealed to Genesis.

> Haven't you read, he replied, that at the beginning the Creator "made them male and female" and said, "For this reason a man will leave his father and mother and be united to his wife, and the two will become one flesh"? So they are no longer two, but one flesh. Therefore what God has joined together, let no one separate (Matt 19:4-6).

According to Jesus, Genesis is normative for the permanence of marriage. What has been "joined" with divine blessing is not to be separated by human faithlessness. And the joining in marriage that has received divine blessing in the creation account is a union of "male and female." Is it only an accident of this statement that Jesus specifies the male-female nature of marriage? Is there anything defining or prescriptive in his words? A more detailed examination of both the Genesis account and Jesus' use of it will come later in this book.

Sex in Its Proper Moral Context

To focus on a handful of texts that speak to same-sex intercourse is too narrow a universe of discourse. That someone has a particular opposite-sex or same-sex inclination, orientation, and/or set of experiences neither validates them to be holy nor condemns them as evil. My conviction is, however, that every marriage text implies something central to the subject at hand. The limited number of texts about departures from the marriage narrative are protections and should be expected to be both less frequent and less detailed than some think would be needed to make this a significant concern to Christian ethics.

For example, Robin Scroggs grants that the Old Testament laws found in the Torah's Holiness Code are "unequivocally opposed to male homosexual activity."[4]

> **Disordered Sexual Pairings**
>
> Fornication fails to honor the image of God in the other person, for it only sees the other as a commodity. Adultery violates the shrine of marital fidelity which houses and keeps sacred the sexual expression. Incest is an effort to achieve union with an image too close to oneself ... Bestiality is the effort to achieve union with an image too different from oneself ... And homosexuality is a confusion, since it involves the effort of achieving union with a "mirror" image of oneself. This "other" is not sufficiently different.
>
> — Michael Ukleja

From that admission, he proceeds to affirm "the New Testament church [is] uninterested in the topic."[5] The path from his admission to his affirmation (by assigning Paul's three statements about homosexual activity to a narrow concern about pederasty) will be traced later. For now, I would only point to his claim that the fact that "only" three New Testament texts (Rom 1:26-27; 1 Cor 6:9; 1 Tim 1:10) name same-sex intercourse implies the earliest Christians were unconcerned about the topic that has caused so much angst in our day.

> We might observe, however that the New Testament commandment to "love your enemies" appears explicitly in only three texts (Matt 5:43-48; Luke 6:26-27; Rom 12:17-21). Yet we should not say that the New Testament is virtually silent on, and that the early church was hardly interested in, loving enemies.
>
> The rhetorical thrust of such arguments is that the church's debate over same-sex union is out of proportion to, and grants the matter relevance unwarranted by, Scripture. Yet I doubt that many Christians would say that the church's concern for loving neighbors and enemies is disproportional to and unwarranted by Scripture. The importance of a matter in Scripture and the relevance of that matter for the church today cannot be gauged simply by its numerical frequency in the biblical canon.[6]

Real-Life Meaning and Implications

If the Bible does in fact affirm that monogamous male-female partnership in marriage is normative for putting sex in a consecrated context for Christians, it *will* matter. If someone who is affirming toward or living a same-sex partnership changes his or her mind, it will have real-life implications. The same is true not only about same-sex intercourse but premarital cohabitation, "friends with benefits," pornography, sexting, and a variety of other behaviors that have been normalized of late. They, too, are implicated.

The disapproving attitude in Scripture toward these behaviors has serious implications. Specifically, it entails a plea for persons in those relationships to see themselves through God's eyes (i.e., to accept biblical truth), change their minds about a lifestyle they have embraced (i.e., to repent), begin to live on God's terms for his beloved human beings (i.e., to pursue holiness), and allow God's presence (i.e., in the form of the indwelling Holy Spirit) to heal and transform them.

The "process" just outlined is the same for all of us – no matter where we are when we begin to seek God. Anyone who is concerned to understand Jesus of Nazareth, follow him as a disciple, and to be part of a Christian community knows the progression just summarized. First, one learns the central message of the gospel. To accept it as true and authoritative to one's life is faith; to reject the Jesus Story as either untrue, irrelevant, or too demanding is unbelief. Second, one who accepts the gospel as true begins a process of moving deeper into a Christ-following life and turning away from ideas, attitudes, and behaviors that are inconsistent with the gospel; the biblical word for this process of faith's turn toward Jesus and away from sin is repentance. Third, this changes a person's life goal from selfish concerns to the God and neighbor concerns that reflect the two great commands of Jesus about love; holiness is the Bible's term for people and lifestyles dedicated or set apart to that pursuit. Fourth, the dynamic for this deep and thorough reorientation of a human life is not personal determination and strength of will; it comes about through the empowering presence of the Holy Spirit in a woman or man's surrendered life.

"Boundaries" Are Necessary

Books that trace this process of life change at various starting points have been and will continue to be written for people. It is what Christian evangelists and teachers believe our calling and duty to be. This book is written to address human sexuality for its implications to Christian discipleship. I am not a "sexologist" and have no competence to address the concerns some would want addressed about sex. It is not the physiology or psychology of sexual relationships but their ethical status that I will address.

Most people acknowledge that sex is more than a physical function. Plants and animals, as well as human beings, are sexual for the purpose of reproduction. In the case of human beings, however, sex is not merely a utilitarian function for continuing the race but important to self-awareness, emotional health, spiritual life, and ethics. On the point of the ethical and moral dimensions of sex, everyone believes there are boundary markers. You may not be a Christian or have any interest in Christian doctrine, but I suspect you believe that female genital mutilation and rape as a "weapon of war" are serious moral offenses. Even so culturally sensitive an institution as the United Nations – which insists that intercultural moral judgments are inappropriate – has named both these assaults on human bodies and human dignity immoral and sees them as pressing challenges to the modern world.[7]

> **Sexual Intimacy and Moral Commitment**
> The man and woman who engage in sexual intercourse are giving their bodies, the most intimate physical expression of themselves, over to the other. Unlike the man who plays tennis with a woman, the man who has sexual relations with her has literally entered her. A man and woman engaging in sexual relations have united themselves as intimately and as totally as is physically possible for two human beings. Their union is not simply a union of organs, but it as intimate and as total a physical union of two selves as is possible of achievement. . . .
> The sexual encounter is a definitive experience, one in which the physical intimacy and merging involves also a merging of the nonphysical dimensions of the partners. . . . Within the lives of those who have so committed themselves to each other, sexual intercourse is a way of asserting and confirming the fullness and totality of their mutual commitment.
> — Vincent Punzo

The point of all this is essentially twofold: (1) to document the fact that all people in all generations believe there are moral boundaries to sexual conduct and simultaneously (2) to short-circuit the claim that only a limited number of ultra-conservative Christians believe it is even appropriate to say where those boundaries are and to defend them against criticism. You may be surprised to learn about the pagan cultural settings for sexual behavior in both Old and New Testament times. The surprise is likely to come in learning how lenient and indulgent the standards of the Ancient Near East, Greece, and Rome were.

If you have been told, for example, that ancient cultures were generally repressive and inhibited about sex, you will find out the opposite is true. If you thought Judaism and Christianity simply reflected ancient sexual taboos in their Scriptures, you will find how mistaken an impression that is. If you have been told that ancient cultures had no significant level of toleration for homosexual and lesbian behaviors and certainly nothing resembling today's "long-term, loving, monogamous commitment by same-sex partners," you will find the documentation for just such relationships in the chapters ahead.

Beginning at the Beginning

But our beginning place to set all this into a Christian framework is not Egypt or Babylon, not even Athens or Rome. We must begin with the biblical materials in Genesis. And we begin with the positive affirmations of marriage and family in the opening book of the Torah. Only against that background can we understand and evaluate for their ongoing value the restrictive texts in the Old Testament about sexual behaviors.

In due course, we will see how the biblical information about marriage is directly relevant to persons who are unmarried – whether straight or gay. And this thorny question will be addressed in due course: What about those who commit themselves to Christ but who see themselves as non-heterosexual and have no desire or intention to marry someone of the opposite sex? Those people are not weird, incomplete, or somehow deficient – but neither are they released from the biblical guidelines that govern *all* sexual behavior.

Instead of giving us constant anathemas against pornography, pedophilia, premarital sex, extramarital sex, adultery, same-sex intercourse, pederasty, lesbianism, bisexuality, transgenderism, prostitution, polyamory, and bestiality, the Old and New Testaments offer a thematic affirmation of what the present social climate describes as long-term, covenanted, monogamous heterosexual relationships. The older term for that rather tedious descriptor is *marriage*. And it is marriage that puts sex in its place – a holy and honorable place before God and humankind.

It is time to open Scripture and seek insights about the natural order of human life. We will begin where the Bible itself begins, not with a study of boundaries and prohibitions but with human life as it was meant to function. Before reading the creation account in Genesis in some detail, however, it might be good to ponder what has happened to undermine "traditional marriage" of late.

ENDNOTES

1. Fred B. Craddock, "The Letter to the Hebrews," *New Interpreter's Bible* (Nashville: Abingdon Press, 1998), 12:163.

2. Elizabeth Stuart, *Just Good Friends: Toward a Lesbian and Gay Theology of Relationships* (London: Mowbray, 1995), 174.

3. The Jewish "certificate of divorce" provided for in Deut 24:1 (cf. Matt 19:7) documented a woman's clean break from a marriage, affirmed her right to marry again, and protected her from being harassed and/or reclaimed by her former mate. Cf. David Instone-Brewer, *Divorce and Remarriage in the Bible: The Social and Literary Context* (Grand Rapids: William B. Eerdmans, 2002), 28-33.

4. Robin Scroggs, *The New Testament and Homosexuality: Contextual Background for Contemporary Debate* (Philadelphia: Fortress Press, 1983), 99.

5. Ibid., 101.

6. Darrin W. Snyder Belousek, *Marriage, Scripture, and the Church: Theological Discernment on the Question of Same-Sex Union* (Grand Rapids: Baker Academic, 2021), 17.

7. In the "Secretary-General's Message for 2022," the UN's chief officer, António Guterres, named female genital mutilation "an abhorrent human rights violation that causes profound and permanent harm to women and girls around the world." (https://www.un.org/en/observances/female-genital-mutilation-day/message). In October 2022, the Secretary-General also released a document to the UN General Assembly titled "Report of the Independent International Commission of Inquiry on Ukraine" that contains findings of human rights violations following the invasion of Ukraine by Russian military forces. Page 14 of the 17-page document says: "In the period and locations under review, the Commission has been investigating cases of rape committed by some Russian armed forces soldiers in localities that came under their control, which are war crimes. Victims range from four to over 80 years old. Perpetrators raped the women and girls in their homes or took them and raped them in unoccupied dwellings. In most cases, these acts also amount to torture and cruel or inhumane treatment for the victims and for relatives who were forced to watch. Other incidents of sexual violence were also documented against women, men, and girls." Accessed at https://www.ohchr.org/sites/default/files/2022-10/A-77-533-AUV-EN.pdf.

> *"The scale of marital breakdown in the West since 1960 has no historical precedent. . . . At no time in history, with the possible exception of Imperial Rome, has the institution of marriage been more problematic than today."*
> – (Historian) Lawrence Stone

CHAPTER 4

Look What We've Done to Marriage!

The fundamental importance of monogamous heterosexual marriage to the enterprise of being human came under devastating assault in the anti-war, anti-establishment, anti-authority decade of the 1960s. We are far enough removed from that era now to see some of the negative impact of that onslaught in bold relief.

The late Chief Rabbi of the United Kingdom, Jonathan Sacks, released his book *Morality* shortly before his sudden death in 2020. Lamenting the widespread loss of a strong, shared moral code in the West and the general disposition of moderns to put self-interest above the common good, his fourth chapter speaks to what he termed "The Fragile Family." The chapter begins with his personal recall of the BBC Reith Lectures of 1967. Edmund Leach, Professor of Anthropology at Cambridge University, made this declaration: "Far from being the basis of the good society, the family, with its narrow privacy and tawdry secrets, is the source of all our discontents."

Upon hearing someone of Leach's academic stature not only reflect but also clearly laud the mood of the sexual revolution of his day, Sacks paid attention.

> That was when I knew something extraordinary was happening. . . . [He] was dismissing, with little less than disdain, the most significant institution of Western civilization, the vehicle through which it is transmitted, genetically and culturally, its past to the future: namely, marriage and family life.
>
> My first thought was: "Speak for yourself, Professor Leach." . . . Marriage is fundamental to the moral enterprise because it is the supreme example of the

transformation of two "I's" into a collective "We." It is the consecration of a commitment to care for an Other. It is the formalization of love, not as a passing passion but as a moral bond.[1]

The Reverberating '60s

Has it actually made a difference that the '60s ushered in a dramatic revolt against the "moral bond" that celebrated love as the self-giving connection of a male and a female in marriage? Does it really matter that our culture has removed any sense of embarrassment about having children outside the moral bond of marriage? Is it meaningful that the turbulent 1960s began the drive toward gender as a mere "social construct" and set us on the path to embrace a concept of "fluid identity"? Shall we abandon reality altogether for the postmodern claim that identity is nothing more than a modernist fiction?

After citing Daniel Patrick Moynihan's solemn-but-scorned prediction about the enormous social jeopardies that would accompany the breakdown of what had been valued for millennia as family, Sacks writes:

> Everything he predicted came true, but the spirit of the moment was unstoppable. For many, sex was no longer associated with marriage, or commitment, and became instead a leisure-time activity. Over the next generation, in Britain and America, fewer people got married and those who did were marrying later. In 1968, 56 percent of Americans between the ages of eighteen and thirty-one were married or heads of households; by 2012, this was true of only 23 percent. An unprecedented proportion of marriages – rising at times to 50 percent, 42 percent in Britain in 2017 – terminated in divorce, and almost one in two children were born outside marriage.
>
> Marriage is often derided as a mere formality, a "piece of paper," while cohabitation has come to be portrayed as an equivalent or substitute.[2]

In a word, I agree with Rabbi Sacks that monogamous heterosexual marriages lived out in covenant fidelity model the *healthy view of human sexuality* envisioned in Tanakh and the New Testament. These marriages put sex in its proper place and prevent it from morphing into a dehumanizing idolatry.

Did every Jewish or Christian couple making a promise to live this way achieve the goal of their sacred writings? No. Were some of the long-term marriages lacking in appropriate security and nurture for children? Yes. Are there terrible accounts of betrayal and abuse within these traditional family units? Of course. It is nevertheless true that "Love as a moral bond in the form of monogamous marriage is one of the great achievements of the West, a remarkable combination of sociological realism and moral and spiritual beauty: marriage as the crucible of the love that brings new life into the world."[3]

> **The Last Forty Years**
>
> "When it comes to sex, isn't the Church taking positions that are just out of step with what's cool?"
>
> "How can the Church oppose homosexual marriages, divorce, premarital sex and abortion? The Church is way out of step with today's progressive society."
>
> These comments assume the Church must eat the fruit of the sexual revolution. . . . Freedom from restraint, commitment, virginity, and commandments has not ushered in the bliss expected in the 1960s. . . .
>
> The wider culture has become a dangerous jungle of seductive, well-subsidized ideologies. The marketplace is now also full of post-modern spirituality preachers and advocates of new moralities. It reminds historians of Rome at the time of Christ.
>
> — Jim Reynolds

Marriage Redefined

Today's agenda that has been embraced by progressive politicians, affirmed by courts up to and including the U.S. Supreme Court, and woven into the storyline of some of TV's most popular sitcoms is that gay is as acceptable as straight. Gay is as normal and natural as straight. Same-sex coupling is as appropriate for honoring God and reflecting his holiness into his creation as opposite-sex marriage. At least, that is what we are asked to believe.

What has been adopted as a lifestyle by some and endorsed by far more celebrities ranging from media stars to professional athletes to the most popular musicians is what their parents once saw as flagrant immorality. Impressionable young people are influenced far more directly and powerfully by their celebrity idols – and the word "idol" will be central to the discussion of biblical ethics in this book – than by their parents, youth pastors, or preachers.

American courts, as well as lawmakers in many nations of the world, have now redefined the word "marriage" from its thousands-of-years, cross-cultural meaning of female-plus-male to include male-plus-male or woman-plus-woman. In some cultures and during certain periods of human history, the term may have included one male and more than one woman (i.e., polygamy) or one female and more than one male (i.e.,

> **The Move to "Redefine"**
>
> In the 20th century sexual roles were redefined once again. For a variety of reasons, premarital intercourse slowly became more common and eventually acceptable. With the decline of prohibitions against sex for the sake of pleasure even outside of marriage, it became more difficult to argue against gay sex. These trends were especially strong in the 1960s, and it was in this context that the gay liberation movement took off. . . .
>
> Large gay urban communities in cities from coast to coast became the norm. The American Psychiatric Association removed homosexuality from its official listing of mental disorders. The increased visibility of gays and lesbians has become a permanent feature of American life despite the two critical setbacks of the AIDS epidemic and an anti-gay backlash. . . . In the 21st century, the legal recognition of same-sex marriage has become widespread."
>
> — Brent Pickett

polyandry), but the cross-cultural meaning of the very word honored the union of male and female as a given. Occasional documented instances of formalized same-sex "marriage" in Greek, Roman, or other ancient cultures were typically written into the history, anthropology, or sociology texts with scare quotes. Writers thereby put themselves and their readers on notice that they were using an equivalent to our English terms so-called, supposed, or pretended.

Whatever the court rulings or legislative actions to change the legal definition of marriage, it strikes me as roughly equivalent to a government enactment that black is now white and blue is henceforth to be known as yellow. The right of every person to define morality in terms of personal desire – "my truth" versus "your truth" – makes about as much sense as letting every cab driver in New York City decide the meaning of red and green traffic lights for himself.

Nevertheless, the court rulings and laws in place stand. As with Sen. Moynihan's prediction about the impact of certain views that undermined the common understanding of marriage across the ages, one can be sure that the effective redefinition of marriage to mean little more than a convenient social arrangement for the purpose of health insurance, taxes, and inheritance will speed up all those negative forces.

To be clear, however, I am not pressing for political action and the reversal of legal definitions. I am proposing that the Christian church – as a minority culture – should continue to live with the definition of marriage it has embraced uniformly for 2,000 years. I am affirming that the 3,500-year-old boundary markers prohibiting premarital sexual license and extramarital affairs are still compulsory to biblical faith and ethics. I am claiming that its historic refusal to officiate and otherwise bless same-sex unions as morally equivalent to heterosexual unions remains the proper course for the church.

Same-sex orientation and desire constitute *temptation*. It is an element of the church's ministry of grace to love, encourage, and support the struggle of its members with temptation – this or any other. But it is not the church's right to disregard Scripture and reclassify one's yielding to same-sex desires as somehow less than sinful because we live now within a postmodern culture that is generally dismissive of moral absolutes.

A Biblical Frame of Reference

Reading Holy Scripture at the most casual level tells us there is something both foundational and formative about marriage. As the Bible opens, a male and female are joined in marriage and commissioned to be partners with God in bearing his image into his good creation and ruling it wisely.

When Abraham was chosen as the one through whose offspring Yahweh would bless all people, the nation that emerged from that promise (i.e., Israel) was portrayed as his bride. In the New Testament, when the promise to Israel is enlarged to include both Jews and Gentiles, Israel's Messiah takes the role of bridegroom in relation to the church as his bride. Finally, the biblical drama reaches it grand conclusion with the celebration of the marriage feast of the Lamb (i.e., Jesus). Along the path of this narrative, the importance of marriage to particular human families – for their spiritual flourishing or floundering – seems too obvious to deny.

The most straightforward way to read the warnings, prohibitions, and anathemas against other forms of sexual coupling posted along the way is to see them as protective moves against the disestablishment of marriage. They are given as guardrails to keep marriage safe. They communicate a consistent and clear message: *marriage exists by divine appointment, and sexual intercourse is reserved to those who have covenanted to be male husband and female wife to each other.*

A breach of that covenant relationship by any type of extramarital sexual relationship(s) was both *porneia* (fornication = illicit sexual contact) and *moicheia* (adultery = violation of one's marital covenant). Unmarried persons could be guilty

> **Justifying a Change of View**
>
> The doctrinal consensus on sex and marriage – sex within marriage only, marriage is a man-woman monogamy only – could be in error or need reform. If that is clearly the case, by no means do I wish to stand in the way of reforming the Christian doctrine of sex and marriage in accord with truth. Yet if that is clearly the case, it should be possible for advocates of innovation to exhibit that error or justify that reform. . . .
>
> By "justify" I mean give reasoned arguments that sufficiently explain why the church should substantially revise doctrine, robust arguments that can withstand careful scrutiny according to Christian convictions. I recognize that my request for reason and rigor in argument sets a high bar for justification; and I acknowledge that other Christians might be satisfied with a lower bar. Yet I think that substantially reforming a Scripture-based doctrine, and doing so in a way that contradicts what the church has always taught and two millennia of faithful Christians have firmly believed, demands no less of those that advocate reformation.
>
> — Darrin Snyder Belousek

of *porneia*, for premarital sexual intercourse is a violation of the divine will; married persons could be liable to the more serious charge of *moicheia*, for within the marital covenant one has certain formal pledges about care and protection, exclusivity and fidelity (cf. Ex 21:7-11; 1 Cor 7:3-5). Within the Torah, the latter incurred a greater degree of guilt and liability to punishment precisely because of the covenant factor.[4] Marriage is sacred and worth protecting, for it puts sex in its morally correct place that has been assigned by both creation and decree.

When the gospel began to be preached among non-Jews of the first Christian century, however, the reality was quite different. These converts from paganism did not have a background in biblical revelation about marital purity. The cultural assumptions, civil laws, ethical norms, and general standards of behavior – evaluated from the point of view of Torah – were lax to nonexistent in the Roman Empire. Trade in human flesh among the Greeks and Romans is well-known and extensively documented, and both the economy and social fabric of the Roman Empire in the time of Jesus, Peter, and Paul were sustained by it. That much of this trade in human flesh was sensual in nature is beyond dispute.

Estimates vary that from 25 to 40 percent of the empire consisted of enslaved souls in the time of Jesus and Paul – with the higher concentration in urban areas and a lower percentage in the outlying provinces and rural areas. Even so, in a city of no more than 12,000 to 15,000 such as Pompeii, archaeologists have been shocked to find so much physical testimony to the widespread presence of erotica (e.g., not only brothels but also pornographic paintings and mosaics in private residences) preserved to us by its sudden burial in ash and lava from the eruption of Vesuvius in A.D. 79. The Roman order of things both allowed and expected free males to exploit their inferiors (whether male or female) – in pagan religious settings as cult prostitutes, at public brothels, as family-personal slaves – in order to satisfy their sexual impulses.

Returning to the Roman Way: Progress?

I have been struck by the fact that both Christian theologians and non-Christian historians see the same parallels between the dehumanizing sexual behaviors of Roman culture and modern Western culture. Both also see the counter-cultural impact the gospel had on Roman culture.

Here, for example, are the observations of one Christian textual scholar:

> It seems that we are now living in a post-Christian society that appears to be growing more similar to first-century Roman society year by year . . . Theological truth seems irrelevant to most people in our society. The heated controversies about same-sex marriage and parenting have relativized the biblical standard of a man and a woman joined in God-ordained holy matrimony as the right and best home into which a baby should be brought. Sexual immorality of all forms is as public as it was in licentious Roman society. The popularity of violence in entertainment rivals the blood-thirsty audiences that crowded the Colosseum to watch gladiators slaughter and be slaughtered.[5]

The coming of the gospel of Jesus Christ into the Roman Empire brought with it a transformative message about the value of every human life. While gendered, social, and ethnic differences still existed among Christ-followers, the notion of privileged versus exploited, included versus excluded, were defied. Thus Paul wrote to the churches of South Galatia: "There is neither Jew nor Gentile, neither slave nor free, nor is there male and female, for you are all one in Christ Jesus" (Gal 3:28). It is difficult to impossible for twenty-first century Westerners to understand how radical a statement this would have been to its original hearers.

A non-Christian historian puts the prevailing understandings that Christianity challenged and undermined this way:

> Sex was nothing if not an exercise of power. As captured cities were to the swords of the legions, so the bodies of those used sexually were to the Roman man.

To be penetrated, male or female, was to be branded as inferior: to be marked as womanish, barbarian, servile. While the body of a free-born Roman was sacrosanct, those of others were fair game. 'It is accepted that every master is entitled to use his slave as he desires.' . . . In Rome, men no more hesitated to use slaves and prostitutes to relieve themselves of their sexual needs than they did to use the side of a road as a toilet. In Latin, the same word, *meio*, meant both ejaculate and urinate. To the presumptions that underlay this, however, Paul brought a radically different perspective. 'Do you not know that your bodies are members of Christ himself?'[6]

Christianity Remains Counter-Cultural

In the context of this transition from the norms of Roman experience to the ethical life called for by the followers of Jesus, one discovers a *healthy view of human sexuality* being offered as an alternative to the old ways of paganism. Rooted in the Bible of first-century Jews and Christians, sexuality was neither unclean, undesirable, nor unmentionable. Beginning in the book of Genesis, a positive structure is envisioned for human sexuality. Although we most often read their Bible – our Old Testament – for the prohibitions against certain sexual behaviors, it would be a mistake to explore them without studying the positive setting for sex that made them necessary. Judaism and Christianity forged a central place for faithful heterosexual marriage to a life of human flourishing. As we have retreated from that biblical view of marriage, family, and commitment, we have become more pagan again. And we are reaping the fruit of devaluing marriage in countless ways.

It should not be overlooked that the sexual behaviors expressly forbidden in the Bible – fornication, adultery, incest, rape, homosexuality, and bestiality – have one thing in common. Each is a sex act other than intercourse

---

Culture or Counter-Culture?

G.K. Chesterton believed that a godly way of life is the best way of all ways. It's the way the world is supposed to work, the way the world is meant to be.

Evangelicals often say that Christianity is a "counter-culture." I think Chesterton would probably say, "No, Christianity is the culture. Heretics are the counter-culture."

What we need to do is rediscover the culture. And the culture includes joy and pleasure.

So often, the church is viewed as this finger-wagging, don't-have-fun institution. Those of us who are in it know that that's a caricature, but that is the impression a lot of people have. Chesterton would say exactly the opposite. He would say: "To have fun, live the way God intended life to be lived – the Christian way."

— Philip Yancey

between a wife and her husband. The very givenness of gendered human bodies in creation speaks to the purpose of God for marriage: one male, one female, one flesh, one lifetime, in covenantal commitment.

I agree with Philip Yancey that the good world God created and meant for us to experience is the culture to which Christian faith is calling us. It is the culture that once was Eden – before sin broke the bond of intimacy between the human pair and their Creator. Innocence. Joy. A world without guilt or shame. Once sin entered, however, the male and female who became disoriented in their relationship to God suffered the same sort of perplexity in their relationship with one another and their environment. With their open-with-God and open-with-each-other world tarnished, living wisely and well in the upside-down world we know only too well began to require a counter-cultural way of life. The intimacy of marriage would soon be corrupted by the coarse and dehumanizing sexual behaviors that would be offered in its place. But I am getting ahead of the biblical story.

Before looking at the counter-cultural opposition to pagan abuses of sex in both Old and New Testaments, then, we must begin by exploring Scripture's positive case about human beings – with particular attention here to the issue of human sexuality. In the next chapter, we will go to the book of Genesis to establish some foundational facts about the nature of creation, a basic theology of the human body, and the establishment of marriage. We will see how this opening to the biblical story establishes a worldview through which all else about human behavior is to be interpreted and measured.

ENDNOTES

1. Jonathan Sacks, *Morality: Restoring the Common Good in Divided Times* (New York: Basic Books, 2020), 61-62.

2. Ibid., 64.

3. Ibid., 68.

4. In Old Testament literature, to commit adultery (Heb, *naaph*; LXX, μοιχεύω) is to sin by breaking faith or violating one's marital pledge to sexual fidelity, particularly on the part of a woman. By contrast, to commit fornication (Heb, *zanah*; LXX, πορνεύω) is different. It is not that fornication is not ethically significant or that premarital sex was not disapproved. But it is clearly viewed as a less serious offense than adultery, for the penalties that could be imposed for the two actions were vastly different in nature and severity. Under certain circumstances, adultery could be punished by the death of the parties (Deut 22:22-24). By contrast, in the absence of a marital pledge or covenant, sexual activity between a man and woman was not adultery but

fornication. It was therefore subject to a very different outcome for the parties involved and did not entail the possibility of capital punishment (Deut 22:28-29; cf. Ex 22:16-17).

5. Karen H. Jobes, *Letters to the Church: A Survey of Hebrews and the General Epistles* (Grand Rapids: Zondervan, 2011), 268.

6. Tom Holland, *Dominion: How the Christian Revolution Remade the World* (New York: Basic Books, 2019), 99.

> *"Whereas the creation mandate [to reproduce]*
> *was intended to be fulfilled only through the experience*
> *of human marriage, the gospel mandate [to make disciples]*
> *can be fulfilled by all believers irrespective of marital status."*
> — Barry Danylak

EXCURSUS

Our Sin Against Singles

The chapter just finished affirms a God-ordained importance for married life. Marriage is, in fact, the oldest and most basic social enterprise of human life. It is the one human relationship within which a man and woman have the right to sexual intercourse – both for procreative and personal bonding functions. Marriage remains both central to species survival and the cultural norm in modern Western civilization – by virtue of the fact that approximately nine of every ten of us will marry at least once in the course of his or her lifetime.

Important and common as it may be, however, marriage is neither commanded by God nor morally superior to being single. There are even times and situations in which I fear we – where "we" means parents and friends, youth group leaders and Sunday-morning preachers, peer pressure and statistical averages – may have sinned against single persons. Let me explain.

"You'd better start looking for a wife/husband!" says dad/mom in their child's junior year of college – if not before.

"You know we want some grandchildren one of these days," mom/dad says. "And we're not getting any younger, you know!"

Let just a few more years pass, and parents are saying things like, "You're going to be all alone – and too old to make a 'good catch' soon" or "At your age, the pool of eligible mates is shrinking pretty fast." Even strangers will offer, "You're still single? At your age?"

It's no better in our churches. Teen classes have quarter-long studies and special seminars on how to *find* the right person to marry, how to *be* the right person for someone to choose to marry, or simply *what to expect* from marriage – where marriage is presumed to be the "normal" adult state. I don't remember ever hearing – and certainly never taught – a class for high school, college, or young professional persons on how to function, thrive, or serve Christ as a single person. That was a mistake.

These not-so-subtle statements and settings could be interpreted to mean that people who remain single into their thirties – and certainly into their forties and beyond – is just a bit strange. "What's wrong with her? Can't she find a man? Do you think she's a lesbian?" Or, "He needs a good woman in his life, don't you think? Can he just not get a date? Is he just 'weird' – or is 'queer' the word for people like him!?"

That sort of condescending and shaming language isn't just insulting, wrongheaded, and shabby. One writer sums up the attitude she senses among church people this way: "Christians treat singleness primarily as a waiting game or a kind of purgatory on the way to marriage."[1]

This is not a biblical view of the single life – whether that of never-married persons, widows, or divorcees. We will circle back to this point with biblical data directly.

The Presumptions and Pressures

Wrong as it is, this negative and disapproving view of the single life isn't new.

Tractate *Yebamoth* of the Babylonian Talmud deals with a variety of issues around levirate marriage, the value of marriage, and conversion to Judaism. Among the many positive virtues attributed to the married state by the rabbis of antiquity, there are a couple of interesting downbeat statements about the single life.

> Rabbi Tanhum stated in the name of Rabbi Hanilai: Any man who has no wife lives without joy, without blessing, and without goodness. 'Without joy,' for it is written, And thou shalt rejoice, thou and thy house. 'Without blessing,' for it is written, To cause a blessing to rest on thy house. 'Without goodness,' for it is written, It is not good that the man should be alone.[2]

Shortly after that, Rabbi Eleazar is quoted: "Any man who has no wife is no proper man; for it is said, male and female He created them and called their name Adam."[3]

No more than Christians intend to be, the Jewish community is not "anti-singleness." But both traditions have done more to affirm and promote happy marriages than to support and empower single people. The emphasis on forming marriages that are healthy certainly should not be diminished, but the lack of positive attention to those who are single needs to be addressed.

I found it interesting that an online publication that targets a Jewish audience has made the same point to its readers that I am stressing here. The writer thinks he may have coined a new term – "the tyranny of singlehood" – in his effort to question what he sees as modern Judaism's "obsession with marriage" that has created "an overwhelming 'culture of couples.'" By his phrase the tyranny of singlehood, he explains that he is "referring to the Jewish community being naturally and neatly organized around couples, leaving only an uncomfortable space for those who are single."[4] Might we not say the same thing about Christian practice? In both populations, the result of engagement parties, elaborate weddings, baby showers, and the like may have the "unfortunate consequence of rendering those who are not married to being 'half class citizens.'" Unintentional though it may be, the result can be so negative that the message received by single women and men can cause them to avoid communal spaces and events that could highlight their status.

It is not the business of the church to "cure" single men and women of their "incompleteness" by our fumbling attempts at matchmaking or by otherwise

> **The Church's Message to Singles**
>
> Most people who enter even the most casual sexual relation are not promiscuous. They are, however, lonely. Beneath our disordered desires lies a loneliness brought about by a failure in the common life God intends for all men and women. The churches in America in many ways simply contribute to this loneliness.
>
> Their common life too frequently is not formed as a society of friends who share one Lord, one Faith, one Baptism. It is rather formed around the needs and expectations of the bourgeois family. Single people at best are tolerated. Nevertheless, the view that sexual relations are intended for marital rather than general social relations is linked to the idea that close bonds between men and women, both single and married, ought to exist in all of life's dimensions. Because of these bonds, sexual relations themselves are not necessary as a cure for loneliness.
>
> What is necessary is the fellowship of men and women in Christ. This is the word beyond "no" the church has to speak to single people. If it dares to speak, it will find not only that its common life is transformed beyond all recognition, but also that its teachings begin to appear to single and married people alike as a treasure to be shared rather than as a burden to be inflicted.
>
> — Philip Turner

implying they are inadequate persons as they are. Do you think anyone ever tried to be a go-between for Paul and a "sweet sister from our church that I just know you would like"? Or even – *can you imagine it?* – having Jesus over for Shabbat dinner and, just by coincidence, having a beautiful single girl from the synagogue there as well? I wonder how Jesus would have reacted to a host who explained, "The two of you have so much in common that I thought you should meet"?

Paul is the New Testament writer who said, "But I wish everyone were single, just as I am." Then, as his concession to those of us who marry, he added, "Yet each person has a special gift (Gk, *charisma*) from God, of one kind or another" (1 Cor 7:7 NLT). The apostle gave this encouragement to the single life under a set of circumstances that he dubbed a "present" (NIV) or "impending" (NRSVue) crisis the saints at Corinth were facing (cf. v.26). But are there not crisis times – the NLT translates the word here (Gk, *anankē*) broadly with "the pressures of life" – faced by multitudes of believers under a variety of circumstances that could make it wise for someone to remain single? Here was the logic behind Paul's counsel:

> I want you to live as free of complications as possible. When you're unmarried, you're free to concentrate on simply pleasing the Master. Marriage involves you in all the nuts and bolts of domestic life and in wanting to please your spouse, leading to so many more demands on your attention. The time and energy that married people spend on caring for and nurturing each other, the unmarried can spend in becoming whole and holy instruments of God. I'm trying to be helpful and

---

One God. A Variety of Gifts.

Marriage is itself a good thing. It answers to God-given gifts – perhaps the gift of needing a partner and the gift of being able to fulfill the needs of another person. But Paul also sees continence and self-control as gifts, allowing the individual to devote herself fully to the work of the Lord.

Those with the gift of continence have the God-given ability to control their sexual urges and to concentrate that energy creatively on other endeavors in which they find personal fulfillment. What is advocated is not sexual repression, but the recognition that self-control and singleness can be a gift for ministry to others. . . .

We as a church need to help people discover their gift. If indeed there are many gifts, including the gift of singleness, then we should not assume that a person must marry to be fulfilled. Personal fulfillment can occur outside marriage for those who have sexual self-control. Personal fulfillment comes through using God's gift for the purpose for which he gave it. Singleness is not less than God's best, but is God's best for those called to a distinctive task.

— Bruce Reichenbach

make it as easy as possible for you, not make things harder. All I want is for you to be able to develop a way of life in which you can spend plenty of time together with the Master without a lot of distractions (1 Cor 7:32-35 MSG).

Paul knew from his own experience as a single[5] person that he had freedoms from family duties that made his travel, evangelistic work, encounters with hostile persons, and the like easier. Or, perhaps "easier" is the wrong word altogether. His single status kept him from putting a wife and/or children for whom he was responsible in the perils he had embraced voluntarily and personally for the sake of the gospel.

And we must not forget that Jesus of Nazareth was a single man. He performed his first miracle at a wedding feast in Cana (John 2:1ff). His presence there with his mother indicates his own positive attitude toward marriage.

> **Singleness as Gift**
>
> Paul believes that the Christian, whether married or single, should be looking and living primarily for the world to come (cf. 1 Cor 7:29-31), but he knows that this is simpler for the single person (if he or she has the gift of singleness) than for the married person, since married people have to work out their devotion to the Lord in the context of a very demanding this-worldly commitment.
>
> In commending singleness Paul is not being anti-marriage or anti-sex; he insists that there are different callings and that each must live the life the Lord assigns him (1 Cor 7:17). But he is being realistic about the complications of marriage and family, and consistent in his Christian priorities. Given a belief in the kingdom of God as the supreme joy and priority in life, there is no point in single Christians getting married for the sake of it. On the contrary the single person, who has the gift of self-control, can give himself or herself undistractedly to the Lord's work in ways that others cannot. Paul was a living proof of the point, as was Jesus, as have been other great Christians since. It is a gift, given only to some, to remain single, not dissimilar to other gifts such as teaching and healing, enabling the person concerned to minister in ways that those with other gifts cannot.
>
> — David Wenham

Although we are assured that "he was tempted in every way, just as we are" (Heb 4:15b), there was nothing about either his sexual need or sense of loneliness that led him to marry. When his disciples asked him later about marriage (in a text we will examine in detail later in this book), some of them offered that "it is better not to marry" (Matt 19:10b). In response, Jesus did not rebuke them. He did not tell them they had missed his meaning. He certainly did not tell them, "No, anyone who wants to be happy *must* get married." He said that they were right – about *some* people. "There are those who choose to live like eunuchs for the sake of the kingdom of heaven," he told them. "The one who can accept this should accept it" (Matt 19:12b).

Given the examples of Jesus and Paul as single people – along with what they both explicitly said about being single – how dare we shame the minority of one in a sea of married twos! How dare we think they need to be "fixed" or "cured" by our actions as marriage brokers. How dare we not invite them to be part of our faith communities as equals. The language of Holy Scripture affirms that two people become one in marriage. It neither says nor implies that two half-persons become whole by getting married.

Biblical Precedent

Perhaps we have so idolized the married state in Judaism and Christianity that we have missed some key things about some of its most well-known and significant personalities. In his appeal for a healthier theology of singleness in the church, Barry Danylak[6] points out that the marital status of several Old Testament prophets was directly relevant to the message Yahweh gave them to communicate to their hearers. Thus, he asks, is it really so inconceivable that the varied life circumstances of believers today can create opportunities to speak with grace and truth into the lives of our contemporaries?

On the one hand, the prophet Isaiah married a female prophet with whom he fathered two sons (Isa 8:3). The two boys – Shear-Jashub and Maher-Shalal-Hash-Baz – were given *symbolic* (as well as hard-to-pronounce!) names. Isaiah lived through the fall of the Northern Kingdom to Assyria and warned the Southern Kingdom the same type fate would come to it, if the people did not repent and turn back to Yahweh. Thus, the two sons were given names as "signs and symbols" (Isa 8:18) of God's plans – the former Hebrew name meaning "a remnant will return" (expressing confidence in God's faithfulness) and the latter meaning "the spoil speeds, the prey hastens" (pledging judgment against the nation's enemies).

On the other hand, Jeremiah did not marry and have children whose names would become part of his message. With the book named for him opening some 60 years after the close of Isaiah's ministry, this was Yahweh's word to him: "You must not marry and have sons or daughters in this place" (Jer 16:1). Both as a prophetic sign that children born in Judah would die by famine and sword and likely because of the difficult ministry he was being given, his life story was much like the sort Paul would later embrace. He was opposed by many of his own people and was eventually carried off to Egypt. Better a single man should face such a trying circumstance than a man carry his wife and children through the ordeal.

When the Southern Kingdom (Judah) was finally overrun by the Babylonians under their King Nebuchadnezzar in 606 B.C., Daniel was among the young men selected for service in the king's administration (Dan 1:3-7). He served in a royal post until the time of King Cyrus of Persia – a period of some 70 years (Dan 1:21). Although there is slight evidence that he may have been castrated – a common practice with slaves put into government positions at the time (cf. Dan 1:3, KJV, ESV) – we do not know for certain. There is, however, no reference in the Hebrew text to Daniel ever having a wife. We are left to presume he was single for his lifetime.

Then we come to Ezekiel. He was married to a woman the biblical text describes as "the delight of his eyes." She died and left him a widower – a widower given this command: "Do not lament or weep or shed any tears" (Ezek 24:15-17). This sort of unmourned grief would be a prophetic sign of the loss the people were about to suffer when Nebuchadnezzar desecrated the Jerusalem temple by burning it in 586 B.C. – the holy site which had been "the delight of [the nation's] eyes" (Ezek 24:18-24).

Finally, there is Hosea. Just as Yahweh took Israel to be his bride and had entered a covenant relationship with the nation, Hosea took the woman Gomer as his wife. Although married and with a child by her husband, Gomer became unfaithful, gave herself to the life of a common whore, and was divorced by the prophet (Hos 2:2).[7] Hosea then – and we call him the Prophet of Everlasting Love – cared enough for her to rescue her from her poverty and disease in order to bring her home again. It is a touching

> **Beyond "Just Do It" and "No"**
> Sexual desire is a very powerful one, and at the moment it is given full license by our society. Everything that confronts single people conspires to say "just do it." It is increasingly rare for a single person, at one point or another, not to be involved in a sexual relation. In Christ, however, these relations need neither to be trumpeted nor denied. They can be brought before God, and as they are presented they will be judged with far more truth and love than we can muster.
>
> Another thing the churches ought to say to single people beyond "no" is come among us and present your life to God as it is. The upward call of God always begins from the place one starts and it takes place in a fellowship of friends who are also seeking to subject their lives to the truth and love of God in Christ.
>
> — Philip Turner

picture of the way Yahweh loved Israel – and how Christ loves his church and every struggling soul.

Again, Danylak's point is that the status of married, single, widowed, or divorced is not only discoverable among well-known characters in the biblical narrative but also serves to carry and reinforce the message they carried to the people of their time and place. And we could add names such as John the Baptist, Mary Magdalene, Lazarus, Mary, Martha, Jesus' own widowed mother, Timothy, and others to the list. We should not be surprised, then, when Jesus and Paul indicate that persons in more than one marital status can and do serve the Kingdom of God from their specific life situation.

Practical Implications

I know of no good reason why we should see either being single or being married as somehow spiritually superior to the other life situation. To the contrary, Jesus clearly affirmed marriage but also supported those who "*choose* not to marry for the sake of the Kingdom of Heaven" (Matt 19:12b NLT). Both marriage and the single life are options, and he did not elevate celibacy – as some would a few centuries later – to the duty of a few who would fill special roles of higher service in churches. It seems more likely that he is challenging the notion some in his day would have that singleness or childlessness within marriage is a divine punishment. No, it is a free choice. One who makes the choice is to be respected.

Paul's experience already cited above confirms and illustrates the point Jesus made. It seems quite significant that 1 Corinthians 7 – which deals with a wide variety of questions about persons who are single, married, divorced, or widowed – places the greatest emphasis here: "Nevertheless, each person should live as a believer in whatever situation the Lord has assigned to them, just as God has called them. This is the rule I lay down in all the churches" (v.17). In other words, Paul's guidance to the churches he planted and mentored focused on *kingdom living* rather than marital status.

One of the practical implications of that emphasis would be for those churches to maximize the potential of their single members for service to the larger body. Do we hear his counsel in today's church? Do we integrate single men and women into ministry opportunities? When the issue is kingdom living rather than meeting eligible singles, might our recruitments to ministry sound a bit different?

For example, young people are generally more comfortable with technology than their parents and grandparents. So, Elm Street Church had a glitchy, bug-filled, highly distracting sound and projection problem. Microphones squealed. Slides were too often out of sync with congregational music. Videos had to be called for, glided clumsily onto a projection screen, and clicked to start – with sound sometimes working and sometimes not. It took very little searching to find two students who were enrolled in program at their community college's program in Information Technology.

> **The Covenant of Singleness**
>
> Celibacy is a free choice before God and not a requirement for higher Christian service, as some believe. But its elevation is, by all accounts a radical turn from Old Testament Judaism. It is also a nod toward the future. Recall our Lord's statement that in the resurrection, none will be married (Matt 22:30).
>
> Most Protestants, and evangelicals in particular, have given little attention to the covenantal nature of singleness – despite remarkable examples of singleness such as Dr. Helen Roseveare, a medical missionary, and John R.W. Stott, an influential pastor and Christian leader. Luther's performing marriages of nuns to priests served as a healthy protest against Catholicism's abnormal emphasis on virginity. But it may have implied that marriage is better than singleness in Protestant circles.
>
> A believer's singleness in service to the triune God can be every bit as covenantal as the oath between a Christian husband and wife. . . . The importance of both single and marital covenants before God begs reiteration in our world today.
>
> — J. Scott Horrell

To their delight and to the relief of the frustrated 54-year-old deacon who had gotten so many dirty looks when things didn't work correctly, they made short work of improving the church's use of its audio-visual equipment. The deacon learned by watching and graciously moved two attendees into service roles. The minister's frustration level dropped dramatically – along with that of the rest of the church. The two students got credit in a couple of their courses for the hands-on experience they were allowed to have. And they showed the deacon a couple of newer pieces of equipment and a program or two that were within his budget that made still more improvements.

As part of my own ministry, I began writing a weekly devotional piece for persons in the Nashville business community back in 1995. With a fax program (anybody remember what a "fax" is?) on a computer donated by Charles and Maggie Merryman, it went out to less than a hundred people the first few weeks. It was slow and inefficient – especially as more people asked to be added to the list. A young man in our church, Bonnie Cribbs, asked if I had thought about moving the distribution from fax machines to email. No, but he did it for me – and soon to a more sophisticated email delivery platform. And for 20 years, Bonnie managed everything about the tech side of that ministry as it grew into an outreach to several thousand souls every week.

Bonnie remains one of my all-time personal heroes. Not only did he make possible an outreach with technology that I never could have created. (I was ready to give up when managing the fax program had to be kept current with less than 300 names!) He was also a Life Coach in our teen ministry and – because he was single – could make softball games or soccer tournaments with young men he was mentoring. To this day, those teens – now adults with jobs, some married with children, others single and serving as their mentor did them – tell me about what it meant to have someone who had the time and spiritual depth to invest in growing their faith. If you are a single male or female whose passion is kingdom living, why not be proactive about getting involved in ministries at your church? I wasn't smart enough to ask for Bonnie's help. But he was kind enough to offer help that I needed.

But what about people at the other end of the age spectrum? What about a widow or widower? A divorcee? Should the primary focus of her or his life be finding a new mate? What if the focus is kingdom living?

It has always astounded me that "senior saints" – whether retired couples, someone who never married, or formerly married church members – were more focused on golf, travel, investment management, watching TV, fishing, or tennis than Christian service. I think I know why it happens so routinely. Churches are simply overlooking this huge pool of talent. Why not recruit retired school teachers to tutor neighborhood kids in math, history, and language arts? Create a corps of "readers" for elementary students who need help during school hours two days a week? (In the town where I live, elementary school teachers went to a service club I had joined and recruited anybody who could give two hours a week to read for second- and third-grade students.) What about English as Second Language (ESL) classes on your church campus?

It isn't just former school teachers who can be creative in their communities. Accountants, nurses, drivers, dentists, artists, factory workers, bricklayers, farmers,

EXCURSUS: OUR SIN AGAINST SINGLES

carpenters – it isn't the educational or experience background that matters so much as a minimum of creative intent with the needs around all our churches. Neither is it even the single or married state that is most critical. It is desire – coupled with the need for relationships.

Relationships Matter

Yes, I still hear someone saying, "But you just don't understand the loneliness I feel. I need someone in my life. A partner. A wife/husband to share what's going on. *You just don't get it!*"

You're right. I don't understand a life situation I am not living. I am writing as a male who is married and who experiences the delight daily of getting to share my life with a woman I love. But I have lived long enough and have had enough experience across a wide range of people to have learned a few things about loneliness.

First, being married doesn't "cure" loneliness. Some of the loneliest people I have ever known are married. Oh, there are some who married unwisely or without really knowing their mates. So they don't feel "connected" or "bonded" with them. But there are couples who love each other, enjoy their time together, and otherwise have a good relationship. Yet, they speak to me about being lonely. And I typically find out with just a few questions that they have chosen to disengage from

---

Loneliness

God created us to be relational beings. In singleness, there are natural created desires for relationship that often go unmet. And it's appropriate for us to recognize that challenge and pray for our brothers and sisters who are single.

The real solution is found in union with Christ. He is the truest companion. He knows us more intimately than any husband or wife ever could. He never leaves us or forsakes us. He is always there – even in the darkest and loneliest deserts. Being united to Christ also means that God unites us to each other. Both singles and married people find companionship in Christ together. Ephesians 2:19 says that "you are no longer strangers and aliens, but you are fellow citizens with the saints and members of the household of God." We're family in the truest sense.

That means we must treat each other like family. We must reach out and come alongside each other and show hospitality. We need to open our homes to one another – married inviting singles over and singles inviting married over. Some is already happening; keep it going. We should work toward building spiritual friendships in Christ with different kinds of people, and not just the people who're like us. We were made and saved for this. That doesn't mean the challenge of loneliness won't return. But it does mean that Christ has made provision for it in giving us himself and giving us one another.

— Bret Rogers

life by isolating from other Christians (e.g., Sunday School, small groups, church events), their neighbors, or even persons who try to relate to them. Maybe it was Covid. Maybe it is the layers of distrust that today's social-political environments have created. Maybe some of us are choosing to isolate ourselves and then blaming others for not being involved in our lives.

Second, whether single or married, other people aren't responsible for my happiness or your sense of well-being. When I counsel couples before officiating their marriage, I usually spend some time on *codependency*. Codependent persons expect for others to fill them up, prop them up, provide constant approval, and get them through life. Codependent relationships are always fragile because they avoid honest communication, hold the other person responsible for one's security (and blame the other party when insecurity surfaces), and live in fear of rejection. Unhealthy people in unhealthy relationships don't magically find their spiritual emptiness filled. More often, they find it revealed.

All of us have some things in our lives we wish were different. All of us have elements of personality and ability in which we are lacking. Every Christian is a "work in progress" – whether single or married, male or female. The cultural message of unbelief seems to be that sex in practically any form you can get it is the key to fulfillment. The cultural message of faith seems to have decided to counter that false thesis with the equally false claim that marriage makes life fulfilling. The only person who can make any of us "complete" is Jesus Christ. As we will explore in more depth later in this book, the righteousness, peace, and joy all believers desire and need comes by the power of the Holy Spirit to those who follow Christ (Rom 14:17-18).

Third, the explicit teachings of Jesus make it clear that functionality in the family of God is what brings fulfillment to his people. Then, as spiritually mature people, his followers can find supportive community and healthy relationships – whether single or married – in the church. Even if you have heard it enough times that it sounds trite, it is nevertheless true that water is thicker than blood. The family created by the water of baptism is even more fundamental and essential than any created by blood.

Told that his blood relatives were standing outside a house where he was teaching, Jesus – without showing disrespect for Mary and his siblings – asked a rhetorical question. "Who are my mother and my brothers?" Then, as he looked at the people with whom he had been sharing his message, Jesus said, "Here are my mother and my brothers! Whoever does God's will is my brother and sister and mother" (Mark 3:31-34).

The Sufficiency of Grace

The church has been too deeply influenced by the culture around us to think that a human being simply cannot be complete without a robust and abundant sex life. Ironically to this point, Jesus said, "Anyone who comes to me but refuses to let go of father, mother, spouse, children, brothers, sisters – yes, even one's own self! – can't be my disciple" (Luke 14:26 MSG). Again, "Mark my words, no one who sacrifices house, brothers, sisters, mother, father, children, land—whatever – because of me and the Message will lose out. They'll get it all back, but multiplied many times in homes, brothers, sisters, mothers, children, and land – but also in troubles. And then the bonus of eternal life!" (Mark 10:29-30 MSG).

> **Today's Business**
> If you are single today, the portion assigned to you for today is singleness. It is God's gift. Singleness ought not to be viewed as a problem, nor marriage as a right. God in his wisdom and love grants either as a gift. An unmarried person has the gift of singleness, not to be confused with the gift of celibacy. When we speak of the "gift of celibacy," we usually refer to one who is bound by vows not to marry. If you are not so bound, what may be your portion tomorrow is not your business today. Today's business is trust in the living God who precisely measures out, day by day, each one's portion.
> — Elizabeth Elliot

If you are single today – whether by choice or by circumstances you would not have chosen – the Holy Spirit who gave you a new life in Christ at your confession and baptism is sufficient to sustain and deepen that new life. Even if you look back on multiple sins in a variety of settings, you have been pardoned and your body has been made a temple of the indwelling Spirit. As the Spirit's powerful presence gives you grace both to love your enemy and control your tongue, to bear the fruit of generosity and reject greed, so also will it enable you to experience supportive intimacy with other Christ-followers and control of your sexual urges that could lead to sin.

The result of such a life will not be morbid self-denial but a flourishing and radiant faith that bears witness to the gift of God's life-transforming presence.

ENDNOTES

1. Jana Marguerite Bennett, *Singleness and the Church: A New Theology of the Single Life* (Oxford: Oxford University Press, 2017), 3.

2. b. Yebamoth. 62b.

3. b. Yebamoth. 63a.

4. David Jacobson, "Is Being Single Acceptable in the Jewish Community?" *eJewish Philanthropy* (online), Feb 5, 2015, accessed at https://ejewishphilanthropy.com/is-being-single-acceptable-in-the-jewish-community.

5. The plural noun Paul uses as a self-description at 1 Cor 7:8 (Gk, ἀγάμοις) includes those never married, widowed, or divorced. We cannot be sure which of these "unmarried" states was specific to him.

6. Barry Danylak, *Singleness in God's Redemptive Story* (Altona, Canada: Friesen Press, 2022). The survey of five Old Testament prophets given here is summarized from pages 25-27 of Danylak's book.

7. Old Testament scholars debate whether Gomer was already promiscuous before Hosea was told by Yahweh to marry her or became unfaithful afterward. That Hosea 1:2 indicates he was told "Go, marry a promiscuous woman . . ." may well indicate she was already known to be faithless. On the other hand, the statement may be proleptic. A proleptic statement describes a person or situation in terms of what would happen later. For example, "John dated Bill's wife when they were in high school." But she wasn't "Bill's wife" back in high school days.

"From Genesis 1 onward, Scripture affirms repeatedly that God has made man and woman for one another and that our sexual desires rightly find fulfillment within heterosexual marriage."

– Richard Hays

CHAPTER 5

How Important Is the Genesis Creation Story?

Genesis is foundational to everything that follows in Holy Scripture. In a synagogue, it is the first unit of the five books of Torah; in a Christian assembly, it is the first volume of the Pentateuch. In the Hebrew Torah, it is called *Bereshith* from its opening word; from its Greek version in the Septuagint, Christian translations name it *Genesis*.

Genesis is quite noticeably the book of beginnings, for it purports to tell the origin of our universe of matter, space, and time (1:1-25). Next comes the origin of male and female (1:26 – 2:23) and marriage (2:24-25). Then, all too quickly, we discover the origin of sin and death (3:1-7) and – because of God's love for his creation – the origin of what unfolds through both testaments as the redemptive promise (3:8-24). Foreshadowing the redemption to come, we read of the origin of sacrifice (4:1-15). The starting point of what we know as civilization is recounted (4:16 – 9:29) – along with the origin of diverse languages and nations (10:1 – 11:32). Finally in the book of beginnings, we see the origin of the Hebrew nation as a specially chosen people through whom the Messiah would come into the world (12:1 – 50:26).

Attributed to Moses in both Hebrew and Christian traditions, Genesis frames the biblical story. All things have their origin in God, and all things have their goal in God. Creation is good, and God's revealed will marks the path for all that is good for human beings. Even his judgments are loving and gracious, for they are divine guardrails to keep men and women created in his own image from defacing that image – thus harming ourselves, depriving us of the good he wants us to experience, and going over the edge into destruction.

Genesis tells the story of beginnings in terms of people – not bloodless abstractions. Thus, we follow the stories of Adam and Eve, Noah and his family, Abraham and Sarah, and life of Jacob. There are high moments of faith and obedience, triumph and blessing. There are also tragic times of doubt and disobedience, failure and penalty. From these narratives, we are expected to find the fundamental life moorings for those of us who read its pages.

Genesis: Anchor for the Human Story

The late theologian and missionary Lesslie Newbigin pointed out what becomes obvious upon reflection: "The way we understand human life depends on what conception we have of the human story. What is the real story of which my life story is a part?" He explains:

> In our contemporary culture . . . two quite different stories are told. One is the story of evolution, of the development of species through the survival of the strong, and the story of the rise of civilization, our type of civilization, and its success in giving humankind mastery of nature. The other story is one embodied in the Bible, the story of creation and fall, of God's election of a people to be the bearers of his purpose for humankind, and of the coming of the one in whom that purpose is to be fulfilled. These are two different and incompatible stories.[1]

So much conflict has centered around question of measuring the Genesis creation account by modern science that it has been easy to miss the point of the story as told. It does not cater to our curiosity about *how* God created all things. The crucial point is to generate a worldview that flows from the fact that he did. To see yourself as God's image-bearer in God's world affects the way you think and act in all situations. Your life purpose becomes God-centered (i.e., seeking his kingdom and his righteousness) as opposed to self-centered (i.e., pleasure).

In terms of the story that expands from Genesis, human nature, responsibility, and accountability emerge. There are fits and jerks in the story, as first one and then another character struggles to find her or his place within it. Some, of course, reject the story to embrace a false god or simply to live without regard to any deity (other than self!) to whom allegiance and obedience will be offered.

It is the responsibility of the church to embrace, narrate, and live out the biblical story that reaches its crescendo in the death, burial, and resurrection of Jesus before a watching and increasingly skeptical world. What non-Christian philosopher or social critic has not cried out for Christians to practice what our Founder taught? For the sometimes-unsightly Body of Christ (i.e., the church) to be aligned with and to reflect the spiritual good looks of its Head? A positive and appealing church must do something with the Bible beyond fighting over it and picking occasional texts to lob into what some would label "the enemy camp."

> **God's Perfect Plan**
>
> This was Adam and Eve's perfect world. Not just fruit and fig leaves, but an entire race of people stretching their cognitive and creative powers to the limit to build a society of balance and justice and joy. . . . Can you imagine it? A world in which Adam and Eve's ever-expanding family would be provided the guidance they needed to explore and develop their world such that the success of the strong did not involve the deprivation of the weak. Here government would be wise and just and kind, resources plentiful, war unnecessary, achievement unlimited and beauty and balance everywhere.
>
> This was God's perfect plan: the people of God in the place of God dwelling in the presence of God. Yet, as with all his covenants, God's perfect plan was dependent on the choice of the vassal. Humanity must willingly submit to the plan of God. The steward must choose this world; for in God's perfect plan, the steward had been given the authority to reject it.
>
> — Sandra Richter

I do not believe Jesus saw the world he came to rescue as enemy territory. He saw it, instead, as the good world he participated in creating but which had become confused and misled by the false stories of human nature, responsibility, and accountability that The Enemy circulates. Thus, Jesus moved among the broken and sinful with great compassion – always modeling in a positive way what their lives were lacking in terms of peace, joy, integrity, and love. The attractiveness of who he was and what he did contrasted remarkably with some of the people and actions surrounding him – and that contrast eventually unleashed their fury against him.

Sociologist James Davison Hunter has written quite perceptively about the "culture war" that has done such harm to the witness of Christian churches in America. On his view, Christianity in this country has become a "weak culture" that – in the words of one reviewer – "mobilizes but doesn't convert, alienates rather than seduces, and looks backward toward a lost past instead of forward to a vibrant future."[2] One of the obvious places where this has happened has been the church's response to the anti-authoritarian cultural revolution of the 1960s and its backlash against so-called traditional Christian sexual ethics just described in Chapter 4.

But the narrative is different when we begin with Genesis' positive account of mankind and the nature of human sexuality instead of beginning at the point of rebuke and anathema. The judgments of the Bible appear harsh and cruel when isolated from their original context of a loving creation. As an example that considers a broader range of conduct than sexual behaviors, consider only one instance of biblical "judgment" that is commonly turned on its head.

The eye-for-eye and tooth-for-tooth language in the Torah (Lev 24:19-21; cf. Ex 21:23-25) is commonly heard in twenty-first century contexts as sanctioned cruelty. It is anything but that. Found within the Old Testament's "Holiness Code" (to which we will return later), this snippet of legislation belongs within the larger context of its intent to put an end to personal retaliation and blood feuds of the Hatfield-McCoy variety. Harm done to me or a member of my family is to be submitted to the civil authorities rather than settled through private retribution. And the guideline for the judge in putting the matter right is that the punishment should be proportional to the crime. As a judicial guideline, practically all countries have some variety of *lex talionis* enshrined in their laws. Outlier nations are seen for their cruelty and inhumane behaviors.

Understood in context, the demand of (*only*) an eye for an eye regulates and curbs violence. Contrary to Gandhi's quip that "an eye for an eye makes the whole world blind," the justice principle it expresses is a critical element of the very thing he was seeking in his various protests against British colonialism. It was never right for India's population to be subordinated, discriminated against, or subjected to unfair penalties and punishments by English overlords. The same can be said of the mistreatment through unfair limitations coupled with harsh penalties for both Native Americans and Black citizens in the United States. In ancient settings, it was ultimately the triumph of public law over personal bigotry that led to a degree of gradually clearing vision where there had been functional blindness.

This is an important principle to keep in mind as we move forward in this book. Certain prohibitions related to sexual behaviors (e.g., rape, fornication, same-sex intercourse, heterosexual adultery) are understood properly only when seen in context.

CHAPTER 5: HOW IMPORTANT IS THE CREATION STORY?

Humans are gendered beings with natural (i.e., God-appointed) drives toward sexual expression. Male and female united in marriage are potential partners to continue the creative work God inaugurated with the creation of the first human pair. The race is propagated and invited into God's will for humans to join in the personal rule over creation. That we have been so created is not only natural but also holy.

In their proper places, there is nothing unclean or problematic about either civil justice or human sexuality. Both are blessed by the Creator and Redeemer of humanity. However, when abused and put to use outside their appropriate places, justice quickly becomes injustice and virtuous sexuality morphs into sexual immorality.

Therefore, the defining Genesis story does not begin with humanity trying to find meaning or make its own way to holiness but with God. "In the beginning God created the heavens and the earth" (Gen 1:1). From the power of his loving presence, space, time, and matter were created, the Creative God of the Genesis narrative acted to call the cosmos into being. Leaving his "fingerprints" all through his handiwork, as it were, David would sing one day of the heavens declaring his glory and the skies proclaiming the work of his hands" (Psa 19:1).

With Moses' task of leading the enslaved Israelites out of Egypt toward freedom in a Promised Land, his purpose in the creation account was to affirm that the God of their father Abraham (not Egypt's deities or those of the Negev and Canaanite population they would encounter on their journey) was their creator, deliverer, sustainer, teacher, and joy-giver. So, Genesis opens with an account of God's creative work that brought his human creatures into existence and commissioned them to be his image-bearers and co-rulers of all that had been made. This is hardly a negative opening act to the story about to unfold.

Specific to their status as humans, Genesis (implicitly) affirms God's creative sovereignty over humankind and (explicitly) declares the stewardship rights and duties of the humans who bear his image. This is a story with real promise. And it only gets better when the writer gives a few more details about the human creation. "So God created mankind in his own image, in the image of God he created them; male and female he created them" (Gen 1:27). Chapter 1 closes with the observation that males and females on Planet Earth – under God's sovereignty and stewarding all he has created – constitute a state of affairs that is "very good" (Gen 1:31).

Marriage

If Genesis 1 serves as a wide-angle shot of creation, Genesis 2 zooms in on the creation of human beings that was already sketched into the story at 1:26-28. At 1:27, the text makes clear that the human race is "in the image of God" – *both* male and female. In other words, differentiation by sex is basic to human identity, and – in the Ancient Near East where women were seriously devalued and mistreated – females as well as males are affirmed to be image-bearers of the One True God. In the words of a feminist scholar on this material, male (Heb, *zakar*) and female (Heb, *neqebah*) are "indispensable to their understanding of humankind by explicit attention to the sexual differentiation of the species." She continues:

> Sex is the constitutive differentiation, observable at birth and encoded in our genes, essential for the survival of the species, and basic to all systems of socialization. It plays a fundamental role in the identity formation of every individual. It must consequently be regarded as an essential datum in any attempt to define the human being and the nature of humankind – and thus provides a primary test for false notions of generic humanity.[3]

In the divine plan, maleness and femaleness are not only appropriate to one another but necessary to the imaging of the God who is Pure Spirit and non-gendered. Furthermore, because God is Triune and Communal in nature – the divine family known in New Testament documents as Father, Son, and Holy Spirit – the gendered nature of the Deity's physical creation is a call to interaction and community between male and female that models itself on the holiness of divine kinship and collaboration.

With no suitable companion for Adam found among all the animal creation, the first thing found to be "not good" in creation is identified. "It is not good for the man to be alone. I will make a helper suitable for him" (Gen 2:18).

Perhaps due to our modern cultural view of marriage as a romantic coming together of two (or more!) parties, Christian teachers and writers – with me among them – have sometimes overemphasized the emotional-psychological state of Adam in his original garden home. We have read this text and pointed to his psycho-sexual need for delight in human companionship and have not seen the ability to reproduce the race as primary. (It may be argued, of course, that Roman Catholics have made procreation so all-encompassing as to the purpose of sex that they have minimized the value of psycho-sexual pleasure and bonding that accompany it. That is a discussion for another time.)

While the discussion of intimacy and emotional unity is not to be ignored, it is not the point of the Genesis account. Creation is being narrated from the point of view of God and his purpose for creating and not from the perspective of human location. In more technical language, we might say Genesis 1-2 is *theocentric* (i.e., God-centered), not anthropocentric (i.e., human-centered).

> **Identity and Sexuality**
>
> Human beings are sexually differentiated. It is significant that the only specific explanation of the image of God is that it exists as "male and female" (Gen 1:27). . . . In other words, the dynamic interaction and fellowship between men and women is a fundamental reflection of the divine image. . . .
>
> God's ideal is that human beings enjoy positive social interaction and ongoing cooperation with one another in spontaneous obedience to the will of God. Only thereby can they truly incorporate the image of God. Further, and much later, Paul would point to the appropriate and healthy relationship of Christ and his bride, the church (Eph 5:23-33).
>
> The significance of a person's individual identity and sexuality can only be apprehended through realizing what one is and means to the other person whom one complements sexually. The mystery of manhood and womanhood and their interrelation is so basic to the social existence of human beings that even at the outset of the biblical revelation one begins to anticipate that severe strictures will be made against any form of sexual perversion.
>
> — Arthur F. Glasser

The text does not tell the anthropocentric story of a (hu)man's need for the alleviation of "loneliness" (i.e., a psychological state) but fleshes out the theocentric narrative of the nature of the human race. It relates *how a human who was alone (i.e., an ontological[4] state) was enabled to achieve the purpose for which he had been created.* Told from the Creator's vantage point, Genesis explains how the woman was fashioned to be the man's "suitable helper" for humankind's twofold task.

Going back to the image of a "wide-angle view" and "zoomed-in shot," here is the articulated role of human beings from the first perspective:

> Then God said, "Let us make mankind in our image, in our likeness, so that they may rule over the fish in the sea and the birds in the sky, over the livestock and all the wild animals, and over all the creatures that move along the ground."
>
> So God created mankind in his own image,
> in the image of God he created them;
> male and female he created them.

> God blessed them and said to them, "Be fruitful and increase in number; fill the earth and subdue it. Rule over the fish in the sea and the birds in the sky and over every living creature that moves on the ground" (Gen 1:26-28).

Here, the human race is viewed collectively (viz, plural pronouns "they" and "them"). The NIV's "mankind" is not a designation for males but is a classification term (i.e., "humans" in NRSVue) for the living beings who alone are in God's own image. Turning to the detailed view of how *and why* "they" (i.e., "male and female" humans) were created, the text explains that male humans were ontologically "alone" and incapable of fulfilling the dual divine mandate about (a) filling and (b) subduing creation. How can he bring to fruition the responsibility envisioned by his Creator to bear the image of God into his good creation in wise and loving ways?

With the man "alone" – whether he was "lonely" is not addressed in the text – but facing a task that obviously would require some form of reproductive partnership and collective work for its accomplishment, we are given the story of woman. Animals are brought before Adam for naming, but there was no creature among them who could complete the assigned human vocation or telos. Each animal was a "living creature" or – perhaps better – an "animate being" (Heb, *nephesh chayyah*), but animals are not in God's image. So the ontological status of being a single male was addressed through the creation of a human female.

> But for Adam no suitable helper was found. So the Lord God caused the man to fall into a deep sleep; and while he was sleeping, he took one of the man's ribs and then closed up the place with flesh. Then the Lord God made a woman from the rib he had taken out of the man, and he brought her to the man.
> The man said,
> "This is now bone of my bones
>   and flesh of my flesh;
> she shall be called 'woman,'
>   for she was taken out of man."
> That is why a man leaves his father and mother and is united to his wife, and they become one flesh (Gen 2:20b-24).

"Suitable Helper": Not a Subordinate Assistant

The Hebrew phrase found earlier at Genesis 2:18 (Heb, *ēzer kenegdo*) occurs again here (2:20b) for its only other occurrence in the Old Testament, where it is translated "suitable helper." In both instances, the NRSVue translates the NIV's "suitable helper" as "a helper as his partner." In both translations, the expression makes it clear that the woman is hardly a postscript to God's creative work but is somehow essential to it.

Because our English word "helper" often (if not typically) identifies an assistant, a subordinate, or perhaps even one's slave, a highly developed convention of reading this text as a subordination of Eve to Adam has evolved in Christian interpretation. That is, this text is read so as to position females of the human race as outranked (though not necessarily inferior) to males of the species. A closer look at the original text makes it clear that no such interpretation is justified. More correctly, to read it that way is to read later cultural ideas *back into the narrative* (i.e., eisegesis) and not *from* it (i.e., exegesis).

To the contrary, the woman of Genesis 2 is a full partner with the man as both image-bearer for God and fellow-steward of creation – as well as his reproductive partner. In the biblical story, there is no hierarchy of husband over wife. God did not create men in his image and follow up to create women in the image of men. That *both* genders reflect God's image into his world allows – perhaps I should say requires – both male (e.g., father, Matt 6:9; warrior, Ex 15:3) and female (e.g., giving birth, Deut 32:18; nursing and comforting Israel, Isa 49:14-15; 66:13) metaphors when Scripture refers to God.

The Hebrew term *ēzer* signifies a "helper" who can rescue, bring deliverance, or otherwise become the ally of someone in need.[5] What was Adam's need? Created to bear the Creator's image and to steward all that had been made, he was "alone" for so daunting a task. In particular, how was the solitary man to "be fruitful and increase in number" and "fill the earth" with offspring? Whatever he was created to be and to do was somehow hampered by him as a male who had no female counterpart in prospect.

Upon awakening to see the new person with him, the man excitedly says, "This is now bone of my bones and flesh of my flesh; she shall be called 'woman,' for she was taken out of man." Sexually different from the male, she was nevertheless seen by him to be the same in her human nature. Their animality as "animate beings" (Heb, *nephesh chayyah*) is shared with such other organisms as fish, wild beasts, and livestock (Gen 2:7; cf. 1:20-21,24). What human beings do not share with other animal life is the "image of God." That image is not only marked by rationality and will, but also by shared life in community that reflects the triune nature of God.

As Old Testament scholars have pointed out, the image-of-God language functions on the model of the Ancient Near East to reflect the identity of an absent king who asserts his sovereignty by placing statues of himself in places where he cannot be present in person. Israel was forbidden to make such statues of their God (Ex 20:4), for he had already stamped his image on the fleshly form of humans.

In the bodily presence of the woman, Adam saw *image-of-God sameness* with his own flesh-and-bones body. At the same time, the *gendered difference* from himself – the woman (Heb, *ishah*) who corresponds to man (Heb, *ish*) – was immediately discerned to express something essential to both man and woman. The female was physically and sexually paired to the male for the purpose of completing humankind. She was equally his social, intellectual, psychological, and spiritual counterpart who was capable of rescuing him from his ontological aloneness that made it impossible for the man to realize the goal for which humanity was designed – tending, ruling, filling with new life, and benefitting maximally from God's good world. Put simply, humans were to exhibit and extend God's reign throughout his good creation. Our life task within the human family, as summarized in the words of Jesus, is to seek God's kingdom rule and righteousness above all else (Matt 6:33).

> **The Role of Genesis**
> The early chapters [of Genesis] serve to set forth the world views and the values of the civilization of the Bible, the pillars upon which the religion of Israel rests. The chapters, thus, comprise the fountainhead of ideas and concepts from which all future developments spring. . . .
> This universal opening serves as the background for the rest of the Book of Genesis and, indeed, for the remainder of the Bible.
> — Nahum M. Sarna

This view of gendered pairing in no way entails the mocking reply, "Then you are saying that a single, divorced, or widowed person is somehow 'incomplete' or 'defective' because of the lack of a mate?" Certainly not. The Genesis story is the account of how our *collective humanity* – regardless of the male or female, single or married state of any individual – works to reach its assigned goal. It is not a description of what each individual must attain to be personally whole.

Sadly, some Christian teachers and writers have not only left the impression but have explicitly said that males and females are somehow "incomplete" until they find a marital partner. Absurd! Otherwise, the elderly prophet Anna (who had been a widow for decades, cf. Luke 2:36-37a), eunuchs (whether born eunuchs or surgically castrated, cf. Matt 19:12), or never-married virgins at Corinth (cf. 1 Cor 7:25-28) were only "half-finished souls"? The singles group at my church is a cluster of "deficient" people? One of my dearest friends and colleagues in ministry is single and chaste by choice. And, lest we forget, so was Jesus of Nazareth. So was at least one of his apostles, Paul.

I suspect it is our Western culture that inclines us to read Genesis 2 and hear "lonely" for the text's "alone." We have come to idealize, fantasize about, and worship romantic love. Eros – the Greek god of desire, lust, and sex whose name became Cupid in Roman mythology – is the god of our time. Stories created for genital arousal dominate the visual media. I have seen articles in the popular press that report pornography is estimated to be a $100 billion global industry, with fully ten to 15 percent of that money coming from the United States. Pornography is a – perhaps even *the* – primary "sex educator" for teens and sub-teens. It has had an obvious trickle-down effect within our culture in terms of moving what people see onscreen and online into our social expectations and standards. Our all-pervasive media not only sell products but also promote ideas, values, and norms of acceptability-desirability.

No Denigration of the Single Life

But the church has been complicit as well. Christian literature and teen classes about sexuality often leave the impression – if not saying it explicitly – that the Edenic ideal for every person is marriage, children, and nuclear family. Without diminishing the beauty and sanctity of marriage, it is not a human partner who makes any one of us whole and fulfilled but one's lived relationship with God. Our larger culture has so romanticized every facet of human existence that we have trained ourselves to read happiness in terms of sexual ecstasy. Romantic bliss. Orgasms. For Christians, that cultural ideal has been adopted uncritically and transposed at times into marital-sexual companionship. This, in turn, has effectively elevated marriage to make it such a church-culture idol that we have denigrated the single life.

The primary distinctions within human culture as defined by God are not skin color, linguistic group, or national origin. There is no hierarchy of value marked by gender (i.e., male or female), sexual orientation (i.e., straight or gay), or marital status (i.e., single or wed). If we take Scripture as normative for this inquiry, the Christian affirmation that water is thicker than blood surely applies here. The family structures humans are allowed to create through covenant, procreation, and nurture are wonderful blessings – yet are mere approximations of the ultimate ideal to which believers are moving. Baptized into Christ, the primary relationship each believer has with him concurrently links us to one another (1 John 1:1-4, esp. v.3).

Does this not imply that we must be inclusive of both single and married people in our network of friends? Are our churches not supposed to be places that practice hospitality in order to fulfill the promise of Jesus that anyone who gives up father, sister, or any other contrary relationship for his sake will receive not only eternal life in the renewed creation at Jesus' return but also "a hundred times as much *in this present age*: homes, brothers, sisters, mothers, children and fields – along with persecutions"? (Mark 10:29-30). Are we taking our family relationships seriously enough that we are meeting the relational needs of those among us who are not married? Whether single by circumstance or choice, nature or nurture is irrelevant to the church's commission to meet those needs.

Anyone currently enmeshed within an LGBTQ+ community is likely to see churches as obstacles to conversion and faithful discipleship until our churches are seen as places where the penitent and public soul – whether called by the gospel from drug addiction, heterosexual prostitution, same-sex marriage, or whatever else you choose to name – can be received, supported, loved, and nurtured to spiritual health. *They must believe it is safe for them to be forthcoming with their backgrounds and sexual orientation. To "welcome" a penitent from whatever background without allowing that person to seek acceptance and nurture by people who actually know his or her "issue" is manifestly wrong and unfair.*

The Normative Function of Genesis 1-2

How much of the Genesis story should we read as normative? Is there a creational pattern to human sexuality we are supposed to find in reading it? As a matter of fact, it is this opening story of the Bible that appears to be at the heart of the consistently negative posture toward all types of same-sex activity – whether exploitative or consensual.

Every indication from the use of this original story through the remainder of the Bible says the original creation stands as the norm for how human relationships are to be understood. Quite obviously, there is not a single example of a same-sex union in the Old Testament that stands as an outlier instance of how marriage, sex, and mutual service to Yahweh are blessed from such a bond. Even when marriage is corrupted after the fall (e.g., polygamy, trivial divorce), the ideal for sexual fulfillment is never offered in any setting other than covenanted unions between males and females. When Jesus is asked to address one of those corruptions in an episode recorded in Matthew 19, he begins with this: "Haven't you read that at the beginning the Creator 'made them male and female,' and said, 'For this reason a man will leave his father and mother and be united to his wife, and the two will become one flesh'?" (vs.4-5).

As was pointed out earlier in this chapter, our modern romantic myth of marriage grounds all human love and love-making in emotional fulfillment. Thus our language of "finding my soulmate," "discovering my reason to live," and "the one who meets my every need." I argued that the biblical account of the original sexual coupling has one man and one woman given each other because it was not good for Adam (or Eve for that matter) to be "alone" in the human task of filling and ruling Planet Earth. To say it another way, sexual intercourse within human experience was principally for God's purpose of allowing humans to be God's agents for his kingdom reign on Earth as in Heaven. *Marriage would be the structure within which a man and woman could make an enduring commitment to one another, experience security within self-giving love, and find joy in fulfilling God's purpose for them.*

This means that procreation is blessed and appropriate to a married couple. It does not mean that reproduction is the only purpose served by their marriage or that their marriage is a failure if they either cannot or choose not to have children. On the one hand, think of the moral and practical harm that has been done to children where perhaps half the babies born today will not have the security of a mother and father to train them to be human. On the other, think of the wisdom of certain couples who realize they are either unable to provide security for a child or believe

> **"One Flesh": More Than Emotional Tie**
>
> Gaining traction in the recent debate for same-sex marriage is the assertion that unlike Gen 1:26-28, Gen 2:24 is not about procreation, but rather, becoming one flesh is focused only on kinship ties. Prototypical of this opinion is Miguel De La Torre who asserts that "if we define the purpose of marriage to be procreation, then, yes, same-sex marriage should not be allowed. But if marriage is more than simply having children, if marriage is to become one flesh by creating a familial relationship, then the race, faith, ethnicity, or gender of the participants ceases to be important." Here De La Torre is setting up a false dichotomy: if marriage is not about procreation but rather kinship ties then same-sex marriage should be allowed. However, the issue is not either/or, but both/and . . .
>
> When God brought the woman to the man the result was a marriage arrangement that certainly included emotional and kinship bonding; no one would deny this fact. However, it does not end there. The man and the woman were to become "one flesh." This is not simply kinship ties as proposed by some affirming scholars; this includes the sexual/procreation facet as well. . . . Indeed, sexual coupling is a central teaching of this portion of Gen 2:24.
>
> — Brian Peterson

their kingdom service precludes having children.

The one-flesh aspect of husband-wife sexual intercourse that generates new life is clearly an important part of marital life. At the same time, it is neither necessary for the marriage to be of service to God's mission for the partners nor sufficient to make God's kingdom presence a reality for them. People who view marriage as idealized romantic bliss are the ones who go to divorce courts quickly and are susceptible to seduction by new faces and bodies that seem to offer more erotic thrills. Unlike mere animals, sex in human relationships is not the only purpose served by genital intercourse. Joined with the spiritual purpose of honoring their Creator and the ability to communicate – non-verbally through sexual intimacy as well as verbally – their loving commitment to one another, sex becomes the experience of the one-flesh intimacy God intended.

Gushee's Awkward View of Genesis 1-2

Having laid out a reading of the first two chapters of Genesis, it seems necessary to look at the way Gushee handles this same material in *Changing Our Mind*. I call his reading "awkward" for the reason that he introduces the material, claims its centrality to the discussion of the issue of same-sex unions, and proceeds to disclaim its relevance to making ethical decisions in our context.

The italicized synopsis for Chapter 14 of his book says this: *"We turn to the most important texts for the LGBTQ issue – Genesis 1-2, Matthew 19, Romans 1 – and the most significant theological issue: God's design for sexuality in creation.*"[6] For these to be the "most important texts" on this issue, it seems strange that Gushee devotes a scant three pages to the Genesis material. He opens the chapter by granting that the creation story of Genesis has been used historically "to suggest the illegitimacy of same-sex relationships based on God's original design for human sexuality in creation"[7] and to argue that such an original design "renders all same-sex relations as 'out of order,' that is, contrary to God's fixed plan for creation."[8] Specifically, the creation story presents "a man and a woman, and only a man and a woman, referenced in the discussions of sex and marriage in Genesis 1-2 – and the fact that only a man and a woman have been able to procreate" to shape "traditional Christian opinion on the LGBTQ issue."

> Christian tradition has taken these texts as prescriptive for all times and all peoples pertaining to the design and purpose of sex, marriage and family life. That has excluded those who are unable to fulfill that prescription due to their sexual orientation. But increasingly today it is noted that core practices referred to in Genesis 1-2, including mutual care for children, helper-partner companionship (Genesis 2:18) and total self-giving, can and do occur among covenanted gay and lesbian couples.[9]

While any Bible student would grant that "total self-giving" love is at the heart of the Yahweh-Israel and Christ-church marriage metaphor, a covenanted same-sex marriage simply does not work for its biblical function.

> This line of thinking falters on several levels, the most important one being that God chose the heterosexual relationship found *naturally* in his good creation as a metaphor for the relationship between God and his people. To suggest that Israel would have accepted a same-sex paradigm for their metaphorical relationship with God is illogical. Second, if self-giving love is the main criterion for allowing same-sex marriage to represent Christ's love for his bride, then why not allow any form of self-giving relationship to reflect God's relationship with his people (father-son; mother-daughter; sister-sister; brother-brother, friend-friend, person-pet, etc.)? The fact remains that God chose what was *natural* to his well-ordered creation.[10]

It would be a mistake to argue that marriage is *only* for the sake of sexual reproduction, but it is equally misguided to overlook or to deny the obvious significance of procreation to the Genesis account of human creation. It is a caricature of the biblical data to argue that the primary purpose of sex is pleasure, intimacy, and devotion. If that were true, it would be as difficult to rule out incest or even non-covenanted relationships. As with all the gendered and paired elements of God's animal creation, the reproductive function of sex informs its purpose. God has placed sex within the context of pleasure, intimacy, and devotion for the sake of providing a secure environment with these features for his or her healthy development.

In a word, Genesis 1-2 presents a world in which maleness-femaleness is central to the biblical story. While the differences between males and females are many, the primary and most obvious distinction – as it is for all animal life (Gen 5:1; cf. 6:19b) – is biological-sexual. The full complement of the "image of God" is at stake in this created order, and to defy that by seeking fulfillment in a single-gender relationship is misguided.

Gushee's acknowledgment of the important placement of sexuality in the creation story runs aground not only by his cursory treatment of Genesis 1-2 but also by his subsequent comments about the inappropriate use of the opening two chapters of the Bible in contemporary discussion of sexual ethics. In what I take to be a careless oversight in his rush to find a plausible defense of his thesis, he stakes out a confusing point about Genesis 3 that is mistaken on its surface and beset with a variety of theological problems.

> **Adam's "Loneliness"**
>
> God does not give the woman to the man to cure his loneliness. Rather, she is given to him because it is not good for him to be alone in his task of filling and subduing the world (Gen 1:28), and guarding and serving the Garden (Gen 2:15). Companionship is not the purpose, or end, of marriage. But neither is procreation. Both are marital goods ordered toward a higher end: serving God's kingdom. Marriage "ought to be considered under the governing ethic of human responsibility (to the Creator) and of the human task (over the Creation)." Marriage is therefore not an introverted family of parents and children. "They have children not for their own sakes as parents, nor for the children's sakes, but for the sake of contributing to the great task entrusted to humankind.". . .
>
> To the extent that an introverted, companionate view of marriage holds sway (marriage as cure for loneliness) it will be proportionately difficult to argue that same-sex marriage is impermissible. But, in the beginning, God ordained marriage as a delightful context in which a man and woman would come to know themselves as male and female as they gave themselves to one another in love for the sake of worshipful obedience to their Creator and joyful service of his kingdom.
>
> — Matthew Mason

Accommodating Scripture to Culture

In his very next chapter, Gushee offers three proposals for responding to "God's design in creation" in view of what "we also now *know* from real human beings and research about them that a very small percentage of the human population is intersexual or transgender."[11]

First, he insists we must accommodate our biblical interpretations to contemporary "scientific descriptions of the world as we find it." The argument of "scientific descriptions" that remove same-sex behavior from moral judgment is, of course, the same case that was made to justify slavery in Greece and Rome, African slavery in the pre-Civil War South, and anti-Semitism in modern Europe and the United States. One cannot help but recall the modern science of "eugenics" pressed by the Nazis in Europe and received eagerly by many in North America. Measuring human behaviors by scientific theories is malleable to time, place, and social pressures; measuring those same behaviors by the nature and will of God is quite different.

Second, because certain claims (e.g., anti-environmentalism, the so-called "curse of Ham," etc.) have "proven remarkably problematic in Christian history, do not rely on them [*ancient biblical texts, RS*] for sexual ethics." From the beginning of controversy over environmentalism or the so-called "curse of Ham," however, there has been serious debate over the use versus misuse of key texts. But that has not been the case about same-sex behaviors – as Gushee himself admits – for well over 1900 years of Christian interpretation of Old and New Testament texts. The interpretation of the texts on that subject has been uniform and consistent.

Third, "we should consider more seriously the implications for sexual ethics of living in a Genesis 3 world." While each of these proposals has seriously debatable components, the third of them is my focus here. It presumes and carries forward the previous two claims.

Rejecting the claim that "God made [humankind] male and female and male for female, and so everyone needs to conform to this pattern or live as a celibate,"[12] Gushee makes the remarkable claim that traditionalists "rarely mention Genesis 3, which (most Christians have said) tells the story of the beginnings of human sin, with the disordering consequences that are so painfully described in Genesis 4 through Revelation."[13] This is a "remarkable claim" for the simple reason that it is so obviously false.

The totality of the biblical narrative not only presumes and underscores the fact of the fall in Genesis 3 but also presses the contrast of that "fallen" state to the "ideal" of the original created order – and appeals consistently for a return to Genesis 1-2 purity against the corruption(s) of our Genesis 3 impurity. I can think of no clearer proof of this than Jesus' words from Matthew 19. When pressed on the issue of divorce, he drew a sharp line between the Genesis 3 world in which "Moses permitted you to divorce your wives because your hearts were hard" and the way things were "from the beginning" (v.8). He then made it clear that the Genesis 1-2 world, which presented the ideal state known "from the beginning," was the standard by which his disciples were to judge themselves.

Life in a Genesis 3 World

Gushee's line of reasoning becomes murky and contradictory on this point. Here are the sequential points he makes about life in what he labels the "Genesis 3 world."

> If we live in a Genesis 3 world, and not a Genesis 1-2 world, this undoubtedly means that *everyone's* sexuality is sinful, broken and disordered, just like everything else about us. Nobody has Genesis 1-2 sexuality. . . . *[W]e go into adult life with the sexuality we have, not the sexuality we might want or wish to have.* No adult is a sexual innocent. Our task, if we are Christians, is to attempt to order the sexuality we have in as responsible a manner as we can. We can't get back to Genesis 1-2, a primal sinless world. But we can do the best we can with the Genesis 3 sexuality we have. . . . *I am suggesting that in Genesis 3 perspective, no one's sexuality is innocent.* Everyone's sexuality is broken in ways known quite well to each of us in our own hearts. Everyone's sexuality needs to be morally disciplined and ordered. Meanwhile, basic standards of Christian humility direct our attention to our own issues rather than those of others.[14]

Because these proposals for Christian sexual behavior are so central to everything here, several key claims made about his "Genesis 3 world" deserve to be critiqued in turn.

First, note his claim that *"everyone's* sexuality is sinful, broken, and disordered, just like everything else about us" – and the italics are Gushee's, not mine. If this means a fallen world is cluttered with temptations to sexual sin, it is true. If it means "Jews and Gentiles [Black and White, straight and gay, males and females] alike are all under the power of sin" and "there is no one righteous, not even one," that is certainly true, too (cf. Rom 3:9-10). But if it means that there is no such thing as

CHAPTER 5: HOW IMPORTANT IS THE CREATION STORY?

a morally pure and chaste sexuality, it is categorically false. Was Jesus' sexuality "broken and disordered"? Was Mary's virginal chastity "broken and disordered"? Is monogamous heterosexual marriage "broken and disordered"? To the contrary, "Marriage should be honored by all, and the marriage bed kept pure, for God will judge the adulterer and all the sexually immoral" (Heb 13:4; cf. 1 Cor 6:9).

Second, "Nobody has Genesis 1-2 sexuality. No adult is a sexual innocent. . . . *I am suggesting that in Genesis 3 perspective, no one's sexuality is innocent.*" (Note: Italics are in the original.) Really? If this means we do not live in Edenic paradise, it is true. If it means there is no sexual experience that is innocent and pure, it is false. Sex within a loving heterosexual marriage is as holy as the intercourse of Adam and Eve in Eden. It is sexual encounters outside a male-female marriage that Scripture forbids. Citing Jesus' own words from Matthew 19 once more, the solution to all forms of corrupted sexual expression is to return to the model given "at the beginning" in Genesis 1-2.

Third, "*[W]e go into adult life with the sexuality we have, not the sexuality we might want or wish to have.*" (Note: Again, the italics are Gushee's.) This statement is either naively mistaken or intentionally designed to go where Gushee is determined to take his readers. He has laid the groundwork for accepting the findings of modern studies that certain people are "born gay" or so conditioned by both nature and nurture that they cannot be other than they are.[15] This claim that "we go into adult life with the sexuality we have" would not only legitimate same-sex covenanted relationships but intersexual, transgendered, and/or bisexual persons living out their "fixed, enduring, unchangeable" sexual orientation – so long as it is in a "covenanted and faithful marriage." If not, why not?

Historically and biblically, there is a far better case to make for polygamy than for same-sex marriage. Yet, only a few pages later, Gushee argues that only *monogamous* relationships are foundational to God's plan for marriage and appeals to Genesis 1-2 as his proof. He makes a plea for Christians who are gay, lesbian, and bisexual who "are asking to be welcomed into the covenantal-marital ethic of the Christian tradition. They want to make a lifetime covenant with one person, in keeping with the witness of the Christian tradition."[16] If he appeals to Genesis 1-2 as the precedent for monogamy in these relationships, one has to ask what became of accommodating

> **How Significant a Story?**
>
> The male/female relationship, woven so centrally into the story of creation in Genesis 1 and 2, is not an accidental or a temporary phenomenon, but is, rather, symbolic of the fact that creation itself carries God-given life and procreative possibility within it. Even to consider the question from this angle poses a sharp contrast to the way in which, in our present culture, sexual activity has become almost completely detached from the whole business of building up communities and relationships, and has degenerated simply into a way of asserting one's right to choose one's own pleasure in one's own way. To put it starkly: instead of being a sacrament, sex has become a toy.
>
> — N.T. Wright

ourselves to life in a Genesis 3 world? But if we *do* return to the Genesis 1-2 model of monogamy, why should we not also embrace the precedent of male-female marriage found there? The reasoning here is simply too inconsistent to be convincing.

Fourth, "Our task, if we are Christians, is to attempt to order the sexuality we have in as responsible a manner as we can."

Of course. I offer unqualified agreement with this statement. But the "attempt to order the sexuality we have" must be consistent with the guidelines of Holy Scripture rather than one being set by the fluctuating romantic sentiments of individuals or the relativistic moral norms of our time that are reflected in media, psychology, or legal statutes. But that is not the thrust of Gushee's claim. He wants his readers to believe he has proved that persons from the LGBTQ+ world are under obligation only to find a best-possible course of action (i.e., forming covenants) to the sexuality they have – and not to change their commitment to same-sex partnerships.

When Paul gave instructions on Christian ethics, he described the previous lives of Gentiles who "have given themselves over to sensuality so as to indulge in every kind of impurity" (Eph 4:19). Their obligation as Christians was not to choose "the most morally commendable course of action available in their particular circumstances."[17] It was radically different and involved repentance and spiritual renewal. We could say that he called a group of Genesis 3 people back to the world of Genesis 1-2. "You were taught, with regard to your former way of life, to put off your old self, which is being corrupted by its deceitful desires; to be made new in the attitude of your minds; and to put on the new self, created to be like God in true righteousness and holiness" (Eph 4:20-24).

The solution of placing an *immoral behavior* within a *covenanted relationship* no more justifies or purifies that behavior than placing a stolen car in a garage I own makes it my car or that Bill Brown raping Sue Brown because she is his legally covenanted wife makes his action into licit and loving sexual intercourse. The uniform testimony of the Bible is that same-sex behavior is judged to be outside the will of God and condemned without regard to the origin of the desire, motive toward one's partner, or covenant/non-covenant context.

Another View of Genesis

Because everyone who addresses the subject matter of this book acknowledges the formative importance of the Genesis story, it simply cannot be ignored. A more promising route to minimizing it than Gushee's various awkward moves is the one made by Karen Keen. Further, since her look at the material is a direct challenge to the case I made earlier in this chapter about the normative function of Genesis 1-2, this seems to be the place where it should be examined. While making her affirmative – she prefers the term "progressive" – case for same-sex relationships, she writes: "Progressives agree that male and female are part of God's good creation, but they believe loyal, covenanted love, not sexual differentiation, is the foundation of biblical marriage."[18] Against the view that the Genesis narratives constitute "a mandate for heterosexual marriage, rooted in creation itself and not subject to cultural changes," her view is that the Genesis materials present male-female marriage "as a blessing and norm, but not a mandate."[19] This view of Genesis as description – rather than prescription or divine norm – is based on two key moves in her books.

First, Keen argues that the story of Adam and Eve is about their "kinship bond" and "demonstrates that marriage is, first of all, a union founded on commonality, not differentiation."[20] She discusses marriage and informs her readers: "Kinship is primary. . . . While Genesis 1 indicates God created sexual dimorphism for the *blessing* (and not mandate) of procreation, Genesis 2 and other biblical texts describe marriage as first and foremost kinship."[21]

The kinship argument is designed to mitigate the biblical emphasis on sex as the basic and constitutive differentiation of humanity. Yes, there is "kinship" between the man and woman that connects them in a way Adam could not be with animal life in general. The importance of species kinship should not be minimized but regarded as highly significant. The text makes it clear, however, that it is the *blessing*

111

of a differentiated kinship for the *mandated* purpose of procreation. As animals were brought to the man for naming, "no suitable helper was found" (Gen 2:20b). Bestiality was not to be an option for Adam and his human progeny!

The language of "bone of my bones and flesh of my flesh" from Adam's mouth (Gen 2:23a) is found elsewhere in Genesis to affirm familial kinship as that between Laban and Jacob (Gen 29:14; cf. Judg 9:2; 2 Sam 5:1; 19:11-12; 1 Chron 11:1). But there is an equally emphatic affirmation of "difference" between Adam and Eve. Not only did the man see "bone of my bone" in species kinship, but he also added that "she shall be called 'woman,' for she was taken out of man" (Gen 2:23b). This is one of those few cases where English reflects a form of the Hebrew text that has wo-man (Heb, *ish-ah*) being taken from man (Heb, *ish*). Kinship is important, but so is differentiation. Both are by God's creative intent and design.

If the primary thrust of the Genesis story is, per Keen's account, to affirm kinship sameness, why not simply create her directly from "the dust of the ground"? (Gen 2:7). Indeed, the Hebrew words for man (*adam*) and ground (*adamah*) have similar phonetic and etymological links. To the contrary, her creation from "one of the man's ribs" – or, as a footnote to the NIV indicates, "part of the man's side" – indicates some degree of depletion or want that the male would henceforth find in the female. What had been "*taken out of* the man" (Gen 2:22b, 23b) now faced him as his female counterpart – neither superior nor inferior, not only alike as human beings but also different as male and female.

Furthermore, it was pointed out earlier that the language of the woman's creation to be the "suitable helper" (Heb, *ēzer kenegdo*) is central to the narrative. The female brought to the man was not his extension as servant or domestic but his sexually differentiated complement. From our standard English translations, we tend to miss the fact that the Hebrew *adam* appears in Genesis 1 as a comprehensive term for "human" – without regard to male-female distinction. Thus "God created *adam* (NIV, mankind; NRSVue, humans) in his own image . . . male and female he created them" (v.27) All the references to *adam* are gender-inclusive until God takes some of *adam*'s flesh[22] and forms the woman as "suitable" or "opposite." *Only at this point in the biblical text is Adam called* ish *(male) and distinguished from* ishah *(female).* The biblical text is at great pains here to differentiate male and female as foundational to human experience.

It follows, then, that Keen's proposal to distinguish the "purpose" of marriage (i.e., kinship) from the "goods" of marriage (i.e., procreation, sexual stewardship, sanctification) – with kinship being primary[23] – is not discoverable within the biblical text. It is the creation of artificial categories for the purpose of redefining marriage. Her sentence written as "Scripture defines marriage as covenantal kinship of mutual support that typically includes the goods of procreation, sexual stewardship, and sanctification"[24] would more accurately begin "A recasting of biblical text would allow one to claim that Scripture defines marriage as . . ."

Second, with an acknowledged awareness of the weight of Genesis to biblical ethics, Keen points to the legitimate distinction between "descriptive" versus "normative" or "prescriptive" ethics. A biblical narrative is descriptive simply by virtue of existing. So there are stories of Abraham's great faith in leaving Ur for a destination unknown to him and his half-truth lies about Sarah as his sister, David's courage before Goliath and his adultery and murder with Bathsheba and Uriah, or Peter's bold confession of Jesus as Israel's Messiah and his cowardly denial of him in Pilate's courtyard. By simply *describing* what took place, one cannot assume the Bible is *prescribing* as good, approved, and normative everything in its pages. At the same time, the narrator's ethical perspective bleeds through in the form the stories take.

The value of this distinction to those who affirm consensual and covenanted same-sex relationships is to situate the first two chapters of Genesis firmly in the descriptive category. After citing her own examples of cases where some cultural peculiarity recorded in Scripture has been made binding (e.g., head-coverings for women in church meetings, authoritarian patriarchal family systems, Hezekiah using fig cakes as a medical remedy), Keen leaves Genesis in suspended animation – with the (minimal) implication that it cannot be made normative.

> Another example is Genesis 1-2. The Bible *describes* the creation of male and female, but this does not mean people with atypical sexual development don't exist. As Jesus acknowledged, some are "eunuchs who have been so from birth" (e.g. intersex people; Matt 19:12). Genesis portrays the majority experience rather than a comprehensive discussion of sexual development.[25]

Since there is a discussion of Jesus' comment about eunuchs to come in Chapter 7, I will defer the matter of "intersex people" to the material there. The concern here will be focused on the broader implication of making Genesis 1-2 descriptive over normative. Or, at the very least, Keen clearly wants her readers to leave open the option that the male-female language found there is not meant to establish the standard for what Christians can regard as marriage.

For one thing, everything in the previous couple of pages of this volume weighs against seeing the female-male, *ishah-ish* language as incidental and merely descriptive. For another, the larger context of Jesus' appeal to Genesis 1-2 in Matthew 19 certainly shows that he regarded something about that account as prescriptive. He appealed to the normative work of God in making the first couple "male and female," uniting the man to a wife (Gk, *gynē* = woman), and the two becoming "one flesh" in sexual union. All this, Jesus said, was based – not on the Decalogue, prophetic statements about Yahweh as bridegroom to Israel, or in anticipation of Christ's relationship to the church as his bride – on reading Genesis. "Haven't you read that at the beginning the Creator 'made them male and female,' and said . . .?"

Curiously, however, Keen is quite emphatic that the opening two chapters of Genesis are normative and prescriptive for the following bullet-pointed items:

> To recap the preceding discussion, we find the following key aspects of marriage in Genesis 2 and Jesus' interpretation of Genesis:
>
> - companionship (not good to be alone)
> - mutual support of a strong ally (*ezer*; not unilateral since Adam is by definition a counterpart [*kenegdo*]; as counterparts they mirror each other)
> - commonality and similarity
> - human spouse (bestiality ruled out; animals are too "other")
> - establishment of "flesh of my flesh" kinship tie (no incest because it's redundant; one does not need to form a kinship bond with someone who is already kin; one must leave family of origin to find a spouse [Gen.2:24])
> - faithfulness (no adultery or divorce)
> - a pair (no polygamous relationships)[26]

I confess that I find it more than unlikely that one can find so many prescriptive elements in Genesis 1-2 and nevertheless insist that the man/male and woman/

female distinction that is denoted explicitly in five places (1:27b; 2:22; 2:23; 2:24; 2:25) is clearly non-prescriptive. At the very least, it is a less-than-obvious reading of these two chapters that finds practically everything in them normative *except* the differentiated kinship of the male-female couple enjoined with the responsibility of implementing them.

Binary Personhood vs. Gender Fluidity

Throughout the material in this book, the issue of how sex and gender relate to the human condition will always be close at hand. Before leaving Genesis, here are a few basics that need to be made specific. As this chapter demonstrates, the embodied human being – whether male or female – was created to bear the image of God into his creation and to be its co-regent. This means the body is important and – unlike later Gnostic theories – not a "prison" to a spirit seeking to be free (i.e., deconstructed?) from its natural limitations. But how do concepts of sex and gender relate to one another?

As we have come to discuss sex, gender, and sexuality in the past half century, *sex* is one's chromosomal pattern and is historically determined at birth by external genitalia. *Gender* is typically defined as a "social construct" that involves cultural traits and conventional expectations. *Sexuality* is generally held to be one's orientation, preferences, and erotic behaviors. The initial concession I hear in discussions among believers and non-believers is that sex and gender are not to be equated, and that sexuality is – at least among non-believers and increasingly among believers – personal choice.

As background justification for his affirming position, a friend whose views have transitioned on the subject-matter of this book writes this: "Humans made in the image of this multi-gendered and non-gendered God may expect that their own sexual orientation, gender identity and gender expression will exist in a variety of forms."[27] This sort of statement is as thoroughly postmodern as it is altogether unorthodox within Christian theology. It is also self-contradictory. God is both "*non*-gendered" and "*multi*-gendered"? One is possible. I'm not sure the other is. But both cannot be true of the same being at the same time. That is like saying John is in Nairobi and Chicago at the same GMT today. He might be in one of those places at that exact time; he cannot be in both. Unless, perhaps, we are speaking postmodern whimsey.

Does it seem at all strange that someone would argue from the nature of the Pure Spirit Being who has no physical form, is outside time, and not subject to limitations of space for the gender fluidity he wants to legitimate? By the canons of common sense, one could as well argue that since God is outside time, humans should not be penalized for failing to keep our time-specific appointments. Neither, since God is also outside space, should we be restrained in our physical location in terms of which house we choose to inhabit in a city or which car we drive out of a parking lot. Yet, when God entered the world of space and time as an embodied person, Jesus of Nazareth exhibited a fixed male gender, was aware of the urgency of completing certain tasks because of time limitations, and was not in Jerusalem while in Nazareth or Capernaum.

Postmodernism is a mid-course correction in the history of philosophy that pushed back hard in the final quarter of the twentieth century against Modernity's reduction of all reality to matter and mathematics. Postmodernism asked: Where are the human and relational aspects of our lives in such a scheme? The postmodern movement generated – as its challenged paradigm had before it did to the opposite extreme – an excessive swing away from facts and evidence as central to the search for truth and substituted connection and authenticity as ultimate. Thus, led by psychologists and joined soon afterward by educators, facts and feelings were afforded equal status in the truth quest[28] – with feelings given priority.

Yes, the all-sufficient God of the Bible can represent himself metaphorically as both father (Deut 32:6) and mother (Isa 66:13), but does this say anything at all about human gender expression? Metaphors help God's people understand something of the relationship of generous provision and tender care. Other figures of speech offer the image of God as a potter shaping his people (Isa 64:8), a rock and fortress for their protection (84:11), and more. Does Yahweh's self-representation as a lion (Hos 5:14; 13:8) somehow sanction the contemporary practice of lycanthropy or, as it is more popularly known on some school campuses, presenting oneself as an "animal person" or a "furry"? Would the representation of God as the sun (Psa 84:11) to Israel have justified the captive Israelites in joining their captors to worship the greatest of Egyptian gods, Ra?[29]

My friend quoted above on "gender identity and gender expression" goes further to the essential abolition of binary language about all human beings. Citing

Amy Peeler's conclusion that the gender identity of Jesus is that of "a male-embodied Savior with female-provided flesh," he draws this conclusion: "In other words, the flesh of Jesus is both male and female."[30] With love for my friend and while suppressing the need to laugh, *then so am I*. As a male-embodied human being, it comes as no shock when I tell you that I brought that male flesh into the world from the female-provided flesh of my mother! No, Jesus' flesh was not both male and female; his flesh was male, with every cell of his body stamped with one X and one Y chromosome. And that XY genotypic body came from the womb of Mary, whose every cell affirmed the genotypic female marker of two X chromosomes. Neither Jesus, my friend, nor I have flesh that is *both* male and female. I have to wonder if it has dawned on him that this incredulous and unscientific statement significantly devalues females for their lack of any male flesh that could have come to them by virtue of being born female from a female body?

> **About Gender Stereotypes**
>
> Gender stereotypes were around in biblical times. . . . Any male who cried in public, showed affection (not just lust) toward women, abstained from sex outside of marriage, or honored lower-class people – the poor, the marginalized, and children – was not considered a real masculine man. A real man would never have washed another man's feet.
>
> Enter Jesus.
>
> Jesus not only turned over tables in the temple but also overturned social views about masculinity and femininity. In addition to his "masculine" table-flipping, Jesus also wept over Jerusalem and longed to "gather your children together, as a hen gathers her chicks under her wings" (Luke 13:34). Onlookers might have considered Jesus masculine when he chewed out the religious leaders in Matthew 23. (Or is that a feminine trait?) But he also let others slap him in the face and smack him on the head, and he rarely stood up for his personal rights. Jesus, in other words, supplies us with a counterculutral view of masculinity.
>
> — Preston Sprinkle

The thoroughly postmodern use of language that allows the nonreason of such an assertion takes me back to the story of Rachel Dolezal. Newspapers around the world carried her story in 2015. President of the local NAACP chapter in Spokane, Washington, and a part-time instructor in African-American Studies at Eastern Washington University, the then 37-year-old woman claimed a transracial Black-White identity. She repeatedly spoke of her African heritage – until her parents revealed that their racial-ethnic background is Caucasian except for a Native American grandmother in both their family histories. When she was exposed for her misrepresentations (i.e., lies), both Black and liberal political leaders accused her of an offensive impersonation and denounced what she had done.[31]

As you might expect, however, there were a few people who defended her right to self-identify as Black. Dolezal initially defended her actions by appealing to the evolutionary theory of human origins in Africa. "We're all from the African continent," she said. In that case, someone wondered aloud, shouldn't every human in America call himself or herself African-American?[32] To the matters raised in this book, might Ms. Dolezal have gotten resounding support if she had chosen to self-identify as male rather than Black – trans-*gender* rather than trans-*racial*.[33] Politicians, psychologists, entertainment media, progressive clergy – all seem to have only praise for the elimination of the binary choice of male or female on federal documents such as passports.[34] The fact remains, however, that there is no evidence for the recognition of either a distinction between sex and gender or anything resembling a "third sex" or "third gender" found anywhere in Scripture.[35]

I am not the only person who took note of an interview Piers Morgan did with noted biologist and aggressive atheist Richard Dawkins in the spring of 2023. For all his public support of the gay community and hostility toward practically all things Christian, he stated his view – flatly and bluntly, as is his custom – that LGBTQ+ activists trying to blur the biological fact of two sexes are promoting "utter nonsense." Said Dawkins: "There are two sexes, and that's all there is to it."[36] Dawkins earlier had made the point raised above about trans-racial and trans-gender identity.

> Race is very much a spectrum. Most African-Americans are mixed race, so there really is a spectrum. Somebody who looks white may even call themselves black, may have a very slight [African inheritance]. People who have one great-grandparent who is Native American may call themselves Native American. Sex on the other hand is pretty d*** binary. So on the face of it, it would seem easier for someone to identify as whatever race they choose. If you have one black parent and one white parent, you might think you could choose what to identify as.
>
> The (London) *Sunday Times* condensed my words into the headline that I have adopted for this piece: *Race is a spectrum. Sex is pretty d*** binary.* This point really is childishly obvious. When a female and a male mate, each offspring is either female or male . . .[37]

CHAPTER 5: HOW IMPORTANT IS THE CREATION STORY?

Put most simply and candidly, the Bible recognizes and celebrates two sexes of humankind – male and female. Only those two. Its narrative tells of males who do things that custom may have associated principally with "feminine" roles (e.g., David's harp-playing and singing, Jesus' public tears) and of females taking on tasks typically thought of as "masculine" (e.g., Deborah's civic leadership as an Israelite judge, Lydia's small-business ownership). The image of a hairy-chested brute calling for his dinner to be brought while he watches football by his dainty wife who leaves her sewing room to rush into her well-appointed kitchen is a stereotypical myth. Some cultures may dictate pink touches for little girls and blues for infant boys, but it is only cultural and not biblical. In fact, I know some women who like sports (and are better at them!) more than their husbands. At our house, my wife increasingly defers to me for making cakes and cookies – a (womanly?) hobby I have taken up after decades of (mannish?) disregard for something I had enjoyed doing in my parents' home decades ago. And she has not been hesitant to work from a cherry picker to paint the exterior of the upper story of our house while I was out of the country on a mission trip! Should we really be surprised that gender-binary humans are multifaceted in skills, interests, and activities?

The interpretive issue here is not to figure out how gender

> **Richard Dawkins on "De-Gendered Language"**
>
> The famous critic of religion spoke with Piers Morgan. The host prompted Dawkins by mentioning how "extraordinary" it is that LGBTQ activists "want to what they call, de-gender and neutralize language."
>
> Morgan was referring to a recent list of problematic words put out by a collection of academics looking to police words that could potentially be found to be politically incorrect. The proposed list contains gendered words such as "male, female, man, woman, mother, father," U.K. outlet The (London) Telegraph reported.
>
> Dawkins had commented on the project last month, telling the paper, "The only possible response is contemptuous ridicule. I shall continue to use every one of the prohibited words. I am a professional user of the English language. It is my native language."
>
> Dawkins immediately discredited the entire movement by saying, "It's bullying. . . . But it's very upsetting the way this tiny minority of people has managed to capture the discourse and really talk errant nonsense." Upon Morgan asking Dawkins how to combat the "nonsense," Dawkins replied, "Science."
>
> He then said, "There are two sexes. You can talk about gender if you wish, and that's subjective." Morgan asked him about people who claim there are "a hundred genders," though Dawkins claimed, "I'm not interested in that."
>
> He said bluntly, "As a biologist, there are two sexes, and that's all there is to it."
>
> — Richard Dawkins interview

fluidity might somehow be derived from reflection on the non-gendered God of Judeo-Christian faith. It is, instead, to pay attention to and to respect the nature of God's creation and to observe whatever commands or prohibitions he has placed on our sexual conduct as human agents. Since it is God who is the Creator, it is his right to define what he has created. And he has defined "mankind" (NIV) or "humans" (NRSVue) as male and female at Genesis 1:27. We do not get to retool that definition

It seems clear from the biblical account of creation that readers are not being offered an account of origins in which Israel's God presented sexuality and gender to be fluid and expressed along a continuum. There are still some of us who believe that this account was produced as the writer was moved by God to relate it (cf. 2 Pet 1:20-21) – not from Egyptian lore with its gender-fluid deities such as Atum, Seth, Hapi, Shai, and others.[38] Thus, we accept the biblical scheme of two sexes, male and female, and that physiology is the primary determinant of one's placement for both sex and gender. In Jewish and Christian theology, humans are embodied beings and our sexuality is expressed through those bodies. It is creation itself that has established the baseline norms for human sexuality.

At several junctures as we proceed, the Genesis material introduced here will be referenced for its importance to the ethical issues being explored. In the next chapter, we will see how the Torah protects the creation-ordained relationship. From there, we will arrive at the Gospels and explore a bit further just how essential Jesus saw the Genesis material to be.

ENDNOTES

1. Lesslie Newbigin, *The Gospel in a Pluralist Society* (Grand Rapids: Eerdmans, 1989), 15-16.

2. James Davison Hunter, *To Change the World: The Irony, Tragedy, and Possibility of Christianity in the Late Modern World* (New York: Oxford, 2010). The reviewer's words are those of Ross Douthat in his opinion piece "A Tough Season for Believers," *New York Times*, Dec 19, 2010, https://www.nytimes.com/2010/12/20/opinion/ 20douthat.html?searchResultPosition=1 (accessed May 6, 2022).

3. Phyllis Bird, "'Bone of My Bone and Flesh of My Flesh,'" *Theology Today* 50, no.4 (1994): 531.

4. The words "ontology" and "ontological" are heavy-sounding words that have no easy synonyms. These terms (and their larger family) point to *the essence of things* or the *fundamental categories of being*. From the Greek words *ontos* (being, essence) and *logos* (word, account, statement). Given various disciplines such as philosophy, mathematics, theology, physics, and others, the precise definition will vary. In the classic sense in which it is used here, the word means "the study of existing things in terms of their basic identity, form, and structure." Thus the claim is being made that the ontological status of the human race is essentially binary (i.e., two-gendered) as male and female. "So God created *mankind* in his own image . . . *male and female he created*

them" is not a poetic or incidental statement; it is definitive to the essence and category of being that is human. Adam's state of being "alone" is not a description of his emotional-psychological state (i.e., loneliness, longing for friendship, aching for a sexual partner) but of his status within creation as a gendered male apart from a gendered female. To be human is to exist as a member of the male-female complementarity that constitutes *homo sapiens*.

5. Of the 21 times *ēzer* occurs in the Old Testament, 14 make Yahweh the "helper" or "rescuing partner" in view. Thus, Moses says to his father-in-law, Jethro: "My father's God was my *helper*; he saved me from the sword of Pharoah" (Ex 18:4). A psalmist reassures Israel: "We wait in hope for the Lord; he is our *help* and our shield" (Psa 33:20). Or twice in the familiar: "I lift up my eyes to the mountains – where does my *help* come from? My *help* comes from the Lord, the Maker of heaven and earth" (Psa 121:1-2). These are not the exceptions but the clear rule for Yahweh as the *ēzer* of those who look to him. When the reference is not to God, the clear meaning of the word points to "help" or "helper" as the party who comes to the aid of someone in need to rescue from trouble. The takeaway from this is that an *ēzer* is anything but a subordinate who lives under the control and functions at the discretion of another. To the contrary, whether speaking of God or a human, the term *ēzer* one who is in position to assist, render aid, or otherwise deliver another from some insufficiency. There is no hint of an asymmetry of power where one partner would dominate the other until after the fall. And that reference in Genesis 3:16 is a *description* of what has come to be called "the battle of the sexes" would play out, not a *prescription* of God's will in the matter of human relationships.

6. Gushee, *Changing Our Mind*, 80.

7. Ibid.

8. Ibid., 81.

9. Ibid., 82. Cf. Achtemeier, *The Bible's Yes to Same-Sex Marriage*, for the same imaginative attempt at a positive case for same-sex marriage by offering a similar revisioning of marriage as God's way "to help people grow in their ability to give themselves completely to another person, following the pattern of Christ's self-giving love. It struck me as I considered this that there seemed to be nothing about this purpose that required an opposite-gender relationship" (58).

10. Brian Neil Peterson, "Does Genesis 2 Support Same-Sex Marriage? An Evangelical Response," *Journal of the Evangelical Theological Society* 60, no.4 (2017): 691.

11. Gushee, *Changing Our Mind*, 91.

12. Ibid., 97.

13. Ibid., 96.

14. Ibid., 96-97.

15. For example, "But we also now *know* [italics in original] from real human beings and research about them that a very small percentage of the human population is intersexual or transgender" (Ibid., 91). "We *know* [italics in original] that Genesis 2 says . . . But we also *know* [italics in original] from real human beings and research about them that about 3.4 to 5 percent of the population cannot find a 'suitable partner' (Genesis 2) in a member of the 'opposite sex' because that is not their (fixed, enduring, unchangeable) sexual orientation" (Ibid., 92).

16. Ibid., 104.

17. This is the course of conduct Gushee advocates for gay and lesbian partners in language quoted from Catholic ethicist Lisa Cahill. Ibid., 97.

18. Keen, *Scripture, Ethics, and Possibility*, 30.

19. Keen, *The Bible and Sexuality: A Course Reader*, 28.

20. Keen, *Scripture, Ethics, and Possibility*, 31.

21. Keen, *Bible and Sexuality*, 64; *Scripture, Ethics, and Possibility*, 30-33.

22. While most English versions of Genesis 2:21-22 have Yahweh taking one of the human's ribs (Heb, *tzela*) and making the woman from it, the Hebrew word is more commonly translated "side" in its 49 other occurrences in the Old Testament. A footnote to verse 21 in the NIV reads: "Or *took part of the man's side*." Therefore, the woman is a part of humankind (i.e., kinship), and without *both* male and female (i.e.,

differentiation) the race is incomplete. The "image of God" is inherent to both man and woman. Their difference allows the possibility of procreation but is not confined to it; their commonality is supportive partnership to one's own species but is not limited to it. What *adam* (human) acknowledges as *ish* (male) is the presence of a distinct but corresponding *ishah* (female) as fulfillment and complement.

23. Keen, *Bible and Sexuality*, 63-64, cf. her footnote 39; 68-70.

24. Ibid., 63.

25. Ibid., 105.

26. Keen, *Scripture, Ethics, and Possibility*, 32-33.

27. Chris Altrock, "Open & Affirming: A Case for Full LGBTQ+ Inclusion in the Church," a two-part class presented on Feb 26, 2023, and Mar 2, 2023, at the Stamford Church of Christ, 6. Notes published online at https://drive.google.com/file/d/1hToCw--yB1NPWGNwtZFFCvriT5lCgnYc/view (accessed Mar 16, 2023).

28. Cf. Justin McBrayer, "Why Our Children Don't Think There Are Moral Facts," *New York Times*, Mar 2, 2015, https://archive.nytimes.com/opinionator.blogs.nytimes.com/2015/03/02/why-our-children-dont-think-there-are-moral-facts/?searchResultPosition=4.

29. In the mythology of Egypt, Ra is the "sun god" who created the world and the lesser gods. Ra is represented in Egyptian art by both the sun-disc and scarab. Cf. Fayza Haikal, "Ra, the Creator God of Ancient Egypt," *American Research Center in Egypt* (online), https://arce.org/resource/ra-creator-god-ancient-egypt (accessed Mar 18, 2023). One of the plagues brought against the Egyptians during Moses' encounters with Pharaoh was a "thick darkness" that showed Yahweh's power over their greatest deity.

30. Altrock, "Open and Affirming," 6.

31. Richard Pérez-Peña, "Black or White? Woman's Story Stirs Up a Furor," *New York Times*, June 12, 2015, https://www.nytimes.com/2015/06/13/us/rachel-dolezal-naacp-president-accused-of-lying-about-her-race.html.

32. Kinsey Clarke, "Making Sense of Rachel Dolezal, the Alleged White Woman Who Passed as Black," *National Public Radio*, June 12 2015, https://www.npr.org/sections/codeswitch/2015/06/12/413887930/making-sense-of-rachel-dolezal-the-alleged-white-woman-who-passed-as-black.

33. A similar problem arose for British-born Oli London. Having already self-identified as non-binary and gender fluid (with public support such as that of Ben Shapiro who tweeted that "only bigots disagree"), he (living then as a female) created a firestorm of criticism by claiming a trans-*racial* identity as Korean in connection with cosmetic surgery to have "Korean eyes." Ryan Smith, "Oli London Insists They're 'Transracial' After Surgery to Get 'Korean Eyes,'" *Newsweek*, June 29, 2021, https://www.newsweek.com/ben-shapiro-supports-white-instagram-star-who-identifies-korean-1605095. More recently, London has stated that his life as a Korean woman gave him only "temporary happiness" and has detransitioned. "I have come to realize, actually, I am a man. And I want to stay as a man. So, I'm going to revert to my original pronouns, which is he/him and KOR/EAN." He further explained that this aligns with his "biology." Iris Jung, "Oli London detransitions from 'Korean' woman to British man,"*Yahoo News*, Nov 14, 2022, https://www.yahoo.com/video/oli-london-detransitions-korean-woman-001720404.html. Further developments to this story are likely to occur.

34. U.S. Department of State, "Selecting Your Gender Marker," updated Nov 7, 2022, https://travel.state.gov/content/travel/en/passports/need-passport/selecting-your-gender-marker.html. "The gender you select does not need to match the gender on your supporting documentation such as a birth certificate, previous passport, or state ID. We no longer require medical documentation to change the gender marker on your U.S. passport. At this time, you can select male (M), female (F), or unspecified or another gender identity (X) as your gender marker if you are applying for a U.S. passport book and selecting routine service."

35. Readers may wish to see the discussion of "eunuchs" in Chapter 5 on this point.

36. Gabriel Hays, "Richard Dawkins declares there are only two sexes as matter of science: 'That's all there is to it,'" *Fox News*, Mar 21, 2023, https://www.foxnews.com/media/richard-dawkins-declares-only-two-sexes-matter-science-thats-all.

37. Richard Dawkins, "Race Is a Spectrum. Sex Is Pretty D*** Binary," *Areo Magazine* (online), Jan 5, 2022. Accessed Mar 23, 2023, at https://areomagazine.com/2022/01/05/race-is-a-spectrum-sex-is-pretty-damn-binary. In the continuation of this quotation with an attached footnote, Dawkins raises and clarifies a

point often misrepresented about intersex or hermaphrodite presentations. "When a female and a male mate, each offspring is either female or male, extremely seldom a hermaphrodite or intersex of any kind. [fn: Anne Fausto-Sterling's *figure of 1.7 percent intersex* is much repeated. It is inflated from the more realistic 0.018 percent by the dubious inclusion of Klinefelter syndrome, Turner syndrome and late-onset adrenal hyperplasia. Whether you take 1.7 or 0.018 percent, the figure is still minuscule when placed in the middle of a frequency distribution, where it is dwarfed by huge peaks on either side. The distribution is overwhelmingly bimodal and sex overwhelmingly binary.]

38. Neel Burton, "Gender Fluidity in the Gods and What It Might Mean," *Psychology Today* (July 9, 2017, updated Mar 15, 2020), https://www.psychologytoday.com/us/blog/hide-and-seek/201707/gender-fluidity-in-the-gods. Cf. Burton, "The Oldest Gays in History: Three Tales of Same-Sex Love in Ancient Egypt," *Psychology Today* (July 14, 2017), https://www.psychologytoday.com/us/blog/hide-and-seek/201707/the-oldest-gays-in-history.

> *"If a man lies with a male as one
> lies with a woman, the two of them
> have done an abhorrent thing; they shall be
> put to death – their bloodguilt is upon them."*
> – Leviticus 20:13 (Tanakh[1])

CHAPTER 6

Have We Missed the Point of All Those Old Testament Texts for All These Centuries?

The language of the biblical text cited at the top of this page has been understood by Jews and Christians in remarkably uniform fashion for well over 3,000 years. For all the differences of Jewish-Christian interpretation, this text has *not* been a battleground passage. Alongside the ethical teachings of the third Abrahamic faith (i.e., Islam), we have agreed that the biblical opposition to same-sex intercourse is absolute, unwavering, severe, and – in cultures such as those of ancient Greece and Rome – counter-cultural.

Have the scholars and laypersons of Judaism, Christianity, and Islam consistently misread their sacred texts on same-sex behaviors for all these centuries?

Granting that it is certainly *possible* for human beings to misinterpret texts and draw incorrect conclusions from the biblical materials, how *likely* is it that no prophet or apostle – not even Jesus himself – would correct such a glaring mistake? One that passes such a harsh judgment on persons created in Yahweh's image? One that emphatically denies intimate sexual companionship to all those who are same-sex attracted? Especially one that had such a severe penalty attached (i.e., death) under the theocratic union of church and state in ancient Israel?

Sexual behaviors, after all, were never on par with such cultic provisions as the separation of Israel as Yahweh's Chosen People by means of circumcision, dietary limits, or Sabbath observance. Sexual relationships were fundamental issues of morality. (The attempt to put both cultic and moral rules into a single category that can be dismissed today will be explored at the end of this chapter.)

But Times Have Changed

As popular media, psychological theory, and polls reflecting a cultural shift in attitude toward gays and lesbians have had their collective impact, same-sex activity has come to the fore. Christian churches – Roman Catholic, Episcopal, Methodist, Presbyterian, Baptist, Churches of Christ, Community Churches, et al. – have both academics and clergy who argue now in defense of covenanted and caring same-sex commitments as an acceptable lifestyle. For most who make such an argument, the issue is not mere tolerance but full affirmation. Some will allow that those who hold the historic position of disapproval toward same-sex behaviors do so from rational conviction. Others lump all such people under descriptors such as homophobic, hateful, or simply ignorant.

The purpose of this chapter is to explore key Old Testament texts germane to the current debate. I will present and defend what is usually called a "traditional" position. I have earlier dared to describe it as the "orthodox" view of the church for all its history until the mid- to late-twentieth century. As the cultures of Europe and North America have worked to normalize same-sex relationships, Progressive Catholics, Reform Jews, Mainline Protestants, and the occasional Evangelical Protestant have pressed their historic communities to change their positions from opposition to affirmation.

Stated positively, I argue that Scripture shows a good God creating a good world and then entrusting it to human beings made in his image. With humans appropriately oriented to their Creator, men and women were authorized to be God's co-regents of the cosmos. Creation was delegated to humans who were given both the right and obligation to manage and preside over all things (Gen 1:26-28; 2:5; Psa 8:3-8). In partnership with God, humans were free to engage everything in creation with the Deity's blessing. Bearing God's image and reflecting honor to him, all things were placed under human stewardship. That same narrative reveals that in every instance where humans turn away from God, however, we are destined to become slaves to the very things God gave us as blessings.

When the One True God is the object of human devotion, all things in his creation are ours to enjoy and experience with his approval; when anything in creation becomes more precious to us than their Creator, we are quickly mastered and enslaved by it and suffer negative consequences. Stated another way, to allow our concern with anything in creation to have greater importance in our lives than their Creator is a form of idolatry. Power, money, and sex are holy when managed responsibly and destructive when worshipped. Case studies of how this has played out with sexual pleasure across the centuries and civilizations can be multiplied.

Living within and interacting with pagan cultures in the Ancient Near East – and tempted as well by their own internal motivations – Israel was not left without guidance. The Chosen People were given instruction through Moses and the prophets about – among many other things – permitted and forbidden sexual behaviors. Thus we turn to examine the key Old Testament texts related to same-sex activity and relationships.

Genesis 19

As David Gushee points out, the story of Sodom has "far greater impact in the rest of Scripture and Christian tradition and its role in the LGBTQ discussion"[2] than any other narrative account. If he had continued and simply made the claim that the story is about a violent behavior that no Christian should endorse, he would have been on safe ground. Indeed, Richard Hays has observed that "there is nothing in the passage pertinent to a judgment about the morality of consensual homosexual intercourse."[3] I fear Hays is a bit hasty in dismissing the story as "irrelevant" to the topic of same-sex behavior. For example, it can be argued reasonably that too much has been made of the Sodom story for this topic or that its disposition to same-sex behavior as its central vice has been overstated. It is more correct in my judgment to say that the extreme depravity of Sodom included a variety of sinful behaviors – with violence, adultery, same-sex intercourse, and gluttony *all* among them. As later prophets such as Isaiah, Jeremiah, or Ezekiel spoke to the sins of their own times, they could use Sodom as a case study for the judgment any or all such offenses might bring. It would be comparable to our use of Hollywood as an example in speaking at different times to the issues of gaudy excess, sexual permissiveness, abuse of executive power by males, shameless exploitation of females, and disregard for the homeless poor.

As I will argue below, the specific matter of violence seems to emerge within the larger context of prior sympathy for and involvement with deviant sexual practices. Gushee's contention is that the story is not really about homosexuality at all. On the reading he offers, it is about violence, gang rape, and the misogynistic attitude of the men of Sodom.

> [T]he men wanted to dominate, humiliate and harm the male visitors precisely *by treating them like defenseless women.* In sexist social systems, the most outrageous thing you can do to a man is to treat him *like a woman*. The Sodom story is about the attempted gang rape of men, because they are strangers, because they are vulnerable, and because they are a juicy target for humiliation and violation. It is about a town that had sunk to the level of the most depraved battlefield or prison.[4]

It is correct to say that anal rape was a common feature of warring cultures in the Ancient Near East for the sake of humiliating defeated combattants. By raping their vanquished enemies, soldiers effectively "feminized" them and shamed them for the loss of a particular battle.[5] However, the fact that rape was involved does not vindicate the same-sex aspect of the intent. It is also correct to point out that the story of Sodom revolves around ancient cultural customs related to hospitality. Contrasted with Abraham's hospitality to the three guests at his tent (Gen 18:1-8) and Lot's reception of the two who journeyed on to Sodom (Gen 19:1-3), "all the men from every part of the city of Sodom – both young and old – surrounded [Lot's] house." Clearly, their intention was neither friendly nor moral. "Where are the men who came to you tonight?" the mob demanded of Lot. "Bring them out to us so that we can have sex with them" (Gen 19:4-5). Or, as in the more literal translation of the NRSVue, "Bring them out to us, so that we may *know* them."

Gushee does not make the claim of some revisionist interpreters that the men surrounding Lot's house were merely wanting to "know" the two visitors in the sense of questioning them to be satisfied they were not spies and enemies to their city. Boswell, for example, claims that the men of Sodom who clamored at Lot's door "meant no more than to 'know' who they were, and the city was consequently destroyed not for sexual immorality but for the sin of inhospitality to strangers."[6] However, their intention was clearly sexual in nature, since the same Hebrew verb (*yada*) is used at verse 8 when Lot makes the despicable offer of his "two daughters who have not *known* a man" (NRSVue) or "two daughters who have never *slept with* a man" (NIV).[7]

Gushee's contentions around the Sodom story are that (a) the intended offense against Lot's visitors was violent gang rape rather than the same-sex character of what came to be called "sodomy" and (b) later biblical references to this episode make no

> **Old Testament Literature and Sex**
> The Old Testament is not a collection of unrelated laws against sexual sin. It articulates an overall understanding of the place for sex: in marriage between one male and one female. Understanding this situations discussion about specific sexual sins within a general understanding of sexual unions. It also helps one see that general references to sexual sin would include any sexual practice outside of marriage between a male and a female....
>
> Indeed, several factors make the case against homosexuality strong in the Old Testament. First, every text addressing the issue portrays homosexual unions as sinful. Second, homosexual unions are forbidden through different genres of biblical writing: in both legal and narrative literature. Third, homosexual unions are inconsistent with the Old Testament view that the place for sex is within marriage between a male and a female – there is rationale for the opposition to this sin, and it is grounded in an understanding of God's purpose in creation.
>
> — Donald Fortson and Rollin Grams

mention of homosexual intent or behavior. If some have erred by using the story to prove too much, the mistake of his approach is to be overly dismissive.

Violence vs. Sexual Offense

On the first point, the questionable claim is that the men of Sodom were interested in "gang rape" rather than simply having sex. "They are more interested in men than in Lot's daughters because in a patriarchal society men held greater worth, and thus their violation was viewed as a greater offense than violating a woman."[8] If this were so, then why not inflict their rage on *both* the male visitors *and* the defenseless females? Would that not speak to the gender humiliation (i.e., feminization of the males) even more dramatically? Would it not have been a dramatic act of inhospitality against the host family in their midst?

Well before the account in Genesis 19, readers have been informed: "Now the people [note: the Hebrew word here (*enosh*) typically specifies males] of Sodom were wicked and were sinning greatly against the Lord" (Gen 13:13) and an "outcry against Sodom and Gomorrah" had come before the Lord because "their sin [was] so grievous" (Gen 18:20). At a minimum, therefore, we may reasonably doubt that inhospitality in this particular case of Lot's visitors – linked to a willingness to resort to sexual violence – was the primary sin for which Sodom had been notorious already. They were fated for punishment *before* this specific event.

The global tenor of Genesis 19 gives the impression of a focus on sexual drives. The men of the city wanted to have sex with Lot's male guests (v.5), Lot offered his virgin daughters to the men for sex (v.8), and Lot's daughters subsequently got their father drunk and committed incest with him (vs.35-36). As opposed to the assumption that the men of Sodom were out for violence – with sexual assault being only one element of that violence – the linguistic evidence certainly does not require that conclusion.

To the contrary, as Paul will claim in Romans 1, cultures that reject the True God and are given over to dark thoughts and impure deeds typically embrace multiple evils simultaneously. He will name more than 20 such immoral behaviors in that chapter alone. Same-sex intercourse in the apostle's day by no means ruled out malice, envy, murder, slander, or any other vice he had seen in Roman culture. Why would we assume otherwise in the days of Abraham and Lot? From the offer of his daughters to the men surrounding his house and the later behavior of his daughters in having sex with him, why should we not assume that Lot's family had been influenced directly by its sexually disoriented and generally corrupt environment?

Other Old Testament References to Sodom

As to his second point, Gushee claims that the later use of the word Sodom in Old Testament literature as a "byword for total human evil and devastating divine judgment" is never associated with homosexuality. "But never once in these intra-biblical references to Sodom is their evil described as same-sex interest or behavior."[9] To the contrary, he insists, Sodom's sins are named in terms of abuses of public justice (Isa 1:9-23), adultery, lying, and impenitence (Jer 23:14), or pride, gluttony, and lack of concern for the poor (Ezek 16:49).

The assertion here is weaker than with the initial claim. Looking at the Ezekiel text specifically, revisionists are quick to focus on this verse: "Now this was the sin of your sister Sodom: She and her daughters were arrogant, overfed and unconcerned; they did not help the poor and needy" (Ezek 16:49). That they fail to cite the next two verses seems revealing: "They were haughty and did detestable things before me. Therefore I did away with them as you have seen. Samaria did not commit half the sins you did. You have done more detestable things than they, and have made your sisters seem righteous by all these things you have done" (Ezek 16:50-51).

The New International Version uses the plural (i.e., "detestable things") – as do the NRSVue ("abominable things") and NASB (i.e., "detestable things") – in verse 50 to translate the Hebrew word *toevah.* Yet the word in the Hebrew text is singular in form. Brian Peterson points out that the translators here

> . . . perhaps following the plural *anomēmata* in the LXX, confuse the translation by rendering *toevah* in the plural. However, it is in the singular, which corresponds to the singular use of *toevah* in the sex laws of Leviticus 18. In Leviticus 18, it is only the sin of homosexuality that is referred to as an "abomination" in the singular (Lev 18:22; cf. Lev 20:13; for the plural see Lev 18:26, 27, 29, 30). What is also of importance is the fact that sexual sins are the focus when Ezekiel uses the singular *toevah* in 22:11 and 33:26. One must also remember that Ezekiel was a priest and would have been familiar with the Holiness Code of Leviticus.[10,11]

It is incorrect, then, to claim that a literate reader cannot see a reference to same-sex behaviors in reference to Sodom outside Genesis 19. Consistent with what Paul will say centuries later, Ezekiel sees the critical problem of Sodom less in terms of either pride or gluttony, insensitivity to the poor or homosexuality but principally as arrogance against God and the refusal to honor him as Sovereign over all things.

> Ezekiel thought that the inhabitants of [Sodom] became "prideful" and "haughty" as a result of the city's prosperity, and in their prosperity they *both* neglected the poor *and* committed a particularly abominable act of sexual immorality. The two evils are linked by a flagrant disregard of God's own priorities, putting the human self at the center of the cosmos. In Ezekiel's view, the overarching rubric for the sin of Sodom is not inhospitality or homosexual behavior but human arrogance in relation to God.[12]

If we were to formulate a multiple-choice question about the destruction of Sodom, the question might be framed this way: "According to the cumulative Old Testament material, the ancient city of Sodom was destroyed because of . . ." Then, possible correct answers then could be stated this way: "(a) injustice, (b) pride in its wealth, (c) lack of concern for the poor, (d) detestable sexual behavior, (e) failure to show hospitality to strangers, or (f) all of the above." Against the tendency of a careless test-taker who might choose any one of the options (a) through (e), the correct answer would, of course, be (f).

While a given prophet such as Isaiah or Ezekiel might choose to focus on Sodom from the perspective of what was most relevant to his audience in the narrative he was developing, the larger story with its direct references to the sexual behavior of the men of Sodom remains intact. No more than the Genesis account rules out Sodom's pride in its wealth and lack of concern for the poor do the statements in Ezekiel eliminate its aberrant sexual practices. Neither should it be overlooked that Ezekiel fails to mention violence, inhospitality to strangers, or gang rape in his rebuke of economic injustice. Ancient and modern writers tell the part of the story that illustrates the point being made. So, Isaiah and Ezekiel – without being unaware of or dismissive toward same-sex intercourse – focused on another element of Sodom's wickedness that fit the message they were stressing about callous indifference toward the poor.

New Testament on Sodom

Having set aside the possibility of any intra-biblical references from the Old Testament to same-sex interest or behavior, Gushee gives equally dismissive treatment to the New Testament.

> The only biblical references to Sodom with any *possible* suggestion of same-sex behavior are Jude 6-8 and the parallel text in 2 Peter 2:6-7, with their references to unholy interest in "other flesh" (Jude 7). In the context of an interpretation of Genesis 19 that is already convinced the story is about same-sex behavior, these two late New Testament texts are read as confirmation. But look closely. They represent fragments of tradition, referring to unholy human interest in *sex with angels*, a theme derived from the book of Enoch, with reference back to the mysterious Genesis 6:1-4 story about angels who had sex with human women.[13]

The standard translation of Jude 7 is that Sodom and Gomorrah "gave themselves up to sexual immorality and perversion" (NIV) or "indulged in sexual immorality and pursued unnatural lust" (NRSVue). Gushee offers the translation "other flesh" for the Greek *sarkos heteras* – which is a plausible rendering that has been included as a footnote to the NRSVue. His interpretation of the expression, however, is not at all certain.

While numerous scholars (e.g., Hays, Gagnon) construe the reference here to humans having sex with angels, it is a point of considerable debate. Other equally reputable scholars (e.g., Keener, Gundry) question such a reading by virtue of the fact that the men of Sodom saw Lot's two visitors as "men" (Gen 19:5) – not angelic beings. Indeed, Abraham had received them previously as "men" (Gen 18:2), giving rise to the later comment in Scripture that he had "shown hospitality to angels without knowing it" (Heb 13:2). Furthermore, based on a comment from Jesus about their nature, angels appear to be asexual in nature (Matt 22:30; Mark 12:25) and have spirit forms rather than fleshly bodies (Heb 1:14; cf. Luke 24:37-39).[14] As Moo points out, the word "flesh" (Gk, *sarx*) would be an unlikely term to apply to angels.[15] Thus the "other flesh" of Jude 7 more likely means "flesh other than what is natural" or "flesh other than that of human females" (i.e., same-sex human intercourse) rather than "flesh other than what is human."

> **The Sodom Story**
>
> What was the sin of the people of Sodom that merited their obliteration?
>
> The traditional view has been that they were guilty of homosexual practices, which they attempted (unsuccessfully) to inflict on the two angels Lot was entertaining. But Sherwin Bailey challenged this interpretation on two main grounds. First, it is a gratuitous assumption (he argued) that the demand of the men of Sodom, "Bring them out to us, so that we may know them," meant "so that we can have sex with them" (NIV).
>
> The Hebrew word for "know" (yada) occurs 943 times in the Old Testament, of which only 10 occurrences refer to physical intercourse, and even then only to heterosexual intercourse. . . . Bailey's second argument was that the rest of the Old Testament nowhere suggests that the nature of Sodom's offense was homosexual. Instead, Isaiah implies that it was hypocrisy and social injustice; Jeremiah – adultery, deceit, and general wickedness; and Ezekiel – arrogance, greed, and indifference to the poor. . . .
>
> But Bailey's case is not convincing for a number of reasons: (1) the adjectives "wicked," "vile," and "disgraceful" (Gen 18:7; Judges 19:23) do not seem appropriate to describe a breach of hospitality; (2) the offer of women instead does look as if there is some sexual connotation to the episode; (3) although the verb yada is used only ten times of sexual intercourse, Bailey omits to mention that six of those occurrences are in Genesis and one in the Sodom story itself (about Lot's daughters, who had not "known" a man, verse 8); and (4) for those of us who take the New Testament documents seriously, Jude's unequivocal statement cannot be dismissed as merely an error copied from Jewish pseudepigrapha. To be sure, homosexual behavior was not Sodom's only sin; but according to Scripture, it was certainly one of them.
>
> — John R.W. Stott

To say the least, the Jude text seems to be a broad reference to the fact that Sodom and Gomorrah "gave themselves up to sexual immorality and perversion" rather than a specific reference to the episode with Lot's guests. There is certainly nothing here to indicate that Jude's reference is to "inhospitable acts" of violence and nonconsensual sex (i.e., rape). "Sexual immorality" is a broad category that would include Sodom's "adultery" (cf. Jer 23:14) and perhaps such sins as pederasty, heterosexual fornication, and/or prostitution *as well as* whatever is meant by the KJV's "strange flesh," the NRSVue's "unnatural lust," or the NIV's "perversion."

All this not only serves to readmit Jude to the list of relevant texts for this topic but also weighs against Gushee's wave of his hand to the idea that "loving, covenantal, same-sex relationships" would not be in view in connection with Sodom.[16] Could it not have been the prominence of same-sex relationships in Sodom – whether consensual, cultic, forced, pedophilic, or loving and covenantal – that caused "the men from every part of the city of Sodom – both young and old" (Gen 19:4b) to surround Lot's house? That long-term, committed same-sex partnerships were known in antiquity will be documented in some detail as we move through the biblical materials.

Finally on this point, the consensus of scholarship is that there is a direct dependence on this text from Jude in 2 Peter 2:6-7. If there is ambiguity in the former reference to the sins of Sodom, there is none in the latter use that would indicate lust for or copulation with angels was in view. Second Peter interprets Jude as a reference to "the depraved conduct (Gk, *aselgeia*) of the lawless." In New Testament literature, *aselgeia* serves to mark out conduct that exhibits a lack of moral restraint.[17] In other words, Peter takes the behavior of the men of Sodom as a case study in what both he and Jude (v.4) saw as human behavior in the pagan culture of their own time that was threatening the moral integrity of the church through the influence of false teachers. The writer's concern was clearly human-with-human behavior, not human-with-angel activity.

Judges 19

Gushee treats the story of Sodom in tandem with an event recorded at Judges 19. In a single chapter that deals with them both, he titles it "The Sins of Sodom (and Gibeah)."[18] One could wonder if the two accounts – which he calls "the Genesis

19/Judges 19 pair" – are put together for the sake of making it easier to dismiss the relevance of the Sodom story. Whether that assumption is correct or not, I have been at great pains to argue that Genesis 19 is appropriate to sorting out a biblical view of same-sex behaviors. In this instance, however, I agree that Judges 19 is *not* a critical text to this topic.

The dominant motif in Judges 19 is hospitality. A certain Levite was shown hospitality in Bethlehem, only to be treated rudely at Gibeah in the territory of Benjamin. Finally, he was taken in for the night by an old man of the town. While eating inside the man's house, "some of the wicked men of the city surrounded the house. Pounding on the door, they shouted to the old man who owned the house, 'Bring out the man who came to your house so we can have sex with him'" (Judg 19:22). This would have been their way of humiliating their fellow-citizen's guest and his host. The story is complicated by an unholy "solution" in which the man hands over his concubine to the men, they gang rape her through the night, and she dies from their repeated violent assaults. This set off a series of events that led to a severe retaliation against the Benjamites by the other tribes of Israel. This story adds little or nothing to the overall discussion of homosexuality per se and relates more directly to misogyny, rape, murder, and violent retaliation.

Leviticus and Behaviors that are toevah

Although "homosexual" and "heterosexual" are nineteenth-century words in terms of their origination, there is no mistaking the meaning of Israel's Torah concerning same-sex intercourse. As Boswell points out with regard to the absence of a word corresponding to our English "homosexual" in Hebrew, Aramaic, or Greek: "There are of course ways to get around the lack of a specific word in a language, and an action may be condemned without being named . . ."[19] One of those ways would be to offer a graphic description of the action itself. In what is known as Israel's Holiness Code of Leviticus 17 – 26, a large block of material functions as a collection of societal, cultic, moral, ceremonial, and lifestyle requirements for the Jewish people. Beginning at 18:1, the specific focus is on sexual behaviors.

The general purpose of the commandments given in this section of the Holiness Code appears explicit and clear. Israel has been set apart to Yahweh from the

Egyptians they had escaped, the Canaanites they were destined to displace, various pagan tribes they would encounter along their route, and the remainder of humankind. As a Chosen People to God, its people are charged with reflecting his holiness to the pagan nations.

> The Lord said to Moses, "Speak to the Israelites and say to them: 'I am the Lord your God. You must not do as they do in Egypt, where you used to live, and you must not do as they do in the land of Canaan, where I am bringing you. Do not follow their practices. You must obey my laws and be careful to follow my decrees. I am the Lord your God. Keep my decrees and laws, for the person who obeys them will live by them. I am the Lord'" (Lev 18:1-5).

There is considerable repetition in places, and there are two specific texts that deal with same-sex behavior. "Do not have sexual relations with a man as one does with a woman; that is detestable" (Lev 18:22). Two chapters later, this explicit prohibition is expanded to include the penalty for its transgression: "If a man has sexual relations with a man as one does with a woman, both of them have done what is detestable. They are to be put to death; their blood will be on their own heads" (Lev 20:13).

As clear as these statements appear to most readers, there are moves from revisionist scholars to either blunt or do away with their impact. Without arguing that the Old Testament guidelines to holiness should be set aside altogether or counted as distinctly Jewish ritualistic concerns, Gushee chides those with a traditional view of same-sex behavior this way:

> Almost no Christian ever quotes the Old Testament book of Leviticus today, a text which mainly, though not exclusively, contains worship instructions rendered obsolete for Jews themselves centuries ago by the destruction of the last Jewish Temple. However, two texts plucked from Leviticus are regularly cited by Christians in the LGBTQ debate . . .[20]

It could be said in reply, of course, that Leviticus is not quoted a great deal today because it is a book that focuses on the duties of the Levites and the worship events associated with the tabernacle. Those duties, services, and worship rituals were unique to an era in Israelite history that have no carryover to us. Basic issues of moral behavior, however, are *grounded in God's own character* and do not have time-bounded or place-restricted relevance.

Chapter 12 of Gushee's *Changing Our Mind* points out that the English term "detestable" (NIV) or "abominable" (NRSVue) – translating the Hebrew *toevah* – is used of a broad range of items in the Old Testament. In Deuteronomy, eating such unclean foods as pork and shrimp is labelled *toevah* (14:3-21). In Ezekiel, oppressing the poor or collecting accrued interest (18:10-13), profaning the Sabbath or wronging widows and orphans (22:6-12), and admitting foreigners to the Temple (44:5-7) are *toevah*. Indeed, within the book of Leviticus, eating rare steak (17:10), paying an employee bi-weekly or monthly (19:13b), planting a field with two kinds of seed (19:19b), getting a tattoo (19:28), or for married heterosexual couples to have sex during the wife's menstrual period (20:18) are all *toevah*.[21] He writes: "It is interesting how few of those other acts or character qualities are ever described as abominations by Christians today."[22] Similarly, Hamilton offers: "Is it God's will that gay and lesbian people be put to death? Few Christians would suggest that this punishment should be applied to gay and lesbian people, so they have already determined that a portion of this Scripture should be set aside."[23] So why should we continue to speak of gay and lesbian sexual behaviors in negative ways?

> **Leviticus: The Holiness Code**
>
> Two reasons are commonly advanced for limiting the scope of the Levitical law – the ritual context of the Holiness Code, and the cultic context of the proscription of Egyptian or Canaanite religion. They may be two sides of the same coin, and are in any case not easily separable. The claim is made that the prohibition is no more of general reference or lasting import than the ban on cutting your beard in a certain way (19:27) or making a garment out of two different materials (19:19) or intercourse during menstruation (18:19) and so on. Since we no longer entertain similar notions of ritual impurity or are faced with homosexual behaviour associated with heathen idolatry, this part of the Mosaic law has nothing to say to the permanent-loving-preference type of homosexuality.
>
> The argument has to recognize that many other unambiguously sinful acts are also encompassed by the Levitical code, such as bestiality (18:23) and child sacrifice (18:21), the immediate neighbours of 18:22, and adultery (20:10) and incest (18:6ff). These chapters undoubtedly place a great mixture of activity and conduct under the ban, but is there no way of discriminating between the more and less grave?
>
> Another way to pose the issue is to ask whether the Mosaic law reprobated behaviour simply because the Canaanites indulged in it. . . . After all, the Israelites did not need, one assumes, to be informed about the Canaanite practice of child sacrifice before they could know whether it was permissible for them to dispose of their children in this way. To put it another way, is it conceivable, from what else we know about Mosaic or Israelite ethics, that child sacrifice or homosexuality would have been tolerated if disinfected of their Canaanite associations?
> — David F. Wright

It is accurate that such things as eating non-kosher foods, adultery, profaning the Sabbath, mistreating widows, sex during a woman's menstrual period, and making a garment from two types of material are all classified as being *toevah* in the Old Testament. With such a variety of actions identified as "detestable," can we know that same-sex intercourse is fundamentally different from making a jacket from two types of cloth? At the least, can we be sure that the same-sex prohibitions are not only against casual or exploitative sex as opposed to what takes place in a caring, committed relationship? If we condemn all varieties of same-sex intercourse from Leviticus 20:13, why do we not also ask for the death penalty for those committing the act? Or, if we now think sex during a woman's period is morally permissible for married couples, how dare we "pick and choose" to continue saying that gay or lesbian sex is not morally permissible? Each of these questions deserves to be answered.

A Word Study: toevah

The Hebrew word *toevah* is a rather generic term for anything God disapproves because it compromises an Israelite's personal or the nation's collective witness to divine holiness. It ranges over everything from idolatry to having pork sausage as part of one's breakfast. Gushee is correct to avoid the revisionist position of some writers that *toevah* refers merely to cultural practices as a kind of boundary marker but not as a moral term.[24] Texts such as Proverbs 6:16-19 make clear that the word can be used as a designation for unethical behavior. The relative seriousness of certain actions is not always apparent, however, except by virtue of what is necessary to remove the uncleanness of the thing/act or to atone for an offense. Giving up something (pork) or washing something (one's body after touching a corpse or an emission of semen) indicates a less serious offense than being banished from the community or suffering capital punishment.

Thus, the real question here becomes this: Is there anything about same-sex relationships that would "violate the character of a holy God" – and thus the witness of the community to him? The obvious answer is this: Yes, for it is ethically "detestable" in its denial of God's created order and its refusal to honor Yahweh's positive intention for human sexuality as initiated in Genesis (Gen 1:27-28; 2:22-24), repeated by Jesus (Matt 19:4-5), and emphasized by Paul (Rom 1:26-27).

Since context is always the most important element of interpreting any passage from Scripture, one should not overlook the grouping of activities within which same-sex intercourse is found. For someone to "have sexual relations with a man as one does with a woman" (Lev 18:22) is forbidden in the context of adultery (18:20) and child sacrifice in the verses immediately before (18:21) and bestiality immediately afterward (18:23). These are moral offenses that God rejects on account of his intrinsic holiness (19:2). They are not unique to Israel – as certain types of beard-trimming, mixing seed in one's field, or combining fabric in a garment – but were forbidden "because this is how the nations that I am going to drive out before you became defiled" (18:24).

Because of its frequent association with the discussion of *toevah*, revisionist interpreters also tend to rely on Boswell's attempt to link the same-sex behavior of the Holiness Code to male cult prostitution among certain of Israel's neighboring cultures. Thus the "abomination" of male-with-male sex is claimed to be its association with idolatry and not the act itself. His claim is that *toevah*

> . . . does not usually signify something intrinsically evil, like rape or theft (discussed elsewhere in Leviticus), but something which is ritually unclean for Jews, like eating pork or engaging in intercourse during menstruation, both of which are prohibited in these same chapters. It is used throughout the Old Testament to designate those Jewish sins which involve ethnic contamination or idolatry . . .[25]

Similar claims to cultic rather than moral implications for the word come from heirs to his work. "To the Jews an abomination was not a law, something evil like rape or murder forbidden by the Ten Commandments," claims Mel White. "It was a common behavior by non-Jews that Jews thought was displeasing to God."[26] Similarly, Peter Gomes has insisted that "homosexuality is an abomination in Leviticus not because it is inherently evil, but because the Gentiles do it and is therefore ritually impure."[27] In other words, the sharp language of Leviticus is really directed at idolatry and not same-sex intercourse and therefore has no spiritual relevance for us – unless what is being done is somehow associated with idolatry.

This tactic does not work for the simple reason that the sexual practices forbidden in the Levitical Holiness Code clearly were not "Jewish sins" or certain acts that made Jews "ritually impure" only when associated with foreign idols. These were the sins for which the pagans of Egypt and Canaan were judged sinful (Lev 18:2), practices by which "the nations I am going to drive out before you became defiled" (Lev 18:24, 27), and behaviors which both the Israelites and "foreigners residing among you" (Lev 18:26b) were forbidden to embrace. The sexual sins for which a death penalty could be imposed were sinful in themselves because they are counter both to God's own holiness and to a life that reflects his image into his creation.[28]

Although it is in the context of his defense of homosexuality, Louis Crompton calls out the common mistake of attempting to tie the Levitical prohibitions against same-sex intercourse to issues of ritual purity as opposed to basic ethical behaviors.

> John Boswell is mistaken in arguing that it was akin to enactments on ritual and not binding on gentiles. Leviticus 18:26 specifically extend the prohibition to "any stranger that sojourneth among you." Such a law was one of the so-called Noachid precepts, binding on all the descendants of Noah – that is, on all humanity.[29]

In response to the challenge about applying the death penalty for same-sex intercourse in our time, there is a perfectly good reason why Christians do not call for capital punishment for persons guilty of bestiality, adultery, or gay/lesbian behaviors. Old Testament Israel was both "church" and "state," so civil penalties were typically attached to religious offenses. One could be fined, cut off from the community, beaten, or executed for certain moral-spiritual defilements. In specific instances, for example, one might even be put to death for picking up sticks on the Sabbath (Num 15:32-36).[30] The issue here is often represented as an instance of extreme punishment for minor infractions of some religious code – thus minimizing, for example, the same-sex offense of Israel's Holiness Code. One would more correctly read all these texts as a case study in the seriousness of any and all behaviors that defy the instructions of a Holy God.

In the Second Temple era, Israel was no longer a theocracy with the right to enforce civil penalties for religious infractions, whether "minor" or "major" on our modern scale. As in the case of Jesus' crucifixion, it was understood that only Rome could mete out capital punishment and then only for a civil rather than religious offense. Since "church" and "state" are now separate entities in Western culture, the church neither (inappropriately) calls for nor (illegally) applies civil penalties for moral infractions. Following Paul's instruction to the church at Corinth, the "extreme penalty" for a moral offense is for the defiant brother or sister to be excluded from the fellowship of believers (1 Cor 5:1-11). It is not the business of the church to clamor for its spiritual and ethical rules to be made part of the state's civil code (cf. 1 Cor 5:12).

Thus, it is hardly inconsistent or even difficult to understand why Christians distinguish between Israel's Holiness Code and its stipulations against both vaginal intercourse between a man and his wife during her menstrual period and anal intercourse between two males without qualifying the circumstance. The former has to do with the ritual impurity that always attached to blood under the Torah. Blood signifies life, blood makes atonement for sin, and blood would eventually cleanse from sin via the sacrifice of Christ (cf. Lev 17:10-12). This was a value attached to the

> **Would/Could God Be So Unclear?**
>
> To suggest that 3,500 years of biblical teaching has been incorrect means that God is one of the worst communicators in the universe. You'd have to believe that although He intended to inspire the biblical authors – by the Holy Spirit – to write down a definition of marriage that could include same-sex couples, the writers ended up foiling His plan and penning a definition of marriage that excludes same-sex couples. Because the biblical witness on marriage was clear to them, every Jew, rabbi, church father, and early Christian thinker would interpret this teaching in only one way: marriage is between a man and a woman. This, of course, doesn't even include the fact that every other time a Holy-Spirit-inspired author addresses homosexual relations, they mention it in a negative and prohibitive way. Scripture never affirms same-sex relations and always condemns homosexual behavior. . . .
>
> It makes more sense that God knew what He inspired the authors to write, they wrote it, and for thousands of years the Church understood what He said. That's where we are today, with the exception of a vocal few who want to amalgamate secular standards of sexuality into biblical ones.
>
> It's true our culture has changed and begun to affirm same-sex relations. . . . The biblical view might not win the approval of the world or be "on the right side of history," but that's not our concern. We're not trying to win the approval of man, but of God (Gal. 1:10).
>
> — Alan Shlemon

worshipping community of Israel. The latter issue of homosexual intercourse has to do with moral impurity that violates the character of a holy God; it deconstructs the image of God that is linked in creation to the male-plus-female factor in Genesis 1. The former is a cultural-cultic distinctive to Israel; the latter is tied to creation and has no link to Israel in any distinctive way. As a reminder, the text explicitly judges the non-Israelite nations being driven out of Canaan for the moral defilements of adultery, child sacrifice, homosexuality, and bestiality. "Do not defile yourselves in any of these ways, for by all these practices the nations I am casting out before you have defiled themselves" (Lev 18:24 NRSVue; cf. Deut 9:5; 12:29-31; 18:9-13).

The Relationship of David and Jonathan

Among other Old Testament texts that surface when same-sex topics are discussed, there is one passage highlighted that some offer as *prima facie* evidence of a same-sex partnership that goes without rebuke. Upon hearing of the death of Saul and his son Jonathan, David composed a lament. Specific to Jonathan, the lament goes as follows: "I grieve for you, Jonathan my brother; you were very dear to me. Your love for me was wonderful, more wonderful than that of women" (2 Sam 1:26). Boswell notes that the background to such a passionate lament includes the biblical background that "Jonathan made a covenant with David because he loved him as himself" (1 Sam 18:3). He comments that the words for "covenant" (Heb, *berith*) and "love" (Heb, *aheb*) here are used elsewhere in Jewish Scriptures of a marriage covenant and sexual passion.[31]

While Boswell is correct about the two words in question, he leaves a false impression about both. The Old Testament does not use *berith* exclusively of marital covenants nor *aheb* of sexual passion. Both words are wide-ranging in their meaning and usage. For example, the noun *berith* is used 284 times. The specific language of "making a covenant" (Heb, *karath berith*) may refer not only to marriage but to a divine covenant with humans (Gen 15:18), a peace treaty between warring parties (Gen 21:27,32), pledges to idols (Ex 34:15), neutrality covenants between national groups (Jdg 9:11), loyalty oaths (1 Sam 11:1), etc. The verb *aheb* appears more than 200 times in the Hebrew text and extends over one's love for food (Gen 27:4,9,14), a slave's love for a master (Ex 21:5), love of foreigners (Deut 10:19), instruction from God (Psa 119:97), quarreling and sin (Prov 17:19), one's neighbor (Lev 19:18), and Yahweh (Deut 6:5).

Most notably, the Hebrew term for sexual desire (*yada*) that plays so prominently in the stories of Sodom (Gen 19:5) and the incident in Judges 19 (esp. v.22) is nowhere to be found in the biblical narratives involving David and Jonathan.

In other words, there is nothing in the biblical language about David and Jonathan that immediately suggests romantic involvement. It seems to be a case of using a verse out of its context to see what modern readers wish to see in it. From his critical analysis of the textual materials, one Old Testament scholar sums up this way:

> A sexual dimension in the relationship between David and Jonathan can only be claimed if the biblical descriptions of this relationship are not taken at face value, but expanded by having recourse to a presumed hidden message. Such inferences, however, disregard the sound principles of a historically oriented exegesis. It may be that the sexual interpretation of the relationship of David and Jonathan that came up during the last three decades or so is related to the wider phenomenon of the sexualization of life in Western societies. The story of the deep friendship of David and Jonathan may act as a counter model by showing how emotionally rich and profound a non-sexual relation between two persons (of the same sex) may be – at times even richer and profounder than sexual relationships. [32]

Biblical scholars from a variety of backgrounds see what Walter Bruggemann has pointed out to be central to the Jonathan-David story. It is an important element within the context of the shift of God's favor from King Saul to his replacement, David. First Samuel 18 sees a shift of covenant loyalty being expressed by Yahweh, Saul's own family (both Jonathan and Michal), and the nation – resulting in Saul's growing fear of David.

> The dramatic language of the narrative enacts the very elevation of David and dismantling of Saul about which it speaks. We watch as Saul is reduced to fear and dread while David exults in popular acclaim. As in vv 10-11, so also in vv 12-16, the failure of Saul's strategy is not luck or accident. Twice we are told concerning David, "Yahweh was with him" (vv 12,14; see 16:18) as Yahweh was no longer with Saul (see 15:11,35). Twice we are told David was "successful" *(maskil,* vv 14,15). As a conclusion to the episode, the narrative employs the decisive word "love" *(aheb,* v 16). Israel and Judah love David. The word "love" will govern the entire chapter. Here the verb serves to contrast David against Saul. Saul by now is unloved by Yahweh, unloved by Israel, and, as we shall see, unloved by his own children.[33]

In context rather than as a free-standing verse, David's eulogy of Jonathan as one whose "love for me was wonderful, more wonderful than that of women" hardly suggests a romantic relationship. Yes, it is testimony to a deep personal friendship. In its essence, however, it is the affirmation of a covenant loyalty that Jonathan honored between himself and King David that had proved itself to be deeper than the blood loyalty a son would have to his father. David, after all, had not always had the best of relationships with females. In summary, the following points seem to be critical.

First, the loyalty pledge of 1 Samuel 18 came on the heels of the young David's shocking victory over Goliath – a victory David attributed not to his skill but to Yahweh's power. "This day the Lord will deliver you into my hands," David had told the giant Philistine warrior. "And the whole world will know that there is a God in Israel" (1 Sam 17:45-47). The covenant between the older adult Jonathan and the boy David was not pederastic but dynastic. That is, it was a notable transfer of allegiance from a rejected king who was in personal-national decline (cf. 1 Sam 15:17-19,26) to the young man upon whom Yahweh's favor had been conferred. It was a pledge of support that had more political than personal force when made. King Saul clearly understood what happened that day in political-dynastic terms (cf. 1 Sam 20:30-31).

Second, that this is principally the language of political attachment rather than romantic connection is supported by parallel uses of the term *aheb* in the biblical text. For example, the same Samuel scroll says that "all Israel and Judah loved (Heb, *aheb*) David, because he led them in their campaigns" (1 Sam 18:16). A few verses later, the same writer tells how King Saul – in arranging the marriage of his daughter, Michal, to David – sent word to his future son-in-law that "his attendants all love (Heb, *aheb*) you" (1 Sam 18:22). Are we to read romantic-sexual overtones into that language? Furthermore, it is the word used much later in Israelite history for King Hiram of Tyre when he congratulated Solomon upon his accession to Israel's throne. Whereas the NIV translates "because he had always *been on friendly terms* with David," the ESV (and the ASV that it tends to follow) reads "for Hiram always *loved* (Heb, *aheb*) David" (1 Kgs 5:1). No Old Testament scholar I have found has suggested this was romantic-sexual "love" in the writer's intent. Why should it be otherwise in the opening verses of the same chapter?

Third, the eulogistic praise of Jonathan upon his death need not be read as anything beyond David's reciprocal acknowledgment of Jonathan for his positive, affirming, and loving praise for his dear friend's covenant faithfulness over time. Yes, every evidence is that their political alliance undergirded and developed into personal affection – as I would affirm for a handful of male colleagues I have come to know in church and academic settings. Hired by elders to serve a church or by an administration to teach at a university, I can name several men whom I met for the first time upon being hired by them and for whom I have since affirmed my appreciation, respect, and love. Indeed, the expansion of the relationship between David and Jonathan is evident from the opening out of their personal covenant of mutual support to one between their families-descendants (1 Sam 20:16-17,42; cf. 23:16-18). It was a covenant commitment the king would honor with regard to Jonathan's surviving family members well after his dear friend's death (cf. 2 Sam 7:1ff).

Fourth, in both ancient and modern times in the Middle East, statements of affection, embracing and/or kissing someone of the same sex, and passionate affirmations of enduring loyalty are not uncommon. Thus Laban embraces and kisses his nephew Jacob (Gen 29:13), as Esau will do with his brother later in the narrative (Gen 33:4). For that matter, the prophet Samuel kissed Saul in connection with anointing him for his future role as king (1 Sam 10:1). And what of the emotionally supercharged language – in the context of embracing and kissing each other – among Naomi, Orpah, and Ruth? (Ruth 1:14-17).

Fifth, linking this discussion to the title for this chapter, there is no evidence in early Jewish writings for an interpretation of the David-Jonathan relationship as anything resembling a homoerotic relationship. Neither is there any evidence of defensiveness in discussing it – as if the possibility had even been suggested or raised for discussion by readers of the sacred text. To the contrary, that their relationship was a "sworn friendship with each other *in the name of the Lord*" (1 Sam 20:42) testifies to their obedience to Yahweh's will as a defining feature of their bond. To suggest then that so glaring a violation of Israel's Holiness Code as some form of same-sex moral infraction was part of their relationship seems more than a bit far-fetched. Since the biblical writers did not flinch at calling out David's violation of Israel's Holiness Code at Leviticus 18:20 (i.e., having sexual relations with someone else's wife), is it reasonable to suppose they would have glossed over his violation of the command that comes only two verses later at Leviticus 18:22 (i.e., a male having sexual relations with another male)?

Sixth, even though some revisionist readers of the Old Testament point to David and Jonathan as same-sex lovers, so public a leader among their number as William Loader has written this:

Others cite the friendship between David and Jonathan as an example of a homoerotic relationship, not least because of the allusion to their love as surpassing the love of women (especially 1 Sam 20:41-42 and 2 Sam 1:17-26), but this is doubtful. Nowhere in early Jewish literature is there any indication that it was read in this way, which would have almost certainly have occasioned efforts to explain it differently. Close friendship between men need not have been homoerotic.[34]

The All-or-Nothing Challenge

At the end of his chapter on Old Testament texts, Gushee strikes a bit of a strident tone in demanding that traditionalists "describe and defend their principle of selection, interpretation, and application" of the Holiness Code in Leviticus.[35] This is his challenge to those he believes "quote selectively" from the Holiness Code to condemn covenanted, monogamous same-sex relationships while setting aside the dietary or blood restrictions already identified. This rhetorical device appears designed to say one must either accept everything in Leviticus 18 (and elsewhere) about actions that are *toevah* or for which one could be punished or excluded from the community or grant his thesis.

"What alternative hermeneutical (a method of interpreting the Bible) principle is to be employed?" he asks. The appropriate response is to say that nothing linked to God's own nature and holiness can be altered, for he is personally unchanging in his nature. The central moral demands the Holy One makes of human beings are the same at all times and under all covenants, for God himself is the same yesterday, today, and forever. The specific principle he seems to want is one that helps us distinguish these eternal moral requirements (e.g., forbidding murder, enjoining compassion, etc.) from cultic, ritual, or temporary statutes that might be subject to change. Here I would use his own language to say that we should distinguish this on the basis of "the character of God as taught and embodied by Jesus Christ."[36] It was Jesus himself who explained that foods, touching corpses, bodily emissions, and the like do not make a person unclean or defiled; instead, genuine uncleanness comes from the heart – murder, sexual immorality, theft, slander, and the like (Matt 15:17-20).

Gushee appears unable to see his inconsistency. In addition to God's character seen in Jesus, he has appealed already to Genesis 2 as normative for monogamy – although not (?) for male-female union as one flesh. Are not both monogamy and male-female coming together elements in a single, unified story? Is there a legitimate hermeneutical principle that says a reader may choose one and omit the other? The holistic nature of the story requires both.

Here it can be noted as well that although it is common to hear the objection that "Jesus never once spoke to the issue of same-sex behavior," the word translated "sexual immorality" in Matthew 15:19 (Gk, *porneia*) is the New Testament term that reflects "an unconditional repudiation of all extra-marital and unnatural intercourse."[37] Furthermore, Jesus

> **Why Focus on the Moral Laws?**
>
> Letha Scanzoni argues that these issues in Leviticus no longer are important for the church. She then goes on to ask "If the Israelite Holiness Code is to be invoked against homosexuals [of the modern day], it should likewise be invoked against practices such as eating rare steak . . . and having marital intercourse during the menstrual period."
>
> In other words, why single out the moral laws and not the dietary and ceremonial ones? The answer is fairly simple: "Because Jesus and Paul, as his follower, did." Scanzoni ignores the distinctions made by both Paul and Jesus. Jesus obliterated the food laws but deepened the prohibition against adultery (Matt 5:17-48; Mark 7:6-23); Paul did the same in Romans 14:13-17 and 1 Cor 6:9-20. Even a superficial reading of Leviticus reveals the Lord God declaring punishment for child sacrifice (20:1ff) and commanding generosity to the needy (19:9-10) as well as forbidding incest and adultery (chapters 18-20). Neither Jesus nor his followers abolished these moral, non-ceremonial laws.
>
> — Jim Reynolds

made it clear that he had not come to "abolish" the commandments of the Torah but to "fulfill" them (Matt 5:17-20). He fulfilled all things related to the purpose of the sacredness of blood by his death. By contrast, he repeatedly affirmed the holiness of God and the responsibility of the community of God's people to honor divine holiness in our discipleship behaviors. That he did not name "same-sex intercourse" no more weighs against it being included among the forbidden acts of the Holiness Code than his non-mention of child sacrifice, polyamory, bisexuality, rape, child sexual abuse, and bestiality means he had no expectation that they should be regarded as immoral and forbidden.

Jesus' willingness to proclaim God's forgiveness through their repentance and faith to persons who have been guilty of the various sexual sins included under the term *porneia* "in no way softens Jesus' condemnation of immorality (Mark 7:21 par.). But it does mean that, along with other sins, it is not to be excluded from forgiveness."[38] But more will be said on Jesus' alleged silence about same-sex relationships in the next chapter.

As will be made clear in the upcoming examination of the relevant texts from the New Testament, there is an ethical continuity between the two covenants. It has always been wrong, is wrong, and will continue to be wrong to rape, murder, have sexual intercourse with animals, violate one's covenant promises, or have sexual intercourse with someone of the same sex/gender.

Only if the holy character of God has changed can the moral standards his people are bound to obey change. Short of affirming God's ethical mutability, we dare not alter the behavioral mandates to which his holiness gives rise. But how did Jesus view the Holiness Code? Did he view the Old Testament material as relevant to the lifestyle required of his followers? Are New Testament Christians expected to accept the authority of the Old Testament texts we have just examined?

These questions remain to be addressed as we continue to work through the biblical materials in subsequent chapters.

ENDNOTES

1. Jewish Publication Society *Tanakh* translation (1999) from Adele Berlin and Marc Zvi Brettler, *The Jewish Study Bible* (New York: Oxford University Press, 2004).

2. Gushee, *Changing Our Mind*, 60.

3. Richard Hays, *The Moral Vision of the New Testament* (New York: HarperCollins, 1996), 381.

4. Gushee, *Changing Our Mind*, 63.

5. Male/male rape has been known as an "instrument of war" from ancient times to modern. This sort of humiliation of a male for whom one wishes to display contempt is thought by some scholars to be involved in the account of Ham and Noah. The language of Genesis 9:20-27, where Ham "saw the nakedness of his father" (v.22; cf. Lev 20:17), is taken to be euphemistic language for having sex – thus making Ham guilty of homosexual rape. Cf. *The Jewish Study Bible*, Genesis 9:22fn.

6. John Boswell, *Christianity, Social Tolerance, and Homosexuality: Gay People in Western Europe from the Beginning of the Christian Era to the Fourteenth Century* (Chicago: University of Chicago Press, 1980), 94.

7. *The Jewish Study Bible* translates these verses as follows: "And they shouted to Lot and said to him, 'Where are the men who came to you tonight? Bring them out to us that we may be intimate with them'" (v.5) and "Look, I have two daughters who have not known a man. Let me bring them out to you, and you may do to them as you please" (v.8a).

8. Gushee, *Changing Our Mind*, 63.

9. Ibid., 62.

10. Brian Neil Peterson, "The Sin of Sodom Revisited: Reading Genesis 19 in Light of Torah," *Journal of the Evangelical Theological Society* 59, no.1 (2016): 21.

11. While English translations such as NRSVue, NIV, and NASB are not consistent with the translations of singular and plural forms of *toevah*, it should be noted that the JPS *Tanakh* renders them consistently – using the terms "abhorrence" (singular) and "abhorrent practices" or "abhorrent things" (plural).

12. Robert A.J. Gagnon, *The Bible and Homosexual Practice: Texts and Hermeneutics* (Nashville: Abingdon Press, 2001), 85.

13. Gushee, *Changing Our Mind*, 63.

14. If angels are non-reproducing spirit beings, the Genesis 6:4 reference to intermarriage between the "sons of God" and the "daughters of humans" ("daughters of men," KJV) is better understood as the righteous lineage of Seth intermarrying with that of Cain. The notion of sexual adventures between lesser gods and/or spirit creatures with human beings is typical of pagan mythologies and not part of the biblical story.

15. Douglas Moo, *2 Peter and Jude*, NIV Application Commentary (Grand Rapids: Zondervan, 1996), 242.

16. Gushee, *Changing Our Mind*, 64.

17. Moisés Silva, "ἀσέλγεια," *New International Dictionary of New Testament Theology and Exegesis*, 2nd ed. (Grand Rapids: Zondervan, 2014) 1:419 [hereinafter *NIDNNTE*]; Otto Bauernfeind, "ἀσέλγεια," *Theological Dictionary of the New Testament* (Grand Rapids: Eerdmans, 1964) 1:490 [hereinafter *TDNT*].

18. Gushee, *Changing Our Mind*, 61.

19. Boswell, *Christianity, Social Tolerance, and Homosexuality*, 92.

20. Gushee, *Changing Our Mind*, 65.

21. Ibid., 66-67. Cf. Hamilton, *When Christians Get It Wrong*, 88.

22. Ibid., 67.

23. Hamilton, *When Christians Get It Wrong*, 89.

24. Vines, for example, insists: "So while *abomination* is a negative word, it doesn't necessarily correspond to Christian views of sin." Matthew Vines, *God and the Gay Christian: The Biblical Case in Support of Same-Sex Relationships* (New York: Convergent, 2015), p. 85.

25. Boswell, *Christianity, Social Tolerance, and Homosexuality*, 100.

26. Mel White, *What the Bible Says – and Doesn't Say – about Homosexuality* (Laguna Beach, CA: Soulforce, n.d.), 12.

27. Peter Gomes, *The Good Book* (New York: Avon Books, 1996), 154.

28. It is interesting (and a bit confusing) that Gomes, after citing Boswell approvingly, seems to challenge the central nature of Boswell's claim. "Boswell argues that a distinction is made between what is ritually impure and what is intrinsically wrong. Homosexuality in Leviticus is condemned as ritually impure, the key to his conclusion being the fact that the word abomination does not usually describe something intrinsically evil, such as rape or theft, but something that is ritually impure, like eating pork. . . . An abomination is by definition what the Gentiles do, but that in and of itself is not necessarily evil." (Gomes, *Good Book*, 154). We are left to wonder why Yahweh had the just right to dispossess the Canaanites of their land if their behaviors were not "necessarily evil."

29. Louis Crompton, *Homosexuality & Civilization* (Cambridge, MA: Harvard University Press, 2003), 33.

30. Death for Sabbath violation was not attached to the Fourth Commandment except in such extreme settings as the one in Numbers 15. As the nation was being taught the significance of keeping the Ten Commandments, this instance became an object lesson in distinguishing non-defiant transgressions from actions of persons who simply thumb their noses at Yahweh. Numbers 15:22-31 is a section of text specifying mercy for "everyone who sins unintentionally, whether a native-born Israelite or a foreigner residing among you" (v.29) from the harsh punishment to be meted out against "anyone who sins defiantly, whether native-born or foreigner" (v.30a). The latter was equivalent to the act of someone who "blasphemes" Yahweh and would result in banishment from the community (v.30b). In connection with the original commandment on this point, a Sabbath-breaker of the latter category was put to death to make the seriousness of such behavior evident to everyone.

31. Boswell, *Same-Sex Unions in Premodern Europe*, 136-137.

32. Zehnder, Markus. 2007. "Observations on the Relationship between David and Jonathan and the Debate on Homosexuality." *Westminster Theological Journal* 69 (1): 174.

33. Walter Brueggemann, "Narrative Coherence and Theological Intentionality in 1 Samuel 18," *Catholic Biblical Quarterly* (Jan 1993): 231.

34. William Loader, "Homosexuality and the Bible," in William Loader et al., *Two Views on Homosexuality, the Bible, and the Church* (Grand Rapids: Zondervan, 2016), 23-24.

35. Gushee, *Changing Our Mind*, 71.

36. Ibid., 72.

37. Friedrich Hauch and Siegfried Schulz, "πόρνη, πόρνος, πορνεία, πορνεύω, ἐκπορνεύω," *TDNT* VI:590.

38. Moisés Silva, "πορνεύω, πορνεία, πόρνη, πόρνος, ἐκπορνεύω," *NIDNNTE* 4:114.

> *"Most scholars today acknowledge that at the center of Jesus' ministry lay his announcement of God's reign, which marked the inauguration of an eschatological epoch (e.g., Mk 1:14).... This focus carried ethical implications. For Jesus the good life is not the quest for happiness but the pursuit of God's kingdom (Mt 6:33)."*
>
> – Stan Grenz

CHAPTER 7

Why Didn't Jesus Talk about Same-Sex Issues?

For a person seeking to understand a Christian view of any subject, the natural first question would seem to be this: *What did Jesus have to say about the subject?* The fact is that – in his recorded teachings in the Four Gospels at least – he never mentioned same-sex orientation, attraction, or behavior. At least, not explicitly.

For that matter, the larger New Testament collection of documents doesn't have a great deal to say about homosexuality. In standard English translations from the King James Version through to the more recent

---

Did God Really Say?

The tactic of revisionists in the same-sex union debate is to create doubt – not make a positive case from Scripture. After all, there is not a positive word about homoerotic behavior that can be found in the Bible.

The strategy for winning widespread support in the United States for normalizing same-sex coupling was outlined in a 1989 book titled After the Ball: How America Will Conquer Its Fear and Hatred of Gays in the '90s. In what some have called a "public relations manual for the gay agenda," Marshall Kirk (ad man) and Hunter Madsen (psychologist) outlined a Madison Avenue-style campaign to alter the country's public mood.

The book called for gay and lesbian activists "to muddy the moral waters, that is, to undercut the rationalizations that 'justify' religious bigotry and to jam some of its psychic rewards." The strategy calls for "raising serious theological objections to conservative biblical teachings." That it has been successful in churches and seminaries of all stripes is too obvious to deny.

Churches that maintained an orthodox position on same-sex acts were dubbed "homo-hating churches" and were to be portrayed as "antiquated backwaters, badly out of step with the times and with the latest findings of psychology."

Perhaps the doubt-making strategy (cf. Gen 3:3) of the campaign is the impetus for pushing the question: "Where did Jesus say anything against same-sex intimacy?"

— Rubel Shelly

versions such as the New International, English Standard, or New Revised Standard Versions, references to same-sex behavior are quite meager. Paul mentions it three times – once in Romans (Rom 1:26-27), once in the Corinthian correspondence (1 Cor 6:9), and once in a letter to his younger protégé Timothy (1 Tim 1:10).[1]

Peter makes no direct reference to "same sex acts." Neither do the four Gospel writers nor James. The anonymous epistle to the Hebrews does not mention it. A reference in Jude 7 that has already been mentioned in Chapter 6 is relevant to the topic. But that's it. The New Testament has only three explicit references to same-sex intercourse, and not one of those is on Jesus' lips.

For some, the data just surveyed is taken to be a sign that Jesus, Peter, Paul, and other central figures of the early Christian movement didn't see our subject as a matter of significant moral concern. One Christian writer, for example, seeks to marginalize the explicit censure of homosexual behavior in Paul by appealing to the lack of such direct a denunciation by Jesus.

> It is puzzling why being against homosexuality, about which Jesus and the gospels have nothing to say and Paul has only these passing references alongside many other sins equally common to heterosexuals, should have become the acid test of what it means to be truly "biblical" in a number of quarters over the years.[2]

The Nature of Ethical Instruction

But is that claim true? For one thing, born from the womb of Judaism, the early Christian church took the Hebrew Scriptures as its Bible – Tanakh, our Old Testament. Jesus was quite clear that he had not come to challenge and do away with that body of literature or to argue against its insights and instructions. He had, instead, come with a very different intention. "Do not think that I have come to abolish the Law or the Prophets," he said in his best-known sermon. "I have come not to abolish them but to fulfill them" (Matt 5:17).

"To fulfill" translates a Greek verb[3] that means more than giving one's personal obedience to Torah and the Prophets, although Jesus certainly did that. It also means more than fulfilling predictions about Israel's Messiah being born in Bethlehem or being despised and rejected by his contemporaries. The sense here and elsewhere is that Jesus' presence, teaching, and activities – especially in terms of his death, burial, and resurrection – would actualize and complete the anticipations of Israel's Holy Writings. The long-awaited Messiah would be identified, and the inauguration of the Kingdom of God would have begun. The ancient covenant made with Abraham and his descendants that "all peoples on earth will be blessed through you" would be realized in the person and work of Jesus (Gen 12:3).[4]

The fulfillment of God's purpose to bless all the families of the earth – both the Jews as Abraham's descendants by flesh and blood and non-Jews as his descendants by faith[5] – is affirmed in Christian Scripture. Thus, the great narrative arc of the Judeo-Christian corpus of God-breathed writing has been fulfilled. God's reign on Earth as in Heaven has begun and is in process of being announced by the church.

The foundational moral commandments contained in the Torah remain central to the faithful teaching of the Word of God and for the life of the church. How could they *not* be the same in both Hebrew and Christian Scripture if God himself is the same yesterday, today, and forever? That is, animal sacrifices foreshadow the cross as their fulfillment and terminus. But the moral demands of a Holy God for his people living in community are constant for the simple reason that God's nature is unchanging. Right and wrong behaviors are not arbitrary – as they were with the pagan gods. In the Greek and Roman myths, their deities lied, seduced, raped, stole, and murdered. They were nothing more than human-type "gods" for whom vices as well as virtues were simply human behaviors – both the noble and corrupt ones – on steroids.

The Deity of Judeo-Christian revelation is different. The oft-repeated call for God's people to "Be holy, because I am holy" (cf. Lev 11:45; 1 Pet 1:15) has meaning because his character is unmixed and pure. The Egyptian, Greek, Roman, and other pagan priests could never give permission for their devotees to behave in human relationships as their pseudo-deities did in their poems and legends. In a well-known section of his *Republic*, Plato laments the stories told by Homer and Hesiod for the bad examples they offer young people in their moral education. The mythical Greek gods seduced one another's wives, ate their own children (e.g., Chronus), plotted countless forms of mischief against one another, and committed acts that would have been judged criminal if performed by mortals in the very cultures where they were being told. Such tales, Plato argued, could cause young people "to take beliefs into their souls that are for the most part opposite to the ones we think they should hold when they are grown up."[6] Who can expect people to behave more uprightly than the gods they worship? To the contrary, what is right or wrong for God's human creation is determined by his personal character. "Be holy, because I am holy" finds its meaning in God's very nature.

We can add to these shocking behaviors various gods who took same-sex lovers (e.g., Zeus, Apollo, and others) or lived as bisexuals (e.g., Hermaphroditus).[7] Whether Plato deemed these sexual behaviors among the Greek gods to be part of the negative influence he feared for Athenian youth might be debated. It doesn't seem likely, however, for he extols the virtues of same-sex love in his *Symposium* (see Chapter 9) and never identifies any of the myths involving homoeroticism in Greek literature among those that he believed should be banned from Athens. As in our own day, Greek and later Roman views varied – although both cultures were extremely lax by any modern standard. Most of us would understand his point about influencing impressionable young men and women by tales of their "gods" lying and stealing, raping and murdering.

In contemporary Western culture, many parents and grandparents have something of the same feeling about actors, musicians, athletes, and politicians who are essentially worshipped by their devotees. Do you think their publicized behaviors

> **The Life Experience of Jesus**
>
> Sadly, in our hypersexualized contemporary culture, it is almost inconceivable that someone could be sexually chaste, even celibate, and experience the fullness of what it means to be human and the peace of sexual contentment. Our culture is such that sexual activity is viewed as the most direct path to personal fulfillment and self-realization – to being truly human and fully alive. So deep-seated is this belief that most people today think that to deny yourself sexual experiences is to undermine your own humanity. Try floating the idea of sexual chastity to a group of college freshmen or young urban professionals, and see what kind of looks you get.
>
> But Jesus' life deconstructs this pervasive and powerful cultural myth. His life says something different. From the story of his life, we learn that sexual activity isn't essential to human flourishing or personal fulfillment. Jesus found contentment with his sexuality in the pursuit of chastity and celibacy. To be blunt, he didn't need sex – not because sex is sinful or somehow beneath his dignity, but because sex isn't essential to being human. . . .
>
> If we want to be fully human, we have to embrace our sexed bodies. But we don't have to engage in sexual activity to be fully human. The life of the Son of God makes that perfectly clear. . . . I like the way the renowned scholar and ethicist Richard Hays summarizes the challenging truth Jesus brings to our sex-crazed culture: "Despite the smooth illusions perpetrated by mass culture in the United States, sexual gratification is not a sacred right, and celibacy is not a fate worse than death."
>
> — Todd Wilson

and pronouncements about sex influences the way their enthusiasts think about premarital sex? Their openness to same-sex experimentation? Their values about the nature of marital commitment and fidelity? What was true in ancient Greece and Rome should alert us to the influences that are molding people's minds in North America and Europe today. That a recent poll or a celebrity's example affirms gay and lesbian lifestyles to be acceptable is enough for many. But the source of moral guidelines for Christians is altogether different.

Lying, for example, is not wrong "just because God said so" but because he could not say otherwise. That is, truth is so central to God's nature – as are love, promise-keeping, goodness, self-control, and the other positive virtues – that he simply cannot lie (Tit 1:3).[8] The "cannot" here is not a limitation of power (i.e., he could not verbalize certain words) but the limitation of essence (i.e., the God who is the personification of truth can no more lie than a circle can be drawn with 90-degree angles). This is the nature of moral guidance in Holy Scripture, whether in the Old or New Testament. Human behaviors are tested against the inherent holiness of God. Actions congruent with his nature are good and moral; actions incompatible with his nature are wrong and immoral.

Testing the Claim of Jesus' Silence

It is to the core moral commandments in the Hebrew Scriptures that Jesus was speaking in his declaration about fulfilling the law and the prophets:

> For truly I tell you, until heaven and earth pass away, not one letter, not one stroke of a letter, will pass from the law until all is accomplished. Therefore, whoever breaks one of the least of these commandments, and teaches others to do the same, will be called least in the kingdom of heaven; but whoever does them and teaches them will be called great in the kingdom of heaven (Matt 5:18-19).

That Jesus' words here include the fundamental ethical instruction found in the Law of Moses is clear from what follows. He addresses six issues of moral teaching in Torah – murder, adultery, divorce, oath-taking, retribution for personal harm, and love for one's neighbor – as case studies in Matthew 5:21-48. The point of his teaching is not to add to the stringency of the laws cited; it is to clarify their original intent over against their shallow reading that had become commonplace. For example, the commandment against murder was never intended to accommodate hatred and lesser machinations against another person, any more than the prohibition of adultery could excuse lust and flirtation.

Unless one wishes to argue that Jesus simply did not know the Holiness Code of Leviticus – a hard case to make for one who believes both that Scripture is God-breathed and that Jesus is a full-fledged member of the Triune Deity of Christian faith – it would be a first-order mistake to say that Jesus did not consider same-sex behaviors to be outside the will of God. The force of the Old Testament texts already examined in this book is thereby verified by Jesus and later reaffirmed by his apostles.

Even if same-sex behaviors had never once been named in the New Testament, the unequivocal endorsement of the moral codes of the Bible read and endorsed by Jesus, the apostles, and the evangelists of the earliest church would mark them as conduct outside the will of God and sinful.

Jesus Was Hardly "Silent" on the Subject

As opposed to the simplistic question at the opening of this chapter, the issue is not whether Jesus specifically talked about LGBTQ+ issues or interacted with lesbian or gay persons. In its simplest form, the purpose of the question is to dismiss the consistently negative statements of Scripture about same-sex behaviors. By his blanket endorsement of the Torah, Jesus became part of the consistent, absolute, and counter-cultural opposition to same-sex intercourse found in the Bible. In effect, he said the ink of the Torah was dry on the subject.

Would it be reasonable to argue that Jesus' silence on any other topic involving human sexuality can be interpreted as endorsement of what the Torah denounces? I doubt that anyone who is serious about interpreting Scripture would be willing to argue such a silence-equates-to-approval thesis.

For example, in the Holiness Code that Jesus and his contemporaries knew only too well, various forms of incest are denounced as sinful (Lev 18:6-18), child sacrifice is proscribed (Lev 18:21), and sex with animals is labelled a perversion (Lev 18:23). Yet Jesus did not speak explicitly about even one of those behaviors either. He did not take time to renew the divine anathemas against those who commit such sins. His silence on these topics has never been taken as approval. It is in this same context (Lev 18:22) that the prohibition of having "sexual relations with a man as one does with a woman" is denounced as "detestable" to Yahweh. If Jesus' non-mention of one of these behaviors (i.e., same-sex intercourse) is deemed to reflect a change of attitude from rebuke to assent, should we not interpret his "silence" to mean the same in relation to all of them (i.e., incest, infanticide, bestiality)? This "argument from silence" is a non-argument.

If the matter of same-sex relationships had been put to Jesus as a question, his refusal to answer would force us to explore a possible difference between his view and what had been taught in the Law of Moses. If he had said "You have heard that male-with-male or female-with-female sex is detestable, but I say unto you that long-term covenantal commitment sanctifies those relationships," the Levitical statutes would have been candidates for revision. (In fact, they would not have been "candidates for revision" but would have been revised immediately by such a statement from his authoritative lips.) But that is not what happened. He was not questioned on the topic because his audience and he

> **Does Jesus' "Silence" Mean Permission?**
>
> The idea of a subject being unimportant just because Jesus did not mention it is unreasonable. Are we really to believe that Jesus did not care about wife-beating or incest just because he said nothing about them? There is any number of behaviors that Christ did not mention by name; surely, we don't condone them for that reason alone! . . .
>
> Jesus clearly says [in Matthew 19:4-6] that God's initial intent for marriage and sexual intimacy was that it be between a man and a woman, monogamous, and permanent. If he set this as the standard with that statement, was it necessary for him to name all other behaviors that were not intended?
>
> An analogy from Joe Dallas that I love is this: When you get on the ramp to enter onto a highway, the local government puts up a sign displaying the speed limit. Where I live, in Ontario, Canada, the speed limit is 100 km per hour. By putting up that first sign, the province has clearly set the standard telling me how fast I can drive. The province does not need then to put up a second sign 10 kilometers farther down the road saying, "Do Not Go 110 Km/hr." And then another sign 10 kilometers after that displaying, "Do Not Go 120 Km/hr."
>
> Why? Because they don't need to. The standard was set with the first sign. Anything over the speed limit of 100 kilometers an hour is a violation of the law. That is what Jesus did when he set the standard by saying that sexual intimacy is to be between a man and a woman, bound together in a monogamous covenant until death. Anything falling outside that standard is sinful, whether it be heterosexual or homosexual in nature.
>
> — Guy Hammond

knew and believed the Holiness Code. His blanket endorsement of "the Law and he Prophets" covered the matter definitively. In a word, there are good reasons for his silence on same-sex relationships other than approval.

It is hardly fair for anyone to claim that Jesus was silent about same-sex unions. When asked questions that move in the direction of sexual ethics, he spoke to the matter. Most specifically and revealingly, he responded to the Pharisees' question about divorce by appealing to what this book has called the "healthy view of human sexuality" reflected in the Genesis account of creation. He linked Genesis 1:27 (i.e., "So God created mankind in his own image, in the image of God he created them; *male and female* he created them") with Genesis 2:24 (i.e., "That is why *a man* leaves his father and mother and *is united to his wife* and they become one flesh"). The one-flesh union of God's creative design is the union of male and female.

Jesus' Comment about Eunuchs

Before leaving the Gospels and Jesus' view of sexuality, marriage, and holiness, it seems appropriate to comment on the claim some make that Jesus did in fact speak positively – by implication at least – to a human situation analogous to that of today's transgendered, gay, or lesbian relationships. We have already surfaced Jesus' appeal to the creation order of Genesis in his response to a question about divorce in Matthew 19. At the end of that pericope, he said, "For there are eunuchs who were born that way, and there are eunuchs who have been made eunuchs by others – and there are those who choose to live like eunuchs for the sake of the kingdom of heaven. The one who can accept this should accept it" (v.12).

> **The Eunuchs of Matthew 19:12**
> The way the disciples see it, men find themselves between a rock (the prospect of a difficult marriage) and a hard place (Jesus' teaching about marriage). So why not "jump out of the frying pan into the fire" of celibacy? At least, that's the way Jesus takes their comment. To him, if a man isn't going to marry, he's making a commitment to a celibate life – no sex. That's why he brings up the example of eunuchs, men who are unable to have sex. Note that Jesus didn't entertain a "third way": not married, not celibate, yet still single. To him, it's either sex in marriage or no sex. So, if you're going to make a commitment to stay single, then you've decided to live like a eunuch – a decision one needs to make for the right reason.
> — Rodney Reeves

Some scholars have argued that "this logion of Jesus questions the privileged position of a heterosexist binary paradigm of identity."[9] Similarly, Bart Ehrman has offered with implicit endorsement a "guest post" that offers Jesus' words as an acknowledgment that gender dysphoria or choosing to go through surgery for gender reassignment is nothing about which his followers should be troubled.

> I think Jesus was acknowledging that some people are sexually different from birth, not through the action of others, or by a later choice of their own. Those who suffered gender dysphoria, feeling like they were born into the wrong gender, had no access to medications, and the only surgical option was castration, and that was only for boys, not girls. So most simply had to live with it and make the best of it. But there is no suggestion in the Bible that it was a sin to feel that way.... Frankly, I think the objection to being transgender has no basis in the Bible; I think it is prejudice, pure and simple. Our human nature makes us suspicious or fearful of those who are different from us.[10]

Linking the words of Jesus to Paul's counsel for believers to "lead a quiet life and attend to your own business and work with your hands" (1 Thess 4:11-12), Dr. Wadeson then concludes that "Paul is basically saying, 'Mind your own business!'" to us about transgender identity. At an altogether popular level, an activist for LGBTQ+ causes used the *Huffington Post* to (mockingly?) link Matthew 19 to Lady Gaga's anthem of sexual liberation.

> It is the first category [in Jesus' statement] that struck me: "born so from the mother's womb." To cite another religious scholar/major diva, Lady Gaga: *Some people are just born that way.* One can assume he was certainly referring to the biologically intersexed (previously known as hermaphrodites).... However they get there, Jesus clearly has the same suggestion in how to treat them. *"He who is able to accept this, let him accept it."* ... Normally, I reject the very notion of using this sweeping work of historical fiction [the Bible] to justify anything — but in this case, I'm gladly raising their Leviticus with a Matthew — and from the mouth of our Lord and Savior Jesus Christ himself, no less. There it is in black and white. People who don't fit into traditional categories of anatomy and gender expression are simply people who don't fit into traditional categories of anatomy and gender expression. No need for panic. No need for demonization. No need, really, to make a fuss. In other words, to paraphrase Jesus: *"GET OVER IT."*[11]

Against both these proffered interpretations, reading Matthew 19:12 in its context shows that Jesus was answering a question about marriage – not sex versus gender, same-sex relationships, or "sexual otherness." Gender identity is not the issue in his statement. He is referring to the possible surrender of one's right to be married.

Specifically, Jesus was responding to the horrified idea among some of the disciples that his strong aversion to divorce meant that it might be best simply never to marry. They apparently felt as many do today, that life without a sexual partner is simply unthinkable. To that notion (and perhaps as a gloss on his own experience we seldom think about?), he spoke to the fact that some people would "choose to live like eunuchs for the sake of the kingdom of heaven."

The "eunuch"[12] to whom Jesus referred was not a third-gender, non-gendered, or transgendered person but a male who was incapable of procreation. Although he and his peers knew of men who were "eunuchs who were born that way" (i.e., congenital abnormality) and "eunuchs who have made been eunuchs by others" (i.e., surgical castration), he envisioned the possibility that some people would "choose to live like eunuchs for the sake of the kingdom of heaven" (i.e., choose to remain celibate in order to commit their lives fully to Christian service). The challenge that "the one who can accept this should accept it" is, therefore, not a challenge for onlookers to accept them or their choice of celibacy. It is a challenge to the acknowledged minority for whom – as for Paul – an unmarried and celibate life could be considered a *charisma* (cf. 1 Cor 7:7). That is, a correct paraphrase of his words is not to have him saying, "Straight people, don't make a fuss over trans or gays," but to hear him saying, "To the relative few who will choose to be single and celibate, do it – but not because you must." Neither Jesus nor Paul indicated that celibacy constituted a superior status over traditional marriage.

Here are a few key facts about Matthew 19 and other biblical references to persons who are identified as eunuchs. First, the word "eunuch" is not used in Scripture of a person with intact sexual organs, anyone involved in same-sex intercourse, or a person attempting to alter his sexual identity. Physically, a eunuch is a male who has been castrated or who was born with a genital abnormality. Thus, metaphorically, one could be a eunuch by choosing a celibate life for continuous ministry in service to God. Second, although Greek and Roman literature can be found that reflects a non-binary view of human sexuality, the Bible knows only male and female. There is a limited sense in which the notion of "gender fluidity" is hardly modern, since both Greeks and Romans saw sex/gender as a spectrum – defined more in terms of beauty than sex.[13] Thus, a male was to pursue beauty, whether he found it in a male or female body. One was either "masculine" or "feminine" based on phallic penetration or receptivity rather than anatomy alone. However, this was never part of a Jewish-Christian concept of personhood.

> **Jesus on the Created Order**
>
> Contrary to common assertion, then, Jesus did have something to say about homosexuality. From the beginning God had designed, intended, and endorsed marriage and sex ("one flesh") solely for long term, monogamous, heterosexual unions. Indeed, gendered human bodies reflect that purpose: men and women designed to function together, to fit each other physically in a complementary way.
>
> Simply put, the man was made for the woman and the woman was made for the man. Reject that function and replace it with another, and you reject God's own good purpose for sex. . . .
>
> Not surprisingly, then, the six sexual activities prohibited in the Bible – adultery, fornication, rape, incest, bestiality, and homosexuality – each involves sex with someone other than one's spouse. This point deserves repeating: All forms of sex condemned in Scripture have a common characteristic: sex other than between a husband and wife.
>
> — Gregory Kouki and Alan Shlemon

Third, a person was never "sinful" for his status as a eunuch. The marginal standing of a eunuch in Israel was due to what the KJV and NRSVue identify as a "blemish" or the NIV's "defect" – comparable to being blind, lame, or otherwise disfigured in bodily form (cf. Lev 21:16-23; Heb, *m'uwm*).[14] Fourth, there is nothing textually or linguistically that links eunuchs with same-sex communities (Gk, *galloi*), the Greek word for bodies that exhibit genitalia and/or other reproductive structures that are part-male and part-female (Gk, *hermaphroditos*), or the term that yields our English "androgynous" (Gk, *androgynos*).[15]

In relation to some of the more emotional claims that attempt to link the status of eunuchs in Scripture with today's gay, bisexual, and transgender persons, an Old Testament statement from Deuteronomy 23:1 has been used inappropriately. Information on this text can be found among the questions addressed in Chapter 15.

The Straightforward Approach: "My Experience Eclipses Scripture"

Some Christian writers are more candid than others and simply admit they have chosen to discard the limitation of Scripture on same-sex relationships in favor of the authority of human experience and the life situations of people in their spheres of acquaintance.

> I have little patience with efforts to make Scripture say something other than what it says, through appeals to linguistic or cultural subtleties. The exegetical situation is straightforward: we know what the text says. But what are we to do with what the text says? . . .
>
> I think it is important to state clearly that we do, in fact reject the straightforward commands of Scripture, and appeal instead to another authority when we declare that same-sex unions can be holy and good. And what exactly is that authority? We appeal to the weight of our own experience and the experience thousands of others have witnessed to, which tells us that to claim our own sexual orientation is in fact to accept the way in which God has created us. By doing so, we explicitly reject as well the premises of the scriptural statements condemning homosexuality – namely, that it is a vice freely chosen, a symptom of human corruption, and disobedience to God's created order.[16]

I respect both the erudition and candor of the biblical scholar who wrote those words. In a respectful public discussion of the Bible's teaching about same-sex relationships, Dr. Johnson and I explored various dimensions of the topic. He readily acknowledges that the Bible censures same-sex behavior – but simply has it wrong for our time. Thus, everything reduces to one issue: *How are we to view the Bible?* Is it truly from God to the degree that we should trust its ethical guidelines over time? Did the Holy Spirit actually empower human writers to speak not only to their own generations but also to us about the nature of God and

---

Demythologizing Sex

The Bible undercuts our cultural obsession with sexual fulfillment. Scripture (along with many subsequent generations of faithful Christians) bears witness that lives of freedom, joy, and service are possible without sexual relations. Indeed, however odd it may seem to contemporary sensibilities, some New Testament passages (Matt. 19: 10– 12, 1 Cor. 7) clearly commend the celibate life as a way of faithfulness. In the view of the world that emerges from the pages of Scripture, sex appears as a matter of secondary importance.

To be sure, the power of sexual drives must be acknowledged and subjected to constraints, either through marriage or through disciplined abstinence. But never within the canonical perspective does sexuality become the basis for defining a person's identity or for finding meaning and fulfillment in life. The things that matter are justice, mercy, and faith (Matt. 23: 23). The love of God is far more important than any human love. Sexual fulfillment finds its place, at best, as a subsidiary good within this larger picture.

— Richard Hays

what his essential holiness means in relation to our aspiring holiness? Or did he expect us to alter those directives by the fluctuating opinions of human understanding? Do polls of public sentiment toward same-sex marriage modify or negate what the Bible requires? Johnson offers a path of "discernment" that would allow us to honor Scripture and still set aside its negative take on same-sex coupling. We will explore that case in detail in an excursus on Acts 15 at the end of Chapter 10.

I do not know how to live within the biblical narrative and discard such obvious teachings as the nature of marriage as a male-with-female covenant and its clear Holiness Code language about same-sex intercourse. In the Messiah's ministry among the Jews, both he and his hearers knew what marriage was. In their world of shared definitions and understandings, he did not address the same-sex issue directly because it was not in dispute. If it had been a subject for debate among his Torah-educated hearers, Jesus could have anticipated and prevented 2,000 years of ongoing misinterpretation by clarifying the divine intent for us.

By contrast, as Paul worked among and wrote letters to predominantly non-Jewish churches, we would expect him to address it because the Christian view was so radically different from that of the Greco-Roman culture of his time. His culture was much more like that of our own generation – pluralistic, relativistic, hedonistic. It is that culture shift between Jewish and Greco-Roman backgrounds that Paul found himself as a Christian evangelist. Trying to be all things to all men so that all he could gain a hearing for the gospel (cf. 1 Cor 9:19-23), his handling of ethical standards in conflict is insightful for our sake.

Culture Shift from Jewish to Roman

As to the apostolic literature that names specific homosexual behaviors, it would be difficult to imagine stronger language than Paul used in denouncing what has come to be called a gay lifestyle. It would be intellectually mistaken and morally wrong, however, to use his denunciation of same-sex intercourse as some have. On the one hand, it is offered as proof that Paul was simply a nasty homophobe by some revisionists. On the other, it has been represented by some traditionalists as the judgment of an inspired apostle to whom it had been revealed that God has a particular aversion toward and punishment waiting for LGBTQ+ persons. It is neither.

So we must look next at the cultural setting of Paul in the Roman Empire of the first century. Then we will be in better position to understand what he has written.

ENDNOTES

1. Some scholars would not include the 1 Timothy passage because of their doubts about its Pauline authorship. It is outside the scope of this book to argue authorship of the various biblical materials.

2. Richard Burridge, *Imitating Jesus: An Inclusive Approach to New Testament Ethics* (Grand Rapids: Eerdmans Publishing Company, 2007), 4. Note: Quite revealingly, it seems, the "passing references" to homosexuality that Burridge dismisses in this quote somehow refer only to the lists of vices in 1 Corinthians 6 and 1 Timothy 1. Paul's treatment of the subject in Romans 1 will be explored later. It can hardly be waved aside as a "passing reference" to same-sex behaviors.

3. Πληρῶσαι is an aorist active infinitive form of the verb πληρόω. "The goal of the mission of Jesus is fulfilment (Mt. 5:17b); according to Mt. 5:17a this is primarily fulfilment of the Law and the prophets, i.e., of the whole of the OT as a declaration of the will of God. Jesus does not merely affirm that He will maintain them. As He sees it, His task is to actualise the will of God made known in the OT. He has come in order that God's Word may be completely fulfilled, in order that the full measure appointed by God Himself may be reached in Him. . . . He actualises the divine will stated in the OT from the standpoint of both promise and demand." Gerhard Delling, πληρόω, *TDNT* 6:294.

4. This covenant promise was not only repeated at various times to Abram/Abraham (Gen 15:5-21; 17:4-8; 18:18-19; 22:17-18), to his son Isaac (Gen 26:2-4), and to his grandson Jacob/Israel (Gen 28:13-15; 35:11-12; 46:3) but also to Moses (Ex 3:6-8; 6:2-8) as an extension from one family to the greater nation that arose from Abraham.

5. Peter quoted the Abrahamic covenant on the first Pentecost Day after the resurrection of Jesus for the sake of affirming its fulfillment to his Jewish listeners on that day (Acts 3:24-24), and Paul claimed the inclusion of Gentiles in that same covenant for non-Jews who placed their faith in Jesus of Nazareth (Gal 3:8-9).

6. Plato, *Republic* 2. 377b.

7. Christine Downing, *Myths and Mysteries of Same-Sex Love* (New York: iUniverse, 2006).

8. Note: People sometimes make the thoughtless statement that "God can do anything." As theologians and philosophers from at least the time of Thomas Aquinas have pointed out, God cannot do either the logically impossible (e.g., draw a geometric square that has no right angles) or that which violates his own nature as holy and loving (e.g., lie). These "limitations" are not due to a lack of divine power but trace to the nature of reality.

9. J. David Hester, "Eunuchs and the Postgender Jesus: Matthew 19:12 and Transgressive Sexualities," *Journal for the Study of the New Testament* 28, no. 1 (2005): 37.

10. Douglas Wadeson, "Is It A Sin To Be Transgender: Platinum guest post by Douglas Wadeson MD," *The Bart Ehrman Blog: The History & Literature of Early Christianity*, Feb 18, 2023. Accessed at https://ehrmanblog.org/is-it-a-sin-to-be-transgender-platinum-guest-post-by-douglas-wadeson-md-2.

11. Mark Olmsted, "When Jesus Agreed With Lady Gaga: What the Bible Says About Transgendered Persons," *HuffPost* (Aug 31, 2017). Accessed at https://www.huffpost.com/entry/when-jesus-agreed-with-lady-gaga-what-the-bible-says_b_59a813cce4b096fd8876c0d1.

12. The word *eunuch* (Gk, *eunouchos*) is formed by combining words for "bed" (Gk, *eunē*) and "have, possess, hold" (Gk, *echō*) – signifying someone in charge of the bedroom. Jesus was making the "standard rabbinic distinction between a 'man-made eunuch' and a 'eunuch by nature'" (*m. Yebam.* 8:4; *m. Zabim* 2:1)." [R.T. France, *Gospel of* Matthew (Grand Rapids: Eerdmans Publishing Co., 2007), 724.] In the case of a man-made eunuch, this would be a chamberlain or harem-keeper (Est 2:3,14-15; cf. 2 Kgs 9:30-32). Males working around females in a royal household were typically castrated for the security of their charges. This would appear

to be the case, for example, of the official in charge of the royal treasury of Ethiopia whom we meet in Acts 8:27-39 – where the word *eunochos* is used five times. The "eunuch by nature" is the person Jesus referred to as someone who is "born that way" – without functional sex organs, impotent, or perhaps in the class identified today as "intersex" by virtue of atypical sexual anatomy or chromosomes. Linguistic data on the term's classical and biblical use is found at Moisés Silva, "εὐνοῦχος," *NIDNTTE* 2:326-328. Cf. *TDOT* 10:344-350.

13. The word καλός had no distinction between "beautiful" and "handsome" with reference to females and males as our English words imply. Whether a given text refers to a male or female is often determined solely by the word's declension. Cf. K.J. Dover, *Greek Homosexuality* (Cambridge, MA: Harvard University Press, 1989), 15-16. For Greeks, the ideal of beauty was the youthful, fit, and disciplined body of a male rather than a female. "While we may instinctively think that the Greeks meant beauty of the mind, that is a prejudiced view we have inherited from the philosophers. Beauty for the Greek was primarily physical comeliness. . . . Ancient pinups [vase paintings, erotica] were much more likely to be of male figures than of female." Scroggs, *New Testament and Homosexuality*, 24. This same focus carried through to the Roman Era. "In the ancient world so few people cared to categorize their contemporaries on the basis of the gender to which they were erotically attracted that no dichotomy to express this distinction was in common use. . . . No one thought it useful or important to distinguish on the basis of genders alone, and the categories "homosexual" and "heterosexual" simply did not intrude on the consciousness of most Greeks or – as will be seen – Romans." Boswell, *Christianity, Social Tolerance, and Homosexuality*, 59. This lack of distinction "on the basis of genders alone" obviously did not apply to Jewish and Christian creation literature and moral codes. Details on this point may be found in Chapters 9 and 10.

14. There would be no moral culpability for "eunuchs who were born that way." Neither could a moral fault be assigned to someone "emasculated by crushing or cutting" (cf. Deut 23:1) by some accidental injury or as an act of torture and humiliation. For that matter, there is no indication of sinfulness per se being attributed to eunuchs in charge of a ruler's harem or in service to a female ruler (Est 2:3,14-15; 2 Kgs 9:30-32; cf. Acts 8:27). Any ethical guilt linked to "eunuchs who have been made eunuchs by others" (i.e., surgically) would have entailed some association with idolatry or groups such as the Cybele cult. See fn15 below.

15. The γάλλοι were communities of eunuch priests devoted to Cybele. The noun ἑρμαφρόδιτος is the name of the mythological Greco-Roman character who is half male (genitalia) and half female (face and breasts) whose name came to designate a human or animal with ill-defined genitalia; such offspring appear to have been seen as bad omens for those to whom they were born. Cf. Livy, *History of Rome* 31.12. And ἀνδρόγυνος is a term used not only of hermaphrodites but also of effeminate males and female-with-female sex partners. Found in extrabiblical literature of the period, these words do not appear in the Septuagint or New Testament. For definitions given here, see Franco Montanari, *Brill Dictionary of Ancient Greek*, 3rd ed. with corrections (Leiden: Brill, 2018).

16. Luke Timothy Johnson, "Scripture & experience," *Commonweal* (June 15, 2007): 15. Gale Academic OneFile. Accessed at https://link.gale.com/apps/doc/A166351549/AONE?u=tel_a_beaman&sid=bookmark-AONE&xid=401fcd16.

> *"Now, if you do not identify with the
> pre-populated list of gender identities,
> you are able to add your own."*
> – Facebook

EXCURSUS

Sex(es) and Gender(s):
The Other 72 Genders?

The quotation at the top margin of this page was posted by Facebook in 2015. The popular social networking site whose owner changed its company name to Meta Platforms, Inc., in 2021 thereby broadened – and helped to popularize even more – the idea of self-chosen gender identities. "Last year we were proud to add a custom gender option to help people better express their identities on Facebook," the posting began. Users could add up to ten gender terms to profiles and also control the audience with whom to share their "custom gender."[1] Because the gender issue has loomed so large in Chapter 7, this is likely the best place to deal with the broader issues that being raised today about gender identity.

The move by Facebook is consistent with a later article in *Forbes* in which a "gender bias expert" stated that "many conditions make assigning a biological sex quite difficult." She closed her article by quoting clinical psychologist Aileen Schast and drawing her final conclusion.

> "What's amazed me the most is that there is such a continuum from the male to the female, and it's really hard to draw a line somewhere neatly in the middle," Schast added. Biological sex, it turns out, is a lot like gender identity – not always male or female, but occasionally somewhere in between.[2]

The *Forbes* article appears to have been something of a footnote to the furor kicked up by a tweet from J.K. Rowling, author of the fabulously successful Harry

Potter books. She had mocked an opinion piece that had used the term "people who menstruate" in place of "women." Quoting the op-ed, she wrote: "'People who menstruate.' I'm sure there used to be a word for those people. Someone help me out. Wumben? Wimpund? Woomud?" she wrote. Accused by various groups of being "transphobic," she failed to stifle the firestorm significantly by replying with a statement that both affirmed support for transgender males but nevertheless insisted that biological sex is real.

> If sex isn't real, there's no same-sex attraction. If sex isn't real, the lived reality of women globally is erased. I know and love trans people, but erasing the concept of sex removes the ability of many to meaningfully discuss their lives.[3]

The discussion of sex and gender as "social constructs" that was promoted by Foucault and others has led to the notion of a "sex-gender spectrum" or "sex-gender continuum" that lies at the root of the sorts of things just documented. An online article from a physician at *MedicineNet* explains the emerging theory of "gender identity" that seems to be accepted as established fact in the LGBTQ+ community this way:

> In today's age, one does not need to fit in with regards to their choices, including their gender identity.
> - Gender is no more regarded as a binary concept where one can either be a male or a female.
> - It has emerged as a continuum or spectrum where one can identify themselves as any of the gender identities.
>
> The term gender identity means how a person identifies themselves concerning their gender. It may be regardless of their anatomy or genetics. Thus, a person may identify themselves as male, female, none, both, or some other category independent of their genitals.
>
> The idea is to make everyone feel comfortable in their skin irrespective of what gender they were assigned at birth.[4]

The "Other" Genders

The article proceeds to list "72 other genders" besides male and female that one might embrace in order to "feel comfortable in their skin." These range from "1. Agender: A person who does not identify themselves with or experience any gender" to "37. Cendgender: The gender identity changes from one gender to its opposite" to "60. Gemigender: The person has two genders that are opposite yet they flux and work together" to "72. Omnigender: Having or experiencing all genders."

The sort of infinite multiplication of gender identities in the *MedicineNet* article seems to risk being dismissed out of hand by virtue of being less than credible to one who confronts it. Furthermore, someone reading this book might well take me to be mocking the notion of gender identity or otherwise attempting to make my thesis more plausible by citing outliers to the scientific community in order to caricature the affirming position. *That is not the case.*

The postmodern mindset that allows people to "declare their personal truth" has so pervaded the larger culture and even the academic-scientific community that these are by no means outlier (i.e., detached, isolated from mainstream views) positions. Practically every major university – including my alma mater[5] – grants the non-binary status as normative and allows students, faculty, and staff to self-identify the pronoun and gender by which to be addressed and allowed to function. Passing through the LAX airport last week, the waiting area for my flight was opposite a triad of restrooms – Men, Women, and All Genders.

The British scientific journal *Nature* carried this declaration as long ago as 2015. "The idea of two sexes is simplistic. Biologists now think there is a wider spectrum than that."[6] The article concludes that "biologists continue to show that sex is a spectrum" and argues that "anatomy, hormones, cells or chromosomes" must yield to one's personal claim of gender identity. The final sentence says: "In other words, if you want to know whether someone is male or female, it may be best just to ask."[7] *Scientific American* gave its stamp of approval to the same thesis by publishing the same piece three years later.[8] Almost simultaneously, the *New York Times* published an opinion piece by Dr. Anne Fausto-Sterling entitled "Why Sex Is Not Binary."[9]

The World Health Organization announced the updating of its *Gender Mainstreaming for Health Managers: A Practical Approach* manual in 2022 to accommodate the non-binary approach to sex and gender. One of the four focus areas for the update was described this way: "3. *Going beyond binary approaches* to gender and health to recognize *gender and sexual diversity*, or the concepts that gender identity exists on a continuum and that sex is not limited to male or female."[10] Chapter 5 of this book called attention to the change made by the United States Department of State to offer a third gender option on passports for those who claim a gender identity other than the one shown on a birth certificate. As of April 11, 2022, citizens were allowed to "select an X as their gender marker on their U.S. passport application."[1]

> **Biological Sex in Healthcare**
>
> The truth of the sex binary is anchored in the mechanism that brings every human into existence.
>
> Humans have two different types of gametes, two types of reproductive systems, two discrete reproductive roles: two sexes. As a result, we have given these two sexes different names: female and male. These will exist whether or not the clinician writes them down, or asks a transgender patient "what is your sex?"
>
> The fact that 0.02% of babies have differences in sex development that cause the usually easy identification of sex to become a more complex affair, does not invalidate sex as one of the most clinically useful categorizations in medicine.
>
> — Sara Dahlen

The key terms throughout these articles, manuals, and official government statements are "continuum" and "spectrum" to describe both sexual and gender identities. As Chapter 7 has pointed out, these terms relate to Greek and Roman thought in relation to beauty rather than sex/gender. In the lax moral environment of the Greco-Roman world, free males were allowed – if not expected – to satisfy their erotic attraction to beauty with young boys, women, and toned older males. Young females in free families were generally protected from such advances because of the importance attached to their virginity at marriage at a young age.

Evaluating the Spectrum Theory

The recent contention that sex and gender are non-binary rests on two claims. The first is rooted in the existence of indeterminate sex features in a percentage of people. The second relies on secondary sex features in body type and behaviors.

First, there is no convincing case to make for regarding sex as a "social construct" rather than the ontological reality presented in Scripture texts examined earlier. Standard scientific determination of male or female is made by the body's *primary sex organs* (i.e, the gonads, which produce the organism's gametes and hormones = ovaries in females, testes in males).[12] The attempt at making an argument against a straightforward male-female (binary) distinction is based on the relatively rare instances of intersex persons. But these "borderline" cases are neither a third sex

EXCURSUS: SEX(ES) AND GENDER(S)

nor evidence for a sliding scale for male-ness and female-ness. The failure to grasp the significance of this fact has implications well beyond the ideological goal of legitimating the transgender movement.

Planned Parenthood, for example, defines intersex to be "an umbrella term that describes bodies that fall outside the strict male/female binary." That definition is followed by the claim that there are "lots of ways someone can be intersex."[13] The same article adds that intersex is "a general term used for a variety of situations in which a person is born with reproductive or sexual anatomy that doesn't fit the boxes of 'female' or 'male.'" Although it gives no number for how many people in the United States are intersex, the piece in question cites undocumented estimates which "suggest that about 1-2 in 100 people born in the U.S. are intersex." Information like this is cited frequently to support the idea of a "spectrum of sexes."

The offer of scientific evidence for this incidence of intersex persons traces to the work of Brown University's Anne Fausto-Sterling. She published what has become a widely cited paper suggesting that the frequency of intersex might well be as high as 1.7%.[14] Although her work has been cited as probative in both the scholarly press and by popular media, the National Institutes of Health, along with a number of researchers and clinicians, have pointed to the misleading nature of her claim.

> Anne Fausto-Sterling's suggestion that the prevalence of intersex might be as high as 1.7% has attracted wide attention in both the scholarly press and the popular media. Many reviewers are not aware that this figure includes conditions which most clinicians do not recognize as intersex, such as Klinefelter syndrome, Turner syndrome, and late-onset adrenal hyperplasia. If the term intersex is to retain any meaning, the term should be restricted to those conditions in which chromosomal sex is inconsistent with phenotypic sex, or in which the phenotype is not classifiable as either male or female. Applying this more precise definition, the true prevalence of intersex is seen to be about 0.018%, almost 100 times lower than Fausto-Sterling's estimate of 1.7%.[15]

Therefore, it is not the case that some 98% of us are clearly male or female, but 99.98% of human offspring are taxonomically distinct. Neither is it correct to say that sex is "assigned" at birth as an arbitrary matter. A newborn's sex is determined by physical observation of the infant's genitalia and can be confirmed by DNA testing.

The great majority of individuals who self-identify as "intersex" or who otherwise claim non-binary identities are not in question as to their sex by scientific standards. For that tiny percentage born with an intersex condition, there should be genuine compassion for their situation. Every human being bears the image of God, is precious in his sight, and is to be treated with respect. *But the rare occurrence of intersex persons does not establish that sex is a continuum.* The infrequent ambiguity in sex taxonomy for a few does not translate to the claim that sex identification is arbitrary for all. There simply is no taxonomic grouping of "third sex" over against male and female.

As an evolutionary biologist wrote in a national newspaper the week I was at work on this Excursus, there are two and only two possibilities for an organism's sex.

> When biologists claim that sex is binary, we mean something straightforward: There are only two sexes. This is true throughout the plant and animal kingdoms. An organism's sex is defined by the type of gamete (sperm or ova) it has the function of producing. Males have the function of producing sperm, or small gametes; females, ova, or large ones. Because there is no third gamete type, there are only two sexes. Sex is binary.[16]

In the words of a genetics researcher from Stanford University School of Medicine, the use of claims such as that of Fausto-Sterling finds no justification in the "hard sciences" related to genetic research.

> All "intersex" conditions, when examined, clearly arise from single-gene mutations or chromosomal aberrations on a genetic background that would have indisputably been producing male or female gametes had these mutations not occurred, and, rarely, due to chimerism (i.e. individuals made up of both male and female cells). True hermaphrodites possessing both sets of functional gonads and genitalia have never been observed in Homo sapiens.
>
> Therefore the "intersex" argument against the sex binary is simply not valid. Intersex individuals exist only because of continuous de novo reintroduction of the relevant mutations in the population, recessive genes becoming unmasked, or disruptions of normal embryonic development.[17]

It is the so-called "soft sciences" of psychology, gender studies, and the like that are misusing data to press an agenda against the sex binary. And that leads to the second attempt to justify a male-female spectrum. It is based on *secondary sex organs* (i.e., the structures that transport and sustain gamete production = e.g., male duct system, seminal glands, penis; female uterine tubes, uterus, vagina). During puberty, sex-related anatomies differentiate themselves in such ways as enlarging breasts and wider hips in females and facial hair, additional musculature, and typically deeper voice in males.

One of the more frequent tools used to teach the sex-as-spectrum model used these secondary organs and traits to make the case that biological sex is better thought of as a continuum than a binary is "The Genderbread Person."[18]

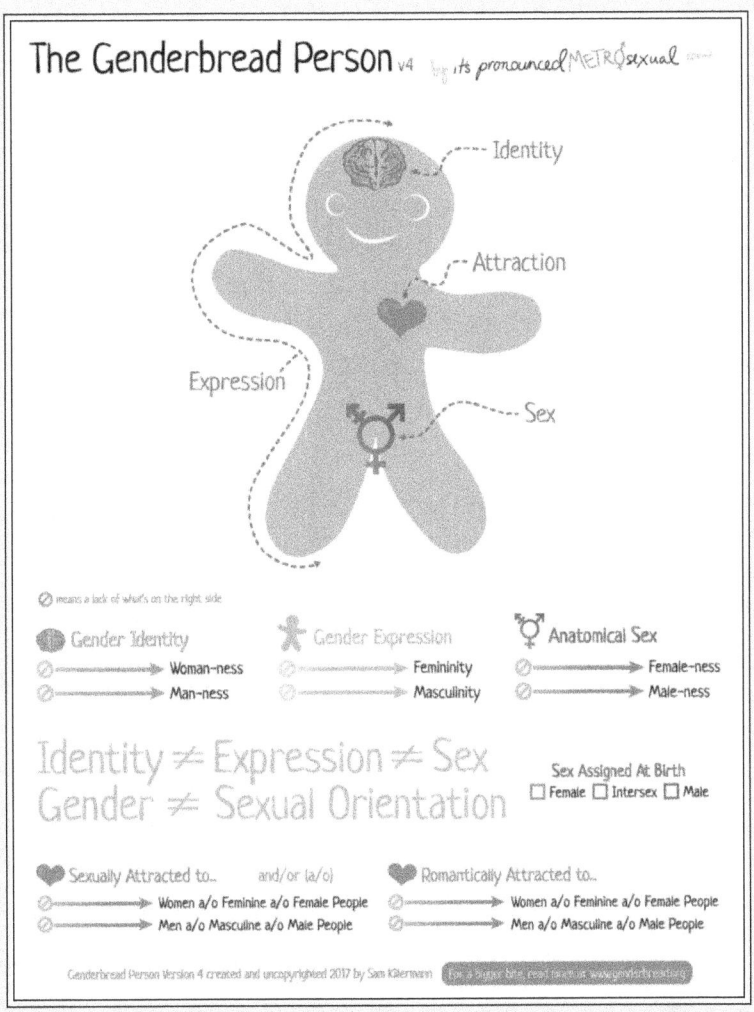

Offered as a "teaching tool for breaking the big concept of gender down into bite-sized, digestible pieces," the cartoon figure features the word *gender* and combines it rather freely – if not synonymously in places – with *sex*. So let me remind you that the biblical account focuses on the human race as male and female. In theological terms, our Bibles use "male" and "female" in the same way most biologists, geneticists, and clinicians use it – defined by the *primary* sex organs of human beings. Our modern word "gender" – although often used as a synonym for "sex" – is a term related much more directly to *secondary* sex organs, behaviors that we typically think of as masculine or feminine, and one's internal (i.e., psychological, emotional) sense of male-female self-identification, and relationships (i.e., preference for social or romantic interaction with the same or opposite sex).

In the case of the Genderbread Person, the accompanying legend for interpreting it avoids the words "male" and "female." Instead, the following explanation is offered:

> Using two continuums for each element (the "-ness" approach), instead of having a scale from F- to-M, allows a person to demonstrate that they embody more of one aspect of gender without that meaning they are less of the complement (i.e., expressing gender masculinely, like wearing a beard, doesn't make a feminine expression, like wearing tight-fitting clothing, less feminine).[19]

The not-so-subtle move here shifts from any distinction between gender as a "social construct" to a sex-spectrum by the category choices around the cartoon figure. Pay particular attention to the heading for "Anatomical Sex" and the graduated scale for *sex* as a variable that ranges from the absence of the right-side qualities of "female-*ness*" and "male-*ness*." And those qualities are defined for users of the material by the quotation above that measures the "-*ness*" qualities by secondary traits of "wearing

---

Sola Experientia

As hard as anyone may try to alter this fact in his or her own body, the most that can be done is artificially remove or augment body parts or use pharmaceuticals to suppress unnaturally the biological and hormonal reality of one's essence as male or female. In other words, psychology usurps biology; what I feel becomes who I am. When denying this physical and genetic reality we allow experience to supersede essence and, more importantly, the image of God. Transgenderism is not exclusively a battle for what is male and female, but rather a battle for what's true and real.

So how did we get here? Transgenderism is the fruit of postmodernity. Postmodernism, coming out of romanticism and existentialism, tells us that "you are what you feel." Thus, experience reigns supreme, and everything else must bow before it. *Sola experientia* ("experience alone") has won out over *sola Scriptura* ("Scripture alone").

— Christopher Yuan

a beard" or "wearing tight-fitting clothes." What is notably missing from the chart is any reference to *primary sex organs* of ovaries, ova, and menstruation for females or testes, sperm, and ejaculation for males. Confusing secondary sexual traits with biological sex is a category mistake of the first order.

Stated in the most basic terms, *sex* is an objective category defined by empirically discernible and set-at-birth qualities, whereas *gender* is a subjective self-perception and option for the presentation of oneself to others. The former is biological, while the latter is psychological. The former states who a person is in terms of bodily taxonomy, and the latter offers what a person may feel about one's placement in the world's social structures. A biological male with a high-pitched voice, shorter-than-average height, and/or wearing a pink shirt is still male. A biological female whose voice has a lower pitch than most of her male peers, who is taller than the man she dates, and/or makes blue her signature color remains female.

> **Analogy: Primary and Secondary Characteristics**
>
> Whether someone is a biker or a cyclist depends entirely on the binary criterion of whether they are riding a motorcycle or a bicycle. This is the primary characteristic that defines bikers and cyclists.
>
> However, there are also many secondary characteristics associated with bikers and cyclists. Bikers, for instance, are more likely to wear leather jackets, jeans, and bandanas. Cyclists are more likely to wear skin-tight spandex. Bikers wear tough clothes because they travel at higher speeds, which necessitate protective clothing in case of an accident and to mitigate windchill. Cyclists, on the other hand, exert great physical effort pedaling their entire body weight plus the weight of their vehicle, which necessitates lighter, breathable, wind-breaking clothing and protective gear. Given cyclists' slower crash speeds, the trade-off in favor of less protective gear is worthwhile.
>
> But a person riding a motorcycle wearing a spandex suit and lighter helmet doesn't become a cyclist (or less of a biker) because they share these secondary traits more commonly associated with cyclists. And a person riding a bicycle wearing jeans and a leather jacket doesn't become a biker (or less of a cyclist) by sharing secondary traits more typical of bikers.
>
> Just as these secondary traits do not define bikers and cyclists, secondary sex characteristics do not define males and females.
>
> — Colin Wright

The prevailing cultural winds seem to be blowing uniformly in the direction of language that chooses the term "gender identity" as all-inclusive and normative. The more serious question of both biblical theology and scientific truth is the choice between locating basic human personhood in *ontological sex* or the current fashion of *gender identity*. Stated as a question for believers, it becomes the following: *Should human physiology be chemically, surgically, and otherwise modified to match one's psychological state – or the other way around?*

Broader Cultural Questions

While this book has biblical-theological placement of these issues as its primary concern, it is undeniable that the practical impact of what is taking place in the broader culture has implications for Christian children and their parents, educators and therapists who prioritize their faith, and churches and Christian schools.

Without any deference to distinctively Christian concerns, a piece written jointly by an American and British biologist points to jeopardies that will confront females in various environments which allow persons to self-select their gender identity.

> Women have fought hard for sex-based legal protections. Female-only spaces are necessary due to the pervasive threat of male violence and sexual assault. Separate sporting categories are also necessary to ensure that women and girls don't have to face competitors who have acquired the irreversible performance-enhancing effects conferred by male puberty. The different reproductive roles of males and females require laws to safeguard women from discrimination in the workplace and elsewhere. The falsehood that sex is rooted in subjective identity instead of objective biology renders all these sex-based rights impossible to enforce.[20]

As to the harm that can be done to young people diagnosed with gender dysphoria, the same writers point out that "the large majority of gender-dysphoric youths eventually outgrow their feelings of dysphoria during puberty" and are better protected from – rather than subjected to – certain widely used protocols.

> "Affirmation" therapies, which insist a child's cross-sex identity should never be questioned, and puberty-blocking drugs, advertised as a way for children to "buy time" to sort out their identities, may only solidify feelings of dysphoria, setting them on a pathway to more invasive medical interventions and permanent infertility. This pathologizing of sex-atypical behavior is extremely worrying and regressive. It is similar to gay "conversion" therapy, except that it's now bodies instead of minds that are being converted to bring children into "proper" alignment with themselves.[21]

While one could wish that the overriding cultural concerns around this issue could focus on the scientific, philosophic, and theological issues this Excursus has highlighted, it appears that the single concern most often highlighted has to do with athletic competition. One of the early instances of controversy in athletics goes back to 1977. Born Richard Raskind, this athletic male – who had adopted feminine dress and mannerisms in childhood – declared a name and gender change in 1975, underwent what was called sex-reassignment surgery, and sued successfully to compete as a female in the 1977 U.S. Open.[22] In 2012, a 50-year-old, 6-feet-6-inches, 230-pound basketball player who was born male competed as a female in college basketball games.[23] There have been transgender females who challenged existing law and won the right to compete in women's football leagues.[24] Something of an uproar was created in New York City when a 29-year-old transgender competitor defeated a 13-year-old girl for a $250 prize in a skateboarding competition.[25]

Papers similar to a study published by The Center for Sports Law and Policy at Duke University have documented the competitive disadvantage of athletes born female against those born male. The paper begins: "If you know sport, you know this beyond a reasonable doubt: there is an average 10-12% performance gap between elite males and elite females."[26] The paper cites the fact that "in the single year 2017, Olympic, World, and U.S. Champion Tori Bowie's 100 meters lifetime best of 10.78 was beaten 15,000 times by men and boys." As to the explanation for such extremes, the authors write: "The differential isn't the result of boys and men having a male identity, more resources, better training, or superior discipline. It's because they have an androgenized body."[27]

Rejecting Conceptual Confusion

While we watch, agonize over certain aspects, and are forced to live within a culture that exhibits increasing bewilderment over the sex/gender topic, Christian teaching and vocabulary need to resist its conceptual confusion. Biblically and scientifically, humans exist as either male or female. To say that sex is binary is simply to say that there are two and only two options. In the relatively rare condition known as "intersex," there is a genital ambiguity or genetic variance – but not a "third" sex. Whatever variation may occur in the 0.018% of the human population that *is* intersex raises legitimate questions of medical care and Christian compassion relative to their bodies. That variation does not invalidate or cast doubt on the unquestionable nature of the 99.982% whose binary status establishes the norm.

While the modern term "gender" may be used to reflect the self-perception of a person of either sex toward comfort with gender expectations (e.g., macho behaviors for males or feminine social requirements for females) or acting against them (e.g., it has not been long ago that doctors were males and nurses females – with females denied admission to medical schools), gender variance does not redefine one's sex. The relationship between sex and gender is therefore tangential at best, and one may legitimately question the "gender expectations" that a given society seeks to impose.

> **Loving Concern**
>
> While there are genuine experiences of gender dysphoria, there is also such a thing as "social contagion" that rests on social constructions of gender fluidity and encourages adolescents who are uncomfortable with their bodies to reject their body's sex and identity as another gender (nonbinary, trans, etc.).
>
> We can lovingly process this dysphoria with people while, at the same time, affirming the biological grounding of gender in their embodied sex. It is a difficult decision to reject the reality of one's body; I cannot imagine that struggle. I know it is terrifying for those who experience it, and they want some peace about how to relate to their bodies. As people of peace, we listen, dialogue, and offer a vision of the gospel that heals wounds rather than creating them.
> — John Mark Hicks

For those who present their struggle against those expectations as a rejection of "antiquated notions of biological sex and my human rights," there are surely cases in which the latter claim about human rights is correct and the former would be a category mistake. Does anyone still believe that only women should cook, change diapers, or weep over a tragedy? That only men can be company CEOs, presidents of universities, or vote? Gender options have shifted along a spectrum of opportunity and recognition of personal ability. There are still only two identifiable sexes – male and female – who either conform, challenge, or are indifferent to those changes. *Gender roles have been fluid enough to undergo modification, while the fixed taxonomy of two and only two sexes has remained immutable.*

In the present climate of cultural disorientation over sexuality, parents will need to be wary of guidance being offered them about replacing common sense with guidance from "experts." One reads pieces in such national magazines as *Time* that have to make all of us wonder how children ever survived with mere parents to nurture them. "When you take the job of education around complex issues out of the hands of experts and educators, you are leaving parents and caregivers and guardians to do jobs they aren't qualified to do," says the executive director of an organization whose stated purpose is to advocate for affirmative learning environments for LGBTQ+ youth.[28] The article offers a single perspective and proceeds to train parents in the proper technique for supporting a non-binary view of human sexuality. While claiming to offer parents "clear, accurate information," it gives garbled opinions that challenge the biblical view offered in literature such as this book.

As an example of the "garbled" views in a newsmagazine many have trusted, the article acknowledges that most children "play" in a variety of gender roles – hair, dress, mannerisms, social functions – with no long-term significance. Yet it suggests books for parents, picture books for children, video series for both, and other educational resources that help parents teach their children that "gender norms are optional" and effectively coach their children into a gender-fluid mindset. While explaining to parents that their children "pick up on subliminal ideas about gender through media as well as interactions with their classmates and family members," the persons quoted throughout the article are quite determined to offer an alternate set of ideas and experiences that foster the blurring and rejection of traditional sexual values. The subliminal message to be feared is clearly the one that presumes that the biological categories of male and female are real and *not* simply "assigned at birth."

Gender dysphoria is real. Most who experience it will work through its minor vestiges as they mature through life experience. For those whose situation is severe and in need of help, a spiritual guide or professional therapist will be helpful when assisting someone to align their subjective inner state with their biological status and injurious to spiritual health by working in the opposite direction.

ENDNOTES

1. "Meta Diversity," *facebook.com*, Feb 26, 2015, https://www.facebook.com/105225179573993/posts/last-year-we-were-proud-to-add-a-custom-gender-option-to-help-people-better-expr/774221582674346.

2. Kim Elsesser, "The Myth of Biological Sex," *Forbes*, June 15, 2020, accessed April 12, 2023, at https://www.forbes.com/sites/kimelsesser/2020/06/15/the-myth-of-biological-sex/?sh=6fca697c76b9.

3. Ryan W. Miller and Hannah Yasharoff, "What's a TERF and why is 'Harry Potter' author J.K. Rowling being called one?" *USA Today*, June 9, 2020, accessed at https://www.usatoday.com/story/news/nation/2020/06/09/ what-terf-definition-trans-activists-includes-j-k-rowling/5326071002.

4. Shaziya Allarakha, "What Are the 72 Other Genders?" *MedicineNet*, medically reviewed Feb 2, 2022, accessed April 12, 2023, at https://www.medicinenet.com/what_are_the_72_other_genders/article.htm.

5. "Teaching Beyond the Gender Binary in the University Classroom," accessed April 12, 2023, at https://cft.vanderbilt.edu/guides-sub-pages/teaching-beyond-the-gender-binary-in-the-university-classroom.

6. Claire Ainsworth, "Sex Redefined," *Nature* 518 (Feb 19, 2015): 288-291.

7. Ibid., 291.

8. Claire Ainsworth, "Sex Redefined: The Idea of 2 Sexes is Overly Simplistic," *Scientific American* (Oct 22, 2018), accessed at https://www.scientificamerican.com/article/sex-redefined-the-idea-of-2-sexes-is-overly-simplistic1.

9. Anne Fausto-Sterling, "Why Sex Is Not Binary," *New York Times* (Oct 25, 2018), accessed at https://www.nytimes.com/2018/10/25/opinion/sex-biology-binary.html.

10. "WHO updates its widely-used gender mainstreaming manual," news release for July 6, 2022, accessed at https://www.who.int/news/item/06-07-2022-who-updates-widely-used-gender-mainstreaming-manual.

11. "X Gender Marker Available on U.S. Passports Starting April 11," press statement of U.S. Department of State on March 31, 2022, accessed at https://www.state.gov/x-gender-marker-available-on-u-s-passports-starting-april-11.

12. It may be important to note that the sex of an individual is not determined by whether or not that person is in fact producing or capable of producing distinctive gametes as a given time. Pre-pubescent males do not produce sperm, and post-menopausal females do not produce gametes. Various forms of infertility may affect adults of either sex to make render them infertile. The anatomical structures of the persons' reproductive anatomies (i.e., ovaries or testes) – regardless of their past, present, or future functionality – determine sex taxonomy. Persons who identify as "trans" or "non-binary" are not exceptions. This entails the conclusion that surgeries on one's reproductive organs does not render his or her sex taxonomy out of date or change it to its alternate category.

13. "What's Intersex?" *Planned Parenthood* (online), accessed April 13, 2023, at https://www.plannedparenthood.org/learn/gender-identity/sex-gender-identity/whats-intersex.

14. Anne Fausto-Sterling, "The Five Sexes," *The Sciences* (March/April 1993): 20-25.

15. Abstract of "How Common Is Intersex? A Response to Anne Fausto-Sterling," *Journal of Sex Research* 39 (Aug 2002): 174-178. Cf. Sax, *Why Gender Matters*, 2nd ed. (New York: Random House, 2017).

16. Colin Wright, "A Biologist Explains Why Sex Is Binary," *Wall Street Journal*, April 9, 2023, accessed at https://www.wsj.com/articles/a-biologist-explains-why-sex-is-binary-gender-male-female-intersex-medical-supreme-court-ketanji-brown-jackson-lia-thomas-3d22237e.

17. Georgi K. Marinov, "In Humans, Sex Is Binary and Immutable," *Academic Questions* 33 no.2 (July 2, 2020): 177.

18. Accessed April 13, 2023, at https://www.genderbread.org. Note the "uncopyrighted" note at the bottom of the document. The website explains that Sam Killermann is a "social justice comedian."

19. "Breaking Through the Binary: Gender Explained Using Continuums," accessed April 13, 2023, at https://www.genderbread.org/wp-content/uploads/2017/02/Breaking-through-the-Binary-by-Sam-Killermann.pdf. Note: This is part of the accompanying material that explains the Gingerbread Person.

20. Colin M. Wright and Emma N. Hilton, "The Dangerous Denial of Sex," *Wall Street Journal*, Feb 13, 2020, accessed at https://www.wsj.com/articles/the-dangerous-denial-of-sex-11581638089.

21. Ibid.

22. Jon Wertheim, "She's a Transgender Pioneer, But Renée Richards Prefers to Stay Out of the Spotlight," *Sports Illustrated*, June 28, 2019, accessed at https://www.si.com/tennis/2019/06/28/renee-richards-gender-identity-politics-transgender-where-are-they-now.

23. Eric Prisbell, "Transgender Woman Gabrielle Ludwig Returns to College Court," *USA Today*, Dec 4, 2012, updated Feb 18, 2021, accessed at https://www.usatoday.com/story/sports/ncaab/2012/12/04/college-basketball-transgender-player-gabrielle-ludwig-robert-ludwig-mission-college/1744703.

24. "Transgender football player prevails in lawsuit against Minnesota team, league," *MPR News*, Dec 22, 2018, accessed at https://www.mprnews.org/story/2018/12/22/transgender-football-player-prevails-in-lawsuit.

25. Snejana Farberov and Selim Algar, "Trans competitor beats 13-year-old girl in NYC women's skateboarding contest," *New York Post*, June 27, 2022, accessed at https://nypost.com/2022/06/27/trans-

woman-beats-13-year-old-in-womens-skateboarding-contest.

26. Doriane Lambelet Coleman and Wickliffe Shreve, "Comparing Athletic Performances: The Best Elite Women to Boys and Men," Duke University School of Law: Center for Sports Law and Policy, no date, accessed April 14, 2023, at https://law.duke.edu/sports/sex-sport/comparative-athletic-performance.

27. Ibid. Note: The meaning of an "androgenized body" is explained in the paper. "Female athletes – here defined as athletes with ovaries instead of testes and testosterone (T) levels capable of being produced by the female, non-androgenized body – are not competitive for the win against males – here defined as athletes with testes and T levels in the male range. The lowest end of the male range is three times higher than the highest end of the female range. Consistent with females' far lower T levels, the female range is also very narrow, while the male range is broad. These biological differences explain the male and female secondary sex characteristics which develop during puberty and have lifelong effects, including those most important for success in sport: categorically different strength, speed, and endurance. There is no other physical, cultural, or socioeconomic trait as important as testes for sports purposes."

28. Solcyre Burga, "How to Talk to Your Kids About Gender," *Time*, June 5, 2023, https://time.com/6284734/how-to-talk-to-kids-about-gender.

> *"In short, the sexual cultures of the Greeks and Romans have proven endlessly fascinating because they lie before the great watershed of Christianization."*
> — Kyle Harper

CHAPTER 8

The Greco-Roman World of Corrupted Sexuality

The most difficult element of serious Bible study in modern settings is generally thought to be ancient languages – Hebrew, Aramaic, and Greek. Challenging as language studies may be, an equally challenging part of biblical exegesis is to read the Torah in the historical context of the Ancient Near East, the Gospel of Matthew from the perspective of a Second Temple Jew, or Paul's epistles with a "feel" for the culture of the Roman Empire midway through the first Christian century. This type of interconnected reading of Scripture is referred to as the *historical-critical method* of biblical study.

In this Postmodern time, the method of Bible "study" we witness most often among both devout church-goers and casual readers is a type of devotional reading whose concern is "What does this text say to you?" Not for a moment do I want to disparage the application of the Bible to life! Nor do I want to eliminate the value of a say-to-you question. But application and personal value of a biblical text should rest on the platform of *informed awareness of a text's original setting and its careful translation into one's primary modern language.* We are fortunate in the twenty-first century to have a variety of good translations available. As to a text's cultural setting, historians, archaeologists, and classicists continue to provide insights into the ancient time periods from which the biblical texts emerge.

Importance of Social-Cultural Settings to Bible Reading

The late Gordon Fee wrote sympathetically of the person who says, "You don't have to interpret the Bible. Just read it and do what it says!" Probably spoken by someone who either thinks her preacher or teacher is "getting into the weeds" with too many complex details, it is her protest that the Bible is not the unique possession of scholars. And I will certainly agree that *the Bible was written for "common folk" – not specialists.* On the other hand, I fear I have heard the same protest lodged by the occasional person who has either had his unfounded or biased reading challenged with a hard fact that torpedoes it or is too lazy to do a bit of spade work in serious study. Here was Fee's response:

> The aim of good interpretation is simple: to get at the "plain meaning of the text," the author's intended meaning. And the most important ingredient one brings to this task is an enlightened common sense. The test of good interpretation is that it makes good sense of what is written. Correct interpretation, therefore, brings relief to the mind as well as a prick or prod to the heart.[1]

To bring clarity and relief to the mind, a student of the Bible must do more than "feel" that a text means this or that; the discipline of getting relevant facts from good sources is simply a must. If we only use the Bible devotionally as a prod to the heart that is separated from an adequate understanding of the original meaning, Scripture becomes more of a Rorschach test than an exercise in listening to the Spirit of God through select human voices. This reduces what should be a serious search for truth into shallow subjectivity.

The orthodox Christian view is that truth is revealed in the biblical text and can be understood adequately – though never wholly, perfectly, and without the need to explore further – through study and prayer. We do not create truth by looking inside ourselves. We receive truth from the revealed words of God. That is why Jesus prayed for his original followers and for those of us who would follow him through their teaching and writings: "Sanctify them by the truth; your word is truth" (John 17:17; cf. 2 Tim 3:16-17; 2 Pet 1:20-21).

Practically, this means getting your hands on a good translation of the text. Better yet, I would recommend having at least two or three good translations at hand for the clarity one may offer and to spot words or phrases that might be particularly difficult to bring into English. It also means investing in a good Bible dictionary and possibly a good commentary or two. The Internet puts resources like these close at hand, but – whether with print copies or online – not everything you will find written or posted is reliable. Go to multiple sources. Test what you find. Use what Fee called "enlightened common sense."

That's what we will attempt to accomplish in this chapter around the New Testament writings. Written over a 50-year span, the earliest of these (likely either Galatians or James around 45 A.D.) to the final among them (the Revelation of Jesus to John in 95) all reflect life under Roman rule. More specifically, since the references to same-sex relationships in the New Testament come from Paul, his letters to churches and friends that we have were written between 45 and 65 – the approximate dates of his earliest epistle (Galatians) and his death as a martyr in Rome during the reign of Nero.

What were the social-cultural conditions of Paul's world – and those of his readers – when he spoke to this topic? What historical influences were in play? What vocabulary did he use? In light of these considerations, what is likely to have been

> **Religion and Ethics: Two Views**
>
> Musonius and philosophical traditions in general appealed to the individual's sense of honor and the avoidance of personal shame, shame in the eyes of others and so also internally, as the basis for the demands of living by their principles. But early Christian texts typically invoked divine commands, appealed to the divine calling laid upon believers to exhibit holiness, and, notably, invoked the mutual responsibility of believers to one another in their behavioral efforts. That is, early Christian teaching made everyday behavior central in one's religious responsibility to the Christian God and thereby replaced social shame with a theological basis for life.
>
> In place of worries about possible embarrassment socially, Christians posited the judgment of God. The difference was profound. Indeed, it is fair to judge that the impact of the distinctive stance of early Christian teaching involved "a transformation in the deep logic of sexual morality.". . .
>
> The early Christian emphasis on, and teaching about, everyday behavior as central to Christian commitment is yet another distinctive feature that has had a profound subsequent impact. In the ancient Roman period and down through human history, what we call "religion" tended to focus more on honoring, appeasing, and seeking the goodwill of deities through such actions as sacrifices and the performance of related rituals. "Religion" did not typically have much to say about what we call "ethics," how to behave toward others, how to conduct family or business, and the formation of character. If we assume today, however, that religion is concerned with such matters, with ordering behavior, this again is likely down to the influence of Christianity in particular.
>
> — Larry Hurtado

the most straightforward meaning of what he wrote to people of his time and place? As Professor Fee pointed out: *"A text cannot mean what it could never have meant for its original readers/hearers."*[2]

Greco-Roman Context for Families

The term "Greco-Roman" is commonly used of the cultural context for the New Testament. The Roman Empire was the single world power during the events of Jesus' life, the spread of the early church, and the death of all the New Testament writers. But that world had been shaped in profound ways by the legacy of Hellenism. Greek philosophy, literature, art, and language continued to frame Roman life. Whether by adopting or rejecting some Greek antecedent, the life and times of Jesus, Paul, Peter, and John were lived in the atmosphere of a Greco-Roman way of life. For example, even though the official court language of the Roman Empire was Latin, the written Scripture of the Jews and Christians in the first century was a Greek translation called the Septuagint. And all the New Testament materials were originally written and circulated in Greek rather than Latin. It was Greek that functioned as the *lingua franca* of the Mediterranean world.

Among other things, this means that the sexual activities, mores, and (in)tolerances were very different at the time the New Testament was written from those of our time – largely because Christian values challenged them so sharply. The common view

> **Sex: Procreational and Recreational**
>
> Studies of the sexual lives of Roman (or Greek) men reveal a typical pattern: males had "procreational" sex with their wives, with whom they shared a home, children, and a family life, and had "recreational" sex with others. . . .
>
> In their sexual recreations, some husbands participated in sex with women while some of these husbands also engaged in same-sex relations on the side. Paul is describing this sort of relationship in 1 Corinthians 6:9, which reads "men who have sex with men" (NIV), but the explanatory footnote clarifies that the words "refer to the passive and active participants." . . . When we ask, "Who were those who engaged in same-sex relations in Paul's day?" we are then to think mostly of married males engaging in same-sex relations recreationally. Since committed same-sex relations were known in the Roman world, 1 Corinthians 6:9-11 could be describing faithful same-sex couples, but this is less likely than a Roman husband's recreational sex with other men.
>
> Lesbianism existed but was not nearly as pervasive as same-sex relations among males. Lucian, writing in the century after the apostle Paul, says, "They say there are women like that in Lesbos, masculine-looking, but they don't want to give it up for men. Instead, they consort with women, just like men."
>
> — Scot McKnight

of pre-Christian Greco-Roman culture would have regarded (and literature of the period discusses) sexual desire from the adult-male perspective almost exclusively and would have regarded a man's sexual attraction to and liaisons with both females and males as normal and expected.

The presumed common image you and I have of family structure would not parallel that of the first Christian century. To begin, the definition of one's "family" or "household" would have been very different in the first century from the one we know. For another, the social revolution created by Christian teaching being implemented within a household would have made that group of people quite distinctive from its pagan neighbors.

As to the basic definition of what constitutes a family, most of us would hear the word to mean something like mom, dad, and the kids. It means what most of us understand by the term "nuclear family." Not so in the first century. "Apart from referring to the slaves and freed slaves attached to a married couple, [the word 'family'] was also used with reference to the kin as well as to the property or family estate."[3] In other words, a Greco-Roman notion of one's household group was more inclusive than the way most of us use the term. "[F]irst-century people . . . would think of 'family' rather as the entire social network of people related to each other by blood, marriage and other intimate social ties, including clientage."[4]

Within a household of that era, the husband and father – usually the oldest male in a Roman family – was the *paterfamilias* (Lat, father of the family) or owner of the estate. He was regarded as title-holder to all the property attached to the family, including not only land and animals but also any slaves in the network. He had near-absolute power (Lat, *patria potestas*) over everyone in its familial arrangement. As will be noted below, the wife – for whatever personal freedom she had in managing the family's daily life – was accountable to the "female virtues" of chastity and fidelity. The punishment for adultery would be severe and could range from divorce (with the loss of her dowry) to public humiliation to possible death.[5] A woman's sole and exclusive sexual partner was to be her husband for the sake of his family bloodline and heirs. Not so with the man. In what is only slightly oversimplified as a summary, men could do what they wanted to do; women did what the men in their lives (i.e., father, husband, slaveowner) told them to do.

A New Testament passage such as 1 Peter 2:18 – 3:7 is clearly an adapted and Christianized form of a Greco-Roman household code. Such codes go back at least to the time of Aristotle and can be found in writings as diverse as those of Seneca, Philo, and Josephus. They survive into post-biblical Christian writings such as *The Epistle of Barnabas* and the *Didache*. First Peter clearly presumes a household where the *paterfamilias* is an unbeliever, whereas similar adapted household codes in Ephesians and Colossians appear to presume a Christian male.

Similar in pattern to non-biblical household codes, this adapted instruction certainly did not endorse everything about Roman family life (e.g., the cruelties of slavery) but put those relationships into perspective for Christ-followers. For example, non-biblical versions focus heavily or exclusively on the authority of the dominant male. They address women, children, and slaves to remind them of their obligation of unlimited subservience. New Testament versions address both the dominant and subordinate parties, with the subordinate parties (i.e., wife, child, slave) addressed first. Just how radical a change to the concept of family was brought to the world by the Christian ethos is hard for us to appreciate.

In the Petrine household code just referenced, slaves who were Christians heard the standard counsel to submit to their masters "in reverent fear of God" (2:18a). Painfully, moderns hear the apostle apply that instruction "not only to those who are good and considerate, but also to those who are harsh" (2:18b). Interestingly, in giving this counsel, Peter reminded his readers that Jesus himself experienced "unjust suffering" without retaliating against his oppressors and thereby left them "an example that you should follow in his steps" (2:18-22). Some of the unjust suffering from harsh owners would have come in the form of squalid living conditions, unrelenting labor, and brutal punishments.

Some would have come in the form of the sexual abuse of both females and males, according to the preference of the *paterfamilias* and/or his blood relatives, guests, or – if he chose – customers to whom he might sell the sexual services of a slave for additional income. Even slaves who were "married" – there was no official status to slave marriages, only coupling with some degree of allegiance – were the possession of the householder for sexual purposes. One of the published graffiti from Roman Pompeii, for example, speaks of these abusive rights: "Take your slave girl whenever you please, for it is your right."[6] Another has a slave named Salvius mocking his fellow male slave for being required by his master to penetrate him in anal sex.[7] These and similar situations are clearly exploitative and abusive within the Roman social order. They were not, however, regarded as criminal or improper. They were the realities of time and place in the New Testament era.

For almost two millennia now, the term "family" has been narrowed from a sprawling term that once included practically one's whole clan – including slaves and other "property" – to our narrower notion of the nuclear family. What is more noteworthy still, there is the sense of dignity that has been brought to all the members of one's family unit. A woman, a child, or a slave is in the image of God and deserves honor and protection. Even more, family life itself is sacred to God and – in all its particulars – part of the service to and worship of the Father of All.

In his book *Dominion*, historian Tom Holland describes the impact of Christianity on the Roman idea of family. His summary is all the more impressive because Holland is an atheist. Yet he sees and appreciates the impact that teaching such as the adaptation of these household codes really had in Christian families and ultimately on Western civilization.

> Here, in this sacral understanding of marriage, was another marker of the revolution that Christianity had brought to the erotic. The insistence of scripture that a man and a woman, whenever they took to the marital bed, were joined as Christ and his Church were joined, becoming one flesh, gave to both a rare dignity. If the wife was instructed to submit to her husband, then so equally was the husband instructed to be faithful to his wife.[8]

The New Testament corpus challenged the traditional household code of the Greco-Roman world with its call for a man to honor his wife with the same exclusivity and fidelity that had been required of her alone.

It was truly revolutionary. Humans are in God's own image, loved immeasurably by him, and capable of loving one another on the model of his self-giving, self-emptying love. And what many pagans eventually saw in this sort of love exhibited by the families of these followers of Jesus Christ turned their heads, captured their hearts, enlightened their minds, and – without a word – won them to Jesus.

The Pagan Alternative

Different as a Christian household would become under the tutelage of Peter or Paul and the other evangelists spreading the Jesus message, Romans in the surrounding culture would have viewed things in quite another way. Males in the Roman Empire who were citizens – as opposed to slaves or freedmen – were presumed to have the right to be sexually promiscuous without shame or rebuke.

> **Roman Erotica as Status**
> They bought and enjoyed objects, or even commissioned paintings for their homes, that frankly represented sexual intercourse in many different forms. We have seen images of men and women making love, but also men making love to boys and sometimes other men, women pleasuring women, and sexual threesomes and foursomes. Artists represented sex in many different ways, varying not only sexual positions but also picturing apparently taboo practices . . .
> By looking at these images – not in museums or in books – but in their original settings, we learn that the ancient Romans, rather than considering these images "pornographic" and hiding them away, usually associated them with luxury, pleasure, and high status.
> — John Clarke

The Greek words for virgin (*parthenos*) and virginity (*parthenia*) seem to have been presumed appropriate for – if not essentially exclusively applied to – females in literature of the time. That is, until the Christian religion began to put sex in its proper place and enjoined chastity for males as well as females. According to classicist Kyle Harper, the non-Christian vocabulary and documents of the period contemporaneous with the writing of the New Testament and extending for a couple of centuries afterward reveal "a whole culture's indifference toward male chastity."

> There was no natural word for male virginity in Greek or Latin. *Parthenia* means "maidenhead," and the ordinary sense of *parthenos* was "maiden." The continent men of the incipient Christian movement searched, awkwardly, for an expression adequate to their unusual ideal. On rare occasions authors would simply appropriate the language of maidenhood for men: the canonical *Revelation* [14:4], for example, or *Joseph and Aseneth*, in which both protagonists are called *parthenos*. *Virgo*, too, primarily means "maiden" or "young, unmarried girl," though it would later be adapted by Christians and applied to males.[9]

In the context of widespread slavery in the Roman Empire in New Testament times, the exploitation of men, women, and children was a built-in and essentially unquestioned feature of sexual life. The elite members of patrician society (e.g., the emperor's family, senatorial class, generals) were notorious for their shameless seductions and the complications resulting from them. Among the plebians (i.e., craftsmen, farm workers, freedmen, slaves), there was a sliding scale of rights and legal protections. Craftsmen and others of the "working class" had a degree of status corresponding to the elites for whom they built, plowed, painted, taught children, tended the sick, cooked, and did necessary tasks. Among these, persons such as Saul of Tarsus – who was a Roman citizen (cf. Acts 16:37; 22:25) – could travel, operate their own small businesses, and have a degree of protection under the law. Non-citizens had few safeguarded rights and slaves essentially none.

Parodied in plays from the period, those with elite status were presumed to have the right to use the bodies of their slaves as they chose. The patrician families and many among the plebs owned slaves and regarded them – in the language of Aristotle – as merely a "living tool" (i.e., a productive implement). Within the Roman class system, the lower classes could not presume to take initiatives, whether sexual or otherwise, with anyone of higher rank. In that honor-shame culture, however, the reverse did not hold true.

> While the body of a free-born Roman was sacrosanct, those of others were fair game. 'It is accepted that every master is entitled to use his slave as he desires.' ... In Rome, men no more hesitated to use slaves and prostitutes to relieve themselves of their sexual needs than they did to use the side of a road as a toilet. In Latin, the same word, *meio*, meant both ejaculate and urinate.[10]

Brothels were thriving businesses in every city of any size, with prostitutes of both sexes on call. Street prostitution competed with the trade in human flesh that was institutionalized in the brothels. Same-sex marriages were not common, but neither were they unknown. Whether defended or derided, we have written testimony to them in literature from the period. The commoner forms of committed same-sex relationships were simply that – long-term loyalties that were not always called "marriage" because that word was understood to denote a male-female union.

The Greek view would have attached no stigma to adult males (perhaps aged 25 to 50) taking younger males (approximately 12 to 20) as sexual partners. The younger man would learn the duties of citizenship and be introduced to persons of influence and wealth as a protégé; the older man received sexual favors in exchange and with

> **We Are Not So Different Today!**
>
> Sex is good. Sex is healthy. Sex is an essential part of our social fabric. And you – specifically – should probably be having more of it. . . .
>
> Not everyone who wants to have more sex is easily capable of doing so. Disabilities, religious objections, asexuality and any set of day-to-day restrictions and responsibilities curtail or close off sex for many. There may be some who simply do not want to have more sex, or any sex at all. But even those who won't have more sex should avoid apathy. Sex is intrinsic to a society built on social connection – and right now, our connections and our sex lives are collapsing alongside each other.
>
> Many people – like some of the young men I have spoken to in my work – have resigned themselves to displacing their sexual desires, relying entirely on porn or other online stimuli, mirroring so many types of relationships that have been subsumed into the digital world. As a balm for loneliness, digital sex can be little better than digital friendship – a source of envy, resentfulness and spite, a driver of loneliness rather than a cure for it. It's no match for the real thing.
>
> So, any capable people should have sex – as much as they can, as pleasurably as they can, as often as they can.
>
> — Magdalene Taylor / NY Times (2/15/23)

the consent of the younger man's family. Although we would classify this as exploitation and call the older man a predator, it was an educational rite of passage in Greek culture. Neither would the Greeks have looked with any disfavor on young men entering such relationships voluntarily in order to have whatever mentoring in a trade or access to social-political standing it could have provided.

Although same-sex relationships were not uncommon among Romans, the passive (i.e., penetrated) partners to anal sex would have been viewed negatively precisely because of their passivity. The Roman ideal of masculinity allowed the penetrating partner to be viewed as powerful and controlling, while his partner would have been judged soft and effeminate.

Because the Roman Empire included so much territory and so many racial-ethnic groups, social-sexual norms and legal regulations about criminal acts varied. But there were commonalities among them.

A noted Oxford classicist and historian points out that "Christians were conscious of standing apart from the pagan world"[11] of Greco-Roman culture in which they lived. In addition to the socially accepted practices of exposure of unwanted infants, abortion, the right of free males to sex with slaves, and freedom for married males to pursue public sexual liaisons that would have been punished severely in a married woman (i.e., adultery was a "female crime"), attitudes toward same-sex relationships were generally very tolerant.

> In many cultural regions, "bisexuality" was also taken for granted, for "Greek vice" *[a Roman term for homosexuality, RS]* had not faded with the classical age. In civic life, homosexuality between young men, or an older and younger partner, was socially acceptable.... In his work on dreams, Artemidorus distinguished "natural" and "unnatural" sex and although he classified lesbianism as unnatural, male homosexuality, he assumed was not. . . . Among Romans, the most acceptable homosexuality was an act conducted by citizens on slaves or foreigners. . . . In Rome, as in Athens, there was special objection to those who were passive partners in a homosexual act. In classical Athens, full physical submission caused a person to be derided."[12]

It is of interest – in light of linguistic data from the New Testament that will come later in this book – that certain elements of the ancient honor-and-shame culture attached to same-sex activity in that era. Although "Greek vice" or "Greek love" was often idealized in relation to Greek philosophers, there were some distinctions. Both man-with-boy relationships and male-with-male adult relationships were socially acceptable, but – as indicated above – the passive (i.e., penetrated) adult was viewed differently than his partner. This would have been true especially of a male prostitute or a man who assumed the passive role outside a long-term "wifely relationship" with a committed partner.

> Although [homosexuality] was idealized, it was considered largely from the person of the active partner. Doctors considered active homosexuality to be natural, though in Rufus's view (c. 100 A.D.) it was more exhausting than heterosexuality because it was more violent. Passive homosexuality was another matter. There had been a familiar medical debate on the causes of this perverse preference, which was compared with the tastes of women "who pursue other women with an almost masculine jealousy." Some said that it was a disease of the mind, others an inherited defect at birth which had become ineradicable ever since it had entered the human race.[13]

From Honor and Shame to Ethical Offense

Strange as it may seem to moderns, there was no "religious" argument against same-sex intercourse in Ancient Greece – only the honor-shame distinction just identified among participants. This will become clearer later, but it was Christianity's dissemination of an ethical norm (already known to Jews) into Ancient Rome that transformed the honor-shame language (i.e., dominant-subservient) into what modern people think of as *moral* language (i.e., sin, transgression). An art historian who has specialized in the Roman Period summarizes:

> Until the Emperor Constantine paved the way for Christianity to become the state religion, Roman attitudes toward sex remained relatively stable. Most people saw sex as a wonderful pleasure to be pursued. Ecstatic sex with a beautiful partner – whether male or female, adolescent or adult – was a gift of the gods, one of life's most important moments. Although it is true that some philosophies and religions stressed sexual abstinence, the pervasive attitude toward sexual pleasure, as expressed in both the law and in art, was highly positive. We read of the Stoic philosophers (like the Emperor Marcus Aurelius himself) practicing self-denial, or the male devotees of the goddess Isis even emasculating themselves, but most Romans saw such sexual practices as unnatural and even perverse.[14]

The same writer points out that the "highly prescriptive" ethics of all three Abrahamic faiths about sexual behaviors would have been shocking – even "absurd" – to the typical Roman. "In their view, when Cupid's arrow stung you, there was nothing you could do but hold on for dear life. It was foolish to resist the power of sexual desire – no matter what the object of that desire."[15]

For example, it would have been *honorable* for a free citizen of Ancient Greece (whether single or married) to have sex with a male or female prostitute, a male or female slave he owned, a friend's male or female slave with the owner's permission, a 15-year-old boy he was mentoring into manhood, or to live a covenanted same-sex union as an alternative to opposite-sex marriage. On the other hand, it would have been *dishonorable* for that same free citizen to permit his wife or daughter to have sex with anyone, to force himself on a 15-year-old boy or girl, or to be "out of control" in a manner philosophers would have criticized as *akrasia* (i.e., self-indulgence, failure of self-control). The Romans altered some of these protocols around sex for reasons mostly related to their ideas of true manhood in a militaristic society.

One of the most offensive elements of Greek culture to modern readers involves the practice of pederasty, to which the Romans also objected and altered. Already mentioned in passing in this chapter as an accepted form of protégé-to-aspirant education in its time, a bit more information will be helpful background to reading the New Testament passages on same-sex relationships.

Pederasty (Gk, *paiderastēs* = lover of boys) involves a sexual relationship between an adult male and an adolescent boy. In Ancient Greece, it was a highly institutionalized and voluntary relationship that introduced the younger party to civic life, responsibility, and even prestige. The older, dominant party (Gk, *erastēs*) would court a young boy from the aristocratic classes with gifts and offer to be his mentor into the Greek polis. Usually arranged with the father of the boy and with some degree of approval by the youth, this years-long relationship was regarded as a privileged form of education when educational structures such as we take for granted were unknown. The younger, submissive party (Gk, *erōmenos*) accepted the opportunity of the relationship to learn, to be the beneficiary of introduction to the older man's circle of wealth and political influence, and to function a primary satisfaction for his sexual needs.[16] This relationship was considered honorable and was not regarded as a form of sexual violation of a child (i.e., pedophilia).[17]

Although the Romans adopted a number of Greek institutions and social norms, pederasty was not one they looked upon with favor. In Athens, the younger partner in a pederastic relationship would be nurtured to full citizenship by means of it; in Rome, the fact of being feminized by virtue of anal sex could be a social-political barrier to one's status in public life. In neither culture, however, would pederasty have been regarded generally as a moral offense – unless the boy in question was taken against his or his family's will or a boy from an aristocratic family was violated by a male from a lower social status.

In Roman culture, the voluntary agreement by a freeborn boy to a pederastic arrangement could have been considered an act of social shame for him and his family. As a recognized and accepted social institution, therefore, man-with-boy sex among citizen families was not widely approved. Anal penetration required the submissive partner to yield his masculinity and to play the part of a female (Gk, *malakos* = soft one) – to be "feminized" in a militaristic culture that prized dominance. This did not mean that man-boy intercourse was forbidden or disapproved for slaves or other lowborn persons, simply that it would be regarded as effeminate and therefore inappropriate between citizens.

But the difference in attitude between Greece and Rome toward pederasty and even a more negative attitude in the latter toward a passive same-sex partner does

> **Sex as Roman Capitalism**
>
> Roman policy toward prostitution has been aptly described as a volatile mixture of "toleration and degradation. Prostitution was legal. It was taxed by the state and . . . was purposefully conspicuous.
>
> Prostitution was a boom industry under Roman rule. In the densely urbanized and highly monetized economy of the Roman Empire, sex was a most basic and readily available commodity. Girls stalked the streets. Taverns, inns, and baths were notorious dens of venal sex. Brothels "were visible everywhere." Companions, trained in various forms of entertainment, could be rented for domestic symposia.
>
> Sex was big business, and although pimps and procurers suffered legal and social stigmas, Roman law allowed slave owners to profit from a slave's entrepreneurial activities, so that undoubtedly some rather illustrious households capitalized, discreetly, on the flesh trade. In the few surviving scraps of evidence for real working brothels, including a handful of papyri from Roman Egypt, what is most notable is the sheer sophistication of the financial instruments undergirding the sale of sex. Prostitution was an exuberant part of Roman capitalism.
>
> — Kyle Harper

not equate to a generally negative attitude toward homosexuality. So long as the relationships were between persons of equal rank and consensual, they were considered appropriate. As in our own time, sexual relationships between male partners in the Roman Empire were a much smaller percentage than heterosexual ones, but they were certainly neither unknown nor disavowed. As noted in a quotation earlier in this chapter from Robin Lane Fox, they would have been "socially acceptable" in the civic life of the empire – likely acknowledged more easily in the larger cities than in most rural areas.

So we turn now from pederastic relationships that were viewed very differently in ancient Greece than by moderns and the exploitative same-sex relationships of Roman times to correct the misinformation that has recently been primary to revisionists. The claim is made that the present-day option of committed, loving, and monogamous same-sex partnerships was never the object of biblical prohibitions for the simple reason that there was no equivalent in biblical times.

Because these claims are so central to the revisionist case, the next two chapters will provide documentation for the awareness and widespread acceptance of long-term commitments between same-sex partners. Chapter 9 examines the Greek background, and Chapter 10 will turn to the immediate context of the New Testament documents in Roman culture.

The chart on the following page is a broad overview of documented references to consensual same-sex relationships that were widely known in the period prior to, contemporary with, and immediately after the New Testament era. To claim that Jews and Christians of that time – especially someone so well-educated and cosmopolitan as Paul – would not have known about them requires considerable naiveté on our part.

Some of these are names of gods and/or public legends. Others are historic characters. They illustrate widespread public awareness of same-sex liaisons, partnerships, and "pseudo-marriages" in Greek and Roman cultures. Collectively, they prove the claim that ancient Greco-Roman culture neither knew nor approved consensual same-sex partnerships of the sort we know today is false. Further, that some of these are accounts of "gods" or "heroes" rather than common people or citizens does not diminish their relevance to the topic: myths were central to the educational process that taught Greeks and Romans what behaviors were acceptable for them as honorable persons.[18] Quite clearly, consensual same-sex love over time was endorsed by these common stories, poems, plays, etc. They were known, documented, and talked about in the New Testament era.

Documented References to LGBTQ+ Activities in Greco-Roman Period

ca. 730 B.C.	Philolaus & Diocles[19]	Aristotle
	adult male lovers with a lifelong commitment to each other that began as a pederastic relationship[20]	
ca. 515 B.C.	Aristogeiton & Harmodius[21]	Thucydides / Aristotle
	adult male lovers who assassinated the Athenian tyrant Hipparchus / both executed	
ca. 400 B.C.	Orestes & Pylades[22]	Greek play by Euripedes
	regarded as models of lifelong adult love in various poems for generations in both Greece and Rome	
ca. 350 B.C.	Boeothian "yoke-mates"[23]	Xenophon
	same-sex unions "sanctioned by the state" / tomb of Iolaus became favored site for taking vows	
ca. 371-338 B.C.	The Sacred Band of Thebes[24]	Plutarch
	famous story of 150 same-sex adult partners as defenders of Thebes	
ca. 400-350 B.C.	Pausanias & Agathon[25]	Plato
	citizens of Athens in committed relationship for more than 30 years	
ca. 335 B.C.	Damon & Pythias	Valerius Maximus
	loyal to each other in the face of accusations of treason by Dionysius I of Syracuse	
200 B.C. – A.D. 200	Cult of Cybele	Multiple sources
	cult that featured transgender and non-binary adult males in various rituals	
100-44 B.C.	Julius Caesar	Suetonius
	widespread stories of same-sex affair with King Nicomedes IV of Bithynia	
70-19 B.C.	Nisus & Euryalus	Poetry of Virgil
	Virgil writes "national epic" of Rome and tells of enduring same-sex love	
3 B.C. – A.D. 69	Galba	Multiple sources
	Notorious in his time for what is generally regarded as exclusive preference for males	
A.D. 5-15	"Warren Cup"	British Museum
	erotic depiction of same-sex intercourse[26] / example of art celebrating male-male sex	
A.D. 37-68	Nero & Pythagoras	Multiple sources
	Nero's "second" marriage in which he appears to have adopted female role for himself	
A.D. 79	Pompeii destroyed	Multiple sources
	archaeological remains show various male-male and female-female erotica	
A.D. 76-138	Hadrian & Antinous	Multiple sources
	"most famous romantic couple" in second-century Rome	
A.D. 203-22	Elagabalus	Multiple sources
	obsessed with idea of changing birth sex to female / sometimes called "gender fluid" or "transgender"	

ENDNOTES

1. Gordon D. Fee and Douglas Stuart, *How to Read the Bible for All Its Worth*, 4th ed. (Grand Rapids: Zondervan, 2014), 22.

2. Ibid., 34. (Italics are in the original text.)

3. Stephen Joubert, "Managing the Household: Paul as *Paterfamilias* of the Christian Household Group in Corinth," in Philip Esler, ed., *Modelling Early Christianity: Social-Scientific Studies of the New Testament in its Context* (New York: Routledge, 1995), 214.

4. Carolyn Osiek, "The New Testament and the Family," in Lisa Sowle and Dietmar Mieth, eds., *The Family* (Maryknoll, NY: Orbis Books, 1995), 1.

5. Historians and classicists can point to documents saying that husbands had the power of life or death over an unfaithful wife, but – as with the Old Testament legislation that authorized the death penalty for adultery – divorce rather than death appears to have been the rule.

6. *Corpus Inscriptionum Latinarum* 4.1863.

7. Ibid., 4.2375.

8. Tom Holland, *Dominion*, 282.

9. Kyle Harper, *From Shame to Sin: The Christian Transformation of Sexual Morality in Late Antiquity* (Cambridge, MA: Harvard University Press, 2013), 52.

10. Holland, *Dominion*, 99. *Note*: The quotation about a master's use of his slaves is from Gaius Musonius Rufus (*ca.* A.D. 25-95), a Stoic philosopher contemporary with Paul, who pointed out the injustice of such sexual indulgences in Roman society. This line is from his *Discourses* 12, "On Sexual Indulgence."

11. Robin Lane Fox, *Pagans and Christians* (New York: Alfred A. Knopf, 1987), 341.

12. Ibid., 341-342.

13. Ibid., 346.

14. John R. Clarke, *Roman Sex: 100 B.C. to A.D. 250* (New York: Harry N. Abrams, 2003), 157.

15. Ibid., 158.

16. These relationships not only admitted the younger male to privilege when successful but also served to impress him with the duty of obedience to authority and understanding the importance of discipline to a well-ordered city. See Jan Bremmer, "An Enigmatic Indo-European Rite: Paederasty," in Wayne R. Dynes and Stephen Donaldson, eds., *Homosexuality in the Ancient World*, Vol 1 (New York: Garland Publishing, 1992), 61.

17. An overview of how pederasty functioned among the elite of Athens is found in Catherine S. Donnay, "Pederasty in ancient Greece: a view of a now forbidden institution" (2018). *EWU Masters Thesis Collection.* 506.

18. In his *Republic*, Plato discusses education in an exchange between Socrates and Adeimantus. Proposing a form of censorship for his ideal city, Socrates explains why its rulers should exercise a degree of censorship over its storytellers or, more literally, its myth-makers (Gk, μυθοποιοί, *mythopoioi*) because of the educational impact such myths have on shaping the character of young people. For example, "Indeed, if we want the guardians of our city to think that it's shameful to be easily provoked into hating one another, we mustn't allow any stories about gods warring, fighting, or plotting against one another, for they aren't true. The battles of gods and giants, and all the various stories of the gods hating their families or friends, should neither be told nor even woven in embroideries. . . . For these reasons, then, we should probably take the utmost care to insure that the first stories they hear about virtue are the best ones for them to hear" (*Republic*, 2.378c-e). Later: "They mustn't attempt to persuade our young people that the gods bring about evil or that heroes are no better than humans. . . . We must put a stop to such stories, lest they produce in the youth a strong inclination to do bad things" (391d-e).

19. "The long trail begins not with a Theban but with a Corinthian, a wealthy aristocrat named Philolaus. Sometime in the 8th century BC this man left Corinth with his male lover, an Olympic athlete named Diocles, and landed in Thebes. The pair were fleeing the incestuous passion of Diocles' mother – a drama worthy of Sophocles, one supposes, but Aristotle, the source for their flight, gives no details. Committed male couples, willing to go into exile together, were as yet uncommon in ancient Greece. Homoerotic affairs were more typically short-lived, ending when the junior partner – who may have been pre-pubescent at the outset – began to grow facial hair. That is the model described by Plato's speakers in the dialogue *Symposium*, one of our fullest sources for ancient sexual mores. But Philolaus and Diocles were both mature men." James Romm, "The Legacy of Same-Sex Love in Ancient Thebes," *History News Network*, June 6, 2021. Accessed Mar 22, 2023, at https://historynewsnetwork.org/article/180453.

20. Affirming writers typically wish to discount same-sex relationships that begin as adult-to-youth bonds. It should be remembered that male-female as well as male-male sexual associations and/or formal marriages that were other than trysts with prostitutes involved adult-to-youth relationships. Most girls were married in their early teens to men old enough to be established in a trade that would allow them to support a family. With both types of sexual initiation, a percentage (e.g., Pausanias and Agathon) evolved into consensual, long-term, and committed relationships that were the cultural equivalent of what Gushee, Hamilton, Keen, and others claim

to have been non-existent. Hubbard calls it a "popular misconception" that Greek same-sex couplings were restricted to man-boy pairs. "Vase painting shows numerous scenes where there is little or no apparent difference between the young wooer and his object of courtship, as well as graphic scenes of sexual experimentation between youths.... Although a youth's attractiveness was thought by many to cease with the growth of his beard and body hair, the window of attraction varied to some degree by individual preferences.... In the Hellenistic period, some lovers swore continued attraction even well into their loved one's adulthood... In Roman times, we have more than one account of soldiers being the object of sexual attention by superior officers; the elderly emperor Galba is said to have preferred mature and masculine men, and Nero supposedly 'married' a freedman named Doryphorus." Thomas K. Hubbard, *Homosexuality in Greece and Rome: A Sourcebook of Basic Documents* (Berkeley, CA: University of California Press, 2003), 5-6.

21. Aristotle in 23 Volumes, Vol. 20, translated by H. Rackham. Cambridge, MA, Harvard University Press; London, William Heinemann Ltd. 1952. Digitized by the Perseus Project: http://www.perseus.tufts.edu/hopper/text?doc=Perseus%3Atext%3A1999.01.0046%3Achapter%3D 19%3Asection%3D1. Cf. "Examples of Love," at http://people.uncw.edu/deagona/lit/Examples%20HA.pdf.

22. Their devotion as lovers is celebrated in various poems and verses. Cf. Lucian's *Erōtes* at https://sourcebooks.fordham.edu/pwh/lucian-orest.asp. Euripides writes of them in texts references at https://www.greekmythology.com/Plays/Euripides/Orestes/orestes.html.

23. "But if, as Romm points out, in Athens and Sparta 'male erôs was "complicated,"' in Thebes and Boeotia it was sanctioned by the state. Male couples could take an oath at the grave of Iolaus, Hercules's own beloved, to live together as *syzygentes*—yoke mates—a term that elsewhere indicates a lifelong marital bond. It is etymologically related to 'conjugal.' (The modern Greek word for 'spouse' is still *syzygos*.)" A.E. Stallings, "Warrior Eros," *The American Scholar* (online), July 24, 2021, https://theamericanscholar.org/warrior-eros.

24. "Theban male lovers swore oaths of loyalty at the tomb of Iolaus. Their pledges were sober commitments, made in the presence of a powerful ghost. A pledge of love, Gorgidas reasoned, might support the new Theban state as much as his old pledge of service. Thinking along these lines, he embarked on an experiment. He recruited male couples, three hundred men altogether, and formed them into an infantry corps: the Sacred Band of Thebes." James Romm, *The Sacred Band: Three Hundred Theban Lovers Fighting to Save Greek Freedom* (New York: Scribner, 2021), 28-29. "The other city for which there is good evidence for the rituals of same-sex pairing is Thebes, home to the 'army of lovers', the Sacred Band of three hundred champions, organised in love-couples. Predictably, the existence of the Sacred Band has been questioned on a priori grounds by David Leitao. Such an army would break all the rules of Greek homosexuality (notably its supposedly transitory and initiatory character). The evidence he must discount, however, much of it from contemporaries, is overwhelming. Xenophon claimed that in Boeotian Thebes, 'man and boy live together, like married people,' in E.C. Marchant's Loeb translation, or, more pedantically, Boeotian men 'form relationships (*homilousi*) once they have been conjugally yoked (*syzygentes*) as man and boy'; the 'like' is Marchant's addition." James Davidson, "Mr and Mr and Mrs and Mrs: Book Review of The Friend by Alan Bray," *London Review of Books*, June 2, 2005, https://www.lrb.co.uk/the-paper/v27/n11/james-davidson/mr-and-mr-and-mrs-and-mrs.

25. Plato, *Symposium*. Details of this relationship are provided in Chapter 9 of this volume.

26. The art historian who authenticated and named the Warren Cup has described the shift that has occurred in understanding how routine same-sex experience and artistic representation were in the New Testament era. "When I first began to study it, the Warren Cup did not even have a name (I named it), and it was virtually unknown, hidden away in a Swiss museum. The reason? Scholars could not bring themselves to believe that such hard-core images of gay sex could have existed in ancient Rome. They thought it was a fake, designed to titillate Victorian gentlemen collectors like E.P. Warren, who acquired the cup in the late 1800s.... My first task was to find out whether there were comparable scenes of hard-core gay sex on vessels that came from documented excavations. It did not take much sleuthing to find many male-male sex scenes that I could date to the same period as the Warren cup, between A.D. 1 and 30. I found a whole range of images of gay sex on a variety of vessels of the period. There were very expensive ones in silver and cameo glass, and cheap, mold-made terracotta imitations produced for poorer folks." Clarke, *Roman Sex*, 78. It is actually a testimony to the counter-cultural attitude of Christianity toward sexual behaviors such as consensual and public same-sex relationships that were quite commonplace in the Greco-Roman world but which came to be "shocking" as Christian teaching and influence spread. Clarke documents "a whole group of erotic cups and bowls produced in the ancient Roman town of Arretium (today's Arezzo) in Tuscany during the period 30 B.C. to A.D. 14. "These 'bisexual' cups and bowls [that alternate images of straight sex with gay sex] helped me to establish that ordinary people prized beautiful images of explicit straight and gay sex." Ibid., 871.

> *"Historical evidence shows that consensual, mutual same-sex practices – even loving, lifelong same-sex partnerships - existed in the Greco-Roman world alongside the abusive practices of pederasty, prostitution, and master-slave sex."*
> — Darrin W. Snyder Belousek

CHAPTER 9

Committed Same-Sex Relationships in Greek Culture

If the previous chapter seemed a bit out of place or even unnecessary, let me explain why it is included. In order to weigh the evidence about same-sex unions in antiquity and, more specifically, to evaluate some of the claims made by modern apologists for loving and committed same-sex marriage, it seems to be essential background. The ancient world had a very different view of sexual morality than the Western world of the past 1,500 years. Both heterosexual and homosexual behaviors were viewed in ways we do not have categories to accommodate. As already pointed out, it was the coming of Christianity that expanded the norms familiar to Judaism into Europe, the Americas, and eventually to much of the world.

In summary, the preceding chapter should have established these basic ideas for readers. First, the Bible is not an ahistorical book; it must be read within the context of the history, personalities, and – most especially – cultural values of its time. Second, the nature of family and how families functioned must be understood in order to read ancient literature of any sort. Third, sexual privileges taken in ancient cultures generally and within family structures in particular are shocking to modern readers. Males who belonged to the elite (i.e., wealthy) and freeborn class had practically unlimited rights to the bodies of slaves – whether male or female. Fourth, exploitation and abuse of slaves was commonplace in the Greco-Roman world that formed the immediate cultural background of the New Testament.

Fifth, Greek culture had fostered a practice among its elite class of introducing young men into public life through a pederastic ritual that was considered moral and appropriate to the wealthy, while being mocked and satirized by many from the "lower" class. Elites of their mid-20s and older exchanged the favor of their status, skills (e.g., law, oratory, estate management), and political prestige for the sexual favors of young males aged between 12 and 20 of the upper class with approval. In age ranges that would qualify as statutory rape in practically all modern cultures, this was an institutionalized practice for the education of teenagers in Greek city states.[1]

Sixth, while adopting many of the practices of the precursor Greeks, the more militaristic Romans did not adopt on a broad scale the *erastēs-erōmenos* (i.e., man-boy) model. Although same-sex intercourse remained common to erotic practice in master-slave contacts, bathhouses, public brothels, and private liaisons, males who consented to anal penetration were regarded as effeminate and looked down upon by their contemporaries.

What one scholar of Hellenistic literature says about the Greeks can be affirmed as well of their Roman heirs – and makes their world very distant from ours. Writing of their use in our modern debates, Jeffrey Carnes has warned against a simple pulling forward of Plato's views into the twenty-first century in some "profoundly ahistorical" manner.

> [N]ot only would Plato probably fail to recognize the categories employed in the debate, but the notion that same-sex affection or sexuality needed defending in the first place remakes Plato in our image. He becomes, like ourselves, a modern, liberal thinker. A better approach – at least in the scholarly world, if not in the courts – might be to leave aside case-by-case arguments about whether Greek philosophers approved of same-sex attraction, kissing, or intercourse, and to argue instead that the Greeks' sexual system was so different from our own as to be for all practical purposes useless as a basis for comparison.[2]

In other words, whether jurists, academics, or novices reading ancient literature, all need to be sure we are comparing like with like. Just as fruitful Bible study requires the sort of linguistic and historical investigation discussed in the previous chapter, we have to be careful in reading Plato, Aristotle, or other Greek writers not to read our experience and modern notions into their documents. The same applies to the works of Cicero, Seneca, or other personalities from the Roman period – including words from Jesus or Paul.

The quotation above calls attention to the complexity of moving between the personalities and literature of those ancient times and our contemporary debates. Tedious and time-consuming as it may be, this is the sort of spadework necessary to get the soil ready for fruitful, reliable results. Yes, writers in the same volume point out, ancient and modern people have similar sexual categories; we express them in different vocabularies and must be careful to be fair-minded in comparing them. No, they did not use our terms "straight" and "gay," but the dichotomy between types of sexual behavior and the motivations between them existed; there is simply no such thing as a noncontroversial view of ancient sexual categories and their possible relevance to modern civil liberties.

In this chapter, we move from an overview of ancient cultures and their genuinely foreign notions of permissible sexual behaviors that frequently involved exploitation and violence to ask if there were non-exploitative and consensual same-sex relationships documented to us. The brief references to same-sex coupling already mentioned need to be expanded. Did ancient cultures know any equivalent to loving same-sex unions? Did they ever liken those relationships to traditional male-female marriage? And what is the likelihood that such non-exploitative alliances were known to biblical writers?

Same-Sex Marriage: Not a Modern Innovation

There seems to be a thematic argument in defense of same-sex marriage that goes this way from Christian writers: "Even if we grant the Bible's consistent negative judgment against male-with-male sex, those justified condemnations are against the only same-sex practices known in those days – pedophilia, pederasty, anal rape of defeated soldiers, and male prostitution. Those evil actions should be condemned. I condemn them. What the Bible never condemns is the sort of loving, committed, and monogamous relationships that are possible in today's more enlightened times."

This type of argument traces to the assertions of writers from the 1980s and has been repeated since by a variety of affirming authors and teachers from various theological backgrounds. For example, Robin Scroggs claims – with the highlighted words here italicized in his original text . . .

Thus what the New Testament was against was the image of homosexuality as pederasty and primarily here its more sordid and dehumanizing dimensions. One would regret it if somebody in the New Testament had not opposed such dehumanization.

If this is so, the necessary criterion of reasonable similarity between the New Testament period and today's model of homosexual relations does not obtain. The ideal, at least, of adult homosexuality today, certainly within Christian groups, is that of a caring and mutual relationship between consenting adults.[3]

> **Temporary and Age-Related?**
> Although writers sometimes infer from the literary stereotypes of fourth-century Athens that all ancient homosexual relationships were temporary and age-related, the evidence suggests that this picture is exaggerated even for Athens, and homosexual relationships in the rest of ancient Europe were certainly far more varied and flexible than this, probably not very different from their heterosexual counterparts.
>
> Plutarch, writing in Greek for a Roman audience of the second century, makes this point explicitly: ". . . the lover of beauty will be fairly and equably disposed toward both sexes, instead of supposing that males and females are different in the matter of love as they are in their clothes" (Erotikos 767B). He suggests, further, that the upper age limit for "lovers" and lower limit for "beloveds" would be precisely the same regardless of the genders involved (Erotikos 754C).
>
> — John Boswell

James Brownson makes a parallel claim: "In the ancient world, such ongoing permanent relationships between persons of the same sex are never documented in the extant literature of the period."[4] Similarly, Achtemeier makes an equally dismissive assertion: "[T]he world of the biblical writers had nothing that remotely resembles the loving, egalitarian, committed gay marriages and partnerships we know today."[5] Stretching himself still further, Achtemeier is willing to affirm more than once: "As in Old Testament times, the Greco-Roman society that Paul inhabited had no concept of sexual orientation and no cultural spaces or institutions that could support egalitarian, committed, same-sex relationships based on mutual love."[6] Hamilton, Gushee, and other affirming writers make the same claim.

Perhaps it is the centrality and emphatic language of such claims that has caused persons relying on them to assume the assertions have merit. Thus, what these writers have published has been taken up and repeated in even more emphatic ways from church pulpits.

> So what Scripture condemns, and rightly so, are certain same-sex practices prevalent in those times – promiscuity, pederasty when an older man would initiate a boy into his manhood including sexuality, prostitution, power-down relations, that is, exploitative relations, for instance, between masters and slaves, between older and younger, between victor and vanquished on a battlefield, as well as behaviors that were just lustful or practiced in pagan cultic circles. Scripture rightly condemns all this, as we would and should. Of course we condemn it for both gays and straights.
>
> What Scripture does not condemn, what it does not address, are life-long, monogamous, mutual and loving gay relationships. Such relationships do not seem to have existed back then, or were kept very, very private. The historical record is essentially silent. Again, some claim otherwise, but on closer look their evidence breaks down, which is not surprising; it was a decidedly hierarchical, top-down society. Such relationships were, as far as I can tell, beyond the horizon of possible meanings for Biblical writers and their audience.[7]

It is easier, perhaps, to forgive a preacher, distressed relative, or same-sex attracted person such a mistaken claim than the authors of their source documents. Maybe it was mere oversight by those authors, yet such an "oversight" is difficult to posit for them in view of the evidence. Could multiple writers simply overlook the data of history and literature of the period in question? Or might there be what logicians call "special pleading"[8] in play? There is abundant and sufficient documentation to prove that monogamous and caring same-sex relationships were indeed known to the Greco-Roman world. As today, they were a minority population in relation to male-female marriages or committed unions among persons of opposite sex.[9]

Although in agreement with Scroggs' (and others') claim that covenanted same-sex unions should be accepted and blessed by modern Christians, William Loader updates their claim that Paul would have been addressing only pederasty and would not have had a broader range of same-sex activity in mind.

> Research since Scroggs has concluded that Paul would have more in mind than just pederasty in Romans 1. In addition, Paul's formulations, especially "for one another" (1.27), suggest mutuality rather than exploitation and so apparently envisage also adult-adult sexual relations of mutual consent. If Paul stands under the influence of the Leviticus prohibitions, his condemnation [of same-sex acts] is likely to have been comprehensive.[10]

Before going to the historical data, however, the essential problem with this position is that it does not square with the most straightforward reading of the biblical text itself.

> **Commitments Beyond Paiderastia**
>
> Pausanias, who seemingly came to know Agathon in the context of paiderastia, thus prolonged this relation until the death of his "beloved." Such permanence in an amorous relationship seems to be the expression, first, of the idealization of paiderastia, and, on the other hand, of the exclusivity of relations between "lover" and "beloved." In addition, there is no doubt about the "visibility" of this couple; it seems to have attracted both praise and blame in classical Athens. . . .
>
> From this point, we may draw three conclusions, which we may generalize with some degree of probability. Despite the semi-institutional practice of paiderastia, the existence of couples formed by adult males was known at Athens. These couples laid claim to genuine exclusivity, for they excluded any relation, in or out of marriage, with women. Above all, they featured an undeniable visibility and permanence.
>
> — Luc Brisson

Language of Mutual Consent

To be sure, every culture in every generation has witnessed sexual exploitation in a variety of its deplorable forms. Vulnerable women are raped or sold for sex by controlling pimps and madams. From antiquity to this day, women in extreme poverty or in situations of distress have sold themselves on streetcorners. Males no less than females have been subjected to sexual abuse. The slavery of the Roman Empire is matched by living cultures of our own time that are known to trade in human flesh. American military personnel were even put under orders in certain regions of Afghanistan to refrain from intervening in cases of sexual abuse of young males in that culture known as *bacha bazi* (i.e., boy play).[11]

There is no doubt among either traditionalist or revisionist scholars that the harsh verdicts in the biblical literature rebuke abusive practices. Even if tolerated at a certain time or in specific cultures, we nevertheless look at such cruel and offensive behaviors and call them evil. There is agreement by practically all parties on this point. But is it reasonable to think it was only these abusive actions that are in view in Holy Scripture?

A cursory reading of the biblical texts hardly leaves the impression that the prohibitions of same-sex behaviors are limited to those involving either force or unusual cultural settings. In the Holiness Code of ancient Israel, for example, the defining element of the forbidden practice is not whether it was cultural or cultic, abusive or exploitative. The single defining feature is that it was between persons of the same sex. "Do not have sexual relations with a man as one does with a woman; that is detestable" (Lev 18:22). There is no qualifying adjective before the term "sexual relations with a man" – nothing equivalent to "forced" or "coerced." There is no word in the original text that implies "cultic sex" or "homoerotic acts in the context of idolatry."

Furthermore, the language of the expanded prohibition that also includes the penalty for violating it contains no language that would imply a perpetrator-victim distinction. That *both* parties were "to be put to death; their blood will be on their own heads" (Lev 20:13) is the language of shared responsibility. By contrast to this severe penalty for both parties, Deuteronomy 22:22-29 makes it clear that there is a difference between the perpetrator of a sexual assault and the victim involved. If the woman assented and/or did not resist her aggressor, she shared responsibility and suffered the same fate as the man. If she resisted his advance only to be forced (i.e., raped), the instruction was altogether different: "Do nothing to the woman; she has committed no sin worthy of death" (v.26a). The text explains that the victim of a sexual assault was to be viewed as a murdered person would be – an innocent victim of another's violence (v.26b). During the entire Greco-Roman period, this would have been the consistent and uniform view of all same-sex behavior within Judaism. Consensual illicit sex was condemned and punished, whereas victims of sexual assault were innocent of transgression.

In view of the aggressor-injured party distinction in the Torah, the significance of Leviticus 20:13 should be clear. Victims are not to be punished, but rescued and helped to heal from their trauma. Partners to an offense or willing participants in a forbidden behavior share both the guilt and the penalty for it. We therefore reasonably conclude that the nature of the sexual act in view here is consensual.

If anything, the New Testament censure of same-sex coupling in the Greco-Roman world that could have been voluntary, caring, and long-term is even more direct. In a larger context that will be detailed in Chapter 11, Paul uses the language of mutuality. After first calling out lesbian sex activity as "unnatural," he continues: "In the same way the men also abandoned natural relations with women and were inflamed with lust for one another" (Rom 1:27a). The phrase "lust for one another" uses the reciprocal pronoun *allēlous* (i.e., one another, mutually, in exchange), which indicates something quite different from exploitation or unwilling participation. It points to the consent of both parties.

From his vocabulary as an educated man, Paul had words at hand which specified rape, pederasty, prostitution, and the like. Instead, he categorically rejects sexual unions of whatever sort between persons of the same sex. As William Loader, a revisionist scholar who affirms the appropriateness of same-sex unions, acknowledges of Romans 1: "Nothing indicates that Paul is exempting some same-sex intercourse as acceptable. It is all an abomination for Paul."[12] In a culture that made distinctions between rich and poor, elite and lower classes relative to their sexual privileges with persons of the same sex, the Bible allows for no exceptions.

The question remains: Does extant literature from the period just prior to and including the New Testament period know of same-sex relationships that are non-exploitative? In addition to pederasty, master-slave abuse, and other forms of bodily violation, is there reliable evidence of consensual and caring partnerships between same-sex couples in antiquity?

The Historical Data

The ancient cultures that were the social context for the writing of the New Testament knew of same-sex marriage. In some of the literature that survives to us, writers actually use the term "marriage" – although, in certain instances at least, clearly with a mocking tone. At other times, without using the word "marriage," a writer is unquestionably citing an instance of what the affirming community of our time would describe as a lifelong, monogamous, mutual, and loving gay relationship.

In fairness, it should be admitted by all parties to this discussion that sexual curiosity, fantasies, experimentations, short-term behaviors, long-term lifestyles, and judgments of one's own and others' sexual lives were surely as varied in the ancient world as they are today. Does anyone really think – whether from a Judeo-Christian historical point of view or from the perspective of an atheist who projects Darwinian evolutionary theories onto human development – that there has ever been a universal norm of sexual behavior? A time when all gendered humans were exclusively heterosexual? Monogamous in their pairings – whether with the same or opposite sex? Committed and faithful to a single partner? All promiscuous and abusive? Enraptured by the possibility of child sex? Eager to murder anyone who would have sex with a pre-pubescent child – whether male or female? I'm sure you get my point by now. You also realize that the "list" of attitudes and behaviors could become infinitely and nauseatingly long.

So does it really seem reasonable to think that the possibility of long-term, committed, authentically caring, and mutually supportive same-sex relationships had not been explored in Egypt, Assyria, Babylon, Greece, or Rome? Five hundred or 1,500 years ago? Centuries before the birth of Jesus of Nazareth? By the contemporaries of Jesus and Paul? Or that they would not have known about such minority experiments in human relations? *Please!* As a matter of fact, we know these "alternative lifestyles" were around in biblical times. And it takes considerable credulity to think that Christians evaluating and reacting to ethical norms and behaviors of their time would be unaware of those modes of living.

At the same time, is it likely that Jesus and Paul would have used twenty-first century terminology with reference to sexuality? Since terms such as "heterosexual" and "homosexual" did not appear in any language before being coined in German in a private correspondence in 1868 and making its way into English in a book published in 1892, we would not expect to find their precise equivalents in Paul's letters. Nor would we find words such as bisexual, pansexual, transexual, or asexual. What about straight or gay – as descriptors of a person's sexual orientation and/or behavior? So, was Alexander the Great gay or bisexual? Was Nero bisexual or gay, married to Sporus[13] or suffering from gender dysphoria?

For fear of being perceived as dismissive and disrespectful of those who are wrestling with these issues, I have no such intent. I am simply trying to make explicit the obvious-but-overlooked fact that there are very few (if any!) new elements to human nature and behavior across history. Altruism, narcissism, unselfishness, explosive temper, middle-child mellowness, optimism, sadomasochism – these are our technical-to-slang terms to name what has always existed and will always reappear in human cultures. As will be made obvious directly, the Greeks even spoke in their myths and musings of gender-reassignment surgeries. (They did not, of course, use our modern expression "gender-reassignment surgery" in naming it.)

> **Greek "Marriage" of Same-Sex Partners**
>
> Such a relationship is both more and less than any variety of heterosexual coupling in the ancient world, most of which were property arrangements – except those of concubine and lover; few were based on emotional or affective considerations or hopes (again, excepting concubine and lover).
>
> In this study, "marriage," "matrimony," "nuptial," "conjugal," and comparable terms have been applied to premodern couplings according to the definition that would have applied at the time – insofar as it can be assessed – rather than in their familiar modern meanings. . . . Because my aim has been in large measure to determine whether forms of premodern same-sex couplings constituted "marriages," and since there is no historical reason to suppose they could not – much as personal distaste or prejudice might predispose some individuals to believe the contrary – I have on the one hand employed the most general phraseology I could ("union," "coupling," etc.) and on the other not shrunk from applying "marriage" or related terms when it has seemed the most accurate description.
>
> Greek terminology regarding marriage was so fluid that it is nearly impossible to infer the precise nature of a relationship from words alone.
>
> — John Boswell

It should also be noted that there were voices raised within pre-Christian Greek society and in later non-Christian thinkers to protest what many regarded as the depravity and excesses of certain sexual practices. Of course, there were the Torah-affirming Jews such as Philo (*ca.* 20 B.C.– *ca.* A.D.50), but they were a small percentage of the population.

Prior to the philosophical musings of Michel Foucault, terms such as "sexual orientation," "sexual identity," and "sex/sexuality as a social construct" either were not part of the discussion of sexuality or were defined differently than in today's professional literature. But these are all illustrations of my point here that *it is the terminology rather than the mental and physical actions that have changed* in the centuries that have come and gone since ancient times.

Plato and His Greek Peers-Heirs

The best-known depiction of a same-sex relationship that has all the earmarks comparable to a marital relationship in Greek literature is found in Plato's *Symposium* – a document that dates from 385-375 B.C. This dialogue offers a Greek perspective on how the human race was created, came to be gendered, why some people are inclined to persons of the same sex – in today's vocabulary, we would say they were born with that "orientation" – and we meet a male-male couple that is something over 30 years in their time as life partners.

The *Symposium* is often called "Plato's poetic and dramatic masterpiece."[14] Titled from a common event in ancient Greek culture called a *symposion*, the dialogue reflects the practice of males retiring after a banquet to a place where they would drink, enjoy entertainment of various kinds (e.g., flute-players, dancers, games), and engage in conversation or debate. The symposiasts in Plato's dialogue have met to celebrate the playwright Agathon's first successful production. The six men agree to make speeches in turn on love (Gk, *erōs*).

The speakers all presume and reflect different elements of the Greek practice of *paiderastia* that the wealthy circles of Athenian society practiced at the time.[15] Specific to the purpose of this book, historians and classicists know that this practice did not always end when the *erōmenos* reached his adult status – signified in both literature and paintings by his growth of a beard. Described as a social convention between an older man and a boy, modern depictions of *paiderastia* often leave the impression of strict rules that put an end to the *erastēs-erōmenos* relationship at the latter's entry into manhood and his move to male-female courtship, marriage, and fatherhood himself – including the right to take an *erōmenos* now himself. A widely published historian and antiquarian anthropologist whose special focus is Platonic studies explains:

> All that has just been said about *paiderastia* might allow us to think that sexual relations between males in archaic and classical Greece were limited to this context of social conventions, obeying very strict rules, and from which desire and pleasure were supposedly banished at least for the younger male; and that these rules excluded permanence. Yet such was not the case. In his speech, Aristophanes insists on the existence of very powerful relations, which are long lasting, between individuals of the same sex. Agathon and Pausanias are examples of this.[16]

The six central speeches in the *Symposium* come from persons of different backgrounds, and – as usual within the Platonic corpus – Socrates is allowed to have the final word. Plato uses his characters to bring various points of view on the god Eros and the human qualities of *erōs* into the evening's discussion. At the end, a drunken seventh person enters and provides still a final insight to the entire night. Without dragging you through the entire document, several key pieces of evidence about Greek views of homosexual orientation, the moral status of same-sex love, and long-term commitments among gay persons are significant to this study.

John Boswell has called attention to the importance of the speech made by Aristophanes to the subject of same-sex orientation, attraction, and intercourse. Although Aristophanes is a comic poet and has been minimized by some affirming writers for that reason, it is important to note that he both begins and ends his speech with a disclaimer of comedic intent. When his turn to speak came, Eryximachus in effect asks if he will be "making jokes" and trying to "say something funny" – against which Eryximachus should "put up my guard against you."[17] Aristophanes explicitly disclaimed any such intent and explained that he feared just such a reaction from a man of science – Eryximachus was a physician – when he was planning to speak of the god Eros. His fear was that he would be seen as a comic and his speech deemed "ridiculous."[18] So he makes his presentation and closes, "Now don't get ideas, Eryximachus, and turn this speech into a comedy. Don't think I'm pointing this at Pausanias and Agathon."[19] (The reference to Pausanias and Agathon will become clear directly.)

Even if someone were to insist, "But I will not relent that Aristophanes was speaking in jest, relating a mere 'myth' about human origins, and perhaps making fun of Pausanias and Agathon for their erotic ties." The stubborn fact remains after such an objection is made that the *Symposium* speaks directly to the topics of male-male and female-female sex. Even if one takes the references to be mocking, they are directed toward persons who are living the experience in the room. Even though pederastic coupling had a significant degree of institutional status, there can be no reasonable doubt that couples other than the one actually involved in this dialogue maintained their relationship as adult males – with exclusivity, permanence, and public awareness.

A Greek View of Sexual "Orientaion"

Aristophanes traces the Greek myth of how Zeus[20] created human beings in order to account for human nature and our varied sexual preferences.[21] Humans were created originally in three forms – male, female, and "androgynous" persons. Formed as offspring of the sun (male), Earth (female), and moon (androgynous), all three had a spherical shape. Furthermore, they were all quite powerful. They had such strength, in fact, that they "tried to make an ascent to heaven so as to attack the gods." To deal with such treachery, the gods originally thought to "wipe out the human race with thunderbolts and kill them all off." But Zeus came up with a plan that split each of the three types of human beings in half. "Now, since their natural form had been cut in two, each one longed for its own other half," explained Aristophanes. However, because of the placement of their genitals, they could not reproduce and were dying.

So Zeus brought about this relocation of genitals, and in doing so he invented interior reproduction, *by the man in the woman*. The purpose of this was so that, when a man embraced a woman, he would cast his seed and they would have children; but when male embraced male, they would at least have the satisfaction of intercourse, after which they could stop embracing, return to their jobs, and look after other needs in life. This, then, is the source of our desire to love each other. Love is born into every human being; it calls back the halves of our original nature together; it tries to make one out of two and heal the wound of human nature.

Each of us, then, is a "matching half" of a human whole, because each was sliced like a flatfish, two out of one, and each of us is always seeking the half that matches him. That's why a man who is split from the double sort (which used to be called "androgynous") runs after woman. Many lecherous men have come from this class, and so do the lecherous women who run after men. Women who are split from a woman, however, pay no attention at all to men; they are oriented more towards women, and lesbians come from this class. People who are split from a male are male-oriented. While they are boys because they are chips off the male block, they love men and enjoy lying with men and being embraced by men; those are the best of boys and lads, because they are the most manly in their nature. Of course, some

> **Lifelong Same-Sex Commitments**
>
> Pausanias thus gives a rationale for Athenians who are attracted to post-adolescent males. In this he challenges the traditional norm: most Greeks considered beardless boys the more appropriate objects of desire. To argue that his is no merely eccentric taste, Pausanias appeals to two other Greek values: pleasure in intellectual converse (which only older youths are capable of) and enduring fidelity.
>
> The love of boys is fleeting, but devotees of the Uranian Aphrodite who choose young men, he claims, "are ready to be faithful to their companions, and pass their whole life with them, not to take them in their inexperience and . . . then run away to others" (Symposium 181b-d).
>
> We know that many Greeks had relations with both women and boys. But Pausanias clearly identifies another class of man – a class who are exclusively devoted to their own sex, approximating the modern conception of the "homosexual." This idea of a homosexual "orientation," though by no means central to Greek thinking as it is to ours, was certainly understood by Plato and his contemporaries.
>
> — Louis Crompton

say such boys are shameless, but they're lying. It's not because they have no shame that such boys do this, you see, but because they are bold and brave and masculine, and they tend to cherish what is like themselves. Do you want me to prove it? Look, these are the only kind of boys who grow up to be real men in politics. When they're grown men, they are lovers of young men (Gk verb, *paiderastousi* = they are boy-lovers), and they naturally pay no attention to marriage or to making babies, except insofar as they are required by local custom. They, however, are quite satisfied to live their lives with one another unmarried. In every way, then, this sort of man grows up as a lover of young men (Gk noun, *paiderastēs* = lover of boys) and a lover of Love, always rejoicing in his own kind.[22]

To this point, Aristophanes clearly is speaking of male-male relationships in terms of Athenian pederastic relationships. The tone is defensive, arguing that there is nothing shameful or effeminate about a young man living as an *erōmenos*. In his relationship with his adult male lover, he is being prepared for his own adult place in society. Interestingly, although he mentions female-female pairing, he does not pursue it further.[23]

At this point, Plato has Aristophanes move from the institutionalized role of pederasty in Athens to a higher level of relationship. He has just observed that it is only the androgenous creatures who naturally seek to unite with their former halves via union with the opposite sex. From this fact, he comments on the phenomenon that both male-female and female-male "seeking the half that matches" has been known to create problems. Specifically, that tendency is designated – whether in the male or the female – "lecherous" men/women (Gk, *philandroi*), with women additionally said to "run after [married] men" (Gk, *moicheutriai*).[24]

It seems rather clear that subcategories of sexual interest and activity are indicated here that reflect Greek sentiment from Plato's time. As one of the most respected Plato scholars of the previous generation put it: "It is well known that homosexual love alone was generally regarded by the Greeks as fulfilling the highest desires of men, and that the love of men for women was little more than a means of procreation."[25] Thus, the least significant feature of erotic attachment would be male-female intercourse, for it is only the sort of relationship "required by local custom." While Zeus nevertheless realized it was pragmatically the most important type of sexual intercourse for keeping the human species alive, the emphasis is clearly on the practical role of male-female sex for reproduction. The highest and purest form of sex is, however, that between males, for – as the closing line says – it is only male-male love that can establish one as a "lover of Love" or "lover of the god Eros." Somewhere in between lies woman-woman love, the class from which lesbians (Gk, *tetrammenai*) arise.

What, then, is to be said of the highest form of love? Is it pederastic in nature? Does it involve an older mentor and younger pupil? It may begin either

> **Aristotle on Nature or Nurture**
> Aristotle was Plato's pupil and studied with him for two decades at the Academy. Their temperaments, however, contrasted. Plato was the poetic utopian, Aristotle the down-to-earth scientist and social observer. . . .
> Nowhere does Aristotle strike the idealizing note of Plato and Plutarch [on pederasty]. On the other hand, his comments on the passive adult in the Nicomachean Ethics are neither contemptuous in the popular style of Aristophanes nor moralizing in the style of Plato. Rather, they smack of the clinician who seeks a scientific explanation for human behavior.
> He thinks that male sexual passivity may sometimes be classified with plucking out the hair or nail-biting as "morbid propensities . . . acquired by habit," as in the case of those "who have been abused from childhood." Other cases appear to result from "natural disposition."
> — Louis Crompton

there or later in life, but it reaches its full potential only as the two continue their same-sex relationship in loving commitment as adults over time. Thus, the following strong assertion emerges:

> And so, when a person meets the half that is his very own, whatever his orientation, whether it's to young men or not, then something wonderful happens: the two are struck from their senses by love, by a sense of belonging to one another, and by desire, and they don't want to be separated from one another, not even for a moment. These are the people who finish out their lives together and still cannot say what it is they want from one another.[26]

The analysis of the *Symposium* offered here is the same in all its essentials with that offered by John Boswell in his *Same-Sex Unions in Premodern Europe*. Boswell's status as a linguistic scholar and the founder of Yale University's Lesbian and Gay Studies Center in the 1980s should establish him as unbiased toward the traditional case I am arguing. At the end of his summary of such key points as the halves of the original female beings – using Boswell's own translations – "have practically no interest in men" but instead form unions with women and that the halves of the male beings "have no natural inclination for [heterosexual] marriage or parenting." From the larger dialogue and from the closing line about how they "finish out their lives together," Boswell comments:

> This tale accounts for precisely the range of sexual preference familiar to modern readers: heterosexuals, male homosexuals, and lesbians, all of whom have, according to the myth, permanent and innate sexual preferences. It suggests, moreover, that each group would form *roughly comparable* lifelong, exclusive attachments. (Note that the halves of the beings would be of the same age and social status.) Although other views of homosexual relations can be elicited from literature of the period, this is one of relatively few *analytical explanations* of erotic interest (as opposed to casual observations of custom), and issues from the pen of an extraordinarily thoughtful and articulate observer, himself involved in both a heterosexual union and same-sex attachments.[27]

Lifelong Same-Sex Commitment

To the claim that only pederasty was known in ancient cultures, where there was a notable difference in age between the male partners, Pausanias' speech in the *Symposium* can be quoted as a direct rebuttal. He first distinguishes between two types of love. The first he calls "Common Aphrodite's Love"; it is the sort of passion that attaches to orgasmic ecstasy in the body, is common to those who take either male or female partners, and "all they care about is completing the sexual act."[28] By contrast, he offers "Love of Heavenly Aphrodite," which is superior; it is attracted to males, "prefers older ones whose cheeks are showing the first traces of a beard" – a sign that they have begun to form minds of their own, and forms lasting bonds. "I am convinced that a man who falls in love with a young man of this age is generally prepared to share everything with the one he loves," insists Pausanias, "he is eager, in fact, to spend the rest of his own life with him.[29]

As a matter of fact, the relationship between Pausanias and his fellow-symposiast, Agathon, is an example of the very sort of lifelong, monogamous, mutual and loving gay relationships that affirming scholars quoted at the beginning of this chapter insist on denying ever existed in ancient cultures. Their committed and exclusive relationship as lovers had extended over more than three decades.[30] So how can writers make a serious claim that the only male-male sexual coupling known from antiquity is the *erastēs-erōmenos* relationship? How can they persist in the assertion that

CHAPTER 9: COMMITTED SAME-SEX RELATIONSHIPS – GREEK

ongoing permanent relationships between persons of the same sex are never documented in the extant literature? How can they say with confidence that nothing comparable to our modern idea of homosexual orientation can be found in that same literature? Such claims fly in the face of hard evidence to the contrary.

It is no less than Pausanias himself who, in his speech prior to that of Aristophanes, scorns the "vile man" and "vulgar lover" whose passion is focused principally on sensual delight in a young man and then casts him aside as the latter's physical beauty fades. The *erastēs* who moves on to yet another youthful *erōmenos* is vile and vulgar precisely because of the infidelity his behavior exhibits. The *erastēs* with the "right sort of character" honors his words of love by remaining true to his beloved "for life." Thus, Pausanias winds up defending Athenian *paiderastia* with language that sounds very much like premarital counsel about fidelity.

> **"Enlightened" Greek Attitudes?**
> Also ironic is the notion that Greek ideas about sexuality should be seen as a liberating force, a counterweight to our own prejudices. Yes, same-sex behavior and affection were given greater leeway in Greece than they traditionally have been in the Judeo-Christian world – but only if they conformed to certain rigid notions of masculinity, in which grown men were expected to be active, dominant, penetrating partners, and were subject to severe disapproval if they varied from this norm.
> Further, if we are to use the Greeks as models of enlightenment concerning homosexuality, does this imply acceptance of their entire misogynistic gender system? For classicists to testify in court about the Greeks' philosophy, their loves, their ideas of friendship and the common good, yet passing over in silence the seclusion and denigration of women that were a contributing, and perhaps a necessary, precondition for the glories of their masculinist culture, seems at best bitterly ironic, at worse a betrayal of our scholarship and our personal moral principles.
> — Jeffrey Carnes

> To give oneself to a vile man in a vile way is truly disgraceful behavior; by contrast, it is perfectly honorable to give oneself honorably to the right man. Now you may want to know who counts as vile in this context. I'll tell you: it is the common, vulgar lover, who loves the body rather than the soul, the man whose love is bound to be inconstant, since what he loves is itself mutable and unstable. The moment the body is no longer in bloom, "he flies off and away," his promises and vows in tatters behind him. How different from this is a man who loves the right sort of character, and who remains its lover for life, attached as he is to something that is permanent.[31]

In his comments on the *Symposium*, Crompton focuses on the sort of same-sex partner Pausanias desired as a partner for the rest of his life

217

> We know that many Greeks had relations with both women and boys. But Pausanias clearly identifies another class of man – a *class* who are exclusively devoted to their own sex, approximating the modern conception of the "homosexual." This idea of a homosexual "orientation," though by no means central to Greek thinking as it is to ours, was certainly understood by Plato and his contemporaries.[32]

An online listing of several documented same-sex couples in classical Greek literature by the History Department at Fordham University includes figures from the fifth through second centuries B.C. Specifically, the list offers "textual references for long-term (in some cases life-long) homosexual relationships in the Greek texts."[33] In addition to Pausanias and Agathon, it includes such couples as Aristogeiton and Harmodius, Athenians credited by Thycydides for overthrowing the tyrant Hippias and establishing a democracy; Philolaus and Diocles, a lifelong relationship between a lawgiver at Thebes and an Olympic athlete, referenced in Aristotle's *Politics*; Orestes and Pylades, celebrated in (Pseudo-)Lucian's *Erōtes* ("Loves" or, sometimes titled, "Two Kinds of Love" in which male-male sexual experience is praised for its superiority to male-female) for their faithful devotion over a lifetime.

Still another example of same-sex devotion is the well-known story of the "Sacred Band of Thebes."

> Theban male lovers swore oaths of loyalty at the tomb of Iolaus. Their pledges were sober commitments, made in the presence of a powerful ghost. A pledge of love, Gorgidas reasoned, might support the new Theban state as much as his old pledge of service. Thinking along these lines, he embarked on an experiment. He recruited male couples, three hundred men altogether, and formed them into an infantry corps: the Sacred Band of Thebes.[34]

The historical background of this fighting band is from Plutarch's *Life of Pelopidas*. The Thebans created a military battalion of 300 warriors as a weapon against Sparta, believing that these 150 same-sex couples would fight more intensely in defense of their partners. A likely element in the decision to create this combat force was the local legend of Heracles and Iolaus. A Greek mortal hero for having assisted Heracles in, among other things, slaying the Hydra, Iolaus' tomb was in Thebes. Building on the reputed love between Hercules and Iolaus, a cult formed around the latter and same-sex lovers were said by Plutarch to go to his grave to pledge their devotion to each other.[35] In translating this section, older versions tend to use the discreet terms "lovers and beloved" to describe them, but Boswell argues for the more inclusive "same-sex lovers."[36] Classics professor Romm writes: "Such pledges of love, perhaps signifying life-long and exclusive commitments – in effect, same-sex marriages – were unique to Thebes."[37] As the evidence already given here would indicate, the word "unique" would be highly suspect.

Non-Literary Evidence of Consensual Unions

More examples of non-pederastic same-sex couples are documented by Mark Smith – along with a reference to the evidential value of vase paintings from the Greek period. Citing the work of Charles Hupperts, he disputes Scroggs' claim that pederasty was the only model of male-male sexual intercourse documented from that time.

> Scroggs knows of no comparable depictions of two adults engaging in homosexual activity. Hupperts, however, has discovered in his study of Attic Black-Figure vases, at least twelve homosexual scenes involving two or more bearded men. From such evidence he concludes, "I think I have shown enough vases to justify my conclusion that paederasty wasn't the only form of homosexual practice in Attica of the sixth century. According to the vases boys, youths or men of equal age could have been involved in a love affair" (263-264). This artistic evidence is cause enough for us to suspect that homosexual activity involving two boys or two men was more than just an exceptional phenomenon.[38]

Thomas Hubbard has also argued from Greek art of the period that man-boy sex was by no means the only type of same-sex practice known in classical Greece.

> Greek homosexual activity, despite popular misconceptions, was not restricted to man-boy pairs. Vase-painting shows numerous scenes where there is little or no apparent difference in age between the young wooer and his object of courtship . . . as well as graphic scenes of sexual experimentation between youths.[39]

The revisionist claim that same-sex relationships in ancient times were either disapproved because they were always exploitative in nature or outside the realm of mutual love and long-term monogamous commitment is a mistake that no one should make who has access to scholarly research of the past hundred years. As this chapter has shown, detailed data and documentation on this point simply are not difficult to find. And Plato, Aristotle, or data about the Theban warriors can hardly be deemed obscure sources about ancient Greek culture that would be hard to find. It seems that one must either accept the literary and artistic evidence for what it is or minimize/ignore it for the sake of an "agenda."

But what about the Roman Empire? What of the immediate attitudes and practices of the time period in which Jesus lived and with which Paul interacted as a missionary and theologian? Had the Romans rejected and eliminated the public acceptance of same-sex unions that involved care and commitment? The next chapter will address these questions.

ENDNOTES

1. Some evidence suggests this process was even more mandatory in Sparta than Athens because of the warrior culture that dominated. Cf. Crompton, *Homosexuality & Civilization*, 6-10.

2. Jeffrey Carnes, "Plato in the Courtroom: The Surprising Influence of the *Symposium* on Legal Theory," in J.H. Lesher, Debra Nails, and Frisbee C.C. Sheffield, *Plato's Symposium: Issues in Interpretation and Reception* (Cambridge, MA: Harvard University Press, 2006), 279.

3. Scroggs, *New Testament and Homosexuality*, 126.

4. James V. Brownson, *Bible, Gender, Sexuality: Reframing the Church's Debate on Same-Sex Relationships* (Grand Rapids: Eerdmans Publishing Co., 2013), 107.

5. Achtemeier, *The Bible's Yes*, 82.

6. Ibid., 92. Similar claims are made multiple times in Achtemeier's book (cf. 77, 110), indicating the significance the writer attaches to the alleged non-awareness of the ancient world of same-sex attraction that could lead to exclusive, long-term, and loving relationships.

7. From a sermon manuscript delivered by Dale Pauls on April 26, 2015, and referenced and distributed by him at the CenterPeace Conference 2022 held on November 5, 2022. The sermon can be found online at https://www.dropbox.com/s/5fgpp4dxyq4ufcu/Affirmation%2C%20And%20on%20his%20way%20he%20met%20an%20Ethiopian%20eunuch.doc?dl=0. Accessed March 15, 2023.

8. Special pleading is an informal fallacy that occurs when a writer or speaker builds a case by choosing to ignore information that is not favorable to what is being argued.

9. The distinction made here between "marriages" and "committed unions" is an acknowledgment that most marriages and their social equivalents in the ancient world were not documented as we would today. Sometimes there was a ceremony where a handshake and statement of intent declared a couple's relationship; more often, a couple simply began life together and formed what what we might today call a common-law marriage. Jewish marital protocols were quite different from Greek and Roman practice and reflect the biblical view of marriage established in the creation narrative of Genesis. The late John Boswell makes some very interesting comments on what should be counted as "marriage" in either ancient or modern cultures and between same-sex or opposite-sex couples in his *Christianity, Social Tolerance, and Homosexuality*, 25-26.

10. William Loader, *Sexuality in the New Testament: Understanding the Key Texts* (Louisville: Westminster John Knox, 2010), 23.

11. Joseph Goldstein, "U.S. Soldiers Told to Ignore Sexual Abuse of Boys by Afghan Allies," *New York Times* (Sept 20, 2015), accessed at https://www.nytimes.com/2015/09/21/world/asia/us-soldiers-told-to-ignore-afghan-allies-abuse-of-boys.html. Five years before this article in the *New York Times*, PBS aired a

documentary on this sordid practice. Cf. "The Dancing Boys of Afghanistan," *PBS Frontline* (April 20, 2010), accessed at https://www.pbs.org/wgbh/pages/frontline/dancingboys. Accessed March 15, 2023.

12. William Loader, *Making Sense of Sex* (Grand Rapids: Eerdmans Publishing Co., 2013), 137.

13. In A.D. 67, Nero had a male slave castrated and then married him in a public ceremony that was complete with dowry, bridal veil, and the trappings of a "wedding night" and celebration of their union.

14. John M. Cooper, *Plato: Complete Works* (Indianapolis: Hackett Publishing Co., 1997), 457. Note: English translation of the *Symposium* are from this edition, unless otherwise indicated.

15. An overview of Greek *paiderastia* is found in the previous chapter of this book. Unlike our modern term "pederasty," which refers to sexual activity between an adult male and a boy, Greek *paiderastia* was a "social institution" that – while involving sexual activity – was accepted without shame as a means of education for young men between the approximate ages of 12 and 20 and introduced them to their mentors' professions and circles of political influence.

16. Luc Brisson, "Agathon, Pausanias, and Diotima in Plato's *Symposium: Paiderastia* and *Philosophia*," in Lesher et alia, *Plato's Symposium*, 235.

17. Plato, *Symposium* 189a.

18. Plato, *Symposium* 189b.

19. Plato, *Symposium* 193c.

20. There are certain Greek myths that seem particularly important to (or constructed for) the "legitimizing" of behaviors likely to be called in question. For example, the myth of Zeus and Ganymede seems particularly framed to justify pederasty. Zeus takes the form of an eagle to capture a beautiful boy named Ganymede, make him his cupbearer and lover, and bestow immortality upon him. If the principal god in the Greek pantheon of deities is permitted to have a male lover, how can mere mortals be wrong in doing so?

21. Plato, *Symposium* 189d-191d.

22. Plato, *Symposium* 191c-192b.

23. It should also be noted that the issue of marriage comes up in this text, and the presumption is that what society regards as a "marriage" involves "making babies" and accommodating "local custom." That is, marriage across the centuries and in Greek as well as Jewish (biblical) culture was the union of a male and female potential for procreation. While there is no lament here that males and females could not "marry" in their culture, the clear presumption is that the "other half" of the bifurcated male and female were inclined to a relationship that paralleled marriage – except for the potential to bear children.

24. The translation here is somewhat complex because of the circumstances being described and the unusual words employed. Plato says that the halved-androgynous person is at risk of becoming φιλογύναικες (a lover of women or one who runs after women) to the degree that [with unattached females] he may be improper and coarse with his attentions or even [with married women] μοικός (a man involved with violating a marital covenant). Similarly, the other half of such a separation is at risk of being φίλανδρος (a lover of men or one who runs after men) and thus is lewd with males or even [with married men] μοιχεύτριαι (a woman who violates a marriage contract). Cooper's translation is likely as good as any. The Loeb translation is more wooden but may bring out the nuance a bit more clearly: "All the men who are sections of that composite sex that at first was called man-woman are woman-courters; our adulterers are mostly descended from that sex, whence are derives our man-courting women and adulteresses." [Plato, *Lysis, Symposium, Gorgias*, trans. W.R.M. Lamb, Loeb Classical Library (Cambridge, MA: Harvard University Press, 1925), III. 141. In both biblical and civil codes in antiquity, seduction of a married person or a married person's seduction of an alternate sexual partner (whether single or married) is considered far more serious and subject to serious punishment.

25. G.M.A. Grube, *Plato's Thought* (Indianapolis: Hackett Publishing Co., 1980), 87.

26. Plato, *Symposium*, 192c

27. John Boswell, *Same-Sex Unions in Premodern Europe* (New York: Villard Books, 1994), 59.

28. Plato, *Symposium* 181b.

29. Plato, *Symposium* 181d.

30. Boswell, *Same-Sex Unions*, 60.

31. Plato, *Symposium* 183d-e.

32. Crompton, *Homosexuality & Civilization*, 57.

33. Paul Halsall, "Greek Couples," a graduate essay posted by Fordham University's "Internet History Sourcebooks Project." Accessed at https://sourcebooks.fordham.edu/pwh/gkcouples.asp.

34. Romm, *The Sacred Band*, 28-29.

35. Plutarch, *Erotikos* 761d.

36. Boswell, *Same-Sex Unions*, 63-64.

37. James Romm, "Ancient Partners in Love and War," *Wall Street Journal*, July 29, 2021, https://www.wsj.com/articles/ancient-partners-in-love-and-war-11627566958.

38. Mark D. Smith, "Ancient Bisexuality and the Interpretation of Romans 1:26-27," *Journal of the American Academy of Religion* 64 (Summer 1996), 234. Note: A footnote to the Smith article explains the significance of the "bearded men" in the vase paintings. "Boys are differentiated from men in the iconography of this period by the boys appearing without beards."

39. Hubbard, *Homosexuality in Greece and Rome*, 5.

> *"[Galba's] sexual inclination was for men, whom he preferred strong and mature. . . . He not only welcomed [Icelus] frankly with the most intimate of kisses, but begged him to prepare for sexual indulgence, and promptly took him aside."*
> – Suetonius, writing of Emperor Galba

CHAPTER 10

Committed Same-Sex Relationships in Roman Culture

As important as the background materials in Chapter 9 are for understanding the culture, norms, and vocabulary of Greece, the fact remains that the New Testament was not written in the heyday of Hellenism. The overlapping lives and careers of Socrates, Plato, and Aristotle are from a time prior to Jesus of Nazareth. So we move here to the prevailing social situation of the Roman Empire in the time of Jesus, Peter, Paul, and the first few generations of Christians.

At the start of this chapter, I probably should warn you that examples of same-sex couples and marriages you will meet in the Roman period may get tiresome. Lest they become offensive, they are duplicated beyond what I think is necessary to show how wrong it is for people to claim that long-term, covenanted, and caring same-sex relationships were unknown then. To say it another way, Scroggs, Gushee, and others are seriously mistaken to claim that the New Testament denunciations of homosexual activity can only be taken to refer to pederasty, prostitution, or rape – and not the sort of relationships they defend for our time.

After Alexander the Great died (323 B.C.), his short-lived empire was fragmented among his warring generals and eventually gave way to the emerging power that was to become the Roman Empire. Following the death of Julius Caesar in March of 44 B.C., the period of the Roman Republic (509-31 B.C.) soon came to an end. Even as the republican period was winding down, however, General Pompey had so enlarged the geography, conquered population, and revenue base that small city-state governing institutions (i.e., the Greek model) had become impractical. Fighting a series of civil wars led by Rome's most famous generals, it was Octavian who emerged the victor. He took the title-name Augustus and established himself as the single imperial ruler. The beginning of what history knows as the Roman Empire (31 B.C. – A.D. 476) traces to his accession to power in 31 B.C.

It was Augustus who called for the census that sent Joseph and Mary from their home in Nazareth to Bethlehem (Luke 2:1-7). Augustus was followed to the throne by his adopted son, Tiberius, upon his death in A.D. 14. It was Tiberius whose reign (A.D. 14-37) extended over the ministry and death of Jesus.

It is important to note, however, the blending of Greek and Roman cultures that occurred during this period. As the Roman Empire was strengthening its military might and ultimately conquering the lesser Greek kingdoms formed after Alexander's death, major elements of Greek architecture, literature, philosophy, art, and language were infiltrating Roman life. The Romans viewed Greek culture to be older and considerably more sophisticated than their own. Hellenization is the term we use to identify the widespread adoption of Greek ways throughout the expanding Roman Empire. Thus, Greek rather than Latin was the *lingua franca* of the Mediterranean world for fully half a millennium after the death of Alexander the Great and is the language in which the New Testament was originally circulated.

How does this interchange between Athens and Rome play out in terms of family, sexuality, and the expansion of the Christian faith? More specifically still, how alike or different were Roman attitudes toward same-sex behaviors when compared to Greek models? What implications are there for our reading of the biblical record that was produced under those cultural assumptions and practices?

When in Rome . . .

Contrary to the erotic portrayals of sex in movie versions of the Roman Empire, Roman culture generally regarded sex simply as a means of necessary satisfaction for an enduring need and pleasure – on par with food, drink, theater, and other entertainments. Among such persons, the "abnormal" mindset more likely would have been exclusive devotion to male or female partners. A man's behavior was seen as "immoral" only if – whether with food, theater, or sex – he exhibited what various writers of the time called *akrasia* (i.e., lack of control over one's appetites). Such an out-of-control person – whether male or female[1] – would likely become an object of contempt. The ethical opposite to *akrasia* both in Greek writers generally and in the New Testament as well (cf. Acts 24:25; Gal 5:23; 2 Pet 1:6) was *enkrateia* (self-control, self-mastery).

As additional cultural context, remember that the concepts of *family* and *marital fidelity* were radically different in the first Christian century than the views we are inclined to read back into the New Testament and other ancient documents from our time. As Longnecker has observed, the role of a wife was to provide legitimate heirs to the householder. Beyond that, she had no expectation or right to demand that her husband's sexual engagements would be exclusive to her. Whatever displeasure or jealousy a wife might have felt or expressed would not have been expected to alter her husband's behavior.

> In fact, Plutarch, the Roman biographer and prolific essayist, peddled the idea that a man's infidelity should actually be seen as a compliment to his wife and a sign of respect for her, since he had chosen to share "his debauchery, licentiousness, and wantonness with another woman" rather than degrading his own wife with them (*Moralia* 140B).[2]

The Moral Code of Rome

The Romans did have an abiding set of moral guidelines called the mos maiorum ("the way of the elders"), a largely accepted and unwritten code of good conduct. . . . The written laws also included sexual offences, including rape, which could carry a death sentence. Prostitutes (and sometimes entertainers and actors) were not given this legal protection and the rape of a slave would only be considered a crime of property damage against the slave's owner.

Marriage itself was, in reality, a lopsided affair. Women who married weren't expected to attain any pleasure or enjoyment from it – they simply wedded in order to abide by the moral code and procreate. Moreover, the subservient wife was expected to turn a blind eye to her husband's sexual infidelity. Males were allowed to sleep around as much as they liked so long as their mistress was unmarried, or, if they were with a boy, he was over a certain age.

Brothels, prostitutes and dancing girls were all considered to be 'fair game', as were older males – on the condition that he was to be submissive. Being passive was considered women's work: men who submitted were considered deficient in vir and in virtus – they were denounced and reviled as effeminate. . . .

There was a strong sexual element in much of Roman religion. The Vestal Virgins were celibate in order to keep them independent of male control, but other religious ceremonies celebrated prostitution.

— Colin Ricketts

While we should not doubt that some pagan marriages saw romantic love and exclusive commitment develop between the partners, the clear picture any student of the period acquires is that Roman marriages were fundamentally transactional. That is, the marriages of both men and women of higher standing were typically arranged by their families.[3] Likely married by age 14 or 15 – and sometimes as young as 12 – the woman's father would have sought some degree of social respectability and financial prospects for her. It would reflect poorly on him to give his daughter to an irresponsible man with a bad reputation. The groom's family – with the man likely some ten or more years older than the bride – would be concerned not to put their son into a marriage beneath their social standing.

Married men in Athens and Rome, Ephesus and Corinth, or any other city of any size in the ancient world had access to public baths where both male and female prostitutes plied their trade. There were also, of course, brothels – such as those preserved in Pompeii with a variety of frescoes that identified the general activity of the house and/or specific services offered by the various providers in that house.

Shocking as these patterns sound to most of us, they were both commonplace and socially acceptable in the world of the larger Roman Empire. Clement of Alexandria (*ca.* 150-215) wrote of shameless women who used nails on the soles of their sandals to leave the message "follow me" as their amorous proposition in the sand.[4] However, the Jewish communities in Roman cities and the Christian movement that grew out of them were exceptional in their uniformly negative attitude toward premarital sex, marital infidelity, and same-sex relationships.

But could all of these not be considered exploitative relationships? Might it be that the biblical language against both heterosexual and homosexual activity is directed only at those perverse and abusive settings? Must we not leave open the option that voluntary, committed, and loving same-sex relationships were not in view? Perhaps that they were unknown in those times?

The Roman View of Same-Sex Relationships

The evidence for widespread awareness and general acceptance of same-sex practices in the Roman Era is equally as abundant as for Greek culture. There are, however, some significant differences between the two.

First, there is general scholarly consensus that same-sex intercourse – while acceptable and presumed to be normal behavior in Roman society – carried negative implications for penetrated partners that was quite different from Greek pederasty. In Athens, Sparta, and other Greek cities, a boy chosen as an *erōmenos* was empowered by the process. His older lover would mentor him and eventually introduce him into public life. Then, in his own adult years, he would in turn be expected to be the *erastēs* to a younger male of his choice. The institutional custom was thereby perpetuated from generation to generation. There was no shame attached to the older, active man for having sex with his apprentice or to the younger, passive youth for allowing it. Even if the lower classes generally mocked the practice of *paiderastia* among the elites, the upper class saw it as appropriate and necessary.[5]

Romans, on the other hand, did not adopt the Greek pederastic model for its privileged class. Their culture was built on power and militaristic expansion. The primary desirable trait among all Roman males was masculinity (Lat, *virtus*[6] = strength, honor, courage). Among other things, this meant that a "real man" had certain lifestyle motivations that were different from Greek ideals. Education, public speaking, and family background were less important than strength, skill, and courage in combat. Therefore, it was much more likely in Rome than in Athens that a slave, gladiator, or soldier could attain citizenship and wealth.

There could be nothing about a Roman male that signaled weakness or vulnerability. To be acquiescent was to be pitiable. Showing mercy to a foe was unthinkable. Thus, any sign of frailty, impotence, or fear was derided as a "womanly" or "effeminate" disposition. This extended into their sexual mores in obvious ways. The truly Roman male was always the phallic penetrator. In an honor-shame culture that predated and later competed with Christian moral norms, it would be dishonorable for a freeborn Roman male to assume the passive role. To be penetrated in a sexual encounter – whether in intercrural, anal, or oral sex – would show that he was less than a powerful man and guilty of disgraceful conduct (Lat, *stuprum*). In the Roman view, it would make him deviant and effeminate and curtail his civil rights. He would be termed a "softie" or "soft one" (Gk, *malakos*) and thereby an object of derision.

Fox comments on first-century assumptions about same-sex relationships and the clear distinction between active and passive involvement.

Doctors considered active homosexuality to be natural, though in Rufus's view (c. 100 A.D.) it was more exhausting than heterosexuality because it was more violent. Passive homosexuality was another matter. There had been a familiar medical debate on the causes of this perverse preference, which was compared with the tastes of women "who pursue other women with an almost masculine jealousy." Some said that it was a disease of the mind, others an inherited defect at birth which had become ineradicable ever since it had entered the human race.[7]

Second, although the pederastic model of sex between older and younger males may have been assented to in particular instances, the Roman disdain for adult-youth sexual encounters likely created a higher percentage of same-sex relationships among persons of the same age than in Greece. In other words, life in the empire during the days of Jesus and Paul would have witnessed more scenes similar to those of modern times that we call "same-sex unions" or "same-sex marriage." Far from being unrelated to the modern loving, committed, and monogamous relationships that some scholars say they have been unable to locate in ancient times, they are the ones more likely to have been known by Paul and the Christian community outside the Jewish homeland.

Thus, one might well suspect that female-female and male-male sexual couplings are the ones he had most specifically in mind when his epistles refer to same-sex acts being against nature, shameful, and contrary to the gospel. This is by no means certain, but the possibility exists. It takes little imagination to sense the disapproval that would be triggered in a man raised as a Pharisee and who was zealous for right conduct based on the Law of Moses.[8] Is it difficult to imagine him walking alongside or overhearing a conversation between same-sex lovers that would offend his "traditional" background and beliefs? Is it not likely that he would have had the same internal flush of awkwardness and discomfort an Orthodox Jew or conservative Christian experiences in comparable settings in our own time?

Chapter 8 gave a cursory overview of Roman sexuality in the broader context of slavery, brothels, and public tolerance of behaviors that would be offensive to practically all modern persons – whether straight, gay, bisexual, or transgender. Think, for example, of the general revulsion of Western society against human trafficking. Although the term "human trafficking" is akin to the terms "homosexuality" and "LGBTQ+ community" as being of recent origin, the behaviors we identify with their use are not modern at all. This includes same-sex unions or same-sex marriage as well.

Consensual Adult Same-Sex Partnerships

Boswell's work observes that Roman same-sex relationships have been less studied than those of Greek culture. However, as the somewhat formal and institutionalized norms of Athens gave way to what is generally seen to be a "riotous and promiscuous sexuality" of Rome, he insists that "there were also many same-sex couples in the Roman world who lived together permanently, forming unions neither more nor less exclusive than those of the heterosexual couples around them."[9] To support his view, he proceeds to list a number of documented instances of same-sex couples – several of which use the term "marriage" of their relationship.

> **Public Recognition of Same-Sex Unions**
> A fourth type of homosexual relationship known in the ancient world consisted of formal unions – i.e., publicly recognized relationships entailing some change in status for one or both parties, comparable in this sense to heterosexual marriage.
> Cicero, though notoriously straightlaced, persuaded Curio the Elder to honor the debt his son had incurred on behalf of Antonius, to whom the younger Curio was, in Cicero's words, "united in a stable and permanent marriage, just as if he had given him a matron's stola" (Philippic 2.18.45). [The stola was the distinctive attire to identify a married Roman woman.]
> — John Boswell

The first instance Boswell cites is documented in the writings of Cicero (106-43 B.C.) and the second – which he terms "the most famous romantic couple in imperial Rome" – is from the second Christian century. Thus, from a century before Jesus and Paul to a century after their deaths, adult sexual coupling existed in the New Testament world. But how public were these relationships? Is it likely that Paul and his original readers would have connected them with his textual denunciations of male-male or female-female intercourse?

In view of the fact that Boswell's work may be suspect for his own bias in favor of an affirming view toward same-sex unions, we should take note of more recent research than his. Specifically, the published work of classicists such as Kyle Harper has pushed our knowledge of how gay persons lived and the literary description – both biblical and non-biblical – of their relationships. In his book that received the 2014 Award for Excellence from the American Academy of Religion, Harper summarizes the current status of work on Roman sexual culture by historians and classicists.

> But the most intriguing novelty, by far, is the evidence for male-male marriage in the early empire. If we had only the extravagant reports about Nero or Heliogabulus marrying their favorites, we might ascribe it to conventional senatorial animus, although the extreme and unnecessary level of detail about the ceremonies would be striking. But there is plenty of evidence besides. . . . Juvenal's second satire, written sometime in the early second century . . . claims that recently a man of wealth and status was given away in marriage to a man; he imagines that the day is near when male-male marriages will take place publicly and be recorded in the state's registers.[10]

As the available evidence has been forthcoming of late, we have also learned more about the existence of female-female sexual partnerships. Brooten – who favors the revisionist view over a traditional one – cites both Greek and Latin sources that reflect familiarity with consensual, mutual, and lifelong same-sex relationships for both males and females.[11] She also speaks to the issue of predisposition or sexual orientation.

> [C]ontrary to the view that the idea of sexual orientation did not develop until the nineteenth century, the astrological sources demonstrate the existence in the Roman world of the concept of a lifelong erotic orientation. Because of a particular configuration of the stars, a girl would be born as a *tribas, virago, fricatirx,* or *crissatrix*; the stars, then, determined a woman's erotic inclinations for the duration of her life.
>
> And yet, unlike the twentieth-century binary notion of homosexuality versus heterosexuality, ancient astrologers conceived of erotic propensities in a far more complex fashion. . . .
>
> In other words, astrologers in the Roman world knew of what we might call sexual orientation, but they did not limit it to two orientations, homosexual and heterosexual. Instead, these ancient writers believed that configurations of the stars created a broad range of sexual inclinations and orientations.[12]

It is not difficult to identity and document a number of persons we would term "high-profile celebrities" from the Roman world who took same-sex partners. Perhaps, as in our own time, it was the fact that such people were flaunting the dominant sexual norm of opposite-sex marriage that made them the object of public gossip and historic record. Against the background of Gibbon's famous quote that "of the first fifteen emperors, Claudius was the only one whose taste in love was entirely correct,"[13] perhaps the imperial residence should be our starting place for establishing several things about the biblical period.

The Rulers of Rome

In the waning days of the Republic, no less a personage than Julius Caesar was rumored to have had a same-sex affair with King Nicomedes IV of Bithynia. While still a young man of about 20, he was dispatched to the king's court, was reported to have spent an undue amount of time there, and later returned under the dubious pretext of collecting money owed to a client of his. This information is related by Suetonius[14] and could be regarded as suspect because of the historian's negative attitude toward Caesar. However, other documentation from the Roman period, lets us know that this view of the relationship between the two men was widespread. Cicero, for example, wrote that Caesar was led into the king's bedroom where he lay on a golden couch arrayed in purple, and that "the virginity of the one sprung from Venus was lost in Bithynia." Gossip and jests about the alleged incident were widespread.[15]

Better documented is not simply an affair but the public marriage – perhaps more than one – of the infamous contemporary of Paul, Nero. After relating several facts about the sexual exploits of the man who was Rome's emperor from A.D. 54-68, Suetonius relates this episode: "He castrated the boy Sporus and actually tried to make a woman of him; and he married him with all the usual ceremonies, including a dowry and a bridal veil, took him to his house attended by a great throng, and treated him as his wife."[16]

Dio Cassius adds information about Nero's union with a freedman named Pythagoras with whom Nero himself took the role of the wife.[17] In what Boswell and others take to be a reference to Nero's marriage to Pythagoras, Suetonius relates how the emperor acted out the role of a bride so as "to imitate the cries and lamentations of a maiden being deflowered."[18]

It is significant to note that Dio Cassius uses the word "marriage" of both opposite-sex and same-sex unions in relating the career of the emperor Elagabalus (218-222). Among the worst of Rome's emperors, Elagabalus' name is sometimes featured in the twenty-first century as "one of the first known gender-fluid Roman rulers" and could "possibly be considered transgender on the basis that [Elagabalus] was obsessed with changing their birth sex and often considered surgery."[19] An element of the scandal around the marriage of Elagabalus to his lover Hierocles is that the latter was a slave who had become a charioteer – not a free citizen of the empire.[20] Boswell cites documentation for the fact that "men who wished to advance in the imperial court [of Elgabalus] either had husbands or pretended they did."[21]

During this period – perhaps especially during the time of Nero when both Peter and Paul would have been active not only in the larger Roman world but also in Rome itself – same-sex partnerships certainly were known. While some would have been nothing more than "mock marriages," there were others that reflect more of the type relationship Agathon and Pausanias illustrate in the *Symposium*.

The Writings of Roman Poets

Virgil (70-19 B.C.) is celebrated as Ancient Rome's most gifted poet. Among his three major works surviving to us, his *Aeneid* is typically regarded as the national epic of Rome. It relates the story of the founding of the nation and asserts its right to civilize the world by bringing the benefits of Roman law, culture, and lifestyle to it. Book 9 tells the story of enduring love between two young males – Nisus and Euryalus – who are soldiers following Aeneas as refugees from Troy in search of a new home. Portrayed by some modern readers as a "touching gay love story,"[22] the two follow a sad and tortuous path that ends with both men dying.

Their relationship can hardly be dismissed as an instance of pederastic love, since both are young soldiers from Troy. The two are introduced in the narrative when Nisus – having slipped and fallen – trips another runner to guarantee his beloved Euryalus will win a ceremonial footrace. Later in the story, the Trojan force appears to be trapped while Aeneas is some distance away. Nisus volunteers to sneak out of camp, break through the enemy lines to get word to Aeneas of their plight, and bring him back. Euryalus pleads to join in the dangerous mission. After some protest,

Nisus agrees and the two set out on their task. "Their love was one," writes Virgil, "and together they charged into battle."[23]

Although they show themselves brave and fearless through a series of challenges, Eurylaus is killed by their enemies. Enraged and determined now to avenge his beloved's killer, Nisis is also killed. The two are decapitated and their heads put on spears. Their love for each other is memorialized by Virgil in the *Aeneid* – very much in the spirit, Boswell suggests, of the lovers Aristophanes and Pausanias in Plato's *Symposium*. He notes that Virgil called them "blessed – *fortunati ambo* (9:447) – and vowed that their devotion would be remembered as long as his poetry."[24]

The Roman poet Martial (*ca.*40-*ca.*103) is best known for his twelve books of 1,561 epigrams composed in Latin. He moved from his native Spain in the mid-60s of the first Christian century and not only wrote of emperors and public figures but also provides vignettes of housing, daily life, and the spectacle that was Rome. As a satirist, he seems to have been particularly popular among the city's literate citizens by writing on such subjects as the gluttony, ambition, furniture, food, and sex lives of his contemporaries.

An unmistakable jibe at what both Martial and his readers apparently knew happened in their midst is found among his epigrams. That the reference is not to an adult-boy relationship but to one between two adults is apparent from the physical descriptions he gives of them.

> Bearded Callistratus as a bride wedded the brawny Afer in the usual form as when a virgin weds a husband. The torches shone before him, a wedding-veil disguised his face, nor were the words of thy song, God of Marriage, unheard. A dower even was arranged. Do you not yet think, O Rome, this is enough? Are you waiting also for an accouchement?[25]

The sarcasm in Martial appears rather tame when compared with that of his contemporary, Juvenal (*ca.*55-*ca.*127). The tone in one of his more famous works is lewd in several places as he attacks the move away from opposite-sex relationships to same-sex unions. Although he is contemptuous of women in various places, this pagan writer nevertheless viewed the abandonment of females as the primary sexual partners for men – and especially for marital commitments – as something to be regarded with contempt.

Throughout the second book of his *Satires*, Juvenal laments the unraveling of civilization (i.e., Rome) through the increasingly effeminate behaviors of its male citizens. In the earliest lines (1-35), he denounces by name certain figures of his day who are passive partners (Lat, *pathicus*) to same-sex intercourse without being honest enough to admit their sexual appetites. Later (62-81), he reproaches Creticus who dressed in an effeminate manner while practicing law in the public arena – and proceeds to affirm that such womanly dress for a man is the gateway to a sort of "stain" that will only "spread further" if unchecked. Indeed, that sort of public dress and manner will – Juvenal predicts (82-116) – lead to more sordid private rites of seduction from which women will be barred and "the goddess's altar open to men alone."

The poem moves to its close (117-148) with a lament to "Romulus, Father of Rome" that the city he founded has come to such a sorry fate. In describing the wedding party of a certain Gracchus, he tells how he was "wearing brocade, the long full dress, and the veil." Then, in the presence of the guests, "the 'bride' reclines in the husband's lap." Thus, Juvenal cries out to Mars, "Can you see a man noted for birth, wealth, wed to another man, and your spear not beat the ground, your helmet stay firm, and no complaint to the Father?" Then, as if to make light of the larger situation Gracchus' wedding foreshadowed, he writes:

> ... "I've a ceremony to attend
> At dawn, tomorrow, down in the vale of Quirinius." "Why's that?"
> "Why? Oh, a friend of mine's marrying a male lover of his:
> He's asked a few guests." Live a while, and we'll see it happen,
> They'll do it openly, want it reported as news in the daily gazette.
> Meanwhile there's one huge fact that torments these brides,
> That they can't give birth, and by that hang on to their husbands."[26]

Beyond the First Century

Finally for our purpose here, there is also the well-known relationship from the second Christian century of the Emperor Hadrian (76-138) and Antinous. Anything but an inept ruler on the order of Nero or Commodus, Hadrian was regarded as an expert military tactician, capable administrator, and clever statesman. During his travels, he met a young man from Bithynia named Antinous and made him part of his entourage – along with his wife, Sabina. The emperor and Antinous became lovers, and Boswell describes them as "doubtless the most famous romantic couple in imperial Rome of the second century."[27]

Although the age differential between the adult Hadrian and teenager Antinous may remind you of Greek *paiderastia*, remember that Roman males generally did not adopt that institution from their predecessors. Any public male-male coupling in a Roman context was simply part of the accepted practice of taking a lover of either sex – almost always younger by several years. The relationship appears to have been one of serious mutual commitment, with no evidence of Antinous attempting to exploit political favors from his lover. Just short of 20, Antinous died. The consensus among historians is that it was an accidental death, but a fourth-century writer named Aurelius Victor advanced the view that Antinous offered himself as a sacrifice. "[W]hen Hadrian was wishing to prolong his life, and the magicians required a voluntary vicarious victim," he wrote, "they say that, upon the refusal of all others, Antinous offered himself."[28] He laid down his life for his beloved.

Regardless of the circumstances of his death, Hadrian had Antinous deified, proclaimed a festival to be celebrated in his honor every four years (that was still observed more than 200 years later), founded a city in his honor on the Nile, erected statues of him throughout the empire (several of which survive), and struck Roman

> **Two Modes of Male-Male Love**
> Maximus of Tyre (ca. A.D. 125-185), though living in the Roman Empire, was a rhetorician and philosopher whose public career built off Plato's work. Forty-one of his Orations have survived. In a series of lectures on Socratic love, he characterized two modes of love between males. Whether either or both is initiated in pederasty may be debated. Both modes involve adults and – in the case of at least one of them – may extend throughout life. His first mode of lover-beloved partnership, Maximus sees as honorable; the second is deemed exploitative and wicked.
>
> "In terms of qualities that belong to each: the first comprises virtue, friendship, modesty, candor, and stability; the second comprises excess, hatred, immodesty, infidelity. In terms of the ways of being that characterize them: the one is Hellenic and virile; the other is effeminate and barbaric. And lastly, in terms of the behaviors in which they are manifested: with the first, the lover takes care of the beloved, accompanies him to the gymnasium, goes hunting with him, into battle with him; he will be with him in death; and it is not in darkness or solitude that he seeks his company; with the second, on the other hand, the lover flees the sun, seeks darkness and solitude, and avoids being seen with the one that he loves."
> — Oration 9

coins with his likeness. Boswell speculates as follows about the popular circulation of stories, literature, and sculpture memorializing the relationship between the two men:

> The enormous appeal of the love between Hadrian and Antinous may have been due in some part to the prevalence of same-sex couples in popular romantic literature of the time. Everywhere in the fiction of the Empire – from lyric poetry to popular novels – gay couples and their love appear on a completely equal footing with their heterosexual counterparts.[29]

This chapter has offered more evidence than is necessary to establish that pederasty was not the only model of same-sex relationship known in antiquity and that long-term, committed, authentically caring, and mutually supportive same-sex relationships are known to have existed in New Testament times. This section can be summarized and closed with this synopsis of the data by Harper:

> It scarcely needs saying that same-sex marriages between women, or men, had no standing or consequence in public law, but that fact hardly diminishes the extraordinary testimony we do have for durable forms of same-sex companionship. In a peaceful and prosperous society, amid a highly urbanized and remarkably interconnected empire where marriage was valorized as an institution of the greatest moral and emotional fulfillment, same-sex pairs openly claimed, and ritually enacted, their own conjugal rights.
>
> It is beyond our ken to say how people truly behaved in any period of history. But at the very least it is time to lay to rest the bizarre notion, which is still sometimes expressed, that same-sex eros was, materially and ideologically, on the wane by the second century. This was the age when an emperor's favorite could become an object of worldwide veneration. When a novelist could claim that male-male love was "becoming the current fashion," when a satirist could claim that marriage between men would soon be officially recognized. The question posed in the debates between marriage and pederasty, which figure so prominently in the literature of the era, was not an idle one. Indeed, same-sex eros was of greater interest to the Latin writers on either side of AD 100 than ever before; and as the Greek sources come to preponderance in the second century, there is no sign of abatement.[30]

With that, we move now to the final question of importance from the historical data available to us: *Did ancient people have a concept of same-sex* orientation *akin to our present-day understanding?*

What of "Sexual Orientation" in Antiquity?

What we now call "sexual orientation" is not new. Psychologists introduced nuanced distinctions between the terms sex and gender in the 1950s, and further subcategories have flowed from it. In hindsight, most scholars credit Michel Foucault[31] (1926-1984) with popularizing the notion that sexuality – along with all other aspects of human behavior – is a social construct. That is, different people groups at different times and places across history establish the norms for acceptable sexual behavior. The chance combination of nature and nurture lead us to set those norms. The revisionist claim is that we are fortunate to have come to a time and place in history where we can rethink the subject of same-sex desire and behaviors and learn to accept what has long been regarded as taboo or sinful.

In a word, revisionists argue that everything in the biblical material is a reaction against the negative social construct of exploitation. Pedophilia, pederasty, exploitation of slaves, cultic prostitution, battlefield rape – yes, they are evil. Yes, they should have

> **Same-Sex "Orientation"?**
>
> What were the ancient categories and how do they correlate with our contemporary categories of heterosexuality and homosexuality? Craig Williams has explored this question extensively. He shows that the Greco-Roman world viewed all people along a spectrum of masculinity and femininity, rather than heterosexuality and homosexuality. In fact, a man could be considered manly even if he preferred to have sex only with men, as long as he was the active partner. Also, a man could be considered feminine if he wore soft clothes and shaved his chest hair – even though he had sex with women.
>
> Working within their own categories of masculinity and femininity, therefore, our modern concepts of heterosexuality and homosexuality do not exactly fit. However, as Williams and others recognize, there were many men who preferred to have sex with the same gender and were even believed to have been biologically oriented this way. Some may have been considered masculine by ancient standards; others may have been viewed as feminine. But such men, who preferred sex with men over women (sometimes exclusively) would have been considered (and considered themselves) at the very least bisexual or even gay today.
>
> Therefore, Brownson's claim that "writers in the first century, including Paul, did not look at same-sex eroticism with the understanding of sexual orientation that is commonplace today" ignores a wealth of historical evidence to the contrary. . . . When Paul therefore says that "men . . . gave up natural relations with women and were consumed with passion for one another" (Rom 1:27), he is not revealing ignorance about sexual orientation; Paul does not necessarily believe that all men are born straight and could not have been born with sexual desires for men. For Paul, the question of orientation is irrelevant. Homosexual unions violate the boundaries of gender established by God at creation.
>
> — Preston Sprinkle

been railed against and forbidden. But, since they knew nothing of a positive form of sexual orientation that affirmed commitment, love, and nurture between same-sex partners, what the Bible condemns is not what we are witnessing now. That, at least, is the counter-claim to this book's thesis.

But is what we are witnessing in the twenty-first century really unique to modern times? Are we simply enlightened enough to practice a different form of same-sex engagement than ancient people fostered as their social construct? Or is this a weak argument that is rooted in a thinly veiled form of chronological snobbery that says ancient people could not have envisioned or framed same-sex relationships that were caring, warm, and other-regarding?

Enough historical evidence has been given already to show that it is a serious mistake for anyone to claim that ancient people had no concept of a natural orientation toward persons of the same sex. While Foucault and revisionists who continue to use "orientation" language to describe a modern social construct, ancient writers simply used their own vocabularies of time and place to describe the same phenomenon. After referring to the speech of Pausanias that explains the inborn male-female, female-female, and male-male sexual longings that drive persons to seek appropriate partners, no less an advocate of same-sex unions than Louis Crompton makes this observation:

> We know that many Greeks had relations with both women and boys. But Pausanias clearly identifies another class of man – a *class* who are exclusively devoted to their own sex, approximating the modern conception of the "homosexual." This idea of a homosexual "orientation," though by no means central to Greek thinking as it is to ours, was certainly understood by Plato and his contemporaries.[32]

Similarly, Hubbard grants the same thing in the introduction to his survey of basic documents from the Greek and Roman periods.

> Close examination of a range of ancient texts suggests, however, that some forms of sexual preference were, in fact, considered a distinguishing characteristic of individuals. Many texts even see such preferences as inborn qualities and thus "essential" aspects of human identity.[33]

Later in the same work, he adds this:

> The coincidence of such severity on the part of moralistic writers with the flagrant and open display of every form of homosexual behavior by Nero and other practitioners indicates a culture in which attitudes about this issue increasingly defined one's ideological and moral position. In other words, homosexuality in this era may have ceased to be merely another practice of personal pleasure and began to be viewed as an essential and central category of personal identity, exclusive of and antithetical to heterosexual orientation.[34]

Returning to a quotation from Bernadette Brooten cited earlier in this chapter, it should have been apparent to scholars other than her that "orientation" in modern sexual theory is what many of the Greeks and Romans would have attributed to fate. Although philosophers have wrestled with the problem of determinism and free will across the centuries, it seems clear that the widespread notion among both the Greeks and their Roman heirs was that fate controlled the destinies of both individuals and nations. Many ancient religions and thought leaders of Egypt, Assyria, Greece, and Rome held deterministic views of human behavior. Indeed, there are several cultures of modern times that preserve such views. And it has not escaped the vocabulary – and perhaps the belief category – of many people who speak still in terms of what is "written in the stars" or events and relationships "just meant to be."

The seers and diviners of the Greek period taught that the stars, other impersonal forces, or the gods "fated" people to ruling status or slavery, prosperity or poverty, and other life outcomes. Thus, the curious-to-most phenomena of astrology, omens, and divination by reading the entrails of sacrificed animals were practiced widely. No less than Plato in several of his dialogues speaks of the role of a "diviner" (Gk, *mantis*) in providing knowledge. While he does not regard divination as the highest form of knowledge, he believed it should be taken into account – as he did himself with regard to the famous Oracle at Delphi's comment to Chaerephon about the wisdom of Socrates.[35] In Plato's *Timaeus*, where his understanding of cosmology and physiology are laid out, he points to the specific importance of the liver "and why it is situated in the region we say – it is for the purpose of divination."[36]

The Roman tradition continued to embrace an abiding fascination with the concept of fate, omens, and divination. Particularly important to this discussion in terms of the

> **Impulses and Behavior Control**
>
> Imagine an Anglo-Saxon warrior in Britain in AD 800. He has two very strong inner impulses and feelings. One is aggression. He loves to smash and kill people when they show him disrespect. Living in a shame-and-honor culture with its warrior ethic, he will identify with that feeling. He will say to himself, "That's me!" That's who I am! I will express that. The other feeling he senses is same-sex attraction. To that he will say, "That's not me." I will control and suppress that impulse.
>
> Now imagine a young man walking around Manhattan today. He has the same two inward impulses, both equally strong, both difficult to control. What will he say? He will look at the aggression and think, "This is not who I want to be, and will seek deliverance in therapy and anger-management programs." He will look at his sexual desire, however, and conclude, "That is who I am." . . .
>
> And where did our Anglo-Saxon warrior and our Manhattan man get their grids? From their cultures, their communities, their heroic stories . . . they are filtering their feelings, jettisoning some and embracing others. They are choosing to be the selves their cultures tell them they may be.
>
> — Tim Keller

interplay of external forces and individual personalities is the Stoic school. From its founder, Zeno (*ca.* 334-262 B.C.), to later writers such as Chryssipus (*ca.*279-206 B.C.), Seneca (4 B.C.-A.D. 65), and Emperor Marcus Aurelius (A.D. 121-180), Stoicism was particularly significant to the ongoing discussion of why humans behave in certain ways. Anticipating the question of why Stoicism is important to a discussion of sexual orientation, the apostle Paul almost certainly knew of and interacted with elements of the Stoic view of fate, human freedom, and moral behavior. Specifically, scholarly interest in the Paul-Stoicism relationship around a variety of topics is a matter of long-standing interest in New Testament studies. This becomes significant in the next chapter of this book and its examination of Paul's statements about same-sex behaviors.

In attempting to explain his belief in the strict determinism of inanimate nature and human agency, Chryssipus illustrated his view with an interesting visual metaphor. As related by Cicero,[37] he imagined a way to explain human behaviors by distinguishing external and internal causes. Pushing a cylinder moves it in a straight line; pushing a cone produces a different effect. Similarly, he argues, the external causes in nature are fixed and determined; the internal properties of human beings – which vary from person to person – cause them to react as they do. Thus, some people react to the world in one way and others in their own distinct manners. As it is sometimes expressed, this Stoic view holds that nothing is up to you, except the way you react to it from your own nature. Although the term was not used in those days, this is a version of what is called "compatibilism" in modern philosophy.

Turning back now to our question of sexual orientation, the Stoic answer appears to run something like this: In the pantheistic world of Stoicism, all things are determined by fate. For the external causes, what we classify as physics and chemistry hold for all things under all circumstances. As to internal causes, living things (i.e., plants, animals, humans) respond to their environments in terms of their unique dispositions so as to act predictably in responding to similar stimuli. Thus, a soldier who is brave in one battle is far more likely to be brave in the next, a mother who neglects or abuses her first child is not likely to treat subsequent children differently, and so on.

This seems to be a different way of explaining what Plato affirmed from a Greek myth about human nature. Males and females of the human race are inclined toward or predisposed to particular sexual choices. As with such terms as homosexual, straight, transsexual, and sexual orientation, those words were absent from the Greco-Roman vocabulary. But the concepts and behaviors were known, witnessed, and discussed publicly.

Is it likely that so literate a man as Paul had no awareness of how his peers discussed causation, fate, and inclination to predictable behaviors? That this resident of a city known for its Stoic thinkers would not have encountered their ideas about internal (moral) causation? That Paul would have discussed same-sex behavior only in terms of exploitative acts? And should we simply ignore the fact that Luke tells us that he engaged "a group of Epicurean and Stoic philosophers" in debate while in Athens? (Acts 17:18).

While some New Testament scholars may wish to grant more to Stoic influence on Paul than seems reasonable,

> **Christianity: An Alternate Attitude**
>
> It scarcely needs saying that the early Christians inhabited a world vastly unlike our own. They moved in a society where same-sex eroticism between males was conceptualized either as pederasty or as passivity. Surely, not all amorous unions fit into one of these two clear channels, but the moral and medical discussion formed around these two poles of experience.
>
> What is significant about early Christian moralizing, from Paul onward is that it drew so little from established modes of criticism. . . . Yet none of this means that the Christian posture toward same-sex love was uncertain. From Paul onward Christian sexual ideology collapsed all forms of same-sex contact, whether pederastic or companionate, into one category.
>
> — Kyle Harper

it is equally unreasonable to presume that Paul had no idea from his combined Jewish and Hellenistic background of inclinations, predispositions, and preferences in personal sexual likings. Such tastes and tendencies are what we now call one's sexual orientation.

Historical Context and Interpretation

For readers who have "never liked history," the three chapters ending here may have been of minimal interest. But I fear we have tended to do too much Bible study in a historical vacuum. That is, we have not done the work necessary to set down Abraham, David, Isaiah, Jesus, and Paul in the space-time context of their lives. This is the backdrop to what I earlier described as a Rorschach-test approach to reading Scripture. "What does this mean to me?" needs to be preceded by "What did this mean at the time the author wrote this?" So we are better prepared now to enter the world of the New Testament and look at the texts that touch this subject with greater clarity.

It simply will not do for anyone to be dismissive of what we are about to read by saying such ill-informed things as "There was no such thing as loving, committed, and monogamous relationships among same-sex persons in biblical times" or "The behaviors rebuked in the New Testament are only such exploitative things as pederasty or rape." It was into this environment that Christianity brought a worldwide message that was already known within the Jewish world but which would be revolutionary in its challenge to pagans.

With a bit of cultural history of the period as background now, it is time to look directly at the New Testament texts themselves.

ENDNOTES

1. Most of our information from both Greek and Roman sources relates to homosexuality rather than lesbianism. This is true because both cultures were patriarchal and female behavior was considered largely in terms of interaction with males. Cf. Bernadette J. Brooten, *Love between Women: Early Christian Responses to Female Homoeroticism* (Chicago: University of Chicago Press, 1996).

2. Bruce W. Longnecker, *In Stone and Story: Early Christianity in the Roman World* (Grand Rapids: Baker Academic, 2020), 204.

3. Marriages within the large slave population of the time were not documented, for only those of citizens were of great enough significance to record in the archives of a city. These relationships were at best *de facto* marriages in which persons may have been alternately "paired up" by their owners as potential for

producing strong children (i.e., as breeding stock), given to one another by a parent, or by some self-selecting circumstance. The indignity of slave life meant that both males and females were at the disposal of their owners for sex or subject to the sexual advances of their fellow-slaves.

4. Clement, *Paedagogus* 2.11.116. "Base, in truth, are those sandals on which golden ornaments are fastened; but they are thought worth having nails driven into the soles in winding rows. Many, too, carve on them amorous embraces, as if they would by their walk communicate to the earth harmonious movement, and impress on it the wantonness of their spirit." Cf. Citing Sue Blundell's "Clutching at Clothes" in *Women's Dress in the Ancient Greek World*, Vearncombe notes: "Archaeologists have discovered a ceramic sandal, presumably an imitation of an actual sandal, with the Greek word *akolouthi* ('follow me') written on the sole. The sole of the shoe was advertisement of gender, sexual status, occupation." Erin Kathleen Vearncombe, "What Would Jesus Wear? Dress in the Synoptic Gospels," PhD diss. (University of Toronto, 2014), 5. Accessed Mar 21, 2023, at https://tspace.library.utoronto.ca/ bitstream/1807/ 68331/1/Vearncombe_Erin_K_201411_PhD_thesis.pdf.

5. When Roman writers use the term "Greek love," a number of their modern readers (including some scholars) equate it to same-sex activity of any sort. The expression refers more narrowly to the widespread disdain for *paiderastia*. Romans presumed the acceptability of same-sex desire and activity – with enemies, slaves, women, and male prostitutes. But the social status of the active-penetrating partner was very different from that of the passive-penetrated partner.

6. The trait of primary importance to Roman females was *pudicitia*, the Latin term for chastity, purity, or modesty. *Virtus* is rarely ever attributed to a female, for its very derivation is from *vir* (Lat, male). This reflects in language something of the misogyny that was so widespread in pagan culture of antiquity.

7. Robin Lane Fox, *Pagans and Christians* (New York: Alfred A. Knopf, 1987), 346.

8. Philippians 3:4b-6.

9. Boswell, *Same-Sex Unions*, 65.

10. Harper, *From Shame to Sin*, 35.

11. Ibid., 42-60.

12. Ibid., 140.

13. Edward Gibbon, *The Decline and Fall of the Roman Empire*, rev. ed. (Grand Rapids: Christian Classics Etherial Library, 1845), 99. Accessed at https://www.ccel.org/ccel/g/gibbon/decline/cache/decline.pdf.

14. Suetonius, *The Life of Julius Caesar* 2.

15. Josiah Osgood, "Caesar and Nicomedes," *Classical Quarterly*, 58(2), (2008): 687-691.

16. Suetonius, *Nero* 28.

17. Dio Cassius, *Epitome* 62.

18. Suetonius, *Nero* 29. Nero's marriage to Pythagoras is also documented by Tacitus, *Annals* 15.37.

19. "Was Elagabalus Rome's First Transgender Emperor?" Accessed Jan 2, 2023, at https://www.history.co.uk/articles/was-elagabalus-rome-s-first-transgender-emperor; also, Alexis Mijatovic, "A Brief Biography of Elagabalus: the transgender rules of Rome." Accessed Jan 2, 2023, at https://outhistory.org/exhibits/show/tgi-bios/elagabalus.

20. Dio Cassius, *Epitome* 80.14-16. In this section of Dio's *Epitome*, the "marriage" is clearly male with male, whereas he also uses the word "marriage" of a desired male-female union. Cf. *Epitome* 79.1.

21. Boswell, *Same-Sex Unions*, 85.

22. Viktor Susnyak, "The Story of Nisus and Euryalus in Virgil's Aeneid," *Roma Optima*. Accessed at https://www.romaoptima.com/roman-empire/the-story-of-nisus-and-euryalus-in-virgils-aeneid.

23. Virgil, *Aeneid*, 9.182. (Mendelbaum trans.)

24. Boswell, *Same-Sex Unions*, 64.

25. Martial, *Epigrams* 12.42. (Ker translation in Loeb.) Note: The word "accouchement" refers to the birth of a child.

26. Juvenal, *Satire II: Effeminate Rome*. Translated by A.S. Kline and accessed at https://www.poetryintranslation.com/PITBR/Latin/JuvenalSatires2.php#anchor_Toc280783785.

27. Ibid., 66.

28. Quoted in Crompton, *Homosexuality and Civilization*, 108.

29. Boswell, *Christianity, Social Tolerance and Homosexuality*, 85-86. Note: Boswell cites examples of the same-sex romantic literature of the period on 86-87.

30. Harper, *From Shame to Sin*, 36.

31. Michel Foucault, *The History of Sexuality. Volume 1: An Introduction*, trans. Robert Hurley (New York: Vintage Books, 1978).

32. Crompton, *Homosexuality and Civilization*, 59.

33. Hubbard, *Homosexuality in Greece and Rome*, 2.

34. Ibid., 386.

35. Plato, *Apology* 20e-21b.

36. Plato, *Timaeus* 72b. Cf. Sarah Iles Johnston, *Ancient Greek Divination* (Malden, MA: Wiley-Blackwell, 2008) for a broader discussion of various types of divination in Greek culture. There is a biblical reference to divination from the liver from the even earlier Babylonian period at Ezekiel 21:21.

37. Cicero, *On Fate* 42.

> *"One of the frightening aspects of loving somebody is the way that love can seem to offer unique access not only to pleasure but to truth."*
> – Eve Tushnet

EXCURSUS

The Book of Acts: A Method for "Changing the Rules"?

In Chapter 7, we made the initial move from the Hebrew Scriptures to the New Testament for this study. The question of Jesus' alleged "silence" on the issue of same-sex relationships versus his quite explicit endorsement of the Old Testament view of sexual morality was discussed. I made a case for the Son of Man having reaffirmed the binary nature of holy sexual expression within covenanted monogamous marriage between solitary male-female companions. God in human flesh as a Jewish male functioning in the prophetic tradition of his people had not come – to use his own words on the value of the Torah – to "abolish" but to "fulfill" what he and his peers in Second Temple Judaism regarded as the Word of God.

In his personal obedience to the Holiness Code of his tradition and in his teaching to the disciples, Jesus of Nazareth modeled human fulfillment as a single and chaste man. In his Genesis-based comments on the nature of marriage in Matthew 19, he endorsed sexual intimacy on the one-man and one-woman model of creation. Nothing outside that paradigm was given his blessing or hinted at as something deemed appropriate – whether as erotic intimacy between persons of the same or opposite sex.

If Jesus had discovered that his contemporaries were misinterpreting the Holiness Code about adultery, *porneia*, and/or same-sex relationships, can we really believe he would have left the matter unchallenged? Would a Redeemer-Messiah who

> **Mirrors and Inkblots**
>
> Some people read the Bible as if its passages were Rorschach inkblots. They see what is in their head. In more sophisticated language, they project onto the Bible what they want to see. If you show them enough passages and you get them to talk about them, you will hear what is important to them, whether it is in the Bible or not! They might see in the "Jesus inkblot" a Republican or a socialist, because they are Republicans or socialists. Or, they may see in the book of Revelation, a favorite of inkblot readers, a sketch of contemporary international strife. Or, they may have discerned in the inkblot called "Paul" a wonderful pattern for how to run a church, which just happens to be the pastor's next big plan! You get the point – reading the Bible as an inkblot is projecting onto the Bible our ideas and our desires. . . .
>
> Instead of being swept into the Bible's story, Rorschach thinkers sweep the Bible up into their own story. Instead of being an opportunity for redemption, the Bible becomes an opportunity for narcissism. This is the problem with taking this shortcut: reading the Bible becomes patting ourselves on the back and finding our story in the Bible, instead of finding the Bible's story to be our story. Instead of entering into that story, we manipulate the story so it enters into our story.
>
> — Scot McKnight

understood being "despised and rejected by mankind" and "held in low esteem" himself (cf. Isa 53:3) have left a scorned subculture of caring and monogamous same-sex couples to their suffering? For the sake of future generations at least, could he not have released those "born that way" or "oriented" to homoerotic fulfillment from marginalization and judgment within Israel? These are not mocking questions but serious expectations I would expect from someone opposed to the harshness religious people could show toward a woman caught in adultery, a man born blind, Samaritans, and even Gentiles.

As we look beyond the Gospels and prepare to examine what Paul said that relates to our subject matter, there is an "intermediate" issue worth considering. It is clear that there is no affirmative case for same-sex pairing to be made from either the Old Testament or the New Testament. As I pointed out earlier, the affirming case for such relationships is made as a negative argument. That is, Jews and Christians have incorrectly interpreted and abusively applied a tiny handful of texts in our Holy Scriptures to make a case that has harmed the LGBTQ+ community.

An "Intermediate" Issue

A respected New Testament scholar from whose work many of us have benefitted over the years has made an argument that deserves notice before moving from the Gospels to the Pauline letters. Luke Timothy Johnson has raised the issue from the Book of Acts about how the faith community of God makes decisions. His altogether reasonable thesis is that the church in Acts and beyond must respond to God's leading on the basis of two realities: *Scripture* and *discernment*. That is, in light of the canonical texts, we look critically at the experiences – both personal and corporate to the people of God – and judge, weigh, and otherwise test events for what they reveal about the will of God. "We might, therefore, define discernment as that habit of faith by which we are properly disposed to hear God's Word, and properly disposed to respond to that Word in the practical circumstances of our lives."[1]

From this non-objectionable orthodox view of how Scripture, life events, and human intelligence come together in seeking to know and live in holiness before God, Johnson proposes to identify a paradigmatic case study from the New Testament. What is learned from that model is then applied to three issues he sees as important concerns for the church today.

> I offer here some thoughts on three kinds of decisions facing churches today. The first deals with leadership and concerns the role of women in the church. The second deals with fellowship and concerns homosexuality in the church. The third deals with stewardship and concerns the church's sharing of possessions. Two of these issues are of a "critical" character, in that they have the capacity to challenge well-established norms. One has a "chronic" character, in that it involves the common and continuing life of every community.[2]

The third of these issues is outside the scope of this book. The second is at the heart of our concern. And the first has a tangential relationship to the second that will be made clear as we proceed. On that second issue, Johnson grants that his case for the church's acceptance and blessing of committed and loving same-sex unions is made problematic because "it challenges what appears to be the uniform and unequivocal testimony of the canonical *texts*."[3] You may recall that an essay from the same writer was quoted in Chapter 7 of this book that bears repeating here because of its straightforward clarity.

> I have little patience with efforts to make Scripture say something other than what it says, through appeals to linguistic or cultural subtleties. The exegetical situation is straightforward: we know what the text says. But what are we to do with what the text says? . . .

I think it is important to state clearly that we do, in fact reject the straightforward commands of Scripture, and appeal instead to another authority when we declare that same-sex unions can be holy and good. And what exactly is that authority? We appeal to the weight of our own experience and the experience thousands of others have witnessed to, which tells us that to claim our own sexual orientation is in fact to accept the way in which God has created us. By doing so, we explicitly reject as well the premises of the scriptural statements condemning homosexuality – namely, that it is a vice freely chosen, a symptom of human corruption, and disobedience to God's created order.[4]

In *Scripture and Discernment*, he grants: "The burden of proof required to overturn scriptural precedents is heavy, but it is a burden that has been borne before."[5] He believes he can produce that "burden of proof" from the New Testament account of an issue related in Acts. So we must explore that case study before moving too quickly from the Gospels to Paul.

The Case Study: Acts 15

Johnson argues that it is "offensive" to challenge the acknowledged biblical injunctions against same-sex behaviors on the basis of "popularity polls" or with such populist claims as "everyone does it" or "surveys indicate." In his words, that approach is "theologically meaningless." To the contrary, "it is important to assert that God *does*, on the record, act in surprising and unanticipated ways, and upsets human perceptions of God's scriptural precedents."[6] The "on the record" instance of direct relevance for him is the biblical account of the so-called Jerusalem Conference given in Acts 15. From that event of "discernment," he insists "the church made bold to reinterpret Torah"[7] and admit Gentiles into its fellowship without circumcision or other elements of proselyting to Judaism for the sake of becoming disciples to Jesus.

The New Testament episode in question is taken to be a watershed event by students of the biblical text. In view of a variety of "experiences" that have taken place involving the outreach of Peter to the household of Cornelius and the preaching tour of Barnabas and Paul that ventured into Gentile territories, certain Judean Christians challenged what was happening. "Certain people came down from Judea to Antioch and were teaching the believers: 'Unless you are circumcised, according to the custom taught by Moses, you cannot be saved'" (Acts 15:1). These critics are later identified as not merely Christians with a background in Judaism but converted Pharisees (v.5). After gathering "the apostles and elders" (v.6) in Jerusalem to consider how to proceed going forward, there was "much discussion" (v.7) – perhaps too tame a translation of the original words here (Gk, *pollēs zēteseōs* = much debate, considerable argument). The upshot of a speech by Peter (15:1-5), the report of their evangelistic work by Paul and Barnabas (15:6-12), and a final speech by James (15:13-21) resulted in agreement by the group on the admission of Gentiles to "full fellowship" in the young church (15:22-29). Luke closes with an account of the good effects that came from what had taken place in Jerusalem (15:30-35).

Johnson rehearses these events and concludes:

> The issue [of whether the church can recognize the possibility of committed and covenantal homosexual love] is analogous to the one facing earliest Christianity after Gentiles started being converted. Granted that they had been given the Holy Spirit, could they be accepted into the people of God just as they were, or must they first "become Jewish" by being circumcised and obeying all the ritual demands of Torah. Remember, please, the stakes: The Gentiles were "by nature" unclean, and were "by practice" polluted by idolatry. We are obsessed by the sexual dimensions of the body. The first-century Mediterranean world was obsessed by the social implications of food and table fellowship. The decision to let the Gentiles in "as is" and to establish a more inclusive form of table fellowship, we should note, came into direct conflict with the accepted interpretation of Torah and what God wanted of humans.[8]

Evaluating the Case Study

There are several noteworthy flaws and inconsistencies in Professor Johnson's case that I think forbid the conclusion he has worked so hard to establish.

First, does it seem ironic at all that his case for discerning that experience can serve as a greater authority than the narrative of Scripture is made from Scripture's narrative? This may be a case where a biblical scholar's instinct about scriptural authority serves to undermine a position his personal passions long to establish. Professor Johnson sounds a warning on this issue that he most likely has had to give students in his classes at various times: "The question is not only how we feel or think or act concerning homosexuality, but also how those feelings, thoughts, and

> **Reading Human Experience**
>
> Experience is itself a kind of text, and texts need interpreters. How often have we thought that we understood our experiences, only to realize later that we had only the barest understanding of our own motives and impulses? We all know how flexible memory can be, how easy it is to give an overly gentle account of our own motivations, how hard it is to step outside our lifelong cultural training and see with the eyes of another time or place. To my mind, Johnson's approach places far too much trust in personal experience. He views our experience as both more transparent and less fallible than it is.
>
> To take personal experience as our best and sturdiest guide seems like a good way to replicate all of our personal preferences and cultural blind spots. Scripture is weird and tangly and anything but obvious – but at least it wasn't written by someone who shared all our desires, preferences, and cultural background. At least it wasn't written by us. And so it's necessary to turn at least as much skepticism on "the voice of experience" as Johnson turns on the voice of Scripture. It's necessary to look at least as hard for alternative understandings of our experience as for alternative understandings of Scripture.
>
> — Eve Tushnet

actions relate to the canonical texts we take as normative for our lives together."[9] Experience is a notoriously flawed criterion for interpreting the text of the Bible. In this case, there is a demonstrable flaw in his case.

Second, what I just termed a "demonstrable flaw" in Johnson's reasoning is becomes evident in Luke's account of the Jerusalem Conference. As indicated above, Peter related to everyone assembled how God had showed him "that he accepted [Gentiles] by giving the Holy Spirit to them, just as he did to us" (Acts 15:8). If the Holy Spirit was given to Cornelius and his household "just as" the Spirit had been given to the apostles in Acts 2, did that not indicate the acceptance of both Jews and Gentiles by faith in Jesus? Then the same group "listened to Barnabas and Paul telling about the signs and wonders God had done among the Gentiles" during their ministries at Antioch, Iconium, Lystra, Derbe, and other places along the route of what we now term the "first" of Paul's missionary journeys (Acts 15:12).

With these experiences related by such credible witnesses, the issue was not yet decided. The final and "clinching" argument on the subject of Gentile inclusion in the community without what Peter had termed the "yoke" of circumcision, dietary restrictions, and other elements of Torah observance (Acts 15:10) came through the speech made by James. He argued not that the experiences just related had somehow either "changed the rules" or – as Johnson put it – surfaced a "direct conflict with the accepted interpretation of Torah and what God wanted of humans." To the contrary, he argued that "the words of the prophets are in agreement with this" (Acts 15:15) and proceeded to quote from Amos 9 as biblical authority for accepting the experiences of Peter, Barnabas, and Paul as God-approved (Acts 15:16-18; cf. Amos 9:11-12).

The consultation about Gentile acceptance as Christ-followers without any requirement of proselyting to Judaism demonstrates how *human experiences must be evaluated in light of Scripture*. It stands both that event and our present obligation as Christians on their heads to reverse the order and somehow to construe that event as a deconstruction-reconstruction of biblical ethics by human experience. It is simply inexcusable, then, for Johnson to say that "a blind adherence to Scripture when God is trying to show us the truth in human bodies is also a form of sin."[10] Against that claim, human experience does not prove the scriptural commands to be in error. When they are in conflict, it is God-breathed Scripture that must be regarded as normative for "teaching, rebuking, correcting and training in righteousness" (2 Tim 3:16). And repentance rather than the evasion of biblical commands is the acceptable path.

Third, the Peter-Cornelius event bears a close reading to see how Peter explained his willingness to go forward with the unprecedented-for-him action of baptizing Gentiles. In the initial account of Peter's sermon to the centurion's assembled household, he ended by relating how the risen Christ had ordered him and his fellow apostles to preach "to the people" (Gk, *tō laō*) that God had appointed him as "judge of the living and the dead" (Acts 10:42). And how had that instruction been understood to date? Peter appears to have taken "the people" to be the people of his own Jewish background. Had the rooftop vision, the arrival of Cornelius' messengers, the account of a vision by Cornelius, and the reflective journey from Joppa to Caesarea caused that vision of "the people" to broaden? Had something of the language about going "into all the world" (Mk 16:15a) or making disciples "of all nations" (Matt 28:19a) bled into his consciousness?

Something of the sort clearly seems to have happened, for he summarized everything that was happening with this climactic inference: "All the prophets testify about him that everyone who believes in him (Gk, *panta ton pisteuonta eis auton*) receives forgiveness of sins through his name" (Acts 10:43). Everyone who believes in Jesus? *Everyone? Yes, even the uncircumcised!* What he would later claim in Acts 15:15 about the language of the Old Testament prophets being "in agreement with" what he was defending to his Pharisaic brothers in Jerusalem, this language implies that Peter was breaking through the Jew-Gentile barrier in Acts 10 based on what Scripture said. Again, please pay attention to the order. What was happening had not altered or contravened the Bible. It dawned on him that this what Scripture had anticipated and authorized.

Fourth, stepping back from Acts 15 and to examine the larger flow of Luke's narrative, the exchange at Jerusalem is a continuation of a theme already well-established in Acts. Luke was among the non-Jewish friends and coworkers of Paul (cf. Col 4:11b,14). Aside from what seems to be a general interest in showing that Jesus and the early church made room for society's marginalized people (e.g., women, children, lepers, disabled persons, etc.), he evidences a particular interest in Acts to affirm the acceptance of Gentiles within the community founded by Israel's Messiah.

> **Relating Scripture to Culture**
>
> One should be prepared to distinguish what the New Testament itself sees as inherently moral and what is not. Those items that are inherently moral are therefore absolute and abide for every culture; those that are not inherently moral are therefore cultural expressions and may change from culture to culture.
>
> Paul's sin-lists, for example, never contain cultural items. Some of the sins may indeed be more prevalent in one culture than another, but there are never situations in which they may be considered Christian attitudes or actions. Thus sexual immorality, adultery, idolatry, drunkenness, homosexual practice, thievery, greed, and the like (1 Cor 6:9-10) are always wrong. This does not mean that Christians have not from time to time been guilty of any of these. But they are not viable moral choices. "That is what some of you were. Buy you were washed . . ." (v.11).
>
> On the other hand, foot washing, exchanging the holy kiss, eating marketplace idol food, women having a head covering when praying or prophesying, Paul's personal preference for celibacy, or a woman's teaching in the church are not inherently moral matters. They become so only by their use or abuse in given contexts, when such use or abuse involves disobedience or lack of love.
>
> — Gordon Fee and Douglas Stuart

It misrepresents Acts 15 as any sort of initiative toward or inbreaking of a new insight about Gentiles. On Pentecost Day of Acts 2, Peter announced the dawn of a new era (i.e., "the last days") and claimed that the experience of the Holy Spirit that day was in fulfillment of Joel's vision of the Spirit being poured out on "all people" (NIV) or "all flesh" (NRSVue). Thus, he quoted from Joel 2:28-32 (cf. Acts 2:17-21) both to explain and to validate as approved by God what the people were witnessing. The gospel is carried to the Samaritans in Acts 8:5ff, and Philip is called away from Samaria to explain

EXCURSUS: ACTS AND "CHANGING THE RULES"?

Isaiah 53 to a eunuch from Ethiopia as that chapter continues (8:26ff). Peter, staying at Joppa in the "unclean" house of a tanner (Acts 10:6; cf. Lev 11:35), fell into a trance while hungry and was told three times to kill and eat "unclean" food (Acts 10:9-23). Refusing each time, he was admonished, "Do not call anything impure that God has made clean" (v.15). This turned out to be the prelude to his positive response to leave Joppa for Caesarea, where he shared the gospel with a Roman Centurion and his household (Acts 10:24ff). Then comes the initial defense of his interaction with Gentiles (Acts 11:1-18), the establishment of a Gentile church at Antioch in Syria (11:19ff), and the First Missionary Tour by Barnabas and Saul (13:3 – 14:28).

From this partial list of outreach events involving non-Jewish people, we find the background to the Jerusalem Conference of Acts 15. Far from being a decision about the possible innovation of missionary work among pagans, it was a clarifying – perhaps, better, a solidifying – event to look at what had been happening for a few years by then. And what "solidified" the church's position about Gentile inclusion in its mission? Scripture was cited to affirm and validate it. If the experiences of Jesus were proof of his messianic claims only because they were consistent with Scripture, and if the experiences of the apostles and earliest Christ-followers needed to be verified in the same way, there is absolutely no justification for us to reverse the order. It is inclusion within the narrative flow of all that Scripture has said that endorses a person, event, or behavior as God-approved. It is never the case that a divergent person, event, or behavior bests or reverses a God-given commandment. Changing the context of the behavior from forced to consensual, from exploitative to caring, or from multi-partnered to monogamous does not bring about a repeal of divine revelation about what constitutes moral behavior. If it does so for same-sex intercourse, why could it not do the same for other forms of prohibited sexual behavior (e.g., bestiality, polygamy, incest)?

Fifth, the "objection" that the eventual overturning of slavery or polygamy and freeing of females for wide-ranging service and leadership illustrate how experience and broader understanding should eclipse long-standing biblical precedent against same-sex marriage is seriously wrong-headed. Anyone who offers a defense of same-sex behaviors on the basis of such an argument is committing the logical fallacy of offering a false analogy.

For one thing, the Bible never commands, endorses, or recommends slavery, polygamy, or female disenfranchisement.[11] What some take to be their approval is better read as counsel to minority groups in cultures they could not change. It seems that most people ignore the fact that Moses delivered the Torah to a minority group forced to function in the Ancient Near East whose dominant culture had established all these social forms long ago. At a time when their "hearts were hard" (cf. Matt 19:8) toward the mistreatment of women generally and the distortion of (male) marital rights in particular within a culture where human dignity was minimal, many things happened that were less than ideal. They were tolerated without being approved. To borrow Paul's language, "God overlooked such ignorance" (Acts 17:30a) as he moved toward the fulfillment of his promises and a fuller display of his holiness. In the meanwhile, the biblical text pointed out the misery produced when Abraham violated his one-flesh union with Sarah, Solomon multiplied wives, and – perhaps most notably of all in the Torah – powerful nations such as Egypt enslaved and brutalized other races and ethnic groups.

For another, the prophets and evangelists of both testaments constantly raised the line of sight for God's people. They pointed to the arrival of the Messiah who would either be the very presence of God or his anointed representative to set right what was still out of harmony with God's will. The prophets were allowed to anticipate and name a time when Israel's "sons *and daughters* will prophesy" (Joel 2:28); Miriam, Deborah, Ruth, and others were hints of the "last days" when such a thing would be commonplace rather than out of the ordinary. The evils of slavery are highlighted throughout the text, and Israel was forbidden to capture and commit other people to perpetual slavery (cf. Amos 1:6). When an Israelite became destitute and sold himself into debt-servitude, it could last no longer than six years – and the released person was to receive a share of whatever wealth he or she had generated for a master (Deut 15:12-15). This is nothing like the hateful African slave trade that flourished in Europe and North America. The Messiah's heart is always for the oppressed to be free, the dignity and worth of every human being to be respected, and for God's creatures to live fruitfully within his will (cf. Luke 4:18-19).

In all these cases, the oppression and injustice are noted. Promises of freedom, justice, and rewards to the righteous are named. The trajectory is always set in the direction of hope and redemption. God's original design in creation for males and females who bear his image into his world put under their management will be realized. *And there is never a glimmer of a hint that the created order of Genesis 2 that established male-female sexuality as God's design would change. It is, in fact, taken to be a representation of the Christ-church relationship that will endure in the New Heaven and New Earth yet to come.*

"You Are to Abstain from Porneia*"*

Finally, that the Acts 15 discernment cannot be used as precedent for releasing anyone from the biblical prohibitions against same-sex coupling is clear from the letter produced by the Jerusalem Conference. The result of their discussion was communicated to the Gentile believers in a document that simultaneously released them from any obligation to circumcision and required that they "abstain from sexual immorality." The Greek word is *porneia*, and the word signifies "sexual intercourse outside marriage."[12] Far from changing the rules about sexual behaviors, the letter from the apostles and elders draws from the understanding of creation language that Paul makes explicit in a letter written perhaps five years later: "Since sexual immorality (Gk, *porneia*) is occurring, each man should have sexual relations with his own wife, and each woman with her own husband" (1 Cor 7:3).

> **The Jerusalem Decision**
>
> Matthew Vines claims, "Gentiles were included in the church, and the church recognized that the old law was no longer binding." Mark Achtemeier, similarly, claims that doing "an end run around the requirement of biblical law" in the matter of same-sex union "would be utterly consistent with this biblical precedent" of gentile inclusion.
>
> The Jerusalem Council, to the contrary, did not do "an end run around biblical law" or decide that "the old law" for God's people was simply "no longer binding." For the apostles and elders went on to discern not whether biblical law should apply to gentile believers but rather which biblical laws were appropriate for gentile observance. . . . The apostolic decree issued by the council condensed those biblical norms into the mandate that gentile believers "abstain" (apechesthai) from "sexual immorality" (porneias). In the New Testament, the generic term "sexual immorality" (porneia) covered various forms of illicit sex (e.g., prostitution, incest, adultery) and effectively encompassed all sexual intercourse outside marriage (including same-sex intercourse).
>
> — Darrin Snyder Belousek

We need not question whether Paul understood the meaning of the word he and his colleagues had used in the Acts 15 communique. Neither can we doubt that he was fleshing out the meaning of that message to the non-Jewish Corinthian church. *Sex outside of marriage is forbidden to Christians, and* porneia *is avoided when a man has exclusive and loving sex with his wife and women with their husbands*. Indeed, the rules had not changed in Jerusalem nor had the groundwork been laid for what would be offered two millennia later to shift the judgment of biblical text to the authority of experience. Scripture delineates the boundaries for acceptable moral behavior.

The orthodox position of the Christian church across twenty centuries stands. All authority in Heaven and on Earth belongs to Jesus Christ, and that authority is mediated to his people most directly in Holy Scripture. In choosing to confess Jesus as Lord and to follow him as a disciple, Christians subject our feelings, desires, and experiences to his authority conveyed in the narrative of the Bible. It is a radical and unwarranted hermeneutical move to exalt our personal or collective experiences over that narrative. To do so creates a new and different narrative in which the authority of Christ has been rejected.

ENDNOTES

1. Luke Timothy Johnson, *Scripture and Discernment: Decision Making in the Church* (Nashville: Abingdon Press, 1996), 110.

2. Ibid., 140.

3. Ibid., 144. The word "texts" is italicized in the original statement and prepares the reader for the conflict that will be acknowledged between the biblical "text" and certain life experiences that contradict the canonical prohibitions of same-sex activities. It is the tension between "text" and experience that will call for "discernment" of the sort he proposes.

4. Johnson, "Homosexuality & the Church: Two Views," *Commonweal* (June 11, 2007): 15. Accessed at https://www.commonwealmagazine.org/homosexuality-church-0.

5. Johnson, *Scripture and Discernment*, 148.

6. Ibid., 144.

7. Ibid., 147. Professor Johnson's argument is a more sophisticated form and perhaps the source for Adam Hamilton's "The rules are changing!" theme in his *When Christians Get It Wrong*. He has the Bible condoning slavery, polygamy, forcing slaves to be sexual surrogates for their masters. Thus, Hamilton has Peter and other Christians who came to understand God's heart of love "recogniz[ing] that what was written in the law and accepted in the New Testament was not necessarily God's timeless will for humanity" (85-86).

8. Ibid.

9. Ibid., 144.

10. Johnson, "Homosexuality & the Church."

11. For a textual justification of this statement, see the response in Chapter 15 to the question about Christians being "on the wrong side of history" relative to slavery and other social issues.

12. J. Diggle et al. (eds), s.v. "πορνεία," *Cambridge Greek Lexicon*, 2 vols. (Cambridge: Cambridge University Press, 2021), 2:1166. Cf. Kyle Harper, "*Porneia*: The Making of a Christian Sexual Norm," *Journal of Biblical Literature* 131, no. 2 (2011): 363-383.

> *"Nothing, however, indicates that he is exempting some same-sex intercourse as acceptable. It is all an abomination for Paul."*
> — William Loader

CHAPTER 11

The Pauline Texts (Part 1): Romans 1:18-32

Because of the importance Christians appropriately attach to the New Testament, the things said about same-sex behaviors by Paul have particular significance. We must remember, however, that Paul wrote out of his own background and extensive training in Hebrew Scripture and in the context of the Greco-Roman culture and vocabulary of the first Christian century. That is why all the material that has come earlier in this book is vital to reading the Apostle to the Gentiles intelligently.

If Paul's Jewish background related to a different set of sexual practices than he deemed now to be appropriate as a Jesus-follower in the first-century Roman Empire, we would reasonably expect that shift in understanding to surface. As we will see, he sensed no need for clarifying or changing what he had been taught from the Torah. His task was to communicate an ethical directive he knew well to a non-Jewish population that generally would find it novel and challenging.

For that matter, if we really believe Jesus said nothing of real relevance to our subject matter, we would be surprised that Paul would not supplement his Lord's teaching by the empowerment of the Holy Spirit he claimed in texts such as 1 Corinthians 14:37. He had provided just that sort of additional Spirit-guided insight on marriage earlier in the Corinthian correspondence. When he could cite the words of Jesus on issues surrounding marriage and divorce, he did so: "To the married I give this command (not I, but the Lord) . . ." (1 Cor 7:12). When asked about matters to which Jesus had not spoken directly, he spoke with apostolic authority: "Now about virgins: I have no command from the Lord, but I give a judgment as one who by the Lord's mercy is trustworthy" (1 Cor 7:25). Nothing of this nature happens with his comments about same-sex relationships.

So we proceed now to give attention to three statements in his epistles that deal with same-sex conduct directly. In this chapter, primary focus will be on his instruction to the church in Rome. Two additional Pauline texts will be reserved for Chapter 12.

Romans 1:18-32

Because Romans 1:18-32 is not only central to the case I am making in this book but also critically important to the general understanding of Christian ethics, it deserves extensive-enough examination both to exegete this section of Romans and to respond to some of the more common ways revisionists have attempted to blunt its force.

Near the end of a three-year ministry in Ephesus, Paul was making plans to go to Rome (Acts 19:21). Leaving Ephesus late in A.D. 56, he was headed to Jerusalem with a collection for needy believers there (Rom 15:25-26) and intended then to visit Rome (Rom 15:23). It is clear from his epistle that he was both hoping to encourage and bless the Roman Christians (Rom 1:11-12) and to solicit their sponsorship for missionary work he was planning for Spain and regions beyond (Rom 15:24). Writing from Corinth during the winter months of A.D. 56/57, he informed Christ-followers in Rome of his planned visit to their city.

> **A Classicist on Paul's Position**
> In the matter of same-sex eros . . . Christian norms simply ate through the fabric of late-classical morality like an acid, without the least consideration for the well-worn contours of the old ways. As with porneia, Christian hostility to venery involving members of the same sex was nurtured in Hellenistic Judaism, imported to the gentile mission, sharpened in its application and expression. Paul's letters again provided an incomplete but, really, unambiguous template for the blanket condemnation of same-sex love in early Christianity. Nowhere is this clearer than in the first chapter of his letter to the Romans.
> — Kyle Harper

The purpose of Paul's letter to Rome was not to explain the details of permitted and forbidden sexual behaviors. He wrote to explain the focus of the gospel he had preached in so many other places and that he was hoping soon to preach in Rome and then to carry further west. In summary, the message Paul outlines in this epistle is that the *righteousness of God* is revealed in the gospel. The good news that God has been faithful in keeping his covenant promise to Abraham that all people would be blessed through his offspring had become reality in the Christ event. Now Paul was preaching this gospel as the basis for the salvation of both Jews and Greeks.

The first seventeen verses of the first chapter constitute an introduction and theme statement for all that follows. They present Paul's view of himself (vs.1-7), his readers (vs.8-15), and his message (vs.16-17). If the theme statement of the Epistle to the Romans is that *Paul's gospel reveals the righteousness of God who has kept his covenant-promise to save both Jews and non-Jews in Jesus the Messiah*, the deep details of the necessity for, means to, and results of that work bear some unpacking now. And that is what Paul launches into in this section of text. Specifically, the Apostle to the Gentiles explains the necessity for God's actions in terms of the staggering mess we humans have made of our Good Creator's good world.

Stated another way, a demonstration of the *unwavering righteousness of God* became necessary in human history because of the *obstinate unrighteousness of human beings*. Because of the failure of the Jewish project to "bless all nations" through Abraham's descendants, God demonstrated his faithfulness to the Abrahamic covenant through Jesus. Yet, he hastens to admit, the failure of the genetic children of Abraham to honor God through faithful worship and moral uprightness was not unique to them. It had been the common failure of all humankind. Males and females of the human race were created to bear the divine likeness into God's creation. Instead, we have together refused to honor our Creator and – by that very rejection of him – have dehumanized ourselves. That failure of mission could not be dismissed as "ignorance"; it was traceable to an inexcusable turning away from God and the truth he has made known.

> The wrath of God is being revealed from heaven against all the godlessness and wickedness of people, who suppress the truth by their wickedness, since what may be known about God is plain to them, because God has made it plain to them. For since the creation of the world God's invisible qualities – his eternal power and divine nature – have been clearly seen, being understood from what has been made, so that people are without excuse.

For although they knew God, they neither glorified him as God nor gave thanks to him, but their thinking became futile and their foolish hearts were darkened (Rom 1:18-21).

The Human Impulse Toward Worship

From a theological point of view, it is not an overstatement to say that the first impulse of every human heart is worship. Of course, many physicalists and secularists would disagree with that assertion. They might argue that what is sometimes called the "religious impulse" is simply an evolutionary holdover from some primitive adaptation or nothing more than the name given at various times to the drive toward responsible behavior by the human race. Then there are those who either deny that such an impulse exists at all or that, if it does, it is a symptom of mental illness. These dismissive postures might be interesting to pursue, but they are not germane here. This book is an attempt to understand and articulate a *biblical* analysis of LGBTQ+ desires, choices, and behaviors. And both Old and New Testaments make the consistent claim that knowing and honoring God is the first-order duty of humans and that our failure to follow through on it results in predictable disaster for us.

Just as newborns discover the world outside themselves before they become self-aware, males and females of the human species instinctively reach to a higher power, parental figure, personified authority, or god/God. This is essentially Paul's claim in the text quoted above. To say that God's "invisible qualities – his eternal power and divine nature – have been clearly seen, being understood from what has been

---

Adam and the Root of False Worship

God accepts that humans have indeed breached the Creator-creature distinction. Not that humans have now become gods but that they have chosen to act as though they are – defining and deciding for themselves what they will regard as good and evil. Therein lies the root of all other forms of idolatry: we deify our own capacities, and thereby make gods of ourselves and our choices and all their implications. God then shrinks in honor from the prospect of human immortality and eternal life in such a fallen state and prevents access to the "tree of life." God has a better way to bring humanity, redeemed and cleansed, to eternal life.

At the root, then, of all idolatry is human rejection of the Goodness of God and the finality of God's moral authority. The fruit of that basic rebellion is to be seen in many other ways in which idolatry blurs the distinction between God and creation, to the detriment of both.

— Christopher J.H. Wright

made" is to side with the claims of what we call *natural theology*. As opposed to revealed theology (i.e., information about God from prophets, seers, and sacred texts), natural theology holds that God has left clear evidence not only of his presence but also his power and genius scattered over his creation. The Creator's fingerprints are all over his creation. Among other biblical figures, David to Israel (Psa 19:1ff) and Paul to the intellectuals of Athens (Acts 17:22-34) affirm as much. While natural revelation is but a stepping-stone toward God and does not reveal either the details of his will or the divine plan to renew a fallen world through Israel's Messiah, it does reveal the existence of its Creator and implies the humility, awe, and worship owed him by all his sentient creatures.

For a variety of reasons, however, humans have chosen to use our divinely given freedom to "suppress the truth." The result is that his image-bearing creatures "neither glorified him as God nor gave thanks to him." This intellectual move of refusing to acknowledge God's existence and his right to our worship has given rise, in turn, to an ethical quagmire that leaves humanity without a moral compass. How so? There always will be someone or something that a person (e.g., money) or culture (e.g., nationalism) will prioritize. By definition, that person, thing, or state of affairs becomes his or her "god" – that which matters most and for which he or she strives above all else. Put most simply, every *human being worships*. And the object of our worship transforms us into its likeness. The choice is not *whether* to worship but *whom* or *what* to worship.

> *You become like what you worship.* When you gaze in awe, admiration, and wonder at something or someone, you begin to take on something of the character of the object of your worship. Those who worship money become, eventually, human calculating machines. Those who worship sex become obsessed with their own attractiveness or prowess. Those who worship power become more and more ruthless. . . . When you gaze in love and gratitude at the God in whose image you were made, you do indeed grow. You discover more of what it means to be fully alive.[1]

When humanity turned aside from its obligation to worship the God in whose image we are made, we were "without excuse" for doing so. There is nothing innocent about the conscious suppression of what God made "plain to them." That innocence is not at stake – and therefore cannot be used as an excuse – explains why divine wrath comes into play.

That human beings lose our humanity upon turning to the worship of something other than the One True God is an ancient claim of the biblical writers. For example, there is the lament over idolatry and those who follow idols "made by human hands" found at Psalm 115. In particular, pay special attention to verse eight: "Those who make them will be like them, and so will all who trust in them." Dead to the likeness of God stamped on us in creation, humans who turn to idols become increasingly insensitive to all that is holy and progressively drawn to evil. The biting sarcasm with which the prophets caricature the false gods of the pagans – and those who succumb to them – sounds offensive to moderns (cf. Isa 40:18-20; 41:7, 29; 44:6-23; 46:5-7; Jer 10:1-5). That offense is not because the language is either improper or undeserved but due to our resurgent cultural deference to pagan ideas and lifestyles.

God's Wrath Against Human Sin

Paul's theme statement for Romans that "in the gospel the righteousness of God is revealed" (1:17a) is followed immediately by an emphatic statement that "the wrath of God is being revealed from heaven against all the godlessness and wickedness of people, who suppress the truth by their wickedness" (1:18). How can this be? God's righteousness and God's wrath are *both* being made known? Redeeming grace and divine judgment are *both* in play? And, we should notice, this is not a warning that his wrath "will be revealed" (i.e., future tense) against godlessness and wickedness. The text says his wrath "is revealed" or "is being revealed" (i.e., present tense) against sin. How, we must ask then, does Paul see the gospel (i.e., good news) and wrath (i.e., bad news) to be so directly linked to one another?

God's wrath in history has come in the forms of plagues against Egypt, Babylon's conquest and exile of the Chosen People, and Ananias and Sapphira falling dead. God's wrath in the future is being stored up (cf. 2:5) for those unprepared for the second coming of Jesus. Correct? Yes, but Paul believed that sin is so toxic that it brings God's wrath into the lives of people long before death and Judgment Day. When you stop to think about it, what he says makes perfect sense. Karl Barth expressed it this way: "The confusion avenges itself and becomes its own punishment. The forgetting of the true God is already the breaking loose of His wrath against those who forget him (i. 18)."² Here is Paul's explanation for how it has come about and how we witness it in every generation.

God has made himself known to us – in nature, through prophets, and in Scripture. No one can plead ignorance of God's existence, and people are "without excuse" (v.20b) for their unbelief. Having rejected God and having refused to honor him as God and recognize his goodness to them, "their thinking became futile and their foolish hearts were darkened" (v.21b). In other words, the intentional rejection of God by a human mind leads to a lifestyle that is anything but happy and carefree by virtue of throwing off moral restraints. With our hearts "darkened," humans turn from God to all things vile and destructive. What we thought would be authentic freedom turns into some form of miserable addiction. This is why Paul will say later in Romans (12:1-2) that "the renewing of your mind" is central to human redemption – so that one can think clearly about the truth and what a Holy God sanctions for her or his welfare. Would it not be an essential part of God's love for his human creatures to call us back when we have gone badly off course with our lives?

> **Clarity of Language in Romans 1**
>
> For the historian, any hermeneutic roundabout that tries to sanitize or soften Paul's words [at Romans 1] is liable to obscure the inflection point around which attitudes toward same-sex erotics would be forever altered. It is precisely here. Paul's originality lay in the violence with which his thought shuttled between and then beyond both Greco-Roman and Jewish strictures to form an unambiguous and all-embracing denunciation of same-sex love.
>
> Paul's overriding sense of gender – rather than age or status – as the prime determinant in the propriety of a sexual act was nurtured by contemporary Jewish attitudes. The very language of "males" and "females" stood apart from the prevailing idiom of "men" and "boys," "women" and "slaves." By reducing the sex act down to the most basic constituents of male and female, Paul was able to redescribe the sexual culture surrounding him in transformative terms. Paul's view of Roman sexual culture captured patterns invisible through the lens of traditional Greco-Roman moralism. One sign of this recategorization, staring the reader squarely in the face, is the equivalence of same-sex love between men and between women.
>
> — Kyle Harper

The "wrath of God" Paul names here is hardly a capricious, coldhearted response on God's part. It is what happens inescapably when people reject the truth for lies, reject upright behaviors for wicked ones. All that is opposed to God and human wellbeing seems to be rooted in Satan's deceptions (John 8:44b), and we have been falling for them since Eden. God allows us to choose between truth and falsehood, but his own upright and just character then allows – or, perhaps, requires – us to live with the consequences of those choices. Is that unjust? Unfair? Three times in this text (vs.24, 26, 28), Paul speaks of the "exchange" we make by rejecting God for idols, holy sexuality for sexual parodies, and virtue for vice. Across time, God "gave them over" to their choices when our ancestors chose to embrace some enticing deception offered them. When people abandon God, however, they are by that same horrible choice abandoned to the "wrath" of pain, chaos, shame, and dehumanization that surely follow. "And, moreover, the uncleanness of their relation to God submerges their lives also in uncleanness. When God has been deprived of His glory, men are also deprived of theirs."[3]

> Although they claimed to be wise, they became fools and exchanged the glory of the immortal God for images made to look like a mortal human being and birds and animals and reptiles.
>
> Therefore *God gave them over* in the sinful desires of their hearts to sexual impurity for the degrading of their bodies with one another. They exchanged the truth about God for a lie, and worshiped and served created things rather than the Creator – who is forever praised. Amen.
>
> Because of this, *God gave them over* to shameful lusts. Even their women exchanged natural sexual relations for unnatural ones. In the same way the men also abandoned natural relations with women and were inflamed with lust for one another. Men committed shameful acts with other men, and received in themselves the due penalty for their error.
>
> Furthermore, just as they did not think it worthwhile to retain the knowledge of God, so *God gave them over* to a depraved mind, so that they do what ought not to be done. They have become filled with every kind of wickedness, evil, greed and depravity. They are full of envy, murder, strife, deceit and malice. They are gossips, slanderers, God-haters, insolent, arrogant and boastful; they invent ways of doing evil; they disobey their parents; they have no understanding, no fidelity, no love, no mercy. Although they know God's righteous decree that those who do such things deserve death, they not only continue to do these very things but also approve of those who practice them (Rom 1:22-32).

In sequence, to reject the knowledge of the True God for an idol – carved or cast, fleshly or mental – is to be given over to foolish and futile ways of thinking. Here are a few examples of those foolish mantras from our own time: "I gotta be me." "Nobody can tell me what to do." "The only thing that matters in life is to be happy."

"It's my life and nobody's business what I do with it." From those self-centered and God-rejecting mindsets, it is both natural and easy to accept that the most direct route to happiness is pleasure – sexual pleasure most particularly.

Why the Attention to Same-Sex Lifestyles?

As a Jew who had been taught the moral boundaries found in the Torah's Holiness Code from childhood, Paul singles out for special mention the abandonment of sanctioned male-female behaviors for same-sex relationships. Although I still meet people occasionally who think gay and lesbian lifestyles have come to public awareness only in modern times, this book has documented that they were well-known in the Greco-Roman world of New Testament times. Yes, contexts varied. Yes, attitudes toward same-sex relationships varied. But they were known and were a topic of conversation in the world of Jesus, Peter, and Paul.

What most readers may be inclined to miss about Romans 1 is that Paul is not simply giving commentary on the City of Rome or the bizarre things he has heard about the moral climate in Emperor Nero's household. Neither is he tracing the trajectory of a particular individual or saying that that every consenting adult who has had a same-sex experience has done so as an act of personal defiance against God. He is offering a broad-stroke overview of human history to explain how the fundamental turn to idolatry lies at the root of sin.

Both Paul and I could describe some of our acquaintances who are not disciples of Jesus but who rank among the most compassionate and ethical people we know. They try to make their communities better, are brilliant teachers, set up programs to keep children away from drugs or sexual predators, and are faithful to their mates and children. Paul is offering a sweeping appraisal of how the larger culture of his time had come to its confused and morally shameful situation. In our own time, we love occasional stories of heroism and sacrifice that make the news but are far more accustomed to reports of war, terrorism, human trafficking, drug addiction, gang violence, political chicanery, and the like. The proliferation of these shameful actions cannot but bring harmful effects into the cultures where they are found. The very consequences of these behaviors count as elements of God's wrath – a divine punishment within history – that follows with sad but foreseeable predictably.

Although Paul names a total of twenty-two sinful behaviors that result from turning away from God and for which human societies experience divine wrath, the most explicit and detailed of these is same-sex encounters. Why choose this as his primary case study?

Out of the many things Paul could have highlighted in the pagan world, he has chosen same-sex erotic practices, not simply because Jews regarded homosexual practice as a classic example of pagan vice, but more particularly because it corresponds, in his view, to what humans in general have done in swapping God's truth for a lie.

> **A Non-Roman Perspective**
>
> Here, in Paul's formulation, was a perspective on sexual relations that Roman men would barely have recognised. The key to their erotic sense of themselves was not the gender of the people they slept with, but whether, in the course of having sex, they took the active or the passive role. Deviancy, to the Romans, was pre-eminently a male allowing himself to be used as though he were a female. Paul, by condemning the master who casually spent himself inside a slaveboy no less than the man who offered himself up to oral or anal penetration, had imposed on the patterns of Roman sexuality a thoroughly alien paradigm: one derived, in large part, from his upbringing as a Jew. Paul had been steeped in Torah. Twice the Law of Moses prohibited the lying of men with other men "as one lies with a woman." Paul, though, in his letter to the Romans, had given this prohibition a novel twist. Among the gentiles, he warned, it was not only men who committed indecent acts with others of their own sex. "Even their women exchanged natural relations for unnatural ones." A momentous denunciation.
>
> — Tom Holland

The underlying logic seems to be as follows. Those who worship the true God are, as Paul says elsewhere, renewed according to the divine image (Col 3:10). When this worship is exchanged for the worship of other gods, the result will be that this humanness, this image-bearing quality, is correspondingly distorted. Paul may suppose that in Genesis 1 it is male and female together that compose the image of God; or he may simply be taking it for granted that heterosexual intercourse is obviously the creator's intention for genital activity. Either way, his point is that homosexual behavior is a distortion of the creator's design and that such practices are evidence, not of the intention of any specific individual to indulge in such practice for its own sake, but of the tendency within an entire society for humanness to fracture when gods other than the true one are being worshiped. The point is: Exchange your God for an idol, and you will exchange your genuine humanness for a distorted version, which will do you no good.[4]

CHAPTER 11: THE PAULINE TEXTS (PART 1)

Having rooted his argument about the world's degenerate state in its rejection of what is evident about God and the divine nature through reflecting on his creation (i.e., idolatry), Paul also links everything he says about human sexuality to the divine order of creation and to God's revealed will for human relationships.

> The reference to God as Creator would certainly evoke for Paul, as well as for his readers, immediate recollections of the creation story in Genesis 1-3, which proclaims that "God created humankind in his own image . . . male and female he created them," charging them to "be fruitful and multiply" (Gen. 1:27-28). Similarly . . . Genesis 2:18-24 describes woman and man as created for one another and concludes with a summary moral: "Therefore a man leaves his father and his mother and clings to his wife, and they become one flesh." Thus, the complementarity of male and female is given a theological grounding in God's creative activity. By way of sharp contrast, in Romans 1 Paul portrays homosexual behavior as a "sacrament" (so to speak) of the antireligion of human beings who refuse to honor God as Creator. When human beings engage in homosexual activity, they enact an outward and visible sign of an inward and spiritual reality: the rejection of the Creator's design. Thus, Paul's choice of homosexuality as an illustration of human depravity is not merely random: it serves his rhetorical purposes by providing a vivid image of humanity's primal rejection of the sovereignty of God the Creator.[5]

Having set forth a traditional view of the New Testament text most central to this discussion, we turn now to a counter-case. In the next chapter, there will be a brief

---

The Language of "Exchange"

Revisionist authors sometimes argue that excess was the real problem. The ungodly in Paul's mind were those who, though capable of heterosexual attraction, became dissatisfied with their usual sexual activity, lusted after new experience, and sought out homosexual encounters. No doubt, much of homosexual practice in the ancient world was by men who also had sex with women, but this does not mean Paul had no concept of orientation or that the category would have altered his final conclusion.

Even if Paul did not use our modern vocabulary, his judgment is still the same. Homosexual behavior is a sin, not according to who practices it or by which motivation they seek it, but because that act itself, as a truth-suppressing exchange, is contrary to God's good design. . . .

The word for natural "relations" (kresis) in Romans 1:27 does not speak to the state of our desires, but to the state of our design, which is why the KJV has "natural use" and the NASB has "natural function." The problem with the consuming passion in verse 27 was not its intensity but that it corresponded to the giving up of man's natural sexual complementarity with women and committing shameless acts with other men.

— Kevin DeYoung

look at the two additional Pauline texts in the New Testament that mention same-sex relationships. Then, at the end of that chapter, Paul's cumulative teaching on the subject will be summarized.

A Revisionist Take on Romans 1

Because the straightforward reading of this text so clearly contradicts any attempted defense of same-sex behavior, David Gushee calls that reading into question by tossing out four alternative possibilities for interpreting it. He offers them after assuring readers that "massive scholarly literature about this text flows in a number of directions."[6] In fairness, he does not commit himself to any one of these positions. Instead, in the spirit of tossing a bit of sand in the air, he apparently wants to leave the impression that modern scholarship is uncertain about – if not thoroughly mystified by – Paul's statements to the Roman church. While revisionist literature has offered these counter readings, his comment seriously misrepresents scholarly textual literature on Romans 1 to suggest significant uncertainty about its altogether negative view of same-sex intercourse.

First, he offers the possibility that the "exchanging" language and references to giving up "natural" for "unnatural" sexual intercourse "may be saying that [Paul] thinks those engaging in same-sex intercourse were capable of 'normal,' natural heterosexual relations but perversely chose same-sex."[7] Setting aside the issue of genetic orientation for one's sexuality, this is hardly a plausible reading of the text. Paul is not discussing individual behavior choices but pagan society at large. His concern is not the occasional opposite-sex person who perversely pursues same-sex genital behavior against his or her natural orientation. He simply names lesbian and gay behavior as "unnatural" and "shameful" (1:26-27). It is the behavior that is judged, not the violation of an individual's genetic given or one's natural sexual orientation. Without regard to either context or motivation, it is the activity itself that is censured.

> On the matter of the genetic determination of one's sexual orientation, there is certainly no evidence of a "gay gene" or a fixed orientation of one's sexual attractedness by genetic factors. In one sense, however, the etiology of homosexual

orientation is not a significant factor for the formation of normative Christian ethics. We need not take sides in the debate of nature versus culture. Even if it could be shown that same-sex preference is somehow genetically programmed, that would not necessarily make homosexual behavior morally appropriate. Surely Christian ethics does not want to hold that all inborn traits are good and desirable.[8]

Second, Gushee advances the possibility that "same-sex behavior in the Greco-Roman world, very often, though not always . . . looked like pederasty, prostitution and master-slave sex." This would mean that these manipulated and/or coerced forms of same-sex behavior are in view but not necessarily those that were "consensual (not to mention loving and covenantal) same-sex relationships."[9] But Paul does not name or describe this relationship as young-old, master-slave, or powerful-vulnerable; he speaks simply and directly of "men with other men" (Gk, *arsenes en arsesin*) at 1:27b. Furthermore, since he also specifically names and reproves females for lesbian behaviors in 1:26, he cannot be naming pederasty (i.e., the exploitation of young boys by adult males). Both males and females are called out for engaging in this activity, so the "unnatural" or "shameful" behaviors here are not the pederastic behaviors of older males against younger ones but all forms of same-sex intercourse.

> **"Degrading of Their Bodies" (v.24)?**
>
> The context indicates that the dishonor lay with the inconsistency of this activity with what was "natural" (*physikos*, 1:26-27). "Natural" means neither "without passion" nor "culturally normal" but "what is obvious from the operation of the physical world" (cf. 2 Pet 2:12). Paul thought that the eternal power and divinity of the Creator were obvious from the physical world and led clearly to the conclusion that people should glorify and thank the Creator (1:20-21). In the same way, Paul probably considered the "natural" character of heterosexual activity to be obvious from the physical anatomy of male and female and from the role of heterosexual intercourse in the production of children.
>
> When human beings chose to revere and serve the creature rather than the Creator (1:25) and irrationally failed to glorify and thank God, their reasoning powers became futile and blurry, and they were shown to be foolish (1:21-22). In the same way, Paul considered homoerotic sexual activity to be foolish at an obvious level: it used the human body in a way contrary to its natural design, and it could accomplish nothing. Because of this, those who engaged in it dishonored themselves, and this is the sense in which they receive "in themselves" the recompense for their sin. At the level of human relations, this was equivalent to worshiping the creature rather than the Creator (1:25).
>
> — Frank Thielman

Third, Gushee takes note of Sarah Ruden's account of "widespread and quite vile Greco-Roman cultural practices authorizing violent anal rape of powerless young men, especially slaves, but really anybody of lower social status."[10] He then cites her view that "this is what Paul had in mind when he thought about same-sex interest and activity, and this is why he links it to other vices of excess and debauchery in Romans 1."[11] Again, this might be persuasive but for the fact that Paul was naming something that was not simply a male problem but also an issue among females. (This is the only biblical text, in fact, that points specifically to same-sex behaviors by females.) While the violation of male children or males of lower social strata in Rome was certainly condemned in Christian moral teaching, that is not what Paul specifically has named in Romans 1. It is any and all genital intercourse between persons of the same sex – whether by force or consent, whether in connection with a pagan temple or by private arrangement, whether as a one-time event or as part of a long-term, covenanted, and monogamous relationship.

Fourth, Gushee suggests that perhaps Romans 1 should be contextualized this way: "Paul was writing to Roman Christians, some of whom had connections in the Roman imperial court, and all of whom would be familiar with the craziness there."[12] Although historians provide graphic accounts of "craziness" in the lives of such emperors as Caligula and Nero, nothing in Romans 1 points to anything so case-specific. The chapter is not about Roman rulers or personal conduct by a subset of identifiable persons. To repeat what was said earlier, it is about the rejection of God by pagan culture generally and the eventual rejection of sexual roles assigned by God in creation itself. Both Josephus,[13] from his Jewish background, and various Greco-Roman moral philosophers cited below make the same distinction in their writings that Paul makes here. What Paul calls "natural" as opposed to "unnatural" sexual drives and behaviors is consistent with their vocabularies. They wrote of the fact that people exchanged "natural sexual relations for unnatural ones" (Gk, *tēn physikēn chrēsin eis tēn para physin* = *literally*, the natural use into the [use] against nature).

Gushee's strategy – characterized earlier as "tossing a bit of sand in the air" to chip away at Paul's unambiguous condemnation of same-sex – falls far short of casting doubt over his clear and unsparing language.

"Natural" vs. "Unnatural" in Paul's Vocabulary

Beginning no later than Plato, the meaning of sexual intercourse that is natural (Gk, *kata physin* = according to nature) versus unnatural (Gk, *para physin* = against nature) is spoken of by philosophers and ethicists. In his *Laws*, for example, Plato has the Athenian say this of behaviors at the gymnasium:

> More especially, the very antiquity of these practices seems to have corrupted the natural pleasures of sex, which are common to man and beast.... [W]hen male and female come together in order to have a child, the pleasure they experience seems to arise entirely naturally (*kata physin*). But homosexual intercourse and lesbianism seem to be unnatural (*para physin*) crimes of the first rank, and are committed because men and women cannot control their desire for pleasure.[14]

A study of primary sources beginning with Plato reveals that the prepositional phrase *para physin* (against nature) is used by a variety of persons – though seldom in their literature of ethical behaviors, for they are more likely to be discussing matters of science, physiology, and medicine – to mean "that which is against its created purpose" and not merely "out of its customary cultural setting." Thus, Aristotle allows that "nothing contrary to nature (Gk, *para physin*) is noble."[15] That Greek and Roman writers understood this language to refer to one's essential make-up rather than to something merely outside social custom has been documented carefully from the first century through the Middle Ages.[16]

Far more significant than this data concerning extra-biblical use of the terms "natural" and "unnatural" is Paul's own contextual usage. Later in Romans, he uses the same language to describe the natural growth of an olive tree and the grafting of a foreign branch into its stump in his explanation of how Gentiles have been made part of God's expanded Israel. "After all, if you were to cut out of an olive tree that is wild by nature (Gk, *kata physin*), and contrary to nature (Gk, *para physin*) were grafted into a cultivated olive tree, how much more readily will these, the natural (Gk, *kata physin*) branches, be grafted into their own olive tree!" (11:24).

Do we reasonably understand Paul to say that "wild" and "cultivated" olive trees are simply outside the ordinary or unconventional experience? Or does even the most casual reader hear the apostle contrasting what is intrinsic and native (Gk, *kata physin*) to a plant with what happens when something acquired and contrary to its essential

> **Josephus on para physin**
>
> Paul's description of same-sex activity at Romans 1 may be compared also to that of another Jewish contemporary, the historian Josephus. Defending Judaism to a Greek audience, Josephus elaborated "our laws about marriage" in this way: "That law owns no other mixture of the sexes but that which nature has appointed (kata physin), of a man with his wife, and that this be used only for the procreation of children. But it abhors the mixture of a male with a male (arrenas arrenōn); and if anyone does that, death is its punishment" (Against Apion 2.199.).
>
> Josephus contrasts sexual relations according to nature (kata physin) and sexual relations against nature; and he categorizes sexual relations as according to or against nature by the "mixture of the sexes" involved: sexual intercourse of "a man with his wife" is according to nature; sexual intercourse of "a male with a male" is against nature. In characterizing male-male sexual relations, Josephus uses generic terms that would apply to any "male" with any other "male" regardless of age, status, or sexual role. In these respects, Paul parallels Josephus: like Josephus, Paul categorizes sexual relations as "against nature" (para physin) by the mixture of the sexes involved (female-female and male-male are against nature); and, like Josephus, Paul characterizes same-sex relations using generic terms for "females" and "males" that cover all possible combinations in unnatural mixtures. Indeed, Paul's phrase "males with males" (arsenes en arsesin) closely parallels Josephus' phrase "males with males" (arrenas arrenōn).
>
> — Darrin Belousek

nature (Gk, *para physin*) happens to it? Wild olive trees put on branches and bear fruit according to their essential natures – unless and until something contrary to their ordered role in nature occurs. This internal-to-Romans use of the same Greek terms makes it most unlikely that he would have used vocabulary essential to these two central arguments in contrasting ways. Would that not be confusing to his readers?

Revisionists are quick to cite Paul's statement from 1 Corinthians 11:14-15 in an effort to cast doubt on the "nature" argument. "Does not the very nature (*physis*) of things teach you that if a man has long hair, it is a disgrace to him, but that if a woman has long hair, it is her glory? For long hair is given to her as a covering." Since it has already been granted that *physis* has a wide range of meaning, it is generally deemed plausible that the meaning here could be "by custom" or "within common expectation." However, that may be too quick a concession for what Paul is arguing here. It is altogether possible that his comment is not a simple parallel to a mother's advice that her son should look neat for his job interview. It well may be a reminder that Christian men are to abstain from effeminate looks and behaviors – regardless of the latest cultural trends of Rome, Europe, or North America.

The Apostle to the Gentiles certainly knew that it was "customary" within certain cultures of his day (e.g., Parthian, German) for men to wear their hair long. Even within Roman culture, Paul would have been able to spot a member of the Cynic school during his Acts 17 conversation with the philosophers of Athens by their tendency to let their hair grow long.

It is equally possible, therefore, to take the term *physis* in 1 Corinthians to mean the same thing as in Romans 1 – even as something of an echo of his argument there. If customary practice in some cultures both allowed and observed males with long hair, there were also settings within which males with long hair signaled an effeminate disposition and willingness to engage in same-sex intercourse. For example, priests of the cult of Cybele would accept castration, dress as women, and grow long hair to appear as females. "Cybele's priests were known as the *galli*; these men wore yellow or multi-colored robes with a tiara, and 'adorned [themselves] with ornaments,' rings, and earrings; they wore white make-up and curled their long hair."[17]

One may therefore argue with plausibility:

> Paul uses *physis* in accordance with its traditional meaning: "the way things are because they were created by God to be so." Thus, Paul's point is not that long hair is impossible for a man to grow but that an effeminate appearance for a man is unnatural. In 1 Corinthians 11:2-16, Paul is saying that men should be men and women should be women, according to nature. While hairstyles are a matter of custom, in Paul's day long hair on men suggested effeminacy in Greek and Roman culture. For a man to have long hair, then, was like cross-dressing – purposefully appearing contrary to his nature.[18]

Not Paul's View of the Matter?

Perhaps a more creative attempt at sidestepping the impact of Romans 1 is some variation of the claim that Paul is not giving his own apostolic view of same-sex relationships in this text. To the contrary, the claim is that he is inveighing against a narrow and legalistic view that would condemn them.

> Romans 1:24 says that God gave people up, or handed them over, to their vile passions and depraved hearts. . . . I think that since this idea does not at all reflect what we see in Jesus, or even what we see elsewhere in the writings of Paul, that we must conclude that something else is going on in the text.

> And what is that something else? It is Epistolary Diatribe.
>
> Romans 1:24 and the surrounding verses are not the ideas of Paul, but the ideas of a legalistic law-based religious teacher in Rome, whom Paul is quoting so that he can then refute him.[19]

By his acknowledgment in the larger piece from which this quotation is taken, the writer bases his claim on an approach to reading Romans that has been offered by Douglas Campbell.[20] Campbell is principally concerned to challenge both the forensic view of justification and the so-called "New Perspective" for interpreting Paul. In attempting to construct what he dubs an "apocalyptic" reading of Romans that few scholars have adopted, he makes the controversial suggestion that the section from Romans 1:18 – 3:20 has Paul laying out views that he is concerned to reject rather than his own position. In a word, as he prepares to indict both Second Temple Judaism and non-Jewish moralists for their self-righteousness toward pagans, Paul is only *describing* the world that an imaginary interlocutor encounters and not *prescribing* the moral stance Christians should take toward it.

Diatribe is an ancient rhetorical device and should not be confused with our common use of the word to refer to an abusive rant or tirade. It makes use of an imaginary discussion partner who asks questions or raises objections to ideas the speaker or writer is affirming.[21] Along with other New Testament writers, Paul certainly knows and uses the technique at times. For example, in the apostle's discussion of the Law of Moses in Galatians, he posits this possible objection from a hypothetical voice: "Is the law, therefore, opposed to the promises of God?" He responds in his own voice to say, "Absolutely not!" (Gal 3:21a). His Greek expression *mē genoito* is a typical marker for diatribe in both biblical and non-biblical writers.[22] Seeing, then, that Paul knows and uses this stylistic device, can his views on same-sex activity in Romans 1 be dismissed as an aberrant view he rejects?

A diatribe is often, but not always, signaled by such markers as "What shall we say, then" (Gk, *ti oun eroumen,* Rom 6:1; cf. 7:7; 9:14) or simply "then" (Gk, *oun*, 3:31; 7:13). No such marker for rebuttal occurs within the listing of behaviors and their consequences here. There is, instead, the straightforward introduction of an imagined objector (i.e., the "you" of 2:1,3,5) who is daring to "pass judgment on someone else" and – in Paul's view – "condemning yourself, because you who pass judgment do the same things" (2:1). Against the traditional reading[23] that his hypothetical critic is (a) presumed to be tolerating one or more of the vices in himself that he eagerly joins Paul to condemn, the Myers-Campbell view argues he is (b) acting as a legalist who thinks the Christian God would be guilty of retributive "wrath" in handing people over to their sins and their consequences.

> Romans 1:18-32 is sort of the introduction to what this other teacher was saying. Therefore, much of what we read in Romans 1:18-32 is not Paul's ideas, but the ideas of someone that Paul wants to refute.
>
> This is extremely significant, for it is only here in Romans that wrath is clearly attributed to God. Also, it is here that we read about God handing people over to their sin.
>
> And all of these ideas do not come from Paul, but rather from a legalistic teacher whom Paul sets out to refute in his letter to the Romans.[24]

In simple terms, this reduces to a simple disjunctive argument of the following form: "If John isn't in his dorm room, he is in the library. Since we just went to his room and found it empty, he must be in the library." By parallel: "Paul is either representing his own view of the acts named in Romans 1:18-32 or is rebuking those who believe the God revealed in Jesus is capable of 'wrath' against humankind." It is not difficult to prove that Paul not only does not have contempt for persons who believe in divine wrath against sin but also affirms it himself.

Paul is consistent to reflect a view of God's holiness that not only permits wrath against sin, but requires it. While Romans 3:21ff explains how the work of Christ has provided release from the eschatological judgment that awaits the impenitent, the theme of a pending reckoning for sin never disappears from the New Testament. Well after the passage in dispute, Paul still speaks of accountability, judgment, and wrath in Romans. For his readers still hoping to attain righteousness through the law rather than by faith, Paul warned that "the law brings wrath" (4:15). And he did not hesitate to repeat the word "wrath" still later to write: "What if God, although choosing to show his wrath and make his power known, bore with great patience the objects of his wrath – prepared for destruction?" (9:23). Even in a beautiful section of the epistle that revels in the power of sincere love, he does not hesitate to give this counsel: "Do not take revenge, my dear friends, but leave room for God's wrath, for it is written: 'It is mine to avenge; I will repay,' says the Lord" (12:19). God's wrath is not the bloodthirsty anger of some pagan deity – meted out capriciously and as the fancy of the deity drives him or her to avenge some slight. It is the fully justified wrath (i.e., judgment, rejection, punishment) that awaits all things dark and sinister that work against the best interests of his creation.

The disjunctive argument is now complete: "Paul is either representing his own view of the acts named in Romans 1:18-32 or is rebuking those who believe the God revealed in Jesus is capable of 'wrath' against humankind. But the apostle cannot be rebuking the very position about divine wrath he continues to press in the same epistle, so we must presume his denunciation of greed, malice, and same-sex behavior is his view of the matter."

The point of the variant reading of Paul's diatribe is to avoid the subjective sense so many seem to have nowadays that it is heartless to hold to some ancient notion of judgment and wrath. It becomes clear that this is the precise conclusion the Campbell-Myers proposal wants to establish.[25]

> Let me say it again: I do not believe that God hands us over to sin and Satan. He does not deliver us up to the destroyer. He does not withdraw His protective hand. He does not "Release the Kraken!" to have its way with us.
>
> As we see in Jesus Christ from first to last . . . God always forgives, only loves, and will never, ever, ever leave us or forsake us, but will be with us, even unto the end of the age.[26]

These few sentences above are, in fact, the conclusion to the Myers article. Reasoning back to front from this conclusion to its premises, something had to be done with the clear language of 1:26-27. One has to wonder if the same sort of argument to have Paul dismissing a legalistic view of same-sex behavior would have been forthcoming if there had been no mention of "unnatural" sexual encounters but only greed, murder, and outright hatred for God. Yet a closer look at the text Paul is alleged to be discounting names those very actions in verses 29-30. And are we really to suppose that Paul believed the failure to show faithfulness, mercy, and love were equally inconsequential in view of the cross? (v.31). If we allow that he dismisses same-sex intercourse but censures murder, how do we make that distinction from Romans 1? Or, if we praise mercy and love, how can we – except by sheer subjectivity?

The sort of argument that seeks to have Paul dismiss homoerotic behaviors as so inconsequential as to be the concern only of a narrow, judgmental, and legalistic soul would have far greater likelihood of sounding plausible if the apostle had drawn attention to them at the end rather than at the beginning of Romans. Beginning at 14:1, Paul identifies a series of topics that were (and *are* yet by some!) viewed as critical to righteousness and discounted their importance. He told the Roman church to steer clear of "quarreling over disputable matters" such as banning certain foods – or perhaps meat altogether – from one's diet (vs.2-3,6b), participation versus non-participation in sacred days (vs.5-6a), and drinking wine (v.21).

This is the blanket of toleration he spreads over all such things: "You, then, why do you judge your brother or sister? Or why do you treat them with contempt? ... Let us stop passing judgment on one another. ... Whatever you believe about these things keep between yourself and God" (vs.10,13a,22a). This is not biblical language about the deity of Jesus or such basic ethical requirements as the protection of marriage. To so redefine Paul's language about idolatry that leads to immoral behaviors from Romans 1:18-32 that it can be equated with his counsel about vegetarianism and wine on the dinner table does a gross disservice to biblical interpretation.

Although Romans 1 is the most extensive and most important New Testament text treating same-sex relationships, two others require attention as well. These, in turn, require a word study of two additional Greek terms. As you might expect, there are new ideas afoot as to how they might be translated and understood. So, we move now to explore 1 Corinthians 6:9-11 and 1 Timothy 1:9-11 in Chapter 12.

ENDNOTES

1. N.T. Wright, *Simply Christian: Why Christianity Makes Sense* (San Francisco: HarperCollins, 2006), 148.
2. Karl Barth, *The Epistle to the Romans* (London: Oxford University Press, 1933), 51.
3. Ibid.
4. N.T. Wright, "The Letter to the Romans," *The New Interpreter's Bible*, Vol 10 (Nashville: Abingdon Press, 2002), 433-434. In his "Reflections" over Rom 1:18-32, Wright adds this: "Paul's comment about homosexual behavior is deeply controversial today. Attempts have been made to mitigate its force by saying (for instance) that he is only referring to a deliberate swapping from heterosexual to homosexual practice, not to what in recent years has been regarded as an innate homosexual condition, or that he was only concerned with practices related to idolatrous cults. As in some other matters, it would be wrong to press 1:26-27 for a full analysis of same-sex desires or practices; but equally it is wrong to minimalize or marginalize what Paul teaches here" (435).
5. Hays, *Moral Vision of the New Testament*, 386.
6. Gushee, *Changing Our Mind*, 85.

7. Ibid., 86.

8. Hays, *Moral Vision of the NT*, 398.

9. Gushee, *Changing Our Mind*, 87.

10. Ibid.

11. Ibid., 88.

12. Ibid.

13. Josephus, *Against Apion* 2.38.

14. Plato, *Laws* I, 636b-c as translated by Trevor J. Saunders in John M. Cooper, ed., *Plato: Complete Works* (Indianapolis: Hackett Publishing Company, 1997), 1330. In the older Loeb Classical Library translation by R.G. Bury, the English is a bit more wooden and reads as follows: "[A]nd moreover, this institution, when of old standing, is thought to have corrupted the pleasures of life which are natural (κατὰ φύσιν) not to men only but also natural to beasts.... [W]hen males unite with female for procreation the pleasure experienced is held to be due to nature (κατὰ φύσιν), but contrary to nature (παρὰ φύσιν) when male mates with male or female with female, and that those first guilty of such enormities were impelled by their slavery to pleasure." E.H. Warmingdon, ed., *Plato in Twelve Volumes*, Vol X, Loeb Classical Library (Cambridge: Harvard University Press, 1926), p. 41. In his *Timaeus*, where Plato gives his account of the physical creation, he "explains" that the Creator wanted all things in his creation ("in the realm of all things *naturally* [κατὰ φύσιν] visible" in the Cooper translation or "such creatures as are *by nature* [κατὰ φύσιν] visible" in Loeb) to be ordered by intelligence; this Creator wanted the cosmos to be "as excellent and supreme as its *nature* [κατὰ φύσιν] would allow" (Cooper) or "so the work He was executing might be *of its nature* [κατὰ φύσιν] most fair and most good" (30b-c). Cf. Roy Bowen Ward, "Why Unnatural? Tradition behind Romans 1:26-27," *Harvard Theological Review* 90 (1997): 263-284.

15. Aristotle, *Politics* 7. 1325b.

16. Cf. S. Donald Fortson III and Rollin G. Grams, *Unchanging Witness: The Consistent Christian Teaching on Homosexuality in Scripture and Tradition* (Nashville: Broadman & Holman Academic, 2016), 27-68. "Though pagan writers wrongly accused Christians of participating in perverse sexual acts, the church consistently denounced fornication, adultery, and all homosexual acts as incompatible with Christian faith. A number of the Fathers wrote commentaries on Paul's epistles and consequently dealt with the apostle's perspective on homosexuality. Early Christians condemned all practices that involved members of the same gender participating in sexual acts with one another. This included pederasty, male dominance/rape, effeminacy, lesbianism, male homosexuality, transsexuality, prostitution, temple prostitution, orgies, and homosexual 'marriages.' It was not merely a specific type of homosexual activity that was considered unacceptable, even though specific texts mentioned specific practices (such as pederasty). The church fathers condemned the immorality underlying *all* such practices" (28).

17. Anna Clark, *A History of European Sexuality* (New York: Routledge, 2008), 28.

18. Fortson and Grams, *Unchanging Witness*, 327.

19. Jeffery Myers, "Epistolary Diatribe in the Letters of Paul (No, really! It's Interesting. I promise!)." Accessed April 19, 2023, at https://redeeminggod.com/epistolary-diatribe-letters-of-paul.

20. Douglas Campbell, *The Deliverance of God: An Apocalyptic Rereading of Justification in Paul* (Grand Rapids: Eerdmans, 2009). Worthwhile reviews of the book can be found in Grant Macaskill, "Review Article: The Deliverance of God" *Journal for the Study of the New Testament* 34, no. 2 (Dec 2011): 150-161 and Douglas J. Moo, "The Deliverance of God: An Apocalyptic Rereading of Justification in Paul by Douglas A. Campbell," *Journal of the Evangelical Theological Society* 53, no. 1 (Mar 2010): 143-50.

21. For a discussion of the diatribe as a literary device in Pauline literature, cf. Abraham Malherbe, "ΜΗ ΓΕΝΟΙΤΟ in the Diatribe and Paul," *Harvard Theological Review* 73, no 1-2 (1980), 231-240.

22. Ibid., 232.

23. Cf. F.F. Bruce, *Romans: An Introduction and Commentary* (Grand Rapids: IVP Academic, 1985), 92-94; N.T. Wright, *Paul for Everyone Romans: Part 1 (Chapters 1-8)* (Louisville, KY: Westminster John Knox Press, 2004), 28-31.

24. Myers, "Epistolary Diatribe in the Letters of Paul."

25. The argument here is a variant of what has been offered earlier by Furnish in V.P. Furnish, *The Moral Teaching of Paul: Selected Issues*, 2nd ed. (Nashville: Abingdon Press, 1985), 78-80; idem. "The Bible and Homosexuality: Reading the Texts in Context," in Jeffery S. Siker (ed), *Homosexuality in the Church* (Louisville: Westminster John Knox Press, 1994), 19. Furnish argues that Paul is not enumerating sins from which people need to repent but preparing to affirm the unconditional grace [e.g., "saving grace is bestowed as a sheer gift (e.g., 3:24), with absolutely no conditions (e.g., 5:6,8)."] which has freed believers from all sin – including perhaps the worst of all sins, judging others.

26. Myers, "Epistolary Diatribe in the Letters of Paul." Note: The "Release the Kraken!" phrase comes from the 1981 movie "Clash of the Titans" and refers to a scene in which the pagan gods determine to release a horrible beast against the humans who have angered them.

> *"The combination of terms,* malakoi *and* arsenokoitai,
> *are correctly understood in our contemporary
> context when they are applied to every
> conceivable type of same-sex intercourse."*
> — Robert Gagnon

CHAPTER 12

The Pauline Texts (Part 2): 1 Corinthians 6:9-11 and 1 Timothy 1:9-11

This chapter will explore the remaining two Pauline texts that deal with the situation of persons who engage in same-sex practices. With that, we will have examined all the New Testament texts on the subject. The references in Jude 7 and 2 Peter 2:6-7, you may recall, have been brought up already in Chapter 6 because of their link to the story of Sodom.

Most students consider Romans 1 to be the heart of all the New Testament texts on our subject because of its straightforward language and the inclusion of both lesbian and gay conduct. Against the efforts of different people to make Paul's subject matter in Romans so narrow as to apply only to pederasty, master-slave sexual abuse, and/ or the carnal "craziness" of Nero, his apostolic judgment against female-female and male-male sex seems clear. The subject is not only exploitative and abusive sex, but also sex by consent (i.e., persons of the same sex who are "inflamed with lust for one another") that is "unnatural" (i.e., outside the created order).

In the remaining Pauline texts to be examined here, two Greek words come into play that require close scrutiny. But standard translations of the Bible into English have been questioned as to whether they have identified same-sex practices correctly. Some scholars have proposed – and a movie has been produced recently to argue – that it is translation mistakes rather than the original biblical text that brought same-sex behaviors under recent social and legal censure.

So we must look at Paul's use of the words *malakoi* and *arsenokoitai*. Are they negative toward same-sex behaviors? Do they refer to anything that relates to same-sex practices at all?

1 Corinthians 6:9-11

From the traditional view, one of the more positive texts on this subject in either the Old or New Testament has Paul celebrating the fact that some of the Jesus-followers in Corinth had been rescued from their pre-conversion lifestyles that embraced a variety of sinful behaviors.

> Or do you not know that wrongdoers will not inherit the kingdom of God? Do not be deceived: Neither the sexually immoral nor idolaters nor adulterers nor *men who have sex with men* nor thieves nor the greedy nor drunkards nor slanderers nor swindlers will inherit the kingdom of God. And that is what some of you were. But you were washed, you were sanctified, you were justified in the name of the Lord Jesus Christ and by the Spirit of our God (1 Cor 6:9-11).

While there is recent literature from affirming writers that calls into question the translation of the final three Greek words of verse nine (*malakoi oute arsenokoitai*) – italicized in the English citation above – the consensus of biblical scholarship is supportive of the words used in our standard English translations. The words are variously translated "effeminate nor homosexuals" (NASB), "male prostitutes, sodomites" (NRSV), "male prostitutes, men who engage in illicit sex" (NRSVue), or "men who have sex with men" (NIV). A footnote to the NIV adds this: "The words *men who have sex with men* translate two Greek words that refer to the passive and active participants in homosexual acts."

Neither Greek nor Latin has a word that corresponds to our "heterosexual," "homosexual," or "bisexual"; instead, both have words that signify the roles taken by participants in the sexual act. Both Greek and Roman cultures were highly patriarchal, thus the submissive (i.e., penetrated) person was seen as effeminate or weak. The dominant (i.e., penetrating) partner was regarded as stronger and controlling. Regardless of linguistic debate, the consensus among scholars is that the word denotes same-sex activity of some sort.

On this point, Gushee rather presumptuously dismisses the text in question this way: "I do not concede that the terms *malakoi* and *arsenokoitai* in 1 Cor 6:9 can definitively be interpreted as meaning the passive and active partners in same-sex male intercourse."[1] I call this wave-of-the-hand statement "imperious" for the simple reason that Gushee is neither a linguistic scholar with the gravitas to be so dismissive nor is he able to cite standard lexicographical sources that support his position. Although not citing him, he appears to be mirroring the claim made by Boswell that *malakos*[2] "is never used in Greek to designate gay people as a group or even in reference to homosexual acts generically"[3] and "the soundest inference is that '*malakos*' refers to general moral weakness, with no specific connection to homosexuality."[4] This unevidenced claim stands against standard reference works on the Greek language.

> **How Best to Translate?**
> Multiple Greek authors attest that malakos was a typical way to designate a man who flouted traditional male gender norms and behaved in ways that showed passivity or various shades of "femininity." For this reason, it was a term readily applicable to men who were penetrated in sexual intercourse with other men.
>
> On the other hand, the term to which malakos is paired . . . is arsenokoites in Greek. A compound word (comprised of, literally, "male" and "bed"), it is not attested in any extant Greek texts prior to Paul. It does, however, have a strong verbal connection to the Septuagint renderings of both Leviticus 18:22 and 20:13, where both halves of the compound are used. This has led many scholars to suggest that Paul probably coined the term himself in dependence on the Greek text of Leviticus. And if that is the case, then this text, like Romans 1, points to the deep embeddedness of Paul's opposition to same-sex sexual acts in Israel's Scripture and, hence, in creation.
>
> — Wesley Hill
>
> [Note: See Appendix 4 "Review of '1946'" for information on a controversy over translation choices for these words in the RSV, NRSV, and NRSVue.]

The fourth occurrence [of *malakos*] is in 1 Cor 6:9, as part of a list that identifies those who will not inherit the kingdom of God: *oute pornoi oute eidōlolatrai oute moichoi oute malakoi oute arsenokoitai*. An attempt at a lit[eral] rendering of these terms would be: "fornicators [NIV, 'the sexually immoral'; see *porneuō* G4519], idolaters, adulterers, soft ones, men who go to bed with men." The precise meaning of the last two terms is difficult to determine. Both the NIV 1984 and the NRSV render *malakoi* here as "male prostitutes"; although there is in fact evidence that the term could be applied thus, usually it appears to have a broader sense. The other term, *arsenokoitēs* G780, prob[ably] had a narrower meaning than "sodomite"

(NRSV) or "homosexual offender" (NIV 1984). The NIV 2011 renders both terms together with the phrase "men who have sex with men," with a note explaining that the words refer respectively "to the passive and active participants in homosexual acts." This understanding is supported by BDAG, which says that the term *malakos* was applied to *catamites*, i.e, "men and boys who are sodomized by other males," whereas *arsenokiotēs* was applied to *pederasts*, i.e., men who use boys (whether prostitutes or not) for sexual gratification.[5]

> **Paul's Positive Message**
> Paul's words are full of grace. They wound in order to heal. In v. 11, he reminds us of the resources that are available in Christ to cover the guilt of sin, to dethrone the dominion of sin, and to mortify indwelling sin, "But you were washed, you were sanctified, you were justified in the name of the Lord Jesus Christ and by the Spirit of our God." Same-sex sin is not unpardonable. It can be covered by the blood of Christ. Neither is a person who wrestles with temptations to same-sex sin consigned to despair before the prospect of unbroken slavery to it. There is grace in Christ that offers sinners hope–hope to be delivered from the tyranny of sin, and hope to live under the wholesome lordship of Christ; hope to put sin to death, and hope to become more and more like the Savior whom they love.
> — Guy Waters

Both Gushee's offhand rejection of the translations cited above – and particularly, it would appear, of the NIV's translation and footnote – and Boswell's earlier claim on which he and others have relied are unwarranted. Boswell either didn't find or chose to ignore Greek writings that unquestionably refer to same-sex activity that have been cited earlier in this book – for both Greek and Roman cultures. Contrary to Hamilton, who claims the two words "may refer primarily to male prostitutes and those who frequented them,"[6] the linguistic evidence cannot be read so narrowly. In particular, the term *malakos* has a significantly broader sense than male prostitute and applies to a variety of settings in which men have intercourse with either young or adult males. While either term would *include* male prostitutes and their patrons, they simultaneously bring in all males – prostitutes, pedophiles, rapists, pederasts, committed partners, covenanted pairs, "married" couples, and any others – who engage in same-sex intercourse.

Non-Biblical Writers on "Soft Males"

Philo (*ca.* 20 B.C. – *ca.* A.D. 50) was a Jewish philosopher-theologian who lived in Alexandria. Writing about a particularly offensive pagan behavior involving man-boy sex (Gk, *paiderastēs*), he broadened his criticism to adult males who pursued sexual trysts by dressing and behaving as females. He thus inveighs against both pederasty and effeminate (Gk, *malakias*) adult males who solicited sex as if they were females. In his commentary on the sixth and seventh commandments, his view about both is made clear. Contra Boswell, it is beyond dispute that the issue is "gay people" and "homosexual acts" – not a vague and general moral weakness.

> Moreover, another evil, much greater than that which we have already mentioned, has made its way among and been let loose upon cities, namely, the love of boys (Gk, *to paiderastein*), which formerly was accounted a great infamy even to be spoken of, but which sin is a subject of boasting not only to those who practise [sic] it, but even to those who suffer it, and who, being accustomed to bearing the affliction of being treated like women, waste away as to both their souls and bodies, not bearing about them a single spark of a manly character to be kindled into a flame, but having even the hair of their heads conspicuously curled and adorned, and having their faces smeared with vermilion, and paint, and things of that kind, and having their eyes pencilled [sic] beneath, and having their skins anointed with fragrant perfumes (for in such persons as these a sweet smell is a most seductive quality), and being well appointed in everything that tends to beauty or elegance, are not ashamed to devote their constant study and endeavours to the task of changing their manly character into an effeminate one. And it is natural for those who obey the law to consider such persons worthy of death, since the law commands that the man-woman who adulterates the precious coinage of his nature shall die without redemption, not allowing him to live a single day, or even a single hour, as he is a disgrace to himself, and to his family, and to his country, and to the whole race of mankind. And let the man who is devoted to the love of boys (Gk, *paiderastēs*) submit to the same punishment, since he pursues that pleasure which is contrary to nature (Gk, *para physin*), and since, as far as depends upon him, he would make the cities desolate, and void, and empty of all inhabitants, wasting his power of propagating his species, and moreover, being a guide and teacher of those greatest of all evils, unmanliness and effeminate (Gk, *malakias*) lust . . .[7]

As with the use of any Greek or English word, it is ultimately context that supplies meaning. So, while there are Greek texts in which a word for "softness" may have a great variety of meanings, discussions of ethical behavior such as this one from Philo leaves no question of meaning and shows the Boswell-based claim repeated by Gushee is mistaken. The language used of men who lotion, perfume, coif

> **Greek Background to Malakos**
>
> The figure of the malakos, the "soft one," also appears in the Pauline vice lists. . . . The essence of malakia was softness, an interior disposition formed of luxuriance, effeminacy, and weakness. Sexual deviance was not the sole mark of softness, but it was a practically inevitable consequence of the inability to impose one's hard will on the enervating poison of desire. Excessive fondness for bathing, fine food, and soft clothing were characteristic of the malakos, but "above all and with the least self-control" he was possessed by "a sharp and scalding madness for sex, for coition with both women and with men, and even for inexpressible and unknown acts of shame."
>
> The malakos was as likely to surrender to the love of women as to the love of men. The desire underlying the sexual behavior of the malakos was not so much deviant as excessive, a surplus of lust dissolving the steely power over the self that was the surest guarantee of manliness in the ancient Mediterranean.
>
> — Kyle Harper

their hair, and otherwise follow feminine routines supports the argument made by Gagnon that – while the word may apply to sexual liaisons other than those between adult males – "*malakoi* should be understood as the passive partners in homosexual intercourse, the most egregious case of which are those who also intentionally engage in a process of feminization to erase further their masculine appearance and manner."[8]

In what is generally taken to be the authoritative dictionary for Classical Greek, the *Brill Dictionary* not only covers the broad usage of the noun *malakia* and adjective *malakos* as they relate to delicate surfaces, soft clothing, and gentle dispositions but also points to a passage in Diogenes Laertius (*ca.*180-*ca.*240) that it offers as a parallel to Paul's usage here. It assigns the meaning "depraved, effeminate."[9] The passage in Diogenes is a rather coarse section in which "belly-thumping" and "thigh-thumping" behaviors by males is characterized as *malakos*. This leaves no room for the claim that some sort of moral weakness "with no specific connection to homosexuality" is indicated by the word.

Pseudo-Lucian on Same-Sex Eroticism

There is also the use of the verb *malakizō* in Pseudo-Lucian's *Erōtes*.[10] Usually referred to in English as either "Two Kinds of Love" or simply "Loves," it is a debate on the nature, appropriateness, and relative value of sexual desire for females and boys. Although focused on pederasty and moving to the conclusion that love (Gk, *erōs* = passion, erotic desire) for boys is superior to love for women because – on what is known to have been a widespread misogynistic view of the Greco-Roman world –

males had superior intelligence and pursued valor over vanity, courage over comfort.

The two disputants are Callicratidas, adamant to defend the pederasty that was common in Greco-Roman culture, and Charicles, who argued that passion for females was to be preferred. Listening to the discussion were two men whose discussion of the topic is the background and setting for the debate; Lycinas is represented as essentially asexual and without interest in sex with either males or females, and Theomnestus is bisexual.[11] The interesting thing to moderns about this debate is that the issue has very little to do with what we think of as "morality." It is about practicality.

Callicratidas presses the claim that sex with boys is preferable because of what he sees as the general male superiority to females. Specifically, the Greek idea was that males care about "virtue" (Gk, *aretē*), whereas women focus on hair, face, and other elements of life that are frivolous. *Aretē* was more about "excellence" – the English word often used to translate *aretē* – in activities ranging from athletics to ruling a city than about the moral

> **Philo on Male-Male Sex**
>
> [Note: Philo (ca.20 B.C.-ca.50 A.D.) wrote from his Jewish background as a contemporary of Jesus and Paul. This quotation is from his "On the Life of Abraham." His view would have reflected the Jewish view of that period.]
>
> The country of the Sodomites was a district of the land of Canaan, which the Syrians afterwards called Palestine, a country full of innumerable iniquities, and especially of gluttony and debauchery, and all the great and numerous pleasures of other kinds which have been built up by men as a fortress, on which account it had been already condemned by the Judge of the whole world. And the cause of its excessive and immoderate intemperance was the unlimited abundance of supplies of all kinds which its inhabitants enjoyed. For the land was one with a deep soil, and well watered, and as such produced abundant crops of every kind of fruit every year. And he was a wise man and spoke truly who said, "The greatest cause of all iniquity is found in overmuch prosperity."
>
> As men, being unable to bear discreetly a satiety of these things, get restive like cattle, and become stiff-necked, and discard the laws of nature, pursuing a great and intemperate indulgence of gluttony, and drinking, and unlawful connections; for not only did they go mad after women, and defile the marriage bed of others, but also those who were men lusted after one another, doing unseemly things, and not regarding or respecting their common nature, and though eager for children, they were convicted by having only an abortive offspring; but the conviction produced no advantage, since they were overcome by violent desire; and so, by degrees, the men became accustomed to be treated like women, and in this way engendered among themselves the disease of females, and intolerable evil; for they not only, as to effeminacy and delicacy, became like women in their persons, but they made also their souls most ignoble, corrupting in this way the whole race of man, as far as depended on them.
>
> — Philo of Alexandria

qualities considered virtuous in Judeo-Christian writings. The pederastic relationship between the adult male (Gk, *erastēs*) and his boy lover (Gk, *erōmenos*) functioned as a mentoring relationship – with presumed sexual "benefits" for the former. When the latter entered early manhood as evidenced by body hair and muscularity, his *erastēs* would eventually choose another young *erōmenos* as he himself would become the *erastēs* to a boy. This self-perpetuating cycle did not, however, mean that the original relationship would end of necessity. The boy who had become a man might well continue a friendship with his original *erastēs*.

That the adult relationship between the two persons of the same sex might well continue to include homoerotic elements is clear from both an initial reference to Socrates' apparent love for the younger Alcibiades in the *Symposium*[12] – an erotic link that continued into Alcibiades' adult years – and also an allusion to the adult relationship of Achilles and Patroclos from the *Iliad*.[13] Charicles argues against Callicratidas' view by pointing out that the human race would simply die off if men had sex only with males. Furthermore, he insisted, if persons such as Callicratidas find greater erotic delight in anal sex, women can not only procreate via vaginal intercourse but can also supply whatever delight anal sex provides as well as boys.

Mind-numbing and even offensive as this detail may be, it allows the following quotation from *Erōtes* to be read intelligently. Charicles explains that the goddess Aphrodite arranged for human reproduction to require the union of both male and female.

> For she allowed males as their peculiar privilege to ejaculate semen, and made females to be a vessel as it were for the reception of seed, and, imbuing both sexes with a common desire, she linked them to each other, ordaining as a sacred law of necessity that each should retain its own nature and that neither should the female grow unnaturally (Gk, *para physin*) masculine nor the male be unbecomingly soft (Gk, *malakizesthai*).[14]

All this combines to demonstrate the mistake made in claiming that *malakos* is "never used in Greek to designate gay people as a group" and has "no specific connection to homosexuality." In connection with both pederasty and adult sexual liaisons, the term has specific reference to same-sex practices – typically indicating the "soft" partner being either a boy or an adult male who is penetrated in the sexual act.

But what of the second of the two terms Gushee wishes to exclude? Since it occurs not only in 1 Corinthians 6:9 but also in 1 Timothy, we move next to examine *arsenokoitai*.

1 Timothy 1:9-11

Because a form of the word *arsenokoitēs* appears not only in 1 Corinthians but also – for its only other occurrence in the New Testament – in Paul's "vice list" in 1 Timothy 1, I have chosen to introduce the latter quotation here to avoid repetition.

> We also know that the law is made not for the righteous but for lawbreakers and rebels, the ungodly and sinful, the unholy and irreligious, for those who kill their fathers or mothers, for murderers, for the sexually immoral, for *those practicing homosexuality*, for slave traders and liars and perjurers—and for whatever else is contrary to the sound doctrine that conforms to the gospel concerning the glory of the blessed God, which he entrusted to me.

In this text, the italicized words parallel the translation of the second word in question from 1 Corinthians 6. More specifically, *arsenokoitēs* is the term that refers to the active (penetrative) participant in same-sex intercourse. Standard Greek lexicons, English translations of the New Testament, and the majority of contemporary scholars understand the word this way. Dunn points out that 1 Timothy 6:9 seems to be laying out a sequence of amplifications of the Decalogue's commandments against dishonoring parents, murder, adultery, theft, perjury. "Today the most controversial of these is the putting of homosexual practice (v.10; the term almost certainly comes from Lev 18:22; 20:13) under the prohibition of

---

Contrary to "Sound Teaching"

Thus, Paul's use of the term (arsenokoitai) presupposes and reaffirms the holiness code's condemnation of homosexual acts. This is not a controversial point in Paul's argument; the letter gives no evidence that anyone at Corinth was arguing for the acceptance of same-sex erotic activity. Paul simply assumes that his readers will share his conviction that those who indulge in homosexual activity are "wrongdoers" (adikoi, literally "unrighteous"), along with the other sorts of offenders in his list. . . .

The 1 Timothy passage includes arsenokoitai in a list of "the lawless and disobedient," whose behavior is specified in a vice list that includes everything from lying to slave-trading to murdering one's parents, under the rubric of actions "contrary to the sound teaching that conforms to the glorious gospel."

— Richard Hays

adultery; the teaching is consistent with Paul's views expressed earlier in Rom 1:26-27; 1 Cor 6:9-10."[15]

There is no point in denying that the history of languages reveals a significant problem with the term(s) we use to describe same-sex intercourse. A few years back, when this topic was just beginning to break open for discussion in churches, a young man put this question to me: "Is it true that Hebrew and Greek don't even have a word for 'homosexual' or 'homosexuality'? So how could the Bible have anything to say about gay people?" He was neither advocating nor opposing same-sex relationships with his question. But he wasn't sure that the person who pressed that information on him wasn't correct in *his* argument that modern Christians were opposing something on which the Bible actually said nothing.

My response was to remind him that we use lots of terms in our conversations today that reflect the evolving nature of language. The fact that our *word* is of recent origin does not mean that the *concept* or *behavior* in question is not in view in Scripture. For example, here are a few of the words both Christians and non-Christians use in our conversations that are not in standard translations of the Bible: Trinity, atheism, rapture, omnipotence, incarnation, halo. Oh, yes. We probably should not omit the word heterosexual. Or Bible. What is the point?

The fact that ancient Jews and Greeks did not have transfer terms for an English word we use hardly means they did not know the concept and could not discuss a given topic. For example, as I explained to my young friend, the descriptive language "have sexual relations with a man as one does with a woman" at Leviticus 18:22 is the basic definition of homosexual or gay sex acts. The writer and/or editors of the Torah did not have a one-word equivalent for our term "homosexuality," but they had the concept. And that concept is unmistakably clear in the biblical text.

Similarly, Foucault and other scholars have pointed out that the ancient Greeks were less concerned with either the concepts or words that equal our "heterosexual" and "homosexual" as they were in the celebration of *erōs*.

> Probably the most frequent assumption about sexual orientation, at least by ancient Greek authors, is that persons can respond erotically to beauty in either sex. Diogenes Laertius, for example, wrote of Alcibiades, the Athenian general and politician of the 5th century B.C., "in his adolescence he drew away the husbands

from their wives, and as a young man the wives from their husbands." (Quoted in Greenberg, 1988, 144) Some persons were noted for their exclusive interests in persons of one gender. For example, Alexander the Great and the founder of Stoicism, Zeno of Citium, were known for their exclusive interest in boys and other men. Such persons, however, are generally portrayed as the exception. Furthermore, the issue of what biological sex one is attracted to is seen as an issue of taste or preference, rather than as a moral issue. A character in Plutarch's *Erotikos* (*Dialogue on Love*) argues that "the noble lover of beauty engages in love wherever he sees excellence and splendid natural endowment without regard for any difference in physiological detail" (*ibid*., 146). Gender just becomes irrelevant "detail" and instead the excellence in character and beauty is what is most important.[16]

While one may grant that a modern word in English,[17] German, French, and other languages is not a direct transfer from our earliest biblical texts, one cannot proceed from that to conclude the Bible says nothing about the concept, performance, or ethical judgment involved. For that matter, the evolution of language about sexual behaviors continues to the present and will remain to the end of time. Apps, videos, and online sites have reportedly in the press to have expanded their "terminology of homosexuality" to include not only the widely known terms gay, straight, lesbian, queer, etc. but also tops, bottoms, verse (versatile), and sides.[18]

A New Word for Christian Vocabulary?

This history of terminology provides background to Paul's use of – many scholars choose to say the "coining" of – the word *arsenokoitēs*. David Wright has made a strong case that other scholars have followed to the effect that Paul or one of his peer Hellenistic Jews formed the word from their reading of Leviticus 18:22 and 20:13 in Greek (i.e., the Septuagint).[19] English readers with no knowledge of Greek at all can visualize how the word was formed.[20]

> Lev 18:22 - *kai meta **arsenos** ou koimēthēsē **koitēn** gynaikos bdelygma gar estin*and with a **male** you shall not lie **in a bed** femininely abomination for it is
> Lev 20:13 - *kai hos an koimēthē meta **arsenos koitēn** gynaikos, bdelygma epoiēsan amphoteroi* and whoever who should lie with a **male** as **in a bed** of a woman, abomination did both

Standard scholarly sources echo essentially the same information on the term:

> The compound *arsenokoitēs* (see *koitē* G3130, "bed, sexual intercourse"), not attested prior to the NT, occurs twice in the Pauline corpus (1 Cor 6:9 [in a list of those excluded from the kingdom of God]; 1 Tim 1:10 [in a list of acts condemned by the law]). The ref. is clearly to someone who practices homosexuality (cf. Lev 18:22, *meta arsenos ou koimēthēsē koitēn gynaikos,* lit., "you will not sleep with a man in the bed of a woman"; sim. 20:13) . . .[21]

The nouns *arsēn* (Gk, male) and *koitē* (Gk, bed, marriage bed, sexual intercourse[22]) appear to have been squeezed into one word by Paul to describe "male-bedders" or "males who have sex with males." It is this linguistic background that justifies the New International Version's "men who have sex with men" at 1 Corinthians 6:9. The footnote to the NIV text explains: "The words *men who have sex with men* translate two Greek words that refer to the passive and active participants in homosexual acts." In other words, the pairing of the words *malakos* (soft one, effeminate male, penetrated partner) and *arsenokoitēs* (active person, masculine one, penetrating partner) yields the NIV language. Paul's use of the two terms in this way removes the qualifications that some have wanted to place on his attitude toward same-sex relationships. Used together, the two words capture male same-sex intercourse *without* qualification and in near-graphic description. Without reference to age or coercion, anonymity with a prostitute or long-term commitment with covenanted partner, Paul identifies male same-sex intercourse as sinful. Since the act itself is sinful and forbidden to Jesus-followers, placing it within the context of "loving, monogamous, and committed relationships" does nothing to legitimate it.

As to the attempt at setting "qualifications" around his use of these words, the entry quoted above from the *New International Dictionary of New Testament Theology and Exegesis* is fair to certain modern writers by acknowledging them. Picking up the quotation where I indicated with an ellipsis that it had been left incomplete, it ends this way: ". . . but many believe that this term has the more specific meaning 'pederast,' i.e., a man who assumes the dominant role in homosexual activity." In other words, rather than taking *arsenokoitēs* to signify homosexual behavior under some general heading or as a technical term to distinguish the penetrating male from his partner, revisionist writers such as Boswell, Scroggs, Gushee, and others offer the limitation that it is a reference to pederasty.

The Pauline Summary

With the background of what has been documented about pederasty and adult same-sex relationships in ancient cultures over against the severe counter-cultural language of the biblical text, the following points should help provide clarity. In particular, the summary statements of the apostle charged with taking the gospel to the non-Jewish world where a same-sex culture was widely known are of primary significance.

Against the claim made by revisionists, there were language-specific words for pederasty, exploitation, and/or violence (i.e., rape) that Paul would have known if only exploitative sex with young men was his intended subject. Paul was among the most brilliant minds of his time and hardly a man of limited vocabulary. A partial list of the terms available to Paul would include such words as the following:

- *Porneia* was a sweeping term that could mean anything from bestiality to prostitution, from sex between unmarried persons to adultery, from pedophilia (i.e., sex with infants and/or prepubescent children) to pederasty (i.e., sex between an adult male and a boy between the ages of approximately 12 to 20). The word means any form of sexual intercourse other than that between a man and woman who are married to each other.

- *Paiderastēs* means "lover of boys" and is, of course, the etymological background to our English words pederast and pederasty. As indicated already, these older-to-younger relationships had different meanings in Greece and Rome.

- *Erastēs* is the Greek term for the dominant – and usually senior in both age and status – partner in a pederastic relationship. Institutionalized in Greek culture, Romans took a dim view of these adult-youth pairings in view of their image of virile manhood.

- *Erōmenos* is the corresponding word for the submissive – and typically younger in age and always in status – partner in a same-sex relationship. The relationship of an *erōmenos* to his lover in ancient Greece would be deemed successful if it led to his intended admission into elite society with a position of some stature. At that point, he could become the *erastēs* to a younger man – although that would not necessarily terminate his relationship to his own mentor-lover. Again, the Roman view was quite different and likely would not have been tolerated among the empire's upper classes.

- *Kinaidos* is yet another vocabulary word with a significantly negative meaning. It identifies an adult who chose a permanent life as an effeminate male whose sexual preference was to be penetrated anally. In both Greek and Roman cultures, this signified the abandonment of masculinity and typically was synonymous with "male prostitute" and was a derogatory term.

- *Biasmos* is the Greek noun occasionally used for rape and is from a family of words that refer to attacking a person, overpowering by force, or forcing one's way on another.

In summary of all this tedious-to-some-readers information, the claim by affirming writers that Paul somehow needed to create a new word that would point to pederasty and exploitative same-sex relationships is fanciful. The wide-ranging list of terms here – which is by no means exhaustive – is offered simply to show that those words had an established usage and were known to literate persons such as Paul. If the target of his indictment had been pederasty or some other form of sexual coercion as opposed to *all* same-sex intercourse, he had the language for doing so without coining a new word. He was not addressing pederasty with the word *arsenokoitai* but simply "men who have sex with men" – whether as pederasts, prostitutes, rapists, or consenting adults. It is a broad term that cannot be restricted to specific types of male-male intercourse.

The respected New Testament scholar Richard Hays discusses the word in question in relation both to its origin and significance this way:

> The other word, *arsenokoitai*, is not found in any extant Greek text earlier than 1 Corinthians. Some scholars have suggested that its meaning is uncertain, but Robin

Scroggs has shown that the word is a translation of the Hebrew *mishkav zakur* ("lying with a male"), derived directly from Leviticus 18:22 and 20:13 and used in rabbinic texts to refer to homosexual intercourse. The Septuagint (Greek Old Testament) of Leviticus 20: 13 reads, "Whoever lies with a man as with a woman [*meta arsenos koiten gynaikos*], they have both done an abomination" (my translation). This is almost certainly the idiom from which the noun *arsenokoitai* was coined. Thus, Paul's use of the term presupposes and reaffirms the holiness code's condemnation of homosexual acts. This is not a controversial point in Paul's argument; the letter gives no evidence that anyone at Corinth was arguing for the acceptance of same-sex erotic activity. Paul simply assumes that his readers will share his conviction that those who indulge in homosexual activity are "wrongdoers" (*adikoi*, literally "unrighteous"), along with the other sorts of offenders in his list.[23]

What Paul wrote about same-sex relationships in 1 Corinthians 6 and 1 Timothy 1 cannot be isolated from his comments in Romans 1. Instead, they must be read in light of them.

Writers such as Robin Scroggs have argued for *malakos* and *arsenokoitai* to be taken as references to exploitative and abusive pederasty and not applicable to consenting, loving, and faithful same-sex relationships. While granting that homosexuality is specified as shameful behavior that is to be loathed by Christians, he argues, "I close with the observation that Paul thinks of pederasty, and perhaps the more degraded forms of

> **Authenticity and Virtue**
>
> Part of the problem about authenticity is that virtues aren't the only things that are habit-forming: the more someone behaves in a way that is damaging to self or to others, the more "natural" it will both seem and actually be. Spontaneity, left to itself, can begin by excusing bad behavior and end by congratulating vice. . . .
>
> Romantic ethics, or the existentialism which insists on authenticity or (in that sense) freedom as the only real mark of genuine humanness . . . tries to get in advance, and without paying the true price, what virtue offers further down the road, and at the cost of genuine moral thought, decision, and effort. That is what I meant by saying that the cult of authenticity or spontaneity was a parody, a caricature, of what virtue would produce when it has its full effect. "Being true to yourself," then, is important, but it isn't the principal thing. If you take it as a framework or as a starting point, you will be sadly deceived.
>
> Over against all these frameworks, which I suspect have conditioned in various ways the thinking and behaving of many of my readers, we urgently need to recapture the New Testament's vision of a genuinely "good" human life as a life of character formed by God's promised future, as a life with that future-shaped character lived within the ongoing story of God's people, and, with that, a freshly worked notion of virtue. This is what we need if we are to answer the question of what happens after you believe.
>
> — N.T. Wright

it, when he is attacking homosexuality."[24] But this is a claim that simply does not fit the evidence.

An obvious negation of Scroggs' assertion lies in the fact that Paul is naming a relationship of mutual attraction. The "shameful acts with other men" are the result of men being "inflamed with *lust for one another*" (1:27b) as opposed to a one-sided desire that leads to exploitation. Furthermore, that his apostolic judgment is not against pederasty is clear from the fact of his reference to women as well as men (1:26b). In other words, the attempt to narrow these texts to young male slaves being forced to have sex by their owners or their being pimped in brothels and gymnasia is artificial and forced. The textual evidence from both Old and New Testaments is of an unqualified prohibition of same-sex intercourse.

To say the prohibition is "unqualified" is, among other things, to say that it forbids both male-with-male and female-with-female intercourse. Both violate the created order and abandon what both biblical and non-biblical writers call "natural" sexual expression. Neither is it to be understood only as the outlawing of coercive and exploitative relationships; the mutual and voluntary nature of what is named is evident not only from the language of Romans 1 but the imposition of the death penalty for both partners in Leviticus 20. Victims deserve rescue rather than punishment. Referring once more to the vocabulary already cited, Paul had very specific words at hand if his intention had been to focus on pederasty and/or prostitution.

The Existential Argument

No one reads the revisionist arguments of our day without discovering very quickly that the argument being pressed most aggressively – and, from my experience, most effectively – is not the textual-linguistic argument. The ink has long ago dried on the Old Testament's censure of "a man [who] has sexual relations with a man as one does with a woman." The same is true for Paul's reference to either males or females who "exchange natural sexual relations for unnatural ones." The claim for an existential argument tells us either that personal experience is more authoritative than biblical commands or that advances in psychology have given us to understand that ancient taboos must yield to modern insights.

Thus, the claim put forward now is that the same-sex behaviors being condemned so clearly in Scripture were qualitatively different in their nature from what is possible in modern cultures. It is affirmed that only in recent times are loving, covenanted, and monogamous same-sex unions capable of being understood for what they really are. Thus, the argument goes, we must update our ethical codes.

> Paul had no conception of the kinds of things some of us are just beginning to understand – that while perhaps 95 percent of the population may be wired to have an attraction toward the opposite sex, there may be five percent who by nature or nurture feel they are different. That five percent, by the time they are older, are drawn to love people of the same sex. It's clear that Paul couldn't see two people of the same sex living as a family together for the rest of their lives, the way he couldn't see that slavery was wrong or that women could speak in church.[25]

Aside from a bit of chronological snobbery and a serious diminishing of biblical inspiration in this claim, Hamilton is simply mistaken on several points. For one thing, Paul *did* challenge slavery both in theory (Gal 3:28) and practice (Phile 15-17); for another, he *did* affirm the right of women to both prophesy (preach) and pray in church assemblies – while respecting the prevailing custom of a modest head covering (1 Cor 11:5-6) – and required silence in those same assemblies of *both* males (1 Cor 14:28,30) and females (1 Cor 14:34) under certain circumstances.

But we will explore these existential claims further in the remaining part of the book. What is significant here is the fact that there is no comparable situation or text in which the Bible's uniform censure of same-sex intimacy is mitigated. There is no statement from any biblical writer that says anything to the effect that –

> **The Message of Hope in Romans**
> My point is that while we need to affirm that Romans 1:26-27 places homosexual behavior under the category of sin, we can offer all men and women, with any kind of sexual struggle, the hope laid out in the rest of Romans, namely, that Christ saves us from the penalty of sin, gradually from the power of sin, and one day from the very presence of sin.
> The relevance of Romans to the "gay issue" is not some kind of cliché message that sinners must "turn or burn" or even "hate the sin but love the sinner." The biblical response embodied by Paul is for all people to "believe in him who raised Jesus our Lord from the dead" (4:24), to confess that "Jesus is Lord" (10:9), to "clothe yourselves with the Lord Jesus Christ, and do not think about how to gratify the desires of the flesh" (13:14), and for the church corporately to "accept one another, then, just as Christ accepted you, in order to bring praise to God" (15:7).
> — Michael Bird

like females prophesying under one circumstance but not another – same-sex acts that have been forbidden under certain circumstances are nevertheless honorable within covenanted, loving, and monogamous relationships. Paul spoke against the prevailing cultural norms with regard to women and slaves; he did not challenge whatever taboos or aversion people – especially with a background in the Torah – may have had about same-sex intercourse. Put most candidly, there is no positive case that can be made from the Bible for homosexual activity.

The questions that remain now are less about the interpretation of biblical texts than their application. How do these moral limitations apply to our twenty-first century context? How well has the church done in helping single women and men live chaste lives? Is there spiritual help available to persons who sense strong same-sex desires but wish to live within the will of God? Against the background of our extended attention to history, language, and the biblical text, we turn now to their pastoral application in a culture that is aggressively affirming of same-sex unions.

ENDNOTES

1. Gushee, *Changing Our Mind*, 152-153.

2. Readers who are unfamiliar with Greek should not be confused by the alternation in text and references here between *malakos* and *malakoi* or *arsenokoitēs* and *arsenokoitai*. They are merely the singular and plural forms of the words under scrutiny.

3. Boswell, *Christianity, Social Tolerance, and Homosexuality*, 107.

4. Ibid., 340.

5. Moisés Silva, "μαλακός, μαλακία," *NIDNNTE* 3:217.

6. Hamilton, *When Christians Get It Wrong*, 91.

7. Philo *The Special Laws* III. 7. 37-39. English translation is that of C.D. Yonge and is found at http://www.earlychristianwritings.com/yonge/book29.html, accessed Aug 19, 2022. Greek text cited is from *Philo*, Vol VII, trans. by F.H. Colson, Loeb Classical Library (Cambridge: Harvard University Press, 1937), 498-500.

8. Gagnon, *The Bible and Homosexual Practice*, 312.

9. Montanari, *Brill Dictionary of Ancient Greek*, s.v. "μαλακία" and "μάλακος."

10. Originally considered part of the corpus of the satirist Lucian of Samosata (*ca.* 120 – *ca.* 200), some scholars now attribute the work to an imitator of his style and date this piece perhaps a hundred years after his death. In this case, the original work may have been produced in the mid to late 200s. For the purpose of this study, the issue is the use of language in a document originally composed in Greek. The document shows that the family of words (adjective/noun/verb) was used to name a particular type of person and activity associated with homosexuality – the "soft" or penetrated male (whether adolescent or adult) in same-sex intercourse.

11. Ormand points out that it is Lycinus and Theomnestus who "frame the dialogue proper" by their extreme positions of being asexual (Lycinus) or able to enjoy sex with both men and women (Theomnestus). "Between the two of them, Lycinus and Theomnestus define the poles of an axis on which every Greek and Roman man had to locate himself. . . . There is evidently no concern about (Callicratidas') love for boys as such. What is odd about his preference is that he loves boys exclusively. . . . Even more noticeable, though, is the

fact that Charicles' predilection for women, and only women, is also thought of as abnormal." Kirk Ormand, *Controlling Desires: Sexuality in Ancient Greece and Rome* (Westport, CT: Praeger Publishers, 2009), 8.

12. Lucian, *Erotēs* 49. The section of the *Symposium* reflected here is 219C. Text and citation from *Lucian*, Vol VIII, trans. by M.D. Macleod, Loeb Classical Library (Cambridge: Harvard University Press, 1967), 226-227.

13. Lucian, *Erotēs* 54. The citation relevant to the adult relationship of the two is from *Iliad* 9.191. *Lucian*, Vol VIII, Loeb Classical Library, 234-235.

14. Lucian, *Erotēs* 19 in Loeb Classical Library, Vol VIII, 180-181.

15. James D.G. Dunn, "The First and Second Letters to Timothy and the Letter to Titus," *The New Interpreter's Bible*, Vol 11 (Nashville: Abingdon Press, 2000), 791.

16. Brent Pickett, "Homosexuality," *The Stanford Encyclopedia of Philosophy* (Spring 2021 Edition), Edward N. Zalta (ed.), accessed Sept 21, 2022, at https://plato.stanford.edu/archives/spr2021/entries/homosexuality/.

17. The consensus appears to be that the word "homosexual" came into English via German from a taxonomic term coined from *homo* (Greek for "same") and *sexus* (Latin for "sex") by Karl Maria Kertbeny around 1869 and later given extended use by virtue of Richard von Krafft-Ebing's use of it in his *Psychopathia Sexualis* (1886 in German) and its translation into English by Charles Gilbert Chaddock (1892).

18. Jim Farber, "Rise of the sides; how Grindr finally recognized gay men who aren't tops or bottoms," *Guardian* (US Edition), June 20, 2022, https://www.theguardian.com/technology/2022/jun/20/rise-of-the-sides-how-grindr-finally-recognized-gay-men-who-arent-tops-or-bottoms. "In mid-May, Grindr added a position called side, a designation that upends the binary that has historically dominated gay male culture. Sides are men who find fulfillment in every kind of sexual act except anal penetration. . . . Some adherents refer to these activities as 'outercourse.'"

19. Wright, David F. "Homosexuals or Prostitutes? The Meaning of Ἀρσενοκοῖται (1 Cor. 6:9, 1 Tim. 1:10)." *Vigiliae Christianae* 38, no. 2 (1984): 125–53; cf. John Granger Cook, "μαλακοί and ἀρσενοκοῖται: In Defence of Tertullian's Translation." *New Testament Studies* 65.3 (2019): 332–52.

20. The relevant lines in the LXX (with emphasis) read as follows: καὶ μετὰ **ἄρσενος** οὐ κοιμηθήσῃ **κοίτην** γυναικός βδέλυγμα γάρ ἐστιν (Lev 18:22) and καὶ ὃς ἂν κοιμηθῇ μετὰ **ἄρσενος κοίτην** γυναικός, βδέλυγμα ἐποίησαν ἀμφότεροι (Lev 20:13).

21. Moisés Silva, "ἄρσην, ἀρσενοκοίτης," *NIDNNTE* 1:407-408.

22. Moisés Silva, "κοίτη, κοίτων, ἀρσενοκοίτης," *NIDNNTE* 2:713-715. At the conclusion of this entry, *NIDNNTE* points to the practice of coining such neologisms as *arsenokoitēs*. "The primary motivation for such a term, however, must have been the use of ἄρσην and κοίτη in LXX prohibitions of homosexuality (Lev 18:22; 20:13). From a morphological point of view, there was a precedent for a compound of this kind in the use of μητροκοίτης ('someone who engages in incest with his mother' . . .)"

23. Hays, *Moral Vision of the NT*, 382-383.

24. Scroggs, *The New Testament and Homosexuality*, 117.

25. Hamilton, *When Christians Get it Wrong*, 90.

> *"Christian discipleship means following the risen Christ, in the power of the Holy Spirit, to the glory and praise of God the Father."*
> – Leonard Allen

CHAPTER 13

Inner Strength from the Holy Spirit

We have reached the part of this book that I consider its most important section. *How does anyone live to the standard of holiness presented in the Bible and modeled by Jesus?*

Please don't hear that question backwards. By "backwards" I mean this: Many people still have the idea that being a Christian is a matter of being a good-enough person that you can be sure God will do good things for you now and eventually receive you to be with him when you die. Frankly, that's a poor definition of anything that resembles Christian identity in Scripture. To be a Christian is to know you are not good enough to deserve what most of us call salvation – but that you are loved so much that God offers you his grace through Jesus of Nazareth. He did not die as an innocent martyr to a defeated or delayed cause. His death and resurrection were at the heart of his mission to defeat evil, reclaim a world that was created by God as a place where he would live with humans, and both mark the path and provide the empowerment for humans to live as fulfilled and flourishing men and women.

People who come to know Christ find new purpose for living. As Paul put it, "If anyone is in Christ, the new creation has come. The old has gone, the new is here!" (2 Cor 5:17). With another of his metaphors, he expressed it this way: "For he has rescued us from the dominion of darkness and brought us into the kingdom of the Son he loves, in whom we have redemption, the forgiveness of sins" (Col 1:13-14). Paul, too, would think it "backwards" to banish the old and be rescued from darkness first

> **Power to Break Free from Sin**
>
> As John Murray says, "The believer's once-for-all death to the law of sin does not free him from the necessity of mortifying sin in his members; it makes it necessary and possible to do so."
>
> The Spirit's presence in our lives inevitably produces fruit pleasing to God. Thus, we are secure. But the Spirit does not do his work apart from our response. I like the careful balance Paul achieves in verse 13: "By the Spirit you put to death the misdeeds of the body" (italics added). Paul puts the responsibility squarely on our shoulders: You need to put sin to death. But at the same time, he makes it clear that we can only do it through the Spirit.
>
> — Douglas Moo

and then come to know Christ. No, the correct order is first to know Christ, then to be made new and brought under his reign, and then to exhibit the renewed life that is the evidence salvation.

Doing good things doesn't save you, but being a saved person shows itself in good character and its fruits. "For we are God's handiwork, created in Christ Jesus to do good works, which God prepared in advance for us to do" (Eph 2:10). This is an emphasis that some Christian disciples and their mentors have lost sight of in recent times.

Eternal Life Starts Here and Now

You likely know what John 3:16 says about God's gift of his unequaled and beloved Son and the promise of eternal life to all who believe in him. And what that verse calls "eternal life" is not about something that happens when you die. Eternal life is human life lived fully and authentically in one's partnership with God that starts here and now and reaches its ultimate fulfillment in the New Heaven and New Earth. Realized at Christ's return, that life will not be playing harps on clouds floating in the sky but is destined to be bodily life in a redeemed world where God will live with us.

John 3:16 needs to be supplemented with this clarification about the mission of Jesus when he came here two millennia ago: "I have come that they may have life, and have it to the full" (John 10:10). Then, looking beyond his immediate intention for you and me, this is the visionary promise of his *parousia* (i.e., Christ's "presence" with us at his return) that was given to the same writer, John, who penned the verses just cited from the Fourth Gospel:

> I saw the Holy City, the new Jerusalem, coming down out of heaven from God, prepared as a bride beautifully dressed for her husband. And I heard a loud voice from the throne saying, "Look! God's dwelling place is now among the people, and

he will dwell with them. They will be his people, and God himself will be with them and be their God. 'He will wipe every tear from their eyes. There will be no more death' or mourning or crying or pain, for the old order of things has passed away" (Rev 21:2-4).

Taken together, all this sounds a bit different from what some of you have heard at church. Or, perhaps I should say, it may sound different from what you *thought* you heard at church. It seems that most people still hear us preachers telling them how to behave so they won't wind up in hell. Okay, I admit that some preachers think that is the gospel. But, far from it, the gospel (i.e., good news) from God is that he is offering us a relationship that makes life worth living as the people we were created to be.

> **The Spirit and the Flesh**
>
> Paul uses the words "flesh" and "spirit" not to designate two parts of human nature but rather to represent two ways of living. Life pursued according to flesh is the life influenced by rebellion and idolatry, in which the entire perspective of the human being is turned in on himself or herself and the person becomes the center of all values. Life in the flesh is essentially life carried on under the lordship of the sinful self. It is a life of self-idolatry.
>
> Life in the Spirit, on the other hand, is life set free from bondage to self and sin, and therefore also law. It is life in bondage to the Creator, which freely acknowledges his lordship in his son Jesus Christ. The power of that lordship has broken the enslaving power of self-idolatry and sin and sets the person free to enjoy a new relationship with the Creator, the relationship of child rather than rebel. . . . This passage describes the reality that led Paul to exclaim to the Corinthians: "If anyone is in Christ, he is a new creation. Old things have passed away; behold, the new has come" (2 Cor 5:17).
>
> — Paul Achtemeier

Humans were not created to be liars and thieves. We were not made to be selfish and mean. We certainly weren't formed as we are to be violent, abusive, and cruel. That's why we cringe to hear reports and see TV footage of the invasion of a weaker nation by a superpower neighbor. It is why we are embarrassed about our own American history of enslaving Africans, displacing Native Americans, and abusing women. We were created to carry the image of God into his created world by loving one another and taking care of our planet home. That we have fallen so far short of that goal is why the mission of Jesus was so crucial.

What I *hope* you have heard at church – and perhaps misunderstood because of either slipshod speaking or careless listening – is that people in a relationship with God are called to live to a standard that people without such a relationship just don't understand. It's not that Christians are smarter or even fundamentally better than they are, but we have a different worldview. Apart from God, it is easy to be selfish, insensitive to others, and focused on such things as money, sex, and power. Living as God's child and wanting to honor him, Christians are learning to love our neighbors as ourselves, care about the welfare of our world, and emphasize traits such as generosity, sexual purity, and serving marginalized people.

There is such a contrast in those two value systems that preachers sometimes get angry about all the negative things around us and spend our time going off on them. We wind up being negative and strident. We look and sound angry. And we leave the impression that Christians think we have the right to be harsh and judgmental. Sometimes, we come across as just downright mean. Please forgive us. Please forgive me for having left that impression at times. *People who are playing the money, sex, and power games are not our enemies. They are victims of our enemy, Satan.*

What if. . .?

If you are fourteen, forty-four, or eighty-four and have been victimized by some of the Enemy's propaganda about gender fluidity, non-binary personhood, or finding your true self in the LGBTQ+ world, I have tried to answer some of the common claims you probably have heard in the earlier chapters of this book. I have taken pains to do so patiently and with careful documentation. And I have tried to use language that is respectful of the intelligence and intent of anyone who would read this book. So, let's assume you are wondering how someone dealing with same-sex feelings or living in some quarter of the LGBTQ+ world could find a way to embrace and live by what this book has argued for as a non-affirming lifestyle.

Suppose I am a young Christian who is trying to negotiate the subculture of my school where drugs and uninhibited sex are commonplace. Can that sort of environment be negotiated successfully? Is using pot any worse than my parents' abuse of alcohol? For that matter, isn't my own drinking at my friends' parties one of those "rites of passage" everybody accepts? Is the Christian ideal of premarital chastity simply unrealistic for my time and place? Does anyone really expect to be a virgin on his or her wedding night?

Don't we live in an enlightened time that allows people to find their own path? Be the persons *they* want to be rather than have their lives dictated by an ancient set of rules the church still tosses around? For that matter, do church people take those rules seriously themselves? There's a lot of hypocrisy in religion! Priests molest children, televangelists scam little old ladies out of their pensions, and scandals of all types make the press regularly.

It isn't unusual to hear it put this way: *"Shouldn't we just leave each other alone – and stop being so judgmental about sex? Why can't we just 'live and let live' – especially with this whole LGBTQ+ business? Let's just do 'the Jesus thing' and love everybody. Let's give each other space to be happy. Authentic. Your own person."*

When I was well over halfway through the writing of this material, I heard from a friend with whom I had not been in contact for a while. After the customary pleasantries, he asked if I had any writing projects going. When I told him about this book, there was a pause. He has the same situation in his family that I have in mine. We both have relatives outside our immediate families who are gay. We both have served churches that sought to minister to persons from the LGBTQ+ community. We both have friends who take strong exception to the traditional, non-affirming view we hold.

I then said something to him that I had not said before about this book. The more I have thought about it, I think the wording was right. "Jim, I'm trying to do a scholar's work with a pastor's heart," I told him. And that is about as clear as I know how to sum it up for you.

It is a *scholar's work* to study a topic, do serious research that takes various points of view into account, and offer his or her best judgment on that topic. You listen, read, and weigh. Without pretending to be objective, you commit to being fair and reasonable. You promise not to bury counter-arguments and evidence that counts for an opposing view. When you offer your conclusions, you do so to have them tested by others who are going through their own time of study and testing of arguments. There is no need for the arrogance that says one could not possibly be wrong or that there is more to learn than has been uncovered. But that is what scholarship does. By definition, a scholar has specialized in a particular discipline, delves deeply into subject-matter he or she believes to be important, and offers points of view to be tested by peers. No real scholar either asks or expects her or his ideas to be swallowed whole, but we also hope not to have them unheard or rejected without careful investigation. *The task of a scholar is to pursue information, and the goal of the pursuit is the discovery of useful truth.*

It is a *pastor's work* to nurture some group of believers to follow Jesus more faithfully by guarding them against various dangers, nurturing their orthodox faith, and encouraging them through times of special challenge. The pastoral metaphor comes, of course, from the ancient role of a shepherd who guards a flock of sheep from predators, sees that they are adequately watered and fed, and tends to their general well-being. If Sunday School stories of David singing to his sheep have deceived us into thinking otherwise, it was demanding and dangerous work to be a shepherd. Pastoral work is equally demanding and dangerous, for there are people and ideas who are enemies of God's purposes for people. Unbelief, false beliefs, temptations, confusion, discouragement – these and more seem always to be lurking to take down members of God's flock. Falsehoods that lead to behaviors outside God's will have been the enemy's best tool since Eden. *The task of a pastor is to love people, and the goal of that love is help oneself and others become fully mature human beings whose lives give honor to God.*

As a Christian whose entire adult life has been spent as a teacher, this book is my attempt to fill my scholarly role by giving solid and documented facts about what I believe the Bible teaches about same-sex behavior and, at the same time, to be pastoral by presenting that information with fairness and respect to people I love. I would try to "win an argument" only for the sake of rescuing someone from the danger of what is false. But I know full well that the goal of the gospel is not to win arguments but to rescue people from the things that are destroying their relationship with God.

Self-Control: Empowered by the Spirit

Part of the work of the Holy Spirit within us is the way he enables us to keep the sinful desires and impulses that still lurk within us under control. Self-control does involve effort of the will but it is an effort inspired and empowered by the Spirit of God as his will bears fruit in our will.

Probably the main thing (but certainly not the only thing) that Paul has in mind as regards what we need to control is our sexual desires. Certainly, his list of "the works of the flesh" begins with sexual immorality, and in several other places Paul includes that among his lists of among his lists of sinful behavior that Christians should put aside altogether (e.g., 1 Cor 5:9-11; Eph 5:3-7; Col 3:5-10).

— Christopher Wright

So, back now to the earlier question: *How does anyone live to the standard of holiness revealed in the Bible and modeled by Jesus?*

First, one has to understand what the biblical standard requires. Second, one has to will (i.e., form a resolute purpose) to conform to that standard. Third, one has to be transformed and empowered by the Holy Spirit.

You Are Not Alone

Between the glorious past event of Jesus' resurrection and the glorious future experience of life in the New Heaven and New Earth, Christians wait. As we wait for his presence with us, we rejoice because of what God has already done through the faithfulness of Jesus. We live in confident expectation of a future that has been promised to us. And we rely on the promise of divine power to live by the standard of holiness revealed in Scripture by the presence of the Holy Spirit in us.

Paul describes two very different perspectives on human life in Romans 8. Some interpreters miss the point here because they have taken the conflict to be the internal struggle of the human fleshly desires against the better things to which a human may aspire, the struggle between "my demons" and "my better angels." This text is drawing a distinction between two conflicting whole-life commitments. If I choose the whole-life path that is dictated by the fleshly, God-resisting, and neighbor-opposing desires that lead me deeper and deeper into the darkness, I am a dead man walking. "Those who live according to the flesh have their minds set on what the flesh desires . . . The mind governed by the flesh is death . . . The mind governed by the flesh is hostile to God; it does not submit to God's law, nor can it do so . . . Those who are in the realm of the flesh cannot please God." But if I choose to travel the path of Jesus, the Light of the World leads me out of this present darkness and into the very glory of God's presence. "Those who live in accordance with the Spirit have their minds set on what the Spirit desires . . . The mind governed by the Spirit is life and peace" (vs. 5-8).

Did you catch the forceful language of verse seven? "The mind governed by the flesh is hostile to God; it does not submit to God's law, *nor can it do so.*" That I *don't* do something is one thing, but that I *can't* is quite something else again. This is the language our culture speaks and understands about *addiction*. Jesus acknowledged the same phenomenon and used the language of *enslavement*. "Everyone who sins is a slave to sin," he said (John 8:34). All of us have seen alcohol and drugs make slaves out of people for whom we care deeply. Money has the same power. And so does sex. Anything taken out of its proper place and misused for a purpose other than God's intention for it becomes an idol. And we have already seen Paul's language from Romans 1 about the "exchange" and "giving over" that occur when someone replaces God with some false image, lie, or unnatural use. "Just as they did not think it worthwhile to retain the knowledge of God, so God have them over to a depraved mind, so that they do what ought not to be done" (v.28).

Addicts can't break their slavery to drinking or using drugs, penchant for lying to or manipulating others, compulsion to same-sex or opposite-sex addiction without an intervention from a powerful source. It does no good simply to tell them "Stop that!" Many who are caught up in these sins would love to stop, but they *can't*. The person who wants to get free of an addiction in order to get healthy has to adopt a completely different *worldview* about what life is worth, the places and people he will be around, and the direction and outcome she wants for her life and the people her life is affecting.

In theological vocabulary, this is *conversion*. It is reorienting one's mind and body, eyes and feet, values and commitments to things that are holy.

The Holy Spirit produces a conviction borne of sorrow and felt need that offers nothing less than spiritual awakening from death. Yet sorrow and an altered worldview are not enough. People are made alive by the power of the Holy Spirit that brings them to new life. That is why Jesus told Nicodemus about birth from above that came by water and Spirit (John 3:3,5). Made alive from the dead *by* the Spirit, we begin to live *to* the Spirit. The Spirit lives within us. We seek the things of the Spirit. We become increasingly sensitive to the internal promptings of the Spirit.

The Holy Spirit didn't go into retirement after guiding a handful of people to write your New Testament. He is very much alive and willing to see to it that you are not alone in struggling with your sexual orientation, sexual temptations, or sexual sins. The Spirit lives in the temple-bodies of God's people. He can make the written word come alive and turn the printed word into a living word. The Blessed Spirit has the power to incarnate all that is true and good and holy into your flesh-and-blood body for the glory of the Christ who saves fallen and confused human beings.

Inner Strength by the Spirit

One of the specific spiritual powers God cultivates in redeemed souls is self-control (Gal 5:22-24). The Holy Spirit both teaches and empowers the virtue of *enkrateia* – temperance, self-control, or self-discipline – in the lives of God's people. We met this Greek word earlier in the writings of some ancient philosophers. In their literature, it is a word for willpower, strength of mind, and human resolve. In its biblical usage, I would suggest using English terms such as "inner strength" or even the more cumbersome "inner spiritual strength that comes from the active presence of the Holy Spirit" to capture its meaning in Paul's letters. This type of spiritual power arises not from one's own energy but by God's power at work in a person.

The noun form of this word occurs only here in all the writings we have from Paul.[1] He employs its adjective form (Gk, *enkratēs*) once at Titus 1:8 to describe the character of someone who could be appointed an elder; "he must be hospitable, one who loves what is good, who is *self-controlled*, upright, holy and disciplined." As a verb, the word from this same family (Gk, *enkrateuomai*) is used only twice – both times in his first letter to Corinth. Interestingly, one of those uses is about sexual behavior.

In 1 Corinthians 7, he counsels people who are thinking about marriage in the near future that their timing – in view of a "crisis" at Corinth of some unspecified nature – might not be the best. However, having given his pastoral advice, he grants this: "But if they cannot *control themselves*, they should marry, for it is better to marry than to burn with passion" (v.9). That is good pastoral advice that tracks with I have told couples at times. There are times when major life changes such as marriage or having children or moving to a new job would be generally inadvisable. But erotic attraction so strong that it is creating constant temptation to sin could well make it prudent for a couple to go ahead with the wedding they have been planning – or to plan one sooner than later. Then, in chapter 9, Paul uses the word again to describe an athlete's preparation for competition. "Everyone who competes in the games *goes into strict training*" (v.25). The idea is pretty clear that certain situations require self-discipline and a determined focus on some clear goal.

What does this word signify about the lifestyle of a Spirit-filled, Spirit-guided, Spirit-empowered person? Perhaps something a bit different from what our customary English word "*self*-control" conveys.

In terms of the practical outcome and what an observer would witness, *enkrateia* is the virtue that enables one to hold back from revenge or stealing or illicit sex. But the ability to arrive at that outcome is different from what non-Christian writers in antiquity (or today) would likely presume. If a true and ultimate spiritual victory over evil takes place in someone's life, it is nothing we may boast of having done because we are strong-willed enough to keep a list of moral rules. Anyone who actually lives by the Spirit is the person who trusts God to do in her what willpower and determination cannot accomplish. To transform her heart. To transport her from the realm where flesh (i.e., all that opposes God) rules through sin to a new kingdom where the Holy Spirit reigns supreme in righteousness. This seems to be less *self*-control than a type of restraint that is empowered by the Spirit of God.

It is significant that biblical religion finds so little place for the concept of *enkrateia* which in the Hellenistic and Greek world is so essentially ethical. The

---

> **The Work of the Holy Spirit**
>
> Given the central role that enkrateia played in Greek philosophical thought and ethics, what is most striking about its usage in the New Testament is its relative infrequency. . . . One might be tempted to conclude that this human problem to which enkrateia was the recommended solution was unknown to the New Testament writers, but this is hardly the case. . . .
>
> If the New Testament writers rarely appeal to that concept (enkrateia) that was at the heart of so much Greek ethics, I believe it was because they sensed that a new power had been made available to them through Christ. This power was not of their own making, nor was it a power inherent in the human person. Instead, this power was intimately bound up with Jesus Christ and made possible a new way of life, a way that could only be described by contrasting it with the old way of death. Indeed, this death of the "old self" liberates us from that self-imposed bondage created by our disordered desires, freeing us to live in God's likeness. . . .
>
> This suggests that whatever the New Testament writers may have meant when they employed the concept of enkrateia, we should not too quickly assume that they meant "self-control," which in our day means something akin to control of the self, by the self for the sake of the self. . . . [Understood as] a fruit of the Spirit's work and not of our own, then we might suggest that its meaning . . . is something akin to "control of the self by the Spirit for the sake of the gospel."
>
> — Philip Kenneson

reason for this is that biblical man regarded his life as determined and directed by the command of God. There was thus no place for the self-mastery which had a place in autonomous ethics. Again, belief in creation cut off the way to asceticism. It saw in the world with its gifts the hand of the Creator. Finally, the gift of salvation in Christ left no place for an asceticism which merits salvation.[2]

When on display among Christ-followers, self-control is a divine gift and comes of being "led by the Spirit." It is not the fruit of superhuman willpower. It is one of the several virtues that God's love generates in a surrendered Christian personality. It is a mature result of Heaven's redemptive work in a human heart, mind, and lifestyle. With specific reference to sex outside monogamous heterosexual marriage, the essence of the Christian virtue of self-control by the Spirit was nothing other than chastity. Abstinence from sexual intercourse prior to marriage – males as well as females – and exclusive fidelity to one's husband or wife after marriage certainly was not the Roman rule and expectation.

In the ancient world, that form of chastity would have been considered abnormal and sexual freedom the norm. Both Judaism and Christianity were mocked for their negative view of Roman promiscuity in its many forms. Since Second Temple Judaism was non-evangelistic in nature, the Jews could be looked upon as mere curiosities. The Christian gospel was different. Its into-all-the-world mandate from Jesus had Christians offering a belief and lifestyle that challenged all and offended many.

It takes no great imagination to hear these two voices from antiquity as spokesmen for their respective worldviews. Of the life he and his fellow-believers had found in Christ, Justin (*ca.*100-*ca.*165) wrote: "We who formerly delighted in fornication, now embrace chastity alone."[3] Of the resentment against Christians in Rome after the great fire in July of 64, Tacitus (*ca.*56-*ca.*116) wrote that many of them were convicted "not so much for the crime of firing the city as of their hatred against mankind."[4] Not only did the Christians not confess Caesar as Lord, but they also rebuked the reckless and impure lives of their unbelieving neighbors (cf. 1 Pet 4:2-4). Then as now, that some find the power for holiness in Christ stands as an enraging rebuke to those who claim they were "just born this way" or, worse, "made this way by the gods/God."

Different Points of Origin

Before Christianity pressed the matter of sexual restraint to mean chastity, Zeno, Aristotle, Epictetus, and other Greek thinkers had praised *enkrateia*. But it had always been envisioned as the self-control that came from a lifelong struggle of the human will. One possessed this good quality by the mastery of his or her inner motivations that succeeded in giving mastery to good impulses over evil ones. On the philosophers' view, it was rooted in the wisdom of weighing outcomes and exercising one's willpower. Even as they praised it, however, they lamented how few people had the strength of will and discipline of habits to achieve it. I venture that their understanding of this virtue is the one most of us retain even now. Think of the representations of an angel on one shoulder and a demon on the other – with each whispering an appeal into some poor soul's ear. In the conventional case, an obese person does not have enough willpower to curb her appetite; the demon offers rich food, and the angel reminds her of the beautiful dress she wants to wear. In the next cartoonish scene, an alcoholic is a moral failure for his lack of restraint with liquor; the demon offers him a drink at a bar from the hand of a beautiful woman, while the angel reminds him of an anxious wife and children waiting for him at home. And so on with smokers, gamblers, people with bad tempers, addicts to pornography, or any number of vices. For all I know, someone reading this may be feeling a sense of personal shame for something you have tried and tried to bring under control by your own strength of will – only to decide you are too weak-willed ever to deal with it.

This is a conversation I have had with countless people: "Rubel, you're right. I understand the gospel. I know I need to commit my life to Jesus – but I'm just not ready. I can't (and the language varies here from 'join the church' to 'be baptized' to 'start my life as a Christian') until I deal with (again, the language varies, from 'my drinking' to 'my bad temper' to 'this awful mess I've created in my family') this challenge. But as soon as I get a handle on it, I will! I promise."

If people could summon the willpower to manage these challenges and put them right by their own efforts, they would be the envy of Zeno and Aristotle. They would be masters of *self*-control and *self*-discipline. And I suppose they wouldn't need Jesus to help them at all. If we could master our wills, resist temptations, and conquer our addictions, we would be what the world calls – not "faithful Christians" but – Zen Masters. We could lay claim to have "quieted the will," and life would be under our control.

Here is how I routinely respond to conversations of that nature: "Listen, you are falling for one of Satan's biggest lies! If you could fix that problem by self-discipline and willpower, you'd be doing the job God alone can do. The blood of Jesus cleanses you of your past failure, and the presence of the Holy Spirit supplies the divine power necessary to defeat your weakness or to deal with your addiction. What you want comes only as a divine gift, but you are trying to turn it into an achievement of your intelligence and iron will.

> **Self-Denial: Martyrdom vs Freedom**
>
> As someone who has not received one iota of the promised "change" in my sexual orientation that some Christians have held out to me, and as someone who also has not been able to embrace a more progressive understanding of same-sex marriage, I often feel like I am fighting a kind of long defeat. I am gay but not seeking a same-sex partner, and what that feels like is best described in the Apostle Paul's rather stark view of the Christian life: "We know that the whole creation has been groaning in labor pains until now; and not only the creation, but we ourselves, who have the first fruits of the Spirit, groan inwardly while we wait for adoption, the redemption of our bodies" (Romans 8:22-23).
>
> Realizing that my gayness is not some fixed script that I must conform to has given me freedom to explore historic Christian, chaste ways to express my love for men. What my culture defines as "gay" – the story my world offers me for who I am supposed to be and how I am supposed to live – is not something I have to embrace. There is freedom in choosing to express my love for men through friendship and service rather than through marriage or romantic partnership. Granted, opting out of the dominant way of understanding "gay" often feels more like martyrdom than freedom. But if traditional Christianity is true, then self-denial – taking up one's cross and following Jesus – is, in fact, regardless of how it feels to us, real freedom.
>
> — Wesley Hill

Give it up and let God's power go to work in your life to handle that problem."

By the word we are examining, the philosophers were pointing to something like one's "moral will" or "resident power" by which he could master urges and temptations. But what if we read the word Christianly to mean "*conferred* inner strength" or "resident power of the *indwelling Spirit of God*" or "life in the realm of *the Holy Spirit's authority*"? Read that way, we are being fully consistent with Paul's contrast between people who live "in the flesh" versus those who live "in the Spirit." Contrary to another common Christian misreading, "in the flesh" doesn't mean "in a mortal body" but "in the sphere of life that is dominated by human desires and lusts" or *in the sphere that is at odds with God*. Similarly, "in the Spirit" doesn't mean "disembodied" or "in your invisible inner self" but *in the sphere of life to which you have been called and empowered by the Holy Spirit.*

Paul's view was different from Aristotle's. Understanding leading to insight that results in a strong will would not be enough. Christopher Wright expresses that difference this way: "Self-control does involve effort of the will, but it is an effort inspired and empowered by the Spirit of God as his will bears fruit in our will."[5]

Both Greek writers and Paul associate illicit sexual desire and lust with an absence of self-control. Human willpower may work for some people in some situations to preserve premarital chastity and marital fidelity or to keep others from acting out their same-sex attraction. Yet Paul does not argue for sexual purity by challenging Christians to be strong-willed and self-mastered. He posits a different starting point for the virtue of self-discipline or inner strength from a source greater than self. He argues that "your bodies are temples of the Holy Spirit, who is in you, whom you have received from God" (1 Cor 6:19).

The love of God – which takes form as the fruit of the Spirit living in Christ's disciples – teaches us to love God enough that we would not dishonor his temple. That same love reminds us, too, that loving our neighbors means not exploiting and using them for erotic gratification. Love for God and others combine to keep us from violating the created order of male-female oneness in covenanted marriage.

Filled with God's Spirit and living by the power of divine love, grace gives the believer an inner strength to resist evil desires and to be faithful in doing what is virtuous and God-honoring. "Like the other virtues mentioned in [Gal] 5:22-23, *enkrateia* is viewed not as a natural human faculty but as a gift from the Spirit, ever received afresh in one's

> **"Cause Your Fruit to Ripen in My Life"**
>
> Heavenly Father, I pray that this day I may live in your presence and please you more and more.
>
> Lord Jesus, I pray that this day I may take up my cross and follow you.
>
> Holy Spirit, I pray that this day you will fill me with yourself and cause your fruit to ripen in my life: love, joy, peace, patience, kindness, goodness, faithfulness, gentleness, and self-control.
>
> That was the prayer that John Stott prayed every day when he first woke up in the morning. It hardly seems surprising, then, that many people who knew John Stott personally said that he was the most Christlike person they ever met. . . .
>
> The more we are filled with God's Spirit, and the more the Spirit ripens his fruit within us, the more we will become like Christ.
>
> — Christopher Wright

commitment to the gospel."⁶ Someone seeing your behavior might applaud your rigid self-discipline and personal mastery of human passions. But this would be your better answer: "I have been crucified with Christ and I no longer live, but Christ lives in me. The life I now live in the body, I live by faith in the Son of God, who loved me and gave himself for me" (Gal 2:20).

Paul's Prayer for Strugglers

Therefore, I dare to conclude this section by saying we have been misled by placing our focus on "*self*-control" as opposed to thinking of the holy gift of grace that is God's power at work in his redeemed people. We are not saved by our willpower but by God's power at work in and through us. We are saved by our willing participation in the Spirit's life-giving power that refreshes and animates us. That understanding allows us to give God the glory for any victory over our weaknesses and any achievements in righteousness – rather than boasting of it as our own accomplishment.

The relevance of this gift from God to a single person seems obvious. The heterosexual who is dating seriously and with marriage in view, someone who is gay and knows that same-sex intercourse is outside God's will, the woman whose husband has died and

> **Psalm 121:**
> **"My Strength Comes from God"**
> I look up to the mountains;
>   does my strength come from mountains?
> No, my strength comes from God,
>   who made heaven, and earth, and mountains.
> He won't let you stumble,
>   your Guardian God won't fall asleep.
> Not on your life! Israel's
>   Guardian will never doze or sleep.
> God's your Guardian,
>   right at your side to protect you –
> Shielding you from sunstroke,
>   sheltering you from moonstroke.
> God guards you from every evil,
>   he guards your very life.
> He guards you when you leave and when you return,
>   he guards you now, he guards you always.
>   — The Message

who is being paid attention by a kind male, the LGBTQ+ person who attempted a heterosexual marriage only for it to fail by divorce – these and many others are challenged to travel the path marked by Jesus that will demand the restraint of sexual desire. It is a path that requires abstinence and chastity. The power needed by such persons is provided by God through the indwelling presence of the Holy Spirit. It no more smacks of unfairness for them to live to God's glory through abstinence than for all the rest of us who commit ourselves to follow Christ to abstain from whatever behaviors we are drawn to by our sinful natures. The strength for any challenge to holiness must come from the very source of holiness himself.

So, let us pray for one another. *Not* that you will "gut it up and try harder" and *not* that I will "summon up my willpower and do what I know is right" but – as Paul prayed for his friends in this same struggle against the flesh –

> . . . that out of [the Father's] glorious riches he may strengthen you with power through his Spirit in your inner being, so that Christ may dwell in your hearts through faith. And I pray that you, being rooted and established in love, may have power, together with all the Lord's holy people, to grasp how wide and long and high and deep is the love of Christ, and to know this love that surpasses knowledge – that you may be filled to the measure of all the fullness of God (Eph 3:16-19).

There is yet another resource to help us with our spiritual struggles that remains to be identified. Perhaps more correctly, there is a *context* within which the Holy Spirit functions more naturally and effectively to provide inner strength for our struggles. We will explore that in the next chapter.

ENDNOTES

1. Lexical information on *enkrateia* here reflects data from Walter Grundmann, "ἐγκράτεια (ἀκρασία), ἐγκρατής (ἀκρατής), ἐγκρατεύομαι," *TDNT*, 2:339-342 and Silva, "ἐγκράτεια, ἐγκρατής, ἐγκρατεύομαι, ἀκρασία, ἀκρατής," *NIDNTTE*, 2:83-85.

2. Grundman, "ἐγκράτεια," *TDNT*, 2:342.

3. Justin, *Apology* 1.14.2.

4. Tacitus, *Annals* 15.44.

5. Christopher J.H. Wright, *Cultivating the Fruit of the Spirit* (Downers Grove, IL: IVP Books, 2017), 146.

6. Silva, "ἐγκράτεια," *NIDNTTE*, 2:85.

"Therefore confess your sins to each other and pray for each other so that you may be healed. The prayer of a righteous person is powerful and effective."

— James 5:16

CHAPTER 14

The Value of Christian Community

The previous chapter argued that the internal dynamic that enables me to deal with my sinful orientations is the same power that enables LGBTQ+ persons to deal with theirs. The Holy Spirit is the indwelling presence and potency for helping Christians cope with our innumerable weaknesses. For our minds (intellects), hearts (passions and emotional drives), and bodies (physical mass) to be authentically human, they must function by the Spirit's power resident in and available to our inner beings. That was the prayer Paul offered for believers in his time and place. Christians in every generation might well use that very same prayer for one another.

When that prayer was quoted at the end of Chapter 13, I hinted at identifying a *context* within which the Spirit's power functions more naturally and effectively to provide inner strength for us. In fact, within Paul's prayer, he names that setting. Immediately after using the word "power," he adds the phrase "together with all the Lord's holy people" (Eph 3:18b). By the power of the Holy Spirit, Paul dreamed of Christ-followers living supportively with one

> **Paul's Prayer**
> I pray that, according to the riches of his glory, he may grant that you may be strengthened in your inner being with power through his Spirit and that Christ may dwell in your hearts through faith, as you are being rooted and grounded in love. I pray that you may have the power to comprehend, with all the saints, what is the breadth and length and height and depth and to know the love of Christ that surpasses knowledge, so that you may be filled with all the fullness of God.
> — Ephesians 3:16-19 (NRSVue)

another in the all-encompassing love of Christ that would allow them to experience what he called "the fullness of God."

Perhaps you noticed that I used the word "dreamed" to name Paul's sentiment in praying that prayer. I think it would be correct even to use the word "fantasized" in that sentence. Neither in Paul's time nor our own do churches always measure up to what they should be. Just read through Paul's correspondence in the New Testament. Among the cluster of churches addressed in Galatians, they were confused about the very nature of the gospel message. Writing to a house church meeting in the home of his friends Philemon and Apphia, he tried very gently to help them work through the ethical dilemma created for Christians by Roman slavery. He wrote to the church at Corinth about the divisions, immoral behaviors, and false doctrines causing incredible problems for its members. What incredibly complex and messy problems existed in those churches. And what a challenge to the faith of the first-generation believers must have been created by them. I have no doubt that lots of people considering this new religion gave up in disgust because of the things they saw happening in those churches.

Sound familiar? What do people point to in churches of our time? Scandal. Hypocrisy. Abuse of power. Division. Weird doctrines. Sexual abuse. Mishandled funds. The list of failings just goes on and on. *Ad nauseum*. But . . .

Then you see a church opening its arms to shelter people after a flood or hurricane – and then help them reclaim or rebuild their houses. You learn that one of those flawed churches is making space available for Alcoholics Anonymous meetings at multiple times during every week. You find about some preacher or Sunday School teacher who invested money, tears, prayers, and incredible amounts of time to give a child who wasn't her own a chance at life the kid would not have had otherwise. These are the things Christians do in these little communities called "churches" around the world. Every day. Outside the glare of scandal and abuse of some in their midst. To the glory of God.

The Story of Someone You May Know

Take, for example, this story of a person who doesn't need to be named. It could be somebody in your hometown, your church, or your family. So the name doesn't really matter. It could even be you. But this comes from my own experience. I hope it reminds you of some parallels that tend to get buried beneath our joint anger and frustration with the embarrassing stories.

She grew up in a city of modest size. In fact, whether to call it a big town or a small city would be anybody's judgment call. Her mom and dad were good folks. He worked for a local building supply store, and she taught third grade at a public school close enough to their home that she walked to work most days. They weren't public figures. Neither of them likely would ever be mentioned in the newspaper until an obituary listing carried their names. Her mom had taught Sunday School occasionally for the church they attended, and her dad was a deacon on the church's Finance Committee. In other words, they were just rather ordinary people living rather ordinary lives.

By the account she shared with me, some "strange feelings" surfaced when she was in eighth or ninth grade. She was on the softball team and had a good time with the sport. The academics were okay, but it was math she really liked and she excelled at it. But the "strange" things were not about liking math and doing well in algebra and geometry. She found herself erotically drawn more to girls than to boys. "I can't tell you exactly when I began to notice it," she said. "It just happened. And I really wasn't sure what to make of it. I guess I thought it would pass eventually." It didn't.

All through high school, the feelings stayed. She had a few dates with boys, and – by her account – they were pleasant enough. Mostly guys who were athletes themselves, they asked her to school events or to weekend parties. There was nothing serious about her dating. She remembers, though, that she didn't enjoy "the romantic stuff." One of the boys at her church – one year older and one year ahead of her in school – wanted to be more serious about dating her. She went out with him a few times but fended off anything more serious because, she reminded him, he would be leaving for college next year. Beyond hand-holding and a few goodnight kisses, there was nothing that resembled sexual involvement with any of the guys she dated. It was different with a couple of her female friends.

"I guess it's the same with you guys," she said. "But girls see each other in the showers after practice. We tease each other. Sometimes we'd sorta wrestle or push each other around – and laugh. I don't think it meant anything to most of the girls on my high school team. Just playing around. You know." So, yes. I get it. It was that way when I played basketball in high school or at summer camp – which, with camp anyway, I didn't like at all. Bugs. Dust. *Heat*. I'm just a wimp at the idea of camping. She laughed at me – and continued her story.

"There was one girl on the team I really liked. We had lots of things in common – even our love of math. After practice, we'd sometimes get a sports drink together or just go to the big park near our high school and talk. Then, out of the blue one day, I was getting out of her car and – and I didn't plan to, really, it just happened – I leaned over and kissed her." There was a long pause. She looked up at me, and I think she was trying to read my face.

Waiting for a Reaction?

Was I shocked? Did she see a scowl on my face? Was I embarrassed by what she was telling me? (I would find out shortly why she had paused and tried to read my reaction.) Perhaps she had no idea that this wasn't the first time I was hearing some version of her story. Sometimes it was male-female. More often these days, it was male-male or female-female. To break the silence and to let her know it was okay to continue her story, I asked, "So, did that get a reaction from her? Cause you to panic or apologize or . . . ?" She picked up her story, speaking a bit faster now.

"I just started to move away to open the car door, and she

Please Don't Minimize

Sometimes straight Christians have tried to comfort me in my loneliness by reminding me that marriage is no cakewalk either – and, in many cases, marriage can exacerbate loneliness. "I'm in a very happy marriage," a friend said to me, "and I still battle loneliness." I appreciate that perspective very much, and I need it, since I have an inveterate romantic streak that I am always trying to temper.

But frankly, the more lasting consolations have come from people like my friend David Mills, who are willing to say things like this: "We ask our homosexual brethren, and our divorced brethren without annulments, to deny themselves something almost everyone else can have: a marriage, two people forming a haven in a heartless world, with someone they actively desire, with all the pleasures of romance that sexual desire brings. We ask them to live as celibates in a sexually-sodden culture where they may never find the alternative of deep, committed friendships. We ask them to risk loneliness we don't risk."

The way I am trying to live often seems very hard, and I appreciate it when my fellow Christians acknowledge that.

— Wesley Hill

reached over, put her hand behind my head, and pulled me to her. She kissed me on the lips. We kissed a couple more times. I don't remember either of us saying anything. And I got out of the car and went inside the house. I just sat on my bed and tried to make sense of what had happened! Didn't cry. Didn't laugh. Just wondered what it meant. To be honest, I didn't feel guilty or bad. It just felt – well, it felt good. And it felt okay."

"That was more than halfway through our senior year, and we were both already committed to different schools. Maybe it was because we knew that, but we didn't really 'get serious' with each other beyond what I just told you. Yeah, we 'had our secret' and spent some of our time talking about what it meant. I think she felt more guilt over it than I did, but we just kept telling each other that we were just being honest about our feelings. Could there be anything wrong with that?"

"On the one overnight trip we made to a softball tournament that spring, we roomed with two other girls. You know, two double beds and your bunkmate at a Holiday Inn. The first real 'sexual experience' either of us had was that night. We thought our roomies were asleep, and we did some things. It went beyond kissing to what I guess would be called 'intimate touching' – and some oral things." There was another pause.

"It turned out that one of the other girls *wasn't* asleep after all. After breakfast and when we were clearing out of the room, she stayed back after her bunkmate left for the bus and said, 'If I'd known Coach was putting me in a room with a couple of lesbians, I'd have asked to sleep on the bus!' I'm sure she probably said something to at least some of the girls on the team. I don't think she said anything to Coach, though. And it never came up again – at least, it didn't come up in so many words. But did the two of us ever get some weird looks from two or three other teammates! And the girl in the room with us that night, I don't think she ever spoke to either of us again. Was I ever glad graduation was only two and a half weeks away.

"But something happened out of all that. I don't know if it was the 'lesbian' remark or the other girls giving us a hard time. It almost 'forced us together' – and I know that's a dumb thing to say. It didn't 'force' anything, but it made us mad and we got really defiant about it. We saw each other a lot that summer, got really involved with each other sexually, and decided we'd go to the same school and room together. That was three semesters ago now.

"We really are in love, and it has been wonderful. I can see life together with her past college. Growing old together. Being there for each other. So we began to be more public about how we felt about each other. We'd occasionally go to a gay club in a town three hours away. It just felt wrong, though, to be sneaking around. We knew it would get out someday. So, we 'came out' as a same-sex couple several weeks ago. It made some things easier for us, and it made some things harder."

Dad, Mom, and Our Church

"I wondered if my parents were going to disown me when I told them about all this. But they didn't. They asked to talk with (my partner) and me, and we sat down with them almost three weeks ago now – and braced ourselves. But it wasn't that way at all. It was a hard conversation, and my Mom and Dad cried more than I did. They told me they loved me – would always and forever love me. They said they believed what (my partner) and I were doing was wrong and not good for us. They asked both of us if we had thought about what the Bible says about it.

"That's when it dawned on me that I had put them in such a hard spot with our church. They didn't know I had stopped going to church when I left for college, but I knew they were still very involved back at home. Dad would have to resign as a deacon. Mom would have to quit teaching Sunday School. They would probably have to find a different church to attend – or maybe they wouldn't be welcome at any church. So I told them I just hadn't thought about what I might be doing to them. It hit me hard. I really started to cry."

There was a pause in our conversation at that point. I walked to a shelf, picked up the box of tissues I keep handy for these moments, and waited for her to regain composure. We were quiet. Again, I think she was trying to read my body language and facial expressions. After a few minutes, she chose to pick up the story.

"Dr. Shelly, I think what happened next is why I'm here to talk with you today. They told me they had talked with our preacher and a couple of our church's elders already about my 'coming out.' When they met with them the Sunday afternoon before we talked, they had given them a resignation letter from their leadership posts with the church. They said they had asked them to pray for us. But they wouldn't let my Mom and Dad resign. They told them they loved them – and loved me. And the last thing they wanted to do with what they were learning was to find someone to punish. They even said they were sorry for their failure to talk about this subject at church and would do anything they could to help them help me. And they prayed for them – and us.

"That's just not what I expected to happen. I'd heard all those terrible horror stories about how mean and judgmental church people are to gay people. And I know that probably has happened lots of times. But it didn't happen with me. So, when the preacher texted me at school that week and asked to talk with me, I agreed to it. And he said it would be okay if I wanted Mom, Dad, or (my partner) to come. I can't say I was eager to meet with him, but I did. I asked Mom to go with me, and the meeting was good. He said our church wanted to be 'welcoming but non-affirming' with people from the LGBTQ+ community – and I had to get him to explain what that meant. He said that 'everybody has something to deal with' and that gay people were just like straight people on that point. We talked a bit about some verses in Romans he wanted us to read. I asked some questions. And that's why I contacted you.

"He said he was just beginning to do some reading and thinking about this subject and had been a 'coward' – that was *his* word – about addressing it before now. He suggested I come talk with you. He said he knew you, knew you had done some teaching and writing about same-sex attraction, and thought it might help if we talked. Thank you for making the appointment with me and for encouraging you to bring (my partner), too."

And the Point of the Story Is . . .

The story I've just told you has no real names attached for obvious reasons. And enough of the details are "disguised" to protect identities. I have had several of those meetings with men, women, parents, church leaders, and same-sex couples. Candidly, this one preserves better memories than most.

I have met with parents *after* they learned of a daughter or son's gay relationship and scolded, threatened, or punished their child. (It's hard to get productive conversations open after starting on that note!) I have met with parents after they went to their church's leaders for help only to be "punished" themselves. (What did you do to him? Did you sexually abuse her? Why didn't you teach her the Bible? And, by the way, you are no longer going to be a deacon or teacher at this church!) Even worse, I have had the occasional chance to meet with a man or woman who has been confronted by parents, preacher, teacher, or well-meaning "church person" in some brutal fashion. ("You know you'll go to Hell for that!")

It is one thing to say "I believe X" or even "I am convinced Y is wrong." It is quite another thing to scold, threaten, or speak God's damnation over someone. Yes, it is shameful that strong convictions on basic moral truth are in short supply today. No, it will not restore or strengthen strong moral convictions to be spiteful and mean-spirited.

> **Gospel-Centered Support**
>
> We have failed to provide gospel-centered support for same-sex attracted Christians. As a 43-year-old single man who did not choose singleness, I know firsthand the challenges of obedience. But there are also blessings, just as marriage involves challenges and blessings. The church must have a robust, practical theology of singleness which involves more than just abstinence programs and the Christian singles ghetto (also known as the "college and career" group). We are not ready to address the issue of homosexuality (or even sexuality in general) if we have not first redeemed biblical singleness.
>
> We have failed to walk alongside same-sex attracted Christians to whom God has provided a spouse – of the opposite sex. [Matthew] Vines limits the power of God by actually believing that there is no possibility for gays and lesbians to marry someone of the opposite sex. He even believes that encouraging such marriages "is not Christian faithfulness," because they would most likely end in divorce. In this, he offhandedly dismisses many marriages that have not failed. Certainly, there are challenges with these relationships, and getting married should never be the main focus. But fear of failure should not trump gospel-centered living. This is true Christian faithfulness.
>
> — Christopher Yuan

The point of the story above is to encourage more people to take the approach less often used with LGBTQ+ persons and topics. It is not a form of spiritual compromise to be kind to people. It is, in fact, a betrayal of the gospel to be unloving. That story says something to parents about starting with love for our children – no matter what has happened in their lives or some colossal blunder they have made. It also tells those of us who are in church leadership something we need to hear: *Truth gets a better hearing in the context of love and generosity toward hurting, struggling, confused, and erring people.* Truth is imperative, but without love it can be unbearable.

Want to know where this story wound up? In the initial meeting I had with the woman and her partner, things seemed to go well. The first thing I learned was that

I would be having two conversations at the same time. While the woman was a Christian with some (limited!) Bible knowledge, her partner knew essentially nothing of the biblical story or message. Her family background had no Christian memory that she could identify, and she had never owned a Bible. So I was talking with a young sister in Christ who knew very little of the Bible but who had a favorable attitude toward its teaching because of her parents – and the way a preacher and two elders had treated her parents. At the same time, I was talking with an intelligent young woman who was at times simply bewildered by discussing ethical claims made by a God she didn't believe in.

To her credit, the unbelieving partner to this relationship seemed to care genuinely for the Christian woman whose conscience was being stirred by the Holy Spirit. She was not dismissive or disrespectful toward the study of Scripture. I think I would describe her as confused for lack of background. That, by the way, was the only meeting I had with her. By my ongoing dialogue partner's account, she never asked her to stop our conversations. She never made light of her obvious need to have a clear conscience on the matter. Over a period of several weeks, we met several more times. I was in no position to demand anything more of her than I can of a student in a classroom or a person in a church pew. My primary responsibility as I saw it was to encourage thoughtful engagement with the Bible, pray for her, and trust the Spirit to guide her to the truth.

Around three months after we first met, she informed me of a decision she had already communicated to her partner – or now, I should say, her former partner. They had mutually agreed to take some time away from each other to "sort out some things." Perhaps time apart simply allowed things to cool down and the two of them to move on. Maybe a deepening faith caused her to make a Christ-honoring decision. And that was my last meeting with her. The reconnection with both her family and the wise leadership of their church would give her the chance to make a responsible decision.

This story in which I played practically no role at all seemed important to include here. For one thing, it isn't about me or any claim that I know how to help people through these situations. Its importance is to highlight the love of two parents and the spiritual maturity of three church leaders. Against the several accounts I could relate of embarrassed and irate parents who drove a wedge between themselves and

> **The Loving Opposition**
>
> We, the church, have the opportunity to demonstrate, in our words and in our lives, God's love for the homosexual person. If we truly love, we will act on that love. We must start by eradicating our negative responses to homosexual people. Stop the queer jokes and insults; they hurt others. We must deal with our own emotional reactions; we must decide to love. We must repudiate violence and intolerance toward persons of homosexual orientation. We must change the church so that it is a place where those who feel homosexual desire can be welcomed. The church must become a sanctuary where repentant men and women can share with others the sexual desires they feel and still receive prayerful support and acceptance....
>
> Now the second part of our call – to speak the truth. If we truly love, we will not shrink from speaking God's view of homosexual behavior. Do not be deceived: increasingly today we are defined as unloving solely for viewing homosexuality as immoral, regardless of the compassion we exhibit. Nevertheless, we must strive to be loving when we voice our opposition. Compassion in no way entails an acceptance of the gay lifestyle any more than it entails affirming an adulterer's infidelity.
>
> — Stanton Jones

a child, this is a better approach. The reaction was not to accept their daughter's behavior simply because they love her. They loved her enough to question and seek help. Then, with a different approach than some churches might have taken, there was compassion and patience. There was even the humility to admit they didn't know quite how to be helpful – but a determined effort not to close their eyes to a family's pain for the sake of protecting the "image" of their church.

For myself, I could have wished for a Christian counselor in the town where they lived and to whom I might have referred them. From some poor experiences I have had, however, the advice to see a therapist for personal or family help with this sort of crisis is limited to people I know and trust. Even among people who present themselves as Christian counselors, some appear to see their role as helping people clarify and accept their feelings and actions – rather than sort out their life situations from the perspective of biblical faith.

The Role of the Community of Saints

When believers offer the prospect of personal self-control or inner strength by the Holy Spirit, we must not overlook the role a local church can play in nurturing it. Here is a text that I believe is relevant to how that can play out:

> "Truly I tell you," Jesus replied, "no one who has left home or brothers or sisters or mother or father or children or fields for me and the gospel will fail to receive a hundred

times as much in this present age: homes, brothers, sisters, mothers, children and fields – along with persecutions – and in the age to come eternal life" (Mark 10:29-30).

It is critical for our church communities to become more sensitive to the needs of their non-married members – whether late teens, single young adults, widowed persons, divorcees, or adults who simply never married. Although I have argued that Adam's "alone" status was judged in relation to the human mission of populating Planet Earth and ruling it wisely in partnership with the Creator, I see no reason to deny the obvious. Adam "alone" for an extended period would have sensed the need for communication, shared experience, creativity, and love with peers. The ontological status of being "alone" ultimately might have evolved into the psychological-emotional state we call "loneliness." That isolation can lead to such negative feelings need not be denied. How those feelings should be satisfied is envisioned in Scripture.

> Sing to God, sing in praise of his name,
>   extol him who rides on the clouds;
>   rejoice before him – his name is the Lord.
> A father to the fatherless, a defender of widows,
>   is God in his holy dwelling.
> God sets the lonely in families,
>   he leads out the prisoners with singing;
>   but the rebellious live in a sun-scorched land (Psa 68:4-6).

The setting for this psalm is impossible to determine. Even the superscription is not clear as to whether the later editors considered Psalm 68 to have been composed *by* David or *about* him. And is the Conquering God of Israel riding on a cloud of judgment against a particular enemy? Is he coming on a cloud to battle the collective enemies of God? Is he coming – as others have suggested – to establish his sovereign reign over all things in time and space? For our purpose here, it does not matter. Whatever "victory" God sets about to claim, his concern is not to vindicate himself in triumphal glory but to make himself known to the most vulnerable. Orphans, widows, prisoners, *the lonely* – all will have their needs met.

Longman points to the word "lonely" in verse 6: "Or perhaps, as in the NIV footnote, 'the desolate in a homeland,' but in either rendition God is taking those who are cut off from social ties and the web of relationships."[1] That is, the point of the assurance to the lonely is not that they will have a lodging place of stone and wood but that their need for community will be met. They will not wither up in a desolate, sun-scorched land. Does the church have any responsibility to the fulfillment of this promise? Do we watch for people without natural family relationships – orphans, widows, single people, persons with disabilities – and mitigate their sense of social isolation? If not, do we bear any blame for the unhealthy relationships they put in place as an alternative to what may feel like sun-scorched lives?

Through my extended work with one church for twenty-seven years and with several others for short seasons of eight to fourteen months as a consultant, there is a phenomenon that stands out. To be honest, it might not have stood out to me if some of the persons involved had not come to me to express their frustration at being left out. In promoting family meals in homes, family VBS or family camp in the summer, and family gatherings for Thanksgiving and Christmas, I have been guilty of appearing to say, "Singles not included," or perhaps, "Only Mom, Dad, and the 2.5 kids welcome here." Of course, that had never been the intent. So I am grateful to a non-married friend who was gutsy enough to tell me "You're making me feel like I don't belong here." *Ouch!* And thank you again.

> **Going Forward . . .**
>
> In addition to living faithful marriages and engaging in loving conversation [with gay persons], I believe evangelicals must take the lead in a cluster of additional vigorous activities related to gay people.
>
> We ought to take the lead in condemning and combating verbal or physical abuse of gay people. . . .
>
> We ought to develop model programs so that our congregations are known as the best place in the world for gay and questioning youth (and adults) to seek God's will in a context that embraces, loves, and listens rather than shames, denounces, and excludes. Surely, we can ask the Holy Spirit to show us how to teach and nurture biblical sexual practice without ignoring, marginalizing, and driving away from Christ those who struggle with biblical norms.
>
> Our evangelical churches should be widely known as places where people with a gay orientation can be open about their orientation and feel truly welcomed and embraced. Of course, Christians who engage in unbiblical sexual practices (whether heterosexual or gay Christians) should be discipled (and disciplined) by the church and not allowed to be leaders or members in good standing if they persist in their sin. (The same should be said for those who engage in unbiblical practices of any kind, including greed and racism.) However, Christians who openly acknowledge a gay orientation but commit themselves to celibacy should be eligible for any role in the church that their spiritual gifts suggest.
>
> — Ron Sider

CHAPTER 14: THE VALUE OF CHRISTIAN COMMUNITY

In my defense, perhaps I never did anything quite so offensive as one pastor witnessed in his congregation. On a day when Communion was shared by having people move to strategic locations in the room to share the bread and wine, the person presiding over the service did the following. After explaining the procedure, he invited families to come to the tables and serve the elements to each other. He saw and participated in something both holy and moving. As the movement of family groups slowed a bit, the same person then said, "Singles, feel free to come forward now and serve yourselves." And we wonder that people who may be both alone and lonely – I remind you, the two are *not* the same – sometimes simply give up on the church. At other times, they find community in unhealthy relationships. Singles seems to be welcomed at bars, for example. And one 29-year-old member of our church found a person who would become his same-sex partner at a bar he visited on a particularly lonely evening.

From my point of view, his story had nothing that resembles a happy ending. He was a senior staff member of a thriving parachurch organization. He was handsome and outgoing. He had a graduate degree in education. Everybody liked him. But he had never really connected with our large Singles Ministry and had few close friends either at work or in our church. Within the week after his episode at the bar, he phoned and asked to come by my office. He had grown up in a Christian home and had always been taught (and still believed) that same-sex intercourse was sinful. He had wrestled with same-sex attraction, however, for as long as he could remember. He felt bad about it. He had prayed to be delivered from it. He felt incredibly guilty for the few half-steps into the world of gay porn and a handful of visits to gay bars.

On the night in question, he had gone to a gay bar on the opposite side of town – to avoid the possibility of being recognized by anyone. He didn't want to lose his job. He didn't want to be embarrassed. Something happened when he met a man that night that I have to compare to what straight people call love at first sight.

"I didn't go there looking for somebody to hook up with. I'd never done that and knew I never would," he began. "He just came over to the table where I was. We sat and talked. And I have to tell you it was magical – like nothing I've ever felt in my life. We left and went to his place. I had sex for the first time. And I didn't feel guilty. In fact, I just felt wonderful. I don't believe God would give me these feelings, if they were wrong. What am I going to do?"

The what-to-do question wasn't about repentance and change. It turns out that it had nothing to do with wanting help with the moral-spiritual implications of what had happened. The question was purely pragmatic about leaving his job, wounding his parents and two sisters, and cutting himself off from the past. That was it. He had no interest or willingness to talk about Scripture. "I know all that – and believe it," he said. "But I'm through playing a game to please other people. These feelings are real. I believe God made me the way I am and won't judge me for choosing to be honest. *I'm gay!* And – no offense to you, Rubel – but you and everybody else in my world had better get used to it! I just don't fit in a 'straight church' that won't accept me for who I am."

I don't browbeat people I think are wrong. I learned a long time ago that being heavy-handed with people simply drives them away and closes off conversation. So I tried a few questions that I thought might lead to something productive. But he was smart enough to say, "I know the discussion you want to have, but no dice. No thanks. I've been so miserable for so long in trying to deal with these feelings that I'm done now with fighting them. Because we've been friends, I didn't want to 'just disappear' and have you wondering why. I'll work it out. And I wish you all the best." He smiled at me. He shook my hand. He walked out.

I have not seen him since that day. During the next few weeks of his notice at work and moving out of town, he would not take my calls or meet to talk. I have no idea where he is today or how his adult life has gone.

Community for LGBTQ+ Persons

It was outspoken Peter who pressed Jesus about the prospects of discipleship. "We have left everything to follow you," he said. What had that been for Peter? Perhaps his fishing business? Friends and synagogue members from his youth who rejected him when he embraced Jesus of Nazareth as Israel's Messiah? He apparently did not have to give up his wife to be a disciple (cf. 1 Cor 9:5). Did he know of others who had? Many a student of the New Testament has heard deep lament in the language of Paul about "my people, those of my own race, the people of Israel" (Rom 9:1-3). Might this have included family – perhaps even Paul's parents or a wife – back in Tarsus? (cf. 1 Cor 7:9).

Whether any of the apostles were single adults by choice, death, or desertion by others, I cannot say. Whether any of them had same-sex feelings for someone in their group, I have no idea. But I can tell the stories of several people I have known and from whom I have heard frustration voiced about their loneliness. Several of these have been persons who are single because their primary attraction is to persons of the same sex. Their attempt to follow Christ as chaste single adults has been made harder for them when they sensed that everything about a church's life is oriented to married couples. The loneliness of some of these sisters and brothers has been made even more intense because they have had to "hide" their sexual orientation – and occasionally sit through demeaning statements about "queers" and "perverts" in their churches.

> **Restoring Spiritual Friendship**
>
> Does the church have anything to say other than, "Sorry, that's just the price of being consistently same-sex-attracted"? What can we do to address this very real dilemma for [my friend] and thousands of others like him?
>
> There are many answers to that question, but at least one thing the church can and should do is to work to restore friendship to its rightful place in our lives and in our relationships in the church. As Christians and as a faith community, we can prioritize those deep, intimate, affectionate, non-sexual relationships we call friendships. We can work to strengthen the friendship culture of the church so that the church becomes a relationally thick and rewarding place – not just for married folks, but for singles, even celibates like my friend.
>
> In short, we can recover the Bible's vision for spiritual friendship – a vision of human connection in which soul is knit to soul, united together in Christ-honoring love for one another.
>
> — Todd Wilson

What if we took up the challenge of Jesus in Mark 10 and actually helped these Christian brothers and sisters by allowing men and women to be as transparently honest about same-sex attraction as others in our churches are allowed to be about their chemical addictions? Many churches either sponsor or host meetings where people dealing with alcohol and drugs can be welcomed without being shamed. Others have Sunday class sessions or host support groups for people in the aftermath of divorce. We have learned that people are helped most in contexts that are safe enough that specific sins and vulnerabilities to sinful behaviors can be named.

Have we learned nothing from Alcoholics Anonymous? Gamblers Anonymous? Eating Disorders Anonymous? Narcotics Anonymous? Or what about related groups such as Al-Anon and Adult Children of Alcoholics? The idea for forming nonjudgmental groups for persons who know they are in some form of self-defeating, self-diminishing behavior has been revolutionary. There is widespread appreciation for what is done in these "recovery groups" that extends quite literally around the world.

I have claimed for decades now that Alcoholics Anonymous had to be created only because churches have failed. I am more convinced than ever of the truthfulness of that claim. Local churches were God's original "recovery groups" where sinners could band together, receive grace from Christ, give grace to one another, and hold one another accountable to the will of God. In churches like that, all of us would accept the divine judgment against our sinfulness and mediate grace to one another in a context of accountability. Sadly, even where support groups are hosted and in churches that focus on welcoming divorced, grieving, or chemically dependent persons, same-sex attracted individuals typically remain exiles. To name and confess practically any other sin can be met with supportive accountability and help, but this one sometimes generates immediate exclusion. That atmosphere must be changed for the sake of honoring honesty and repentance with acceptance, grace, and accountability.

Loving "Different" People

The focus of this book has been theology, and I don't pretend to know all the steps needed to help persons who want to escape the addiction of same-sex behaviors or cope with same-sex attraction that tempts them to behaviors they know are sinful. I just don't know how to create a program you can ask your church to implement.[2] But I am convinced that the Holy Spirit is the *agent of deliverance* from the power of sin and that the local church is the *context for freedom* within which the Spirit's power best operates.

I have had limited experience in facilitating three small groups modeled on Alcoholics Anonymous for persons dealing with same-sex behaviors. All three involved only Christian males who were committed to celibacy. The key biblical text that guided all three groups was this: "Confess your sins to each other and pray for each other so that you may be healed" (Jas 5:16a). The context for this verse exhorts Christians to pray for the physical health of one another. Indeed, a wide variety of illnesses can be traced to sinful behaviors. Early on, however, believers acknowledged the need for transparency in the whole of one's spiritual life – not just in cases where physical illness and pain resulted. A second-century document used to instruct persons in the faith gives this exhortation: "Confess your transgressions in the church, so you will not come to prayer with an evil conscience."[3]

A common theme among these men was that they were in their first Christian setting that allowed them to name the specific sin they had committed (or in which some still were involved) and to which they were constantly tempted. No one was shamed or scolded. The word "sin" was never avoided; neither was it applied exclusively to their experiences. The overarching theme of all those meetings was God's grace that leads to holiness. The rebuke of a Scripture-formed conscience had been enough for any one of them to know he had done wrong. But where does one find release from the guilt? Where find hope for overcoming a weakness? Where look others in the eye without hoping they "never find out"? What we have learned about alcoholism is true about sexual addiction: *shaming and humiliating a person tends to drive them deeper into an addiction.* On the other hand, transparency and accountability have a liberating power.

The power that is freed to work in such an environment is the power of God's love. Scot McKnight has attempted to untangle what he calls the "four elements of love" described in the Bible from our culture's wrong ideas about love.[4] He proposes that

> **Faithful Witness**
>
> Faithful witness is the reason Christian ethics have always held open two paths for Christian sexual fidelity. . . . In marriage, we bear witness to the world to the quality of the divine-human relationship. As in a faithful marriage, God is faithful to us. The husband and wife who are faithful to one another, while being different from another, are a sign of the ways that God is faithful to us, while being different from us. Singleness is a sign equal to marriage as singleness too points to God's faithfulness. In both marriage and singleness, we are embodying something about God's radical fidelity. . . .
>
> In Rome, some people (potential wives, for instance) got protection and honor, and some (prostitutes and slaves, for example) did not. In the kingdom, everybody's body is honored. In Rome, bodies were for power or pleasure or the state or the market. In the kingdom, bodies are for the Lord. In Rome, sexual ethics were governed by different rules for men and women. In the kingdom, we are called to be chaste, all of our bodies are not for porneia (sex that denies who God is and tells lies about what it means to be human), but for the Lord. In Rome, if you were sexually shameful, there was no going back. In God's kingdom, there is forgiveness and healing and grace and freedom.
>
> Here's the kicker: in Rome, you were either a slave or you were free. In the kingdom of God, we are all free. As a witness to this, we value singleness and marriage as two routes, two ways of life, in which the Christian may be truly sexual and truly free.
>
> — Beth Felker Jones

God's love – and the love he can engender among his people – begins as a "rugged commitment" to another. It works itself out in being "with," "for," and "unto" that person. Being *with* someone is to be present, supportive, and staying with him or her through the toughest of challenges. Being *for* another is to be an active advocate on that person's behalf. Finally, the biblical idea of love means being *unto* the holy goal of God's purpose to transform us in the direction of such kingdom realities as holiness and the imitation of Christ.

When McKnight applies this view of love to same-sex issues, he pleads for local churches to see themselves as the context for redemption God wants to use for the LGBTQ+ person. While granting the historic failure of the church in this regard, he nevertheless insists "we are called to a rugged commitment to all, including those who experience same-sex attraction."[5] A Christ-follower who has never felt the tug of same-sex attraction must get past what one writer has termed "the yuck factor" of gay sex among "those people" to a sense of *us* – where "us" is the class of sinners in need of a Savior.

> If we are called to love one another, we are called to be "with" gays and lesbians (this means physical presence over time), and we are called to be "for" in the sense that these folks will know they are loved, and we are summoned to walk with gays and lesbians toward the kingdom of God and toward sexual holiness. Love does not mean "I will love you if you do what I want," or "We will accept you in our church if you live our way." That's not love; that's coercion. But neither does love mean toleration: you do what you want and I'll leave you alone, and I'll do what I want and you leave me alone. Love is a rugged commitment to someone, which involves presence, advocacy, and a companionship over time as we walk toward the kingdom of God – which means growing in holiness, love, and righteousness together.[6]

How Different? How Alike?

As indicated earlier, some churches use the language of "welcoming but not affirming" in relation to the LGBTQ+ community. Shouldn't that be our language toward *all* of "us" sinners? Without approving or encouraging a person's involvement with *any* forbidden behavior, we can all be agents of God to support the new-creation renewal that is central to Christian experience.

> What shall we say, then? Shall we go on sinning so that grace may increase? By no means! We are those who have died to sin; how can we live in it any longer? Or don't you know that all of us who were baptized into Christ Jesus were baptized into his death? We were therefore buried with him through baptism into death in order that, just as Christ was raised from the dead through the glory of the Father, we too may live a new life.
>
> For if we have been united with him in a death like his, we will certainly also be united with him in a resurrection like his. For we know that our old self was crucified with him so that the body ruled by sin might be done away with, that we should no longer be slaves to sin – because anyone who has died has been set free from sin (Rom 6:1-7).

This is the lesson the church is called to learn anew in every generation. Grace is anything but permission to continue in something God has forbidden. It is the atmosphere of forgiveness and empowerment by the Spirit of God in which we put sin to death and come alive to the things of God. Can God grant some complete freedom from their same-sex attraction? Yes. Just as he may provide immediate sobriety to some, instantaneously release some from greed to become incredibly generous, or heal the rift in some families overnight. In my experience, however, those breathtaking events we love to hear about are far less common than his gift of daily grace to people who struggle with people, places, and events that repeatedly tempt them to cross boundaries they know God has set for their lives.

In either circumstance, victory comes only through the power of God's Holy Spirit and is meant to be supported by churches that can provide love, accountability, and nurture for the Spirit's transforming work. It is in these communities of faith that we most appropriately find our path to being the authentic, whole, and fully human beings God created us to be. It is in these environments that we are able to give life's most significant and most holy consent – *consent to God's work of transforming us into the image of Jesus Christ.*

ENDNOTES

1. Tremper Longman, *Psalms: An Introduction and Commentary*, Tyndale Old Testament Commentaries 15-16 (Downers Grove, IL: Inter-Varsity Press, 2004), 258.

2. While admitting my limitations on forming or critiquing various programs that attempt to help persons who are struggling with same-sex issues, one of the resource groups I have seen in operation and whose

leadership I trust is based in Middle Tennessee. A dear friend, Dr. Leonard Allen, serves on the board of Equip. Information on its ministries may be found at https://equipyourcommunity.org/how-we-help.

3. *Didache* 4.14.

4. Scot McKnight, *A Fellowship of Differents* (Grand Rapids: Zondervan, 2014), 53-61.

5. Ibid., 130.

6. Ibid.

> *"And [God] said to the human race,*
> *'The fear of the Lord – that is wisdom,*
> *and to shun evil is understanding.'"*
>
> — Job 28:28

CHAPTER 15

Questions People Ask

I can imagine that some people who read this book will start with this chapter. It isn't that this is a textbook with the answers at the back. But TV, bumper stickers, and text messaging have reduced the attention span of most of us. It certainly has done that to me. I want a quick, direct answer to my question. If I can get that, I'm done and will move on. I wish more of us were a bit more thoughtful about the whys and wherefores.

So you may have come to this final chapter to see if your specific question(s) of interest are in this list – and what one person's idea for answering it looks like. Okay. I'm not scolding you. But, if you are starting here, I hope you will read this chapter for what it is: *These are short answers to questions that require more than my word for it on these tough issues.* So most of the answers given here will refer you to chapters where you can get additional supporting data for what is said.

In other words, please don't take one of these answers as definitive without looking at the facts and reasoning behind them. For that matter, it is even more important to me that you not dismiss an answer given here because you don't like it or agree with it – until you have paid serious attention to the supporting evidence.

While there are more questions that could have been included, these are among the most frequent I have been asked. There is no particular order of importance or frequency of encounter with them.

* * * * * * *

The same-sex relationships the Bible condemns (i.e., exploitative behaviors like pedophilia, pederasty, or anal rape) are not the same-sex relationships today's LGBTQ+ persons affirm (i.e., loving, covenantal). Why can't people see the difference?

First, let's agree that the Bible unquestionably condemns exploitation and violence in all sexual relationships. Second, when the Bible names same-sex behavior in either the Old or New Testament, it is the activity itself – not the context or motive – that is judged wrong. There is ample evidence from both neutral historians and pro-gay sources that caring and exclusive same-sex unions existed in ancient Greece and Rome. (See Chapters 9 and 10.) Third, the Greek vocabulary of so well-educated a man as Paul had words for rape, pederasty, and other forms of predatory sexual violation that he would have known. (See Chapters 11 and 12.) Fourth, the same-sex behaviors rebuked so severely in both Testaments were mutual, not predatory. Therefore, Leviticus has both parties to the act punished, and Romans specifically says the persons "were inflamed with lust for one another" in their intercourse.

Ancient cultures knew as wide a range of sexuality as we know in our own world. There was also a wide range of attitudes toward same-sex activities and the people involved. Judaism and its Christian offspring were both known for their absolute and counter-cultural opposition. In simplest terms, there is no distinction to be found in the Bible between one-nighters, sex with a stranger-prostitute, sex in a pagan cult, or covenantal same-sex relationships. All were covered by Scripture's consistent censure. (See Chapters 6, 11, and 12.)

There is an obvious trajectory in Scripture on topics like race and the treatment of women. If the rules changed on those issues, why can't they change on same-sex relationships?

From the call of Abraham forward, it has been the declared intention of Yahweh that all peoples on earth will be blessed through him and his offspring (Gen 12:1-3). At various times and under a variety of circumstances, Abraham's descendants mistook their spiritual separation for holiness to entail (or to be equivalent to) racial segregation. Thus, when Moses married an African woman, Miriam and Aaron expressed their disapproval and were punished by God (Num 12:1). Such women as the Canaanite Tamar (Gen 38:27-30), the Canaanite Rahab (Josh 2:1ff), the Moabite Ruth (Ruth 1:4; cf. Deut 23:3), and Bathsheba whose Hittite husband indicates she was also either Hittite herself or a Jewish woman who had married outside Israel (2 Sam 11:3) are significant to the biblical record. The inclusion of the Gentiles was part of the messianic hope outlined by the prophet Isaiah (Isa 2:2-4).

When the Messiah came, he issued his to-all-nations mandate with the gospel (Luke 24:47). Holdouts in the Jerusalem church debated it with the apostles and elders around 48 A.D. and said Jews and Gentiles were to be one in Christ. Interestingly, however, the outcome of that assembly of Christian leaders was a letter to Gentile churches that specifically forbids *porneia* – the New Testament word for all forms of sexual intercourse other than that between a married heterosexual couple in their covenanted life as husband and wife (Acts 15:22-29).

It is clear that God has always purposed and moved toward the embrace and blessing of all people from all races and ethnic groups into his single and united spiritual family. There is never a hint in either Judaism or Christianity of a divine purpose to receive and sanction those who practice same-sex intercourse – whether with children or adults, in temple settings or private bedrooms, as promiscuous souls or as covenanted and monogamous partners for life.

The same essential point is true of the enlarged roles of service most churches offer to women today. Scripture has never oppressed and restrained females in service to God the way churches have across history. As with slavery, racial segregation, and racial prejudice, the Bible has been abused to justify wrongdoing against half of the human race.

For example, there are multiple cases in both testaments of God's choice of women to *lead* in ministry to his people – Deborah, Esther, Priscilla, Phoebe, Junia, and others. It is of no minor significance that many Samaritans came to believe on Jesus "because of the woman's testimony" he met at Jacob's well (John 4:39) and that the resurrected Christ chose women to be the first to testify to his resurrection (Matt 28:8-10; Luke 24:9-12). With reference to the life of the church, Peter claimed on the first Pentecost following the resurrection that an Old Testament prophecy was being fulfilled that the Spirit of God would produce the result that "your sons *and daughters* will prophesy" (Acts 2:27; cf. Joel 2:28-32). To say the very least, there are no comparable texts in which persons actively engaged in same-sex relationships were called to special ministries, honored for their faith, or promised approval that previously had been denied them. The only references to same-sex erotic activity forbid them to the people of God. Put most simply, there is uniformity in the Bible's negative witness relative to same-sex behaviors, while students with the most conservative view of female ministry in churches concede diversity on the issue of "women's role" in Holy Scripture.

There is no analogy between the breaking down of racial-ethnic barriers and the removal of sex-gender distinctions to the current pressures to legitimize same-sex intimacies. Instead of a trajectory toward the inclusion of same-sex behaviors, there is a uniform and unyielding opposition.

Since everybody knows that the Bible approves slavery – and was clearly wrong on that point – why can't you "Bible thumpers" admit it is wrong about same-sex love? Churches were on the wrong side for centuries on slavery and are on the wrong side today about gay and lesbian people!

There is quite a "sharp edge" to this question, and I want to avoid being overly defensive in responding. In fact, let me acknowledge that churches and their preachers *were* on the wrong side of racist slavery in the pre-Civil War South, in South African apartheid, and in other settings. But I must challenge the questioner's view about what "everybody knows" about the biblical view of this subject.

The Bible story plays out in cultures where slavery was such an integral element of economic and social life that neither tiny Israel in the Ancient Near East nor a fledgling and persecuted church in the Roman Empire could have abolished it. For that matter, attempting a full-frontal assault on institutional slavery could have led to both being wiped out! A view that I think is more fair and true to reality is that Moses, Jesus, Paul, and their believing peers had to *tolerate* a society they did not create, worked to minimize some of the more obvious negatives of slave-based cultures, and laid the groundwork for dismantling them.

First, the Bible "approves slavery"? Hardly! The center of the Old Testament story focuses on Israel suffering enslavement – first in Egypt and later in Babylon.

The narrative presents slavery as oppressive, hateful, dehumanizing – and Yahweh acting to provide a deliverer (Moses) whom he would empower to free them. Jesus spoke negatively about slavery and used it as a metaphor for the effects of sin in human lives – and offered to make people "free indeed" (John 8:34-36). And while both Paul and Peter counseled enslaved Christians to make the best of bad situations, what are we to make of "if you can gain your freedom, do so"? (1 Cor 7:21). That doesn't sound like an approving attitude toward slavery.

Second, Old Testament laws relating to slavery in ancient Israel show something very different from what the word means to most of us. It was usually a way of working off debt and didn't resemble Greek or Roman slavery. The "slave" lived at home, did agricultural and domestic work, went home to their families at night, and had legal recourse to protection from abuse. After six years, an Israelite slave had to be given the right to freedom. Not a few people have made the point that calendar-limited work to pay off a debt in ancient Israel looks far more humane than imprisonment in our modern setting. Some texts relevant to these points are the following: Ex 21: 26-27; 23:9; Deut 15:12-18; 16:9-12 (esp. v.12).

Third, the Bible nowhere presents slavery as a "natural" or "desirable" state of affairs – as, for example, both Plato and Aristotle viewed it. The first mention of slavery in the Bible is in the context of a curse (cf. Gen 9:25-27). It is not how God purposed part of his human creatures to live. Women, slaves, children,

> **Slavery and True Freedom**
> The book of Exodus insists that one cannot speak of liberation as a freeing from all restraints; it is not a declaration of independence. Exodus moves from one kind of slavery to another, from bondage to Pharaoh to the service of Yahweh. One cannot bypass Sinai on the way to the promised land. Hence, any who would use Exodus as a paradigm for liberation should then move to the question, Whom will we serve now? Exodus would claim that true freedom is found only in the service of Yahweh.
> — Terence Fretheim

prisoners, all classes of "the oppressed" – these were the people to whom Jesus came to proclaim freedom and favor (Luke 4:16-21). And have you read the little Book of Philemon for its subtle take on slavery?

With regard to the LGBTQ+ community, the same gracious offer still stands. Because every human being is in God's image and dearly loved by him, he offers liberation and grace. We are back to the theme of this book again: the *why* of God's love is that every person is great enough that Jesus would die to set us free from our various slaveries and addictions, and the *how* of acknowledging and accepting his love is repentance and faith that lead to a transformed life (cf. Mark 1:15; 1 Cor 6:9-11).

Jesus loved people and took their human needs into account when he interpreted things like Sabbath restrictions. He let his disciples fix food on the Sabbath (Matt 12:1ff). And he healed a lame man in the presence of his critics on the Sabbath (John 5:1ff). Why can't we do the same thing when interpreting biblical prohibitions on same-sex relationships? Doesn't everybody feel the same human need for companionship and love?

In both cases cited here, Jesus explained that his critics' interpretation of the Law of Moses had been mistaken. The Law of Moses had never forbidden the kindness of feeding a hungry person or relieving suffering on the Sabbath. The "orthodoxy" of some of his contemporaries had turned what was meant to be a day of rest and joy into an oppressive day to be dreaded.

There is no similar case in which Jesus either rebuked his Jewish contemporaries for their counter-cultural (to Roman practices) teaching that sexual privilege attached to monogamous male-female marriage. To the contrary, he affirmed the moral code of the Law of Moses both in his general comments about it (Matt 5:17-20) and in his application of its teachings (cf. Matt 5:21-48). A point that many people miss is that the moral teachings of the Bible are based on the character of God and are not arbitrary and subject to change. For example, God could never change his law against lying for the simple reason that truthfulness is essential to his nature (Tit 1:3). Therefore, while dietary rules, worship rituals, and the like *can* change, fundamental moral commandments about marriage and sexuality cannot. They are the same under the Old and New Testaments. (See Chapter 6.)

I recently heard someone claim that anyone who holds a complementarian or egalitarian view of female participation in church leadership has taken a position that inevitably leads to accepting same-sex marriage. I didn't understand what he meant. Was he correct?

I am as confused by that claim as you are. As a supplement to the question addressed earlier about a "trajectory" of inclusion in Scripture, let me add a bit more here that will be specific to so-called submission, complementarian, and egalitarian views of church leadership.

For clarity, let's define terms. All three doctrinal views in question hold that men and women are both "in God's image" and fully equal in their value as persons; male and female have equal access to salvation in Christ. The *submission* view – also called "male headship" – holds that females are required by Scripture to submit to male leadership in both church and family contexts. Therefore, responsibility for the final word in family decision-making, filling elder-deacon roles in churches, and teaching or preaching to mixed-gender groups belongs exclusively to males. A *complementarian* opinion claims that men and women should fill roles in church and family that complement each other's involvement in service to God and one another. This generally means that women are encouraged to be active in church ministries, with primary roles such as elder and preacher reserved to males. Finally, an *egalitarian* position maintains that there should be no gender-based limitations on service or leadership, with roles filled on the basis of ability and gifting rather than gender. This implies equality not only in worth but also in positions women may fill in the home or church with God's blessing.

Godly and intelligent people in a wide variety of denominations argue for these positions. There is neither space nor requirement to stake out my view of these positions to answer the question that has been asked. *There is nothing about any one of them*

About Gender Roles

Whatever position we take in the complementarian-egalitarian debate on gender roles, it is important that in our teaching and preaching we take seriously the givenness of creation, and particularly the givenness of our embodied existence as male and female.

Scripture's prohibitions on same-sex sexual relationships are not arbitrary. Nor are they simply cultural constructions of an ignorant, repressive age. Creation has a pattern, like the grain of a piece of wood or marble. A wise sculptor recognizes the givenness of this grain and works with it, knowing that this constraint frees her to bring what is most beautiful out of her materials.

Likewise, biblical sexual ethics call on us to cut with creation's grain in our sexual lives and warn that a life or a society that cuts against the grain will warp, splinter, and fragment.

— Matthew Mason

that entails a given view on the issue of monogamous, loving, and faithful same-sex relations. It is easy to explain why.

In both Old and New Testaments, there are unquestioned instances of female prophets (e.g., OT: Miriam, Deborah, Huldah; NT: Mary, Anna, Philip's daughters). Similarly, the New Testament both declares that "both men and women" would receive the Holy Spirit in order to prophesy (Acts 2:18) and records instances in which females shared in the ministry of the Word of God to others (Acts 18:26; 1 Cor 11:4). People who hold submission, complementarian, and egalitarian views do not argue over female inclusion; their disagreement is over the private versus public or informal versus official setting of their work. (Submissionists might argue that women prayed and taught only women and children, complementarians that women were in support roles to males who were leading, and egalitarians that males and females served as fully equal partners in ministry.)

On the other hand, there is no instance in Scripture of a same-sex union being modeled, predicted, blessed, or otherwise affirmed. To the contrary, every reference to sexual intercourse between persons of the same sex in both the Old and New Testament rebukes it. The only morally approved context for sexual intercourse is within male-female marriage. In support of the use made of Hebrews 13:4 throughout this book, note Paul's agreement in writing to Christians in an ancient city known for its sexual license: "Because there is so much sexual immorality, each man should have his own wife, and each woman should have her own husband. The husband should fulfill his wife's sexual needs, and the wife should fulfill her husband's needs. The wife gives authority over her body to her husband, and the husband gives authority over his body to his wife" (1 Cor 7:2-4 NLT).

There is nothing about one's view of female service to and/or leadership in the church's life that entails either a positive or negative view of same-sex marriage. The two issues are unrelated in the biblical text and should not be conjoined in contemporary discussions. Tying them together is probably a rhetorical move to incline others to favor or reject a given point of view by linking it to another position one is known to embrace or dislike.

Jesus taught us to read the Bible through the lens of love – love for God and love for neighbor. That seems to me to make contemporary same-sex relations that are covenantal, caring, and committed possible for us. If not, why not?

It is certainly correct to say that Jesus saw what some interpreters of the Bible have missed: Commandments may not be divorced from the loving intent of God that is behind them or our loving application of them to one another's life situation. The mistake I see some people making today is to think and teach that love either removes the commandments God has given or else allows for time, distance, and public opinion to revise his requirement. Why would the Holy Spirit reveal something in one's personal experience that contradicts what the same Spirit revealed in Holy Scripture as public truth? If God is showing us a changed message about same-sex activity through the lives of thousands of (practicing) gay and lesbian Christians, I was surely wrong to challenge my very effective fellow-theologian's claim that God was showing him a new path to happiness through the affair he had begun with his student.

In light of the teachings of Jesus, the first possibility is clearly wrong. "If you love me, keep my commands" (John 14:15) is very specific and clear. The loving intent of God in giving a certain commandment in the first place is to help us know and do what is in our best interest. The practical requirements against murder, breaking promises, and sexual activity outside marriage are in place to protect us. They make it clear that God loves us enough to protect us against harm and to put light on the path we should follow to be authentically human.

But what of the "close alternative" option? I must admit I had never heard of this approach before, but it is my way of describing what David Gushee calls "living in a Genesis 3 world." In rejecting the claim that either "God made [humans] male and female and male for female, and so everyone needs to conform to this pattern or live as a celibate,"[1] Gushee makes the rather remarkable claim that traditionalists "rarely mention Genesis 3, which (most Christians have said) tells the story of the beginnings of human sin, with the disordering consequences that are so painfully described in Genesis 4 through Revelation."[2] I call this a "remarkable claim" because it is so obviously mistaken.

The totality of the biblical narrative not only presumes and underscores the fact of the fall in Genesis 3 but also presses the contrast of that "fallen" state to the "ideal" of the original created order – *and appeals for a return to Genesis 1-2 purity against the corruption(s) of our Genesis 3 impurity.* There is no clearer proof of this than Jesus' words from Matthew 19. When pressed on the issue of divorce, he drew a sharp line between the Genesis 3 world in which "Moses permitted you to divorce your wives because your hearts were hard" and the way things were "from the beginning" (v.8). He then made it clear that the Genesis 1-2 world, which presented the ideal state known "from the beginning," was the standard by which his disciples were to judge themselves.

It was the love of God that placed Adam and Eve in an ideal relationship that they corrupted by their sin. Since their fall from the ideal state, God's purpose has been to restore – not dumb down, accommodate, or otherwise diminish – the "very good" state of his original creation. (See Chapter 5 for more on the idea of sex in a "Genesis 3 world.")

Gender and Language

The understanding of language portrayed in Genesis contrasts starkly with the view that dominates contemporary debates about gender. Most gender theories hold that what we think of as "reality" is a linguistic and social construction. Our use of the words "woman" and "man," so this theory goes, creates the illusion that sex is a binary.

I want to point out that the constructionist view of language is a complete inversion of the correspondence view depicted in Genesis. In this divinely revealed origin story, our language does not project meaning onto things. Rather, meaning intrinsically exists in what God creates. Moreover, this meaning is intelligible to us, and language, a mark of God's image in us, enables human beings to proclaim that inherent meaning.

— Abigail Favale

I have heard the term "gender fluidity" recently. What does that mean?

Lots of new terms have come into our discussions around human sexuality of late – gender nonconforming, nonbinary, pansexual, misgender, and many others. "Gender fluidity" refers to the claim that one's gender identity as male or female is not fixed by genetic factors but may be expressed as "flowing through" different gender categories. The claim is that a person may choose to change or "weave together" different gender identities.

The notion of "choosing" or "changing" one's gender has emerged from Foucault's idea of gender as a social construct that need not be tied to biological sex. It is a postmodern curiosity without biblical precedent or warrant. Biblically and theologically, I see no way to make gender something ultimately separate from the given status of one's birth. It is not a "social construct" subject to choice and change. Yes, males may exhibit what are generally thought of as "feminine traits," just as females may do the opposite. But is crying or writing poetry "feminine"? Is doing yardwork or playing a given sport "masculine"? These divisions of gender-linked activities really are quite arbitrary.

My psychologist friends describe events of "gender confusion" and the emotional-psychological confusion some persons experience around sexual issues because of contemporary trends and subjective experiences. Christian counselors who are trained to help people sort out these confusions may be helpful to persons or families struggling with this complex issue. (See the following question on "sex" and "gender.")

How can you or anyone else claim that to be "homosexual" is a sin, since the word didn't even exist until the nineteenth century? The Bible condemns rape, prostitution, and pederasty, but those ancient writers had no concept of someone being "homosexual" – a person whose sexual orientation is exclusive to his or her own sex and who lives a loving, committed, and monogamous relationship with someone else who is same-sex oriented.

Terminology about everything from food to sex varies from culture to culture and across the centuries. So we should not be surprised that the medical-psychological term "homosexual" or "homosexuality" is not in ancient literature. And I am not referring to the English word, of course, but to a linguistic equivalent. As best I can determine, it is correct that our word "homosexual" (borrowed from German) was first used in the late 1800s. By the way, the word "heterosexual" was coined at the same time. But did either *concept* exist in ancient cultures?

Scholars of both traditional and revisionist positions come down on different sides of the question of a heterosexual-homosexual *concept* in antiquity. In my view, the Bible doesn't really address the topic of "homosexuality" or "being homosexual" – at least, not as we most often use those terms. (You might want to check the "about terminology" page in this book. It comes just after the "Table of Contents.") The Bible speaks of men having sex with men and women having sex with women. It names *behaviors* and *modes of sexual contact*. That is why I have tried to use the terms "same-sex behavior" and occasionally "homosexual acts" in this book. That is different from the term "homosexuality" as a predilection, preference, or orientation. I think I have found the *concept* of such persons (i.e., those who prefer or are exclusively given to same-sex intimacy) in ancient literature (e.g., Plato's *Symposium*), but Hebrew, Aramaic, Greek, and Latin do not have a word matching that use.

We have something of the same thing with the words "sex" and "gender." I cannot make a case for the two ideas being distinct from each other in Scripture. In contemporary usage, one's biological sex is typically assigned at birth based on external genitalia and scientifically by paired XY (male) or XX (female) chromosomes. Gender, however, is a term that ranges over one's internal sense of identity to masculine-feminine clothing choices and mannerisms. I do not find this distinction in the Bible or other ancient literature. Instead, we meet the binary distinction between male-female, man-woman, or husband-wife. Looking back with our distinctions, someone might say the female Deborah expressed masculine traits in leading a military campaign. The same person might see feminine traits in David's poetry, songs, and tears. Every attempt that has been made across centuries to collect and codify sexual difference fails. The lists that have been produced are more "fluid" than the gender distinctions they try to categorize for a theory of gender fluidity.

Confusing as it is, I have tried to avoid speaking of "homosexuals" because I have known chaste Christians who self-describe with the word. They are same-sex oriented, but they do not engage in same-sex intimacies. I have a friend who would tell you that he is homosexual, but you should not assume by that self-designation that he is – and this is how he explains the difference – "a *practicing* homosexual." (See Appendix D.)

CHAPTER 15: QUESTIONS PEOPLE ASK

Brian McLaren seems to imply in his book* A New Kind of Christian *that the account of the Ethiopian Eunuch (Acts 8) signals a change in the status of a eunuch and perhaps anyone else whose sexuality is different from "the norm" and who, in his language, "was condemned forever by the sacred Jewish Scriptures."

Several arguments have been made similar to this. In Chapter 7, I looked at Jesus' statement about eunuchs in Matthew 19:12. Be sure to add that information to what is said below. The claims I have run across involving eunuchs and the attempt to parallel their situation with transgender and same-sex situations are more emotional than historical-factual. For example, I read one article that discussed "Philip and the Sexual Deviant." *Really?* Let me offer some perspective on what all this means. The Hebrew Scriptures never equate being a eunuch with sin, some form of gender violation, or a sexual transgression. While excluded from certain cultic activities of the Jewish people – along with others who had a variety of physical injuries or blemishes – they could serve Yahweh and receive his blessing.

First, the Old Testament never identifies a eunuch as "condemned forever." Neither are eunuchs listed in the Holiness Code as sexually "deviant" or transgressive. Deuteronomy 23:1 does bar a eunuch from "enter[ing] the assembly of the Lord." But this does not mean he is no longer an Israelite or condemned forever by Yahweh. Frankly, scholars debate what it does mean. For example, children from "a forbidden marriage (bastards, KJV) nor any of their descendants" (v.2), Ammonites, Moabites, nor any of their descendants (v.3), and others are also forbidden to "enter the assembly." But Ruth was a Moabite (Ruth 1:4) – the same Ruth who was King David's great-grandmother and in the lineage of Jesus of Nazareth. Others in the biblical narrative are identified as children of Israel and attain honor among God's people.

The prohibition may mean that such persons could not participate in certain festival events or serve in the nation's military. It may be a banning of men who had been castrated as part of some period of prior devotion to a pagan deity. Or it may bar those – as with anyone of Aaron's descendants wishing to serve as a priest at the altar – who were not physically whole (i.e., deaf, with "crippled hand or foot," with "damaged testicles," etc.) in terms of being free of presenting bodily deformities (cf. Lev 21:16-23). *The Jewish Study Bible* identifies the "assembly" or "congregation" denied to a eunuch as Israel's "national governing body, akin to a popular legislature, that was charged with a broad range of judicial, political, and policy matters (Judg. 20:2)."[3]

Second, since one's status as a eunuch was not within the category of sexual sin, there is no Old Testament provision for either purification or punishment – such as the purification for those who had sex during a woman's menstrual period (i.e., unclean for seven days, Lev 15:24) versus the extreme punishment for same-sex intercourse (i.e., death, Lev 20:13). This clearly separates eunuchs from sexual transgressors. It is not a status equivalent to one's choice to be transgender by virtue of hormonal and/or surgical intervention. A eunuch – whether born so or castrated later – was still a male in the linguistic categories of both Scripture and biological science.

Third, consistent with what has been said here (and in Chapter 7), Isaiah 56:1-8 may help with the interpretation of the status of a eunuch in the Old Testament. Typically read as either a post-Torah repeal of the Deuteronomy restriction on eunuchs, other scholars challenge that view. Unlike the Torah reference, the eunuchs of Isaiah 56 are not being viewed in relation to the "assembly of the Lord" – however one understands that term – but with regard to their lack of hope for children and a namesake.[4] Thus, the metaphor a "dry tree" is used (v.3b; cf. Jer 11:19). The "fear" of this text is not that a eunuch is "condemned forever" but that such a person – along with any "foreigner" in Israel – will not have progeny to participate in the nation's restoration to glory. To this the prophet speaks for Yahweh to declare that both the eunuch and foreigner who keep Sabbath (vs.2b,4a), avoid doing evil (v.2c), and hold fast to the covenant (vs.4b,6b) will be given "a memorial and a name better than sons and daughters" (v.5a). For eunuchs who are Israelites and for the "foreigners who bind themselves to the Lord to minister to him" (i.e., foreigners who convert), there would be acceptance and blessing.

In summary, then, the eunuchs of either ancient Israel or the New Testament era (e.g., Acts 8:26-40) were alike in having experienced physical trauma, were subject to personal and social limitations of various kinds, but were promised a future through holding fast to the covenant provisions announced by the Lord's prophets.

There are no implications whatever from the references to eunuchs in Deuteronomy, Isaiah, or Acts for the setting aside of the covenant prohibitions of same-sex behaviors.

People who are still opposed to loving and monogamous LGBTQ+ relationships are simply "on the wrong side of history." People are increasingly inclined to accept gay rights.

Yes, I understand that more and more people are responding to surveys and polls to say they "approve" same-sex marriage. (By the way, I accept and have advocated publicly for the "rights" of gay and lesbian persons.[5] They should not be denied employment, housing, or basic civil rights because of their sex lives. Otherwise, should we lobby for apartment complexes to refuse rentals to unmarried couples? Should hotels be sure a married man and woman checking in are married to each other and not committing adultery?)

> **Where to Find Truth**
>
> Truth is not a ballot measure. God does not consult us to determine right and wrong. It's we who must go to revealed Scripture to find out what we should believe. Our culture appeals to whatever now is; God appeals to his intentions and design, to what ought to be. . . .
>
> The test of whether Scripture is my authority is this: Do I allow God's Word to convince me to believe what I don't like, what's contrary to what I've always believed or wanted to believe? Do I believe it even when it offends me? Am I willing to bow my knees before God and accept his truth even when my life would be easier, for the moment, if I didn't?
>
> "Truth is truth even if no one believes it; a lie is a lie even if everyone believes it."
>
> — Randy Alcorn

The fact that our culture is increasingly willing to approve same-sex marriage (civil union, etc.) says nothing about its moral status. Any number of things that are legal in the United States are not moral (e.g., lying, adultery). A Gallup Poll can provide good statistical data, but questions of biblical truth and moral uprightness are not answered with statistics and public opinion surveys. Richard Hays put it this way: "If Paul were shown the poll results, he would reply sadly, 'Indeed, the power of sin is rampant in the world.'"[6]

Good theology stresses that God is relational in nature – a Trinity of Father, Son, and Spirit in loving unity. Don't you think being "in God's image" means that we are relational beings? That we are built for relationship? And that sexuality is central to being relational?

It is true that part of the "image of God" that attaches to human beings is our need for relationships. Just as Father, Son, and Holy Spirit exist in ideal community, humans thrive best when we have the acceptance, love, and nurture that come from healthy relationships.

The question is not the need for relationships in our lives, but *what kind* of relationships. It was Paul who warned against some relationships by writing this: "Bad company corrupts good character" (1 Cor 15:33). Loyal relationships within a criminal gang would be included in that warning. So would any association with thieves, addicts, or human traffickers. Right? So the real question here is not about the importance of relationships. The question is about the moral legitimacy of a certain type of sexual relationship.

Twenty-first century Western culture is hyper-sexualized. We are asked to believe that life is incomplete without sex – lots of sex. But that is more Darwinian than biblical. We are not mere animals who act by instinct to breed with any available and willing partner. If God created us for relationship, surely it is God who knows best about the type of relationship that serves our best interests. That, in turn, takes us to Scripture to find out what he approves and what he prohibits. (See Chapter 5.)

Strange as it sounds to many of us, the first priority for a human life is not a joyous sexual relationship. It is neither homosexuality nor heterosexuality. It is not marriage and children. The most important thing in life – a *Christian's* life, anyway – is to honor God by living within his will. Remember the words of Jesus? "But seek first his kingdom and his righteousness, and all these things will be given to you as well" (Matt 6:33). Romantic attraction is an impulse created by God to assure the reproduction of the race. More than that, it is an instrumental good to enhance marital commitment and to provide a nonverbal means for expressing intimate delight in another. But sensual delight in another person is not the essence of being human. It is not the goal or highest good of human life. It can, in fact, be frustrating, confusing, ugly, and painful. Holy in its God-ordained proper context, the power of sensual attraction can stir passions that in improper and ethically distorted settings blind people to what is true, pure, and holy.

Christians cannot follow the cultural trend of making an idol of sex and fostering lust of all sorts – for same-sex or opposite-sex persons. Our calling is different: "It is God's will that you should be sanctified: that you should avoid sexual immorality; that each of you should learn to control your own body in a way that is holy and honorable, not in passionate lust like the pagans, who do not know God; and that in this matter no one should wrong or take advantage of a brother or sister" (1 Thess 4:3-6).

Do you make a distinction between "homosexual orientation" and "same-sex behavior"? Didn't Jesus say that lust was as bad as forbidden sex – at least, with regard to a man lusting after a woman?

Anyone struggling with a concern about his or her sexual "orientation" should make the same distinction that exists in the Bible itself. There is a difference between same-sex *inclination, orientation, predisposition, and the like* — whether one argues for its genetic, psychological, or cultural origin — and same-sex *activity*. The sin is not with the inclinations or desires we have but with giving in to them. Feelings of same-sex attraction are not sinful, but one's decision to act on those feelings by lust or more overt sexual behavior is wrong. The former is temptation; only the latter is sin.

This sort of distinction is not "artificial" at all but seems to be in texts such as this one: "When tempted, no one should say, 'God is tempting me.' For God cannot be tempted by evil, nor does he tempt anyone; but each person is tempted when they are dragged away by their own evil desire and enticed. Then, after desire has conceived, it gives birth to sin; and sin, when it is full-grown, gives birth to death" (Jas 1:13-15).

A few short observations. First, this text seems to warn against the idea that "God made me this way" or "God put this desire in me" counts as justification for any negative feelings (e.g., bad temper, hatred, greed) we humans might have. We have lots of "feelings" that don't come from God. Second, there are certain "evil desires" – perhaps simply "desires" (Gk, *epithymia* = cravings or desires, not always "evil" in nature, cf. Matt 13:17; Phil 1:24, etc.) – that humans feel that are not sinful unless acted upon. *Epithymia* is the word in both Jas 1:14 and 1:15. Third, for someone to be "drawn to" or "to have feelings for" another person – male or female, single or married, etc. – is not necessarily equal to lust. Lust is the cultivation of those feelings so that they become sexual fantasies. Third, this text makes it clear that the "craving" or "desire" is something like a conception, but that "sin" is the full birth that comes later. In other words, no "orientation" is sinful as such, only the indulgence of it in erotic fantasies or actual sex acts.

> **"It Really Helped . . ."**
>
> It really helped me to have a few good friends in the church to whom I could run, at all hours of the night and day.
>
> It helped to know that the crushing loneliness that seemed to be obedience's first fruit could be broken in the time it took to dial the phone.
>
> It helped when I called these inner-circle friends, they didn't jolly me out of my problems, but guided me into deeper repentance.
>
> It helped that these were orthodox Christians and therefore they didn't say, "There is no sin in your feelings; God just made you that way."
>
> It helped that these friends believed in an Almighty Christ, one who changes his people at the root. My inner circle was not satisfied by the illusion of safety of some insular Christian culture that had no real impact on the world in which we lived. They believed – and I did too – that only total abandonment to Jesus could heal what ails us.
>
> — Rosaria Champagne Butterfield

Your book says that people have come to you about this topic as a church leader, and you have tried to help them. I'm not a Bible scholar or teacher. What could I do to help somebody who is dealing with same-sex feelings or who is already into same-sex behavior?

Yes, let me emphasize that I am a *teacher* who has written a book focusing on the textual and theological issues that face LGBTQ+ persons. I am not a therapist who spends his time in counseling or walking people through these issues at a personal level. But let me take a step back to where this question seems to originate.

When I was a sophomore in college, a good friend confided to three of us that he had been struggling with the idea that he was homosexual. (Nobody in the dorm room was sophisticated enough to know the terms "orientation," "same-sex attracted," or other terminology used in this book.) Not one of the three of us with him gasped, walked out, or shamed him. Looking back, we did some things that might have been helpful. (1) We let him talk and explain his "feelings" and what they had prompted him to think about or do with those thoughts. (2) We prayed for him – and promised to keep on praying for him. I presume the other two students did at least as much praying for him as I did. (3) We promised to "hold him accountable" by checking in occasionally to ask him about the issue he had trusted us to name and to be available to talk with him as needed.

Did that unsophisticated and untrained response help him? I don't know. I hope so. I pray that it did. What I *do* know is that he got married to a Christian girl three years later who had gone to school with us, and they have three grown children. They have been active members of their church. Every indication I have had is that his adult life has been one of marital fidelity and Christian maturity.

The concept of "sexual orientation" is new to Christian thought and cannot be equated to what the Bible condemns. John Boswell proved that the "unnatural" thing Paul wrote about in Romans 1 is for people who disregard their heterosexual orientation for same-sex encounters. What if he is right?

Boswell was a brilliant historian who taught at Yale in the twentieth century. He did, in fact, argue a case that was latched onto by his fellow-revisionists that the "unnatural" sexual liaisons of Romans 1:26-27 were those in which persons naturally inclined to the opposite sex (i.e., heterosexuals) abandoned their natural desire for the sake of having sex with persons of the same sex/gender. His claim was that "the persons Paul condemns are manifestly not homosexual: what he derogates are homosexual acts committed by apparently heterosexual persons."[7] While much of Boswell's historical research about same-sex relationships in ancient cultures is valuable, his linguistic attempt to redefine the character of "natural" (Gk, *kata physin*) and "unnatural" (Gk, *para physin*) in Romans 1 has been abandoned by the majority of scholars on either side of this discussion.[8]

The sexual behavior that the apostle named and condemned as *para physin* in Romans 1 is documented to us from a variety of Greek sources to describe same-sex intercourse. Stoic writers in particular argued that sex between persons of the same sex was against the order of creation. (See Chapter 11.)

I have a female friend who tells me, "I was born this way. I have always been attracted to girls. If God made me this way, how can it be 'wrong' or 'sinful' for me to have a committed, loving partner to give myself to in marriage?"

First, I don't feel compelled to deny that some people are "born that way" in terms of same-sex attraction. In a fallen world, there is brokenness everywhere – the environment, genetic defects that cause Down Syndrome, cancer. Since we are confident that behavioral issues such as alcoholism, for example, involve genetic factors, we should not be surprised that sexual behaviors do also. We all participate in the brokenness of this world in different ways.

Second, there is no scientific evidence to date of what used to be called "the gay gene" or some combination of genetic markers that make anyone's sexual orientation or practice inevitable. If same-sex couples were predestined to their lifestyles biologically (i.e., "born that way"), the prevalence of gay and lesbian involvement would not fluctuate so dramatically. In ancient Greece, various forms of sex-same relationship were accepted and institutionalized. A mere century ago, what was commonplace in ancient Athens would have been illegal in practically every Western country.

Third, instead of biology alone as an explanation for LGBTQ+ inclinations and behaviors, there is more likely some knotty mixture of nature (i.e., genetics) and nurture (i.e., environment) that accounts for any specific person's sexual inclinations and patterns of behavior.

Fourth, regardless of the cause(s) of one's sexual inclinations, the *ethical question* remains the same: What shall I do with these feelings and desires? All of us have both positive and negative impulses in our personalities – some of which are occasional and some constant. Your friend who has a hair-trigger temper, my fourth-generation-in-his-family alcoholic friend, my own dramatic impatience, your _____ (or maybe you're different from the rest of us?) – are we "off the hook" if we feel these are inborn traits? Should we feel free to act on them because they are "just part of who I am"? Or do we have some obligation to contain certain impulses and avoid certain negative behaviors?

Fifth, the Bible still prohibits same-sex intercourse. The idea that God "made me this way" to do things he has forbidden me to do borders on blasphemy. In the generations since Adam, people have been born with countless biological, mental, and emotional

> **Why Purity Is Not a "Celibacy Mandate"**
> Unmarried Christians – both heterosexuals and those with same-sex attraction – are commanded to abstain from all forms of sex. That's not celibacy. It's simple sexual purity. Married couples are also to be sexually pure in a way appropriate to their situation (note Prov. 5:15-20).
> Celibacy, on the other hand, is more than merely abstaining from sex. It's a life wholly devoted to God. Singleness allows a believer to dedicate his time, talents, and resources completely to Kingdom concerns, unfettered by the demands of marriage and family (1 Cor. 7:32). Celibacy entails sexual abstinence since marriage is the only place sexual desires may be satisfied, but it is more than mere abstinence. The requirement of purity applies to all Christians, incidentally, regardless of their gifting.
> — Alan Shlemon

CHAPTER 15: QUESTIONS PEOPLE ASK

features that are other than ideal. The questions "Is this part of my natural state?" and "Is this compatible with the will of God?" are separate issues.

The Bible says that celibacy is a "gift" or "charisma" to a limited number of people. I think it is wrong for you to say that celibacy is God's mandate for gay and lesbian Christians.

This claim confuses quite different aspects of Christian life. Yes, it is true that some Christ-followers are called to be celibate "for the sake of the kingdom of heaven" (Matt 19:12b; cf. 1 Cor 7:9). This appears always to have been a small percentage of believers. But that does mean that persons who have not been called to that level of devotion to kingdom service are free to indulge their sexual desires as they choose?

Celibacy as a special calling on one's life is not the same as the duty of every Christian to "put to death" certain temptations to "sexual immorality, impurity, lust, evil desires, and greed" (Col 3:5). It is a more precise use of terms to call a life commitment to serve God as a single person *celibacy* and the general requirement of sexual purity that all Christians are obligated to honor *chastity.*

What you have written in this book is harmful to people in the LGBTQ+ community. You are the one who is sinning by shaming and condemning people you don't know and don't know how to love them.

I understand that response to what the Bible says about any limitation to sexual freedom. But my response is always the same: I am not attempting to shame or condemn but to teach the Word of God. I believe I stand in the shadow of other Christian teachers who said things like this: "Have I now become your enemy by telling you *[what I am convinced is, RS]* the truth?" (Gal 4:16). That is not my intention. I think the "harm" would be in failing to call people to repentance who are living outside God's will.

The most unloving thing I can imagine would be to watch someone walking into the path of a car, about to drink something I know to be poisonous, or disobeying a clear teaching of the Bible and say nothing. Do nothing. Make no effort to warn that person of the risk he or she is taking. The loving thing to do in each of these cases would be to take some action to try to spare the harm that lies ahead. It is not an act of love and grace to defend and enable a person who is involved in sinful behavior.

I am a teacher. That is what I believe to be God's "calling" on my life. Teachers address topics of concern to their time and place. There is no topic of more general concern in my time and place than same-sex behavior. Is homosexuality sinful or simply an alternative lifestyle? Have Jewish and Christian teachers misread and misused a limited number of biblical texts to foster prejudice, exclusion, and abuse against what we now call the LGBTQ+ community? Are those biblical texts referring to exploitative and abusive same-sex behaviors rather than loving and committed relationships between persons of the same gender? Or have people of our time been swept along by permissive social currents to affirm behaviors that are under divine judgment?

Other teachers have already addressed this subject, and I am not so arrogant as to think I have a breadth of knowledge or depth of wisdom and insight they lack. I do, however, have a responsibility to live up to my own calling as a teacher. Knowing what I know at any given moment, I remain open to learning more and being corrected. I have had to change my view on topics before and feel no embarrassment over it. The other option would be to refuse better information that has come to light and to be dishonest.

Jesus said that you know a good or bad tree by its fruit. You cannot tell me that the "good fruit" I see in the lives of LGBTQ+ people I know doesn't prove that their relationship with God is just as holy than yours. Only someone who is in a right relationship with God can bear good fruit that honors and glorifies him.

For both straight and LGBTQ+ persons, what we see and judge to be the "good fruit" of a righteous life or "fruit of the Spirit" may or may not tell the whole story. All of us about whom some good things can be said also have some negative or unfavorable traits. Likely none of us is as ideal a person as some may think, and no one would want to be known for his or her worst failing.

I want to be very, very careful here not to leave the wrong impression. By the stories I am about to relate, I do not mean to imply that the persons to be named or someone you may know who is gay or lesbian is hypocritical or hiding some terrible sin. These are stories of flawed people living in a fallen world. In a word, they are the stories of sinners. I, too, am a sinner and have confessed in the opening pages of this book some of my own failings in relation to LGBTQ+ persons. The "impression" and understanding I want to leave is this: *Someone who is in so many ways admirable and good may also be seriously mistaken on some point or ethically wrong in a given behavior.* Who among us has not known some "good person" in whose life we saw great kindness or gentleness – named as fruit of the Spirit in Galatians 5 – but perhaps abused alcohol, used racist language, or displayed some other less-than-holy trait at times?

Here are a few public cases where it would be a mistake to affirm that the "good fruit" seen in someone's life could not be appealed to as a total life endorsement or as proof that some questionable behavior should go unchallenged.

I worked with a number of pastors and churches to bring Ravi Zacharias to Nashville to speak to several thousand people in our downtown arena on the first Sunday of the new millennium. All of us who invited, paid for, and urged people to attend that event were convinced we saw the fruit of the Spirit in his life and lectures, writings and ministry. It has since been learned that he was raping females repeatedly at day spas and in hotel rooms during that very period of his life. He then lied about it when charges began to be brought by multiple victims. There are the additional sad stories of Karl Barth, Bill Gothard, Gene Robinson, Mark Driscoll, Carl Lentz, Bill Hybels, and ministers/pastors I have worked with personally during my ministry. All these people were "heroes of faith" to countless people they taught. There will surely be people with God in the New Heaven and New Earth who came to know Christ under their teaching and (perceived to be good!) influence. But they did abominable things.

A subjective test of what you or I perceive as "fruit of the Spirit" in someone is not the definition of right or wrong moral behavior. That is not a polished form of legalism but a simple respect for the truth and authority of Scripture. The biblical standard of right and wrong is not somehow eclipsed by a sweet spirit and kind actions. (See Chapters 1 and 2.)

Christians serve under the authority and teaching of the New Testament. Why does anyone reach back to Leviticus for its judgment against men having sex with men? Do you think we should still offer animal sacrifices, too?

If the Old Testament prohibition of same-sex intercourse had not been repeated in the New Testament, this argument would have significant weight. Jesus came to bring the Torah and Prophets to their ultimate end or goal (Gk, *telos*) – not to abolish them, but to bring them to a divinely appointed objective or outcome. And surely no one would argue that anything found in the Old Testament is irrelevant to Christians, for the same controversial Holiness Code of Leviticus 17 – 26 contains what Jesus himself cited as the second commandment of Torah – "Love your neighbor as yourself" (Lev 19:18; cf. Matt 22:39).

The New Testament makes it clear that his death as the lamb of God made all future animal sacrifices pointless and unnecessary; his death "fulfilled" or satisfied all that had been prefigured in countless animal sacrifices under the Law of Moses (cf. Heb 7:1 – 10:18). Jesus explicitly said the kosher dietary requirements were no longer binding (Mark 7:18-23). His apostles made it clear that circumcision was not mandatory (Gal 5:6) and that holy days were optional (Rom 14:5-6). In fact, the old covenantal distinction between Jews and Gentiles has been removed in favor of the "fulfillment" of the purpose of God to bring all nations together in the Messiah (Acts 10:1 – 11:18; cf. Gen 12:1-3; Isa 2:1-2). There is no statement in the New Testament that suggests a change in the nature of marriage to include same-sex unions or a hint of blessing Jesus or an apostle gave to a same-sex relationship.

To the contrary, when the gospel began to be preached among Gentiles (i.e., pagans), the moral assumptions every Jew had known already about fornication, adultery, same-sex relationships, incest, bestiality, and the like – all of which were widespread among pagans – the apostles were at pains to name *porneia* as a condemned and disallowed practice among those who wished to confess Jesus as Lord. Rather than leave them to understand that *porneia* – translated "sexual immorality" in the NIV – included all sexual coupling outside the covenant bond of marriage between one man and one woman, the writers were specific. For example, Paul not only rebuked the sweeping category of sexual immorality but also the specific sins of incest (5:1-5), adultery (6:9d), same-sex intercourse (6:9e), prostitution (6:15-17), and polygamy/polyandry (7:2) when he wrote 1 Corinthians to Christians living in what may have been the most libertine city in the Roman Empire of his day.

Leviticus is important background to understanding the moral demands laid out in the New Testament. The important point for us to grasp is that the classification of same-sex intercourse as sin is emphatic in both. (See especially Chapters 6 and 12)

I have felt drawn to people of my own sex at times. I am 17 years old and don't really enjoy dating boys. I'm much more comfortable with my girlfriends – especially a couple of them. Am I "same-sex attracted" and going to hell if I am? Please help me figure this out!

This anonymous question needs more than a short answer toward the back of this book. If you have a trusted spiritual advisor – I would hope your parents, the minister at your church, a respected older Christian – I would encourage you to trust that person with your question. It needs to be answered very personally and by someone who knows you.

This much, however, is probably important for you to hear: Any "feelings" that you have are just that. Feelings. And most of the unsolicited feelings or inclinations we have are normal to a set of circumstances. Somebody insults you, and you get mad. You see clothes you think would look good on you, and you want them. You are treated well by someone (male or female), and you have "feelings" of attraction toward him or her. The issue is not the "feeling" you have, but what you do with that feeling, inclination, or desire.

When you are mad at somebody, getting into a fight or plotting some sort of revenge would be the wrong reaction; trying to work through the issue and resolve it would be a right reaction. Stealing clothes you want would be wrong; saving your money to buy them would be right. Both teens and adults "feel" things for other people in a variety of settings. He thinks a woman is pretty, or she thinks a man is handsome. He thinks a male friend understands him better than anybody ever has, or she finds herself staring at a girlfriend and wondering what it means.

The sin with a feeling, predisposition, or orientation is not in having it; sin is when you give in to a feeling to do something that is wrong. Anger can become hatred or harm. Desire can become greed or stealing. Feelings of attraction can become lust or illicit sex. In the Bible, this is the difference between temptation and sin.

James 1:14-15 speaks of the progression in temptation. My oversimplification of it here would look something like this: contact > desire > lust > choice > act. There is no trace of sin in view here until the third step. Let's define "lust" to mean "too much desire" for what you have seen or felt. That, in turn, leads to a "choice" to pursue or get the object of your desire by some inappropriate method where you break a law or a moral command in the Bible. Finally, of course, is the "act" of doing something you should not do.

To have the good sense and strength of the Spirit to interrupt the progression is what the community of faith called "church" is supposed to help all of us achieve. That's why I said earlier that I really hope you have a warm-bodied and Christ-centered friend available to talk with about this. I wish we were across a table and could talk. (See Chapter 14.)

"God is love." So what can be wrong with two men sharing their love? Or two women? Don't you believe God wants us to experience love in our relationships – and to be happy?

I'm sure God would be pleased for all of his creatures to be "happy" – if they find their happiness in holy relationships and morally praiseworthy behaviors. But happiness has never been the goal he has placed before his people. And being in love does not mean that everything about one's relationship is wholesome.

> **God Is Love**
> The steadfast love of God must not be confused with a blanket affirmation or an inspirational pep talk. No halfway responsible parent would ever think that loving her child means affirming his every desire and finding ways to fulfill whatever wishes he deems important. Parents generally know better what their kids really need, just like God always knows how we ought to live and who we ought to be. God is not tolerant of all things. . . . We must love what God loves.
> — Kevin DeYoung

Happiness depends on the "happenings" in a person's life. And some people are happy in unholy affairs and evil activities – at least for a time, perhaps until the consequences of their actions catch up with them. Therefore, the Book of Proverbs urges people to allow wisdom and the fear of the Lord to rescue us from those "who have left the straight paths to walk in dark ways, who delight in doing wrong and rejoice in the perverseness of evil" (2:13-14). The prophet Jeremiah knew of apostates who – even in Yahweh's temple – "engage in your wickedness, then you rejoice" (Jer 11:15). There can be a great deal wrong about situations that appear loving, pleasant, and gratifying to a human being. After all, it was Jeremiah who spoke of how "deceitful" the heart (i.e., feelings, intuitions, beliefs) can be (Jer 17:9).

The "blessed" life (Matt 5:3-12) that experiences "joy" from the Holy Spirit (Gal 5:22) comes from pursuing holiness. It begins with a transformative event that Jesus described as being "born from above"[9] (John 3:3) or being "born of water and the Spirit" (John 3:5). This is the effective power God supplies to deal with our natural inclinations and/or the external appeals that tempt us to do things that are wrong.

In our spiritual brokenness, we are selfish and focused on pleasure. Thus, the notion of "love" that appeals most naturally is sensual and immediate rather than the self-giving notion of serving God and our neighbors. In the former mindset, we say things like "It's my body and nobody can tell me what to do" or "It's my life and I'll live it as I choose." In the latter, we say "I have been purchased by Christ's blood and am not my own" (cf. 1 Cor 6:19-20) or "I choose to live for the one who died for me" (cf. Gal 2:20). (See Chapter 2.)

Those Old Testament texts that condemn same-sex relationships also make it a sin to eat pork sausage and shrimp. They say it is "detestable" to mix two kinds of cloth in a garment or for a husband and wife to have sex during her period. Do you teach those things? If not, why not?

The word "detestable" (Heb, *toevah*) does cover a lot of ground in the Old Testament! It refers to any and all behaviors that range from social injustice to mixing fabrics. Some of the things mentioned as "detestable" are simply "strange" to most of us – because we are so far removed in time and data from their setting.

> **Why Bother with the Old Testament?**
> The ethical teaching of the Old Testament is first and foremost God-centered. It is founded on the identity of the Lord, the living God of the biblical revelation.
> It presupposes God's initiative in grace and redemption; it takes its content from the words of God revealed in the cultural context of Israel; it is framed by the purposes of God, who is sovereign in what he has done and will do in history; it is shaped by God's ways and character; it is motivated by personal experience of God's goodness in his dealings with his people.
>
> — Christopher Wright

Nobody really knows why the mixing of fabrics was detestable. From Deut 22:11, the specific fabrics that could not be mixed are wool and linen. Some Bible students think – since the High Priest was to wear a garment made of wool and linen (Ex 28:6-8; 39:4-5) – that the point was to stress the priest's unique role in Israel. Could be. The formula for the priests' anointing oil was so special that anyone else blending by it was to be "cut off from his people" (Ex 30:31-38). We just don't know. But that's a pretty good guess. Don't take what is holy to the Lord and make it common or ordinary?

A husband and wife having sex during the woman's menstrual period is a bit different. Because of the sacredness attached to blood in Israel (cf. Lev 17:11), any contact with blood made a person ceremonially unclean (but not morally tainted!) for a specific length of time and until a ceremonial washing took place. The same thing applied, of course, to the blood of a woman's monthly period. The details are fairly complex and can be found at Leviticus 15:19-33. Again, the text clearly states that contact with blood is "detestable." But the matter is resolved by time passing, washing clothes and bed covers, bathing, and offering a minor sacrifice (i.e., two birds).

That the sexual behaviors mentioned in the Holiness Code are different from the mixed fabrics or blood rituals should be obvious. The penalty for violating the prohibition against same-sex intercourse was far more serious than rebuke, washings, and a sacrifice. Both parties involved were to be put to death! Things regard as *toevah* in the Holiness Code vary greatly, and the best way to determine the seriousness of the offense in Yahweh's eyes would be to compare the penalties.

As to which of these I teach and observe as a Christian, I have a very simple rule of thumb: If it is repeated in the New Testament, I believe I must teach and observe it today.

As to why I don't rally the church to impose the death penalty on same-sex offenders, two factors seem relevant. First, unlike ancient Israel, church and state are separate entities in the New Testament. The church does not raise an army, fund a police force, or administer civil penalties for anything. Second, there is a severe penalty attached to fornication, incest, same-sex activity, adultery, or bestiality *if unrepented*. The person who will not repent is to be "handed over to Satan" (i.e., excluded from the church's fellowship) in hopes of his or her eventual remorse for sin, repentance, and reunion with the Body of Christ (1 Cor 5:3-5; cf. Matt 18:15-18). (See Chapter 13.)

The essence of marriage is love, commitment, and fidelity. Having babies isn't necessary to a marriage – just think about infertile couples or elderly people who get married. Same-sex couples can provide love, commitment, and fidelity. So why should they be denied the right to be married?

Theologically, the "essence of marriage" is not the human impulse to love, commitment, and fidelity. It is not a private relationship rooted in an emotional commitment between two parties. Marriage is God's answer to the problem of Adam's inability to fulfill the human mission of reproducing the human species and functioning as God's partner in ruling his creation with wisdom, creativity, and love. So, Eve was created to be his reciprocal helper-rescuer in the divine project. The purpose for sexual expression in the Genesis narrative is procreation with the context of love, commitment, and fidelity. In other words, to remove sex from its primary purpose in creation is to morph it into a caricature of itself.

Contrary to the popular notion that dominates even in some religious teaching, sex was not created to be the ultimate demonstration of romantic love. Individual humans are created to honor God by reflecting his image into his creation – whether single, married, divorced, or widowed. Marriage exists for the glory of God – with each sex/gender (the Bible makes no theological distinction between the two concepts) bringing a complement to the other that creates the platform for society.

"Faithfulness": Alternative to Procreation?

According to Karen Keen, Jesus views marriage not as a gendered institution, but merely "the unity of two people.". . . Marriage is the union of two people. But it is not any two people. Taking his cues from Genesis, Jesus believed marriage was meant to be the permanent union of one man and one woman who become "one flesh" for one lifetime.

Nevertheless, Keen believes marriage is about faithfulness, not procreation. Thus, she notes that a lack of children does not annul a marriage bond (such as in the case of Elkanah reassuring his wife Hannah that their marriage was valid, even though she was barren).

Keen notes: "One can have marriage without children, but one cannot have marriage without fidelity." This is true insofar as it goes. But it misses the point. Children are the natural result of the "one-flesh" union of a man and a woman. Even if a child does not result, a man and woman can still enter the kind of "one-flesh" union that is oriented towards procreation. Hannah and Elkanah entered into the "one-flesh" union of marriage, even though she was barren. The same cannot be said for same-sex relationships, which by their very nature cannot be barren, because they are not biologically oriented towards children.

— Sean McDowell

Children born into a marriage are nourished by the legal, physical, emotional, and spiritual relationship of their parents.

The biblical narrative was interpreted consistently by rabbis, the church fathers, and Bible readers for millennia to mean that marriage is the union of a male and a female who partner to create a household-family. At the same time, every mention of same-sex intercourse was read negatively and prohibitively. Suddenly, in the last fifty to 100 years, we have discovered that the Bible was unclear and that its few inspired (e.g., Jesus and the apostles with the Torah) and countless uninspired-but-serious interpreters have been misreading it all along? That is quite a stretch.

A male and a female human have the moral right to pair off from others, covenant to fidelity with each other, and experience sexual intimacies because of the Genesis narrative into which that experience fits. They have become part of a narrative that finds affirming parallels not only in creation but in both the Yahweh-Israel relationship and the Christ-church connection. By contrast, same-sex marital unions are a result of the fall rather than an element found in the creation narrative. The prohibition in Scripture against same-sex unions is part of the divine protection of marriage as God designed it. (See Chapters 4 and 5, especially a version of this claim made by Karen Keen.)

People who are same-sex oriented have the same need for companionship as their counterpart opposite-sex attracted friends. Can we deny them their right to a committed companion in the name of Christian ethics?

All people need healthy companionship as part of their lives. We are social beings.

But the attempt to apply our need for "companionship" as somehow an argument with the power to negate the moral prohibition against same-sex marriage is not only implausible but would allow far too much. Ever know estranged married heterosexuals who needed "companionship" because of one partner's coldness? Would the need for "companionship" not justify one-night stands or a "friends with benefits" arrangement as well? The issue from Eden forward has not been the psychological need for "companionship" but the created order of God-ordained sexual partnership. From Eden to church to the marriage feast of the Apocalypse, "covenanted relationships" with sexual privilege are always and only between male and female.

The subjectivism of the companionship argument is not enough to discount and set aside the objective statements of Scripture. (See Chapter 14.)

I didn't choose to be born "homosexual" any more than you chose to be born "heterosexual." If God made me this way, how can it be sinful for me to live this way?

Although we hear the statement often, it is a serious mistake to assign everything about human personality to the will of God. In a fallen world, people are born with genetic mutations that cause (or contribute to) such physical problems as breast cancer, sickle cell disease, different types of diabetes, and a host of others. People are born with varying mental abilities and with emotional issues that appear to have generational (i.e., genetic) roots.

To equate "I was born with such-and-such trait" with "God made me this way" would mean not only that Person A should have moral permission to live in a committed, loving, and monogamous same-sex relationship but also that Person B should be granted the same moral permission to be violent or alcoholic. There is more evidence for the inheritability of alcohol addiction, for example, than for same-sex attraction. Even at the level of conditions we know to be inheritable in the human body, should a person whose cancer or sickle cell disease has genetic roots be encouraged to accept and express that condition? Or seek effective ways to contain and correct it?

Is it *harmful* to live with genetically-rooted diabetes? Yes. So, allow the best medical help you can find to treat it. Is it *sinful* to have sexual intercourse with a same-sex partner? Yes. So, allow the redemptive power of God to help you deal with it. The "shame" is not to have diabetes, to be same-sex attracted, or to be a woman who has prostituted herself to men; the "shame" would be to refuse the forgiving and redemptive presence of the Holy Spirit to change. (See Chapter 13.)

Don't you ever feel guilty for being so self-righteous and judgmental toward anybody who is part of the LGBTQ+ community of people? Do you hate Jews and Black people, too?

I know my own heart and life circumstance well enough to assure you that this lost-but-for-Christ man has not written this book with a "self-righteous and judgmental" spirit. I pray for God to guard my heart from – among other things – racism and homophobia. No, I don't hate Jews, Blacks, women, children, trans persons, lesbians, or anyone in the LGBTQ+ world.

Neither do I want to be intimidated from teaching what the Bible says about sin and redemption. Everybody agrees that some things are wrong – torturing animals, trafficking children, genocide. Christians believe the things God has forbidden are wrong – selfishness, greed, and sex outside marriage between one man and one woman. I also understand that people have the civil right to do some things that Christians believe are sinful – premarital sex, using God's name as a profanity, blaspheming Jesus of Nazareth.

Christians in every generation have been given negative nicknames by people who either misunderstood their message or felt its sting. In the first few centuries, Christians were called "atheists" (for refusing to worship the Roman gods) and "cannibals" (for their rite of Communion). One Roman writer says that Christians were regarded as "haters of mankind" because the lifestyle they pursued – including, but not limited to, premarital chastity and marital fidelity – was so out of step with the culture of their time.[10]

Sadly, then, but inevitably I suppose, Christians will always be subject to the accusation of being "killjoys" and "bigots" for teaching the righteous standards of Scripture. It is even worse when Christians do not take those standards more seriously than some of us seem to in a lenient culture, for it makes the charge of being a "hypocrite" believable. By prayer and in the power of the Spirit, we must always try to avoid bitterness, pride, and disdain for those who choose to live as non-believers. (See Chapter 2.)

I hear the language of churches being "welcoming but not affirming" toward gay people. What is that supposed to mean?

Let's start with a broad perspective in order to get to the specifics of this question. Whether it is the best or your preferred term to describe gay or lesbian persons,

CHAPTER 15: QUESTIONS PEOPLE ASK

people who are members of the larger LGBTQ+ community, or straight people who argue that God approves consensual, loving, and committed same-sex relationships, it is in common use. Sally Gary, who shares a background in Churches of Christ with me, has written a book to defend the thesis "that God could affirm a same-sex relationship"[11] with the word as her title – *Affirming*.

A faithful church is "welcoming but not affirming" toward all people – regardless of the specific weakness she is working to overcome or his criminal record. The "welcoming" attitude says that we understand that God wants everyone to hear the gospel message and accept Christ. The "not affirming" part means that we cannot endorse – or even "just stay quiet" about – things that are outside the will of God.

For that matter, the church has welcomed *me* – with all my quirks, partial insights, moral weakness, and failures. When the church functions as God intended, all people with all sorts of questions and doubts, concealed weaknesses and public humiliations, gay or straight are welcomed. And, I should add, all are *affirmed* for their human dignity. More than that, they are *affirmed* as loved and sought after by God. What is *not* affirmed in any of us who interact with a faithful church is our conscious rebellion against the will of God as made known to us in the Bible.

For people and their families dealing with issues around LGBTQ+ persons, "welcoming but not affirming" says that everyone attending or asking for help from that church will be treated with respect as a person in God's image. It also says – in the confused environment of the "culture wars" going on today – that the church in question does not endorse same-sex unions. In my experience with churches using that phrase to describe themselves, it is not meant to be a mark of hostility toward LGBTQ+ persons, but honesty. In its teaching, preaching, literature, or counseling, persons should know this church holds to the traditional Christian view of sexual ethics. Since the word "affirming" is used for self-identification by many who are gay or lesbian, to be "*not* affirming" is to say that a church or individual does not endorse same-sex unions as conforming to God's will as revealed in the Bible. It should never be the case that a Christian fails to affirm the essential dignity and worth of another person.

The gospel, you see, can only be accepted in connection with one's repentance. And to repent is to accept God's judgment about a behavior I may want to approve

– either because someone I love does that thing or because it is part of my own life experience. Accepting divine judgment against greed or abuse of power, lying or stealing, repentance rejects the continued practice of that thing in my life. Perhaps it can happen immediately and completely. More likely, it will happen incrementally and over time. But the determined effort to put a stop to sinful behaviors is the heart of repentance. Paul described Christians as people who "have taken off our old self with its practices and have put on the new self, which is being renewed in knowledge in the image of its Creator" (Col 3:9-10).

It is that process of "being renewed" by God's grace that is at the heart of the gospel. The welcome of Jesus leads to repentance, and repentance is the first step toward renewal. "Godly sorrow brings repentance that leads to salvation and leaves no regret" (2 Cor 7:10). (See Chapters 13 and 14.)

ENDNOTES

1. Gushee, *Changing Our Mind*, 97.

2. Gushee, *Changing Our Mind*, 96.

3. *The Jewish Study Bible Tanakh Translation,* Adele Berlin and Marc Zvi Brettler, eds. (New York: Oxford University Press, 2004), 418. Cf. Phillip G. Camp, *Living as the Community of God: Moses Speaks to the Church in Deuteronomy* (Rapid City, SD: Crosslink Publishing, 2014), 120-122.

4. Cf. Wright, Jacob L, and Michael J Chan. 2012. "King and Eunuch: Isaiah 56:1-8 in Light of Honorific Royal Burial Practices." *Journal of Biblical Literature* 131 (1): 99–119. In this article, Wright and Chan offer "findings [that] destabilize the problematic interpretation of Isa 56:3-5 as simply a legal abrogation of Deut 23:2-9" (p.116) and give insights consistent with the reading offered here. Their examination of the linguistic and historical setting of the text does not explore ethical implications for the modern LGBTQ+ discussion.

5. Rubel Shelly, "Gay Rights Bill: Shall We Compare Sins?" *The (Nashville) Tennessean*, Feb 9, 2003. This op-ed is an article I wrote during a controversy over gay rights more than 20 years ago. This "Nashville Eye" column was written at the request of the then-editor of the *Tennessean* after I went to her office – together with L.H. Hardwick (Pentecostal) and Charles McGowen (Presbyterian) – to object to what we perceived to be an identification of the conservative Christian community of Nashville with the recent antics of the pastor of Westboro Baptist Church who had come there to rally support for a city ordinance that would have been unfair to gay and lesbian citizens of the city.

6. Hays, *Moral Vision of the New Testament*, 398.

7. Boswell, *Christianity, Social Tolerance, and Homosexuality*, 109, cf. 112-113.

8. Cf. Richard B. Hays, "Relations Natural and Unnatural: A Response to John Boswell's Exegesis of Romans 1," *Journal of Religious Ethics*, (Spring, 1986), 184-215.

9. Commonly translated "born *again*" – which can sound like simply "starting over" or "turning over a new leaf" – the better translation is "born *from above*." The word in question is the adverb *anōthen*. While "again" (reading the word as an adverb of time) is a possible translation, the fact that John uses the same word at 3:31 – where it can only mean "from above" (adverb of place) makes it likely that the emphasis is the same throughout. Whether with regard to money, sex, power, or any other source of temptation, God's offer is not the challenge to summon up one's willpower to try again but the offer of a new internal dynamic "from above" (i.e., the Holy Spirit) to empower what humans cannot do in our own strength. Jesus told Nicodemus that

earthly (biological) birth from the seed of Abraham was insufficient. To share in the Kingdom of God, heavenly (spiritual) rebirth is needed. This is the language and hope of new creation that every person who is humble enough to recognize his or her need for renewal and transformation can appreciate.

10. Tacitus, *Annals* 15.44.

11. Sally Gary, *Affirming: A Memoir of Faith, Sexuality, and Staying in the Church* (Grand Rapids: Eerdmans, 2021), 13.

SPECIAL NOTE:
*This sermon was preached for the Harpeth Hills Church of Christ
and is essentially unedited from that presentation.*

APPENDIX A

Single to the Glory of God

*"Now to the divorced and the widows . . .
[and] about never-married persons" (1 Cor 7:8,25).*

Introduction

One day Jesus was being put to the test by some Sadducee opponents. Because they didn't believe in the resurrection of the dead, they challenged Jesus with a knotty problem: Suppose a woman is married, her husband dies, and she remarries – not once but seven times. "Whose wife will she be of the seven, since all of them were married to her?" they asked. Then they must have crossed their arms, looked at one another in triumph, and waited to see Jesus try to squirm his way out of their "knockout punch." It had always worked with the Pharisees, you see, because their notion of resurrection was everyone would be raised from the dead in the age of the Messiah – and pick up life right where they had left off when they died.

Here was Jesus' answer: "You're off base on two counts: You don't know what God said, and you don't know how God works. At the resurrection we're beyond marriage. As with the angels, all our ecstasies and intimacies then will be with God" (Matt 22:29-30 MSG).

I'm sure I don't know everything I'd like to know about what that means! But this much seems clear. *The way we think about and experience marriage, having children, and celebrating Mother's Day here on Earth is not going to define experience in the*

New Heaven and New Earth. We won't be pairing off, having 2.5 children and a puppy, and hoping the kids will let us spend time with the grandkids – and show up for our funeral. Life will be so different there. Nevertheless, we need not only to look forward to the future but also to live our present experience more fully to the glory of God – and with consistency with what lies ahead.

And another thing. Single people won't feel like "fifth wheels" when there is a family event or Family VBS for the church. They won't be pressured by Mom and Dad to get married and have us some grandchildren. Or asked at church what's wrong that they "haven't found somebody yet." We'll *all* be family. We will *all* be loved and accepted. We'll *all* know we are loved because we are home. Really, truly, finally *home*!

> PRAYER: *Holy God, help us to see each other more clearly through your eyes and within your will. Less through the lenses of American cultural idols and more in the image of your one perfect Son Jesus. Less in terms of nuclear families by DNA and more as your family by the blood of Jesus shed on that holy, horrible cross. In Jesus' name, Amen.*

A Confession of Discomfort

Some parts of Scripture are more commonplace, natural, and easy for me to preach. They are the texts that describe *me*. The *majority* of us. The *statistically dominant group(s)* whose perspective on life I share. That's probably a bit murky, so let me try to clarify my meaning.

I don't do well trying to preach on "women's issues" – and seldom get invited to present anything to a Women's Retreat or to Sunday School classes that are all-female; I'm not a woman, can't read reality through a female perspective (just ask my wife!), and am prone to putting my foot in my mouth because of my unintentional chauvinism that comes of reading everything from my male perspective. To get a female perspective on worldviews and relationships or on religious and ethical issues, it is smarter to ask a female than a male. Yet, because I am a theologian and Bible teacher, I dare to make occasional comments to and about women because of explicit scriptural statements to or about female believers.

I can say the same thing about biblical statements made to and about members of the military. I did not serve in our armed forces and therefore don't understand most of the issues that would be distinctive to that role. (John the Baptist and Jesus weren't soldiers either, but both of them said some things to and about how soldiers were supposed to do their jobs in order to honor God.) Are you beginning to get my point?

It is simply easier for me to preach texts that I more naturally identify with personally – texts that talk to and about men, verses that apply to husbands and fathers, or instructions in the Bible to those of us who are called to preach and teach Scripture. That means I have "blind spots" that contribute to my limitations in communicating the Word of God. So, I have worked hard over the years to study the history, culture, and social-political-religious backgrounds relevant to the biblical texts to fill in some of the gaps that would otherwise mar my work.

For example, I read the Bible from my Greco-Roman, European-American, Southern-Male background. Therefore, I have been shocked and embarrassed – then, thankfully, enlightened – more than once by having someone whose background is Jewish point out facts and meanings from the Old Testament that I had missed because of my non-Jewish upbringing. I have been ashamed more than once of racist takes and even language I was habituated to using when some African-American person helped me see and hear it from his or her perspective.

Faithful Discipleship for Single Persons

I have belabored that point as background to a text I am going to preach this morning. As we continue this sermon series, we are continuing to focus on *faithful discipleship*. And what we are doing now is looking at the meaning of a distinctly Christian lifestyle for people in a variety of life settings. That is the way Paul and Peter served their original readers in writing to their situatedness, for example, in master-slave relationships. Thank God, we don't have that one to face in Brentwood today – at least, not directly and immediately, although what they said about those situations has relevance to some employer-employee situations and even to the topic of racism we will be exploring soon in this same series.

This morning, I am going to work directly from 1 Corinthians and to the interconnected life situations of persons who are divorced, widowed, or who have never married. Collectively, this is the community of *single persons* in our church. At my request last week, our office personnel went into our database at Harpeth Hills and found that roughly 25% of our church body is made up of widowed, divorced, or never-married people. Of that number, 68% are women.

Now do you see why I needed to begin this sermon with the confession that I feel more comfortable dealing with some biblical texts than others because of my own life situation? I am *not* someone who has never been married. (I'm guessing that you English teachers caught the double negative there!) Thankfully, I am not a widower. By God's grace to me and the patience he has engendered in Myra, I am not a divorcee. So, if you are inclined to stiffen and say something like "How dare you presume to tell me about something you don't know about because it isn't your experience!" I get it. But I am not going to address this from my limited experience. (I don't have personal experience either of being a business owner or politician, thief or drug addict, female or gay, African or Jew, but I do have the responsibility of reading and trying to understand what the Bible says to them as well.)

With a second confession that I probably have said less on this topic than I should have over the years, I am going to take you to 1 Corinthians 7 and do my best to explain what Paul said about people who – by virtue of death or divorce, circumstance or choice – live as single men and women. Is there a word from God to you? If so, what is that word? How does a single man or woman live to the glory of God in either a first-century or twenty-first-century world? And how are those of us who are not in your life circumstance supposed to relate to you?

May I try that last question first? I suspect we could be kinder and more Christlike to you by making it clear that *you are full-fledged members of this church!* There is nothing "defective" or "second class" about being single. By the way, the statistics cited earlier pointed out that though we have almost 25% of our members in the single or single-again category, the general population has just over 45%. Maybe we haven't been very welcoming to you. Maybe that's why singles are less likely to be part of today's churches – especially single men. Maybe today can be the beginning of doing better to invite, welcome, and involve single people?

If we are inclined to advertise VBS or church picnics "for mom, dad, and the kids," let's just have "all-church picnics" and VBS that "will have something for everybody." Let's not hear a wedding announcement and turn to the single person beside us and say, "Hey, maybe your turn will come one of these days." Please, don't ask some 25- or 30-year-old person, "What's wrong with you that you haven't gotten married?" Please don't refer to anyone as an "old bachelor" or "old maid." Those are stereotypes and tend to marginalize folks. They have to hurt people.

"Why are you still single?" or "Hey, want me to fix you up?" is another way of saying, "Something's wrong with you, and you need to be fixed!" Really? You are about to hear a Spirit-led apostle of Jesus Christ say that being single is sometimes better than getting married. Before we're through, you are going to hear Jesus say that single and celibate is God's calling and gift to some of his people. Some of those people may be in this room right now, and it is not our calling and gift to discount their place in God's scheme of things. Again, you are going to hear Jesus and Paul say that marriage is a holy relationship, but we still must be careful not to make marriage into a cultural idol or imply it is somehow *more* holy than being single.

Reading 1 Corinthians 7

Paul invests an entire chapter of our 1 Corinthians – one of the longer chapters, by the way, with 40 verses – to questions about sex and singleness, marriage and divorce, being widowed and getting remarried. Here is how he starts: "Now for the matters you wrote about: 'It is good for a man not to have sexual relations with a woman.' But since sexual immorality is occurring, each man should have sexual relations with his own wife, and each woman with her own husband" (vs.1-2).

Corinth was a wild, wide-open seaport city known for its brothels and uninhibited culture of drunkenness and debauchery. Female prostitutes, transgenders, same-sex couples, non-binaries, all that our culture identifies as the LGBTQ+ community – Corinth had (at least!) everything we know about in our hyper-sexualized culture (maybe more!) and Paul knew about it. He had gone there on his second missionary tour in early A.D. 50 and lived there for a year and a half (cf. Acts 18:11). He moved from there to Ephesus and wrote this letter back to the Christian community he had founded there.¹ As the opening line suggests, he was replying to several written questions that had been sent to him.

For our purposes, it is important to note that Paul doesn't think you have to buy into either the Corinthian or American myth that sex is the central point of living. That lots of sex means a fulfilling life. That being single and celibate is a "failure to thrive" as a human being. Some sort of "crisis" (v.26a) situation in Corinth led Paul to give this counsel: (a) if you are "bound" either by an engagement or existing marriage, this is no time to break the engagement or get a divorce, and (b) if you are single or single again, this is not the time to be planning a wedding. This is my literal-as-possible rendering of verse 27: "Are you currently joined (bound, tied) by a past commitment to a woman? Do not seek a divorce. Do you stand as already divorced from a woman? Do not seek a woman."

Paul is not anti-marriage. But it is clear that being married is not the goal every Christian is called to pursue under all circumstances. In his view, either singleness or marriage can be a "gift from God" (v.7). Christians who do get married have sexual rights to each other that unmarried believers do not, and wedded persons should be guided by their mutual awareness of each other's needs to be generous with their sexual attentions (vs.3-6).

Turning now to what we call "single-again" persons, he says essentially the same thing: "Now to the unmarried and the widows I say: It is good for them to stay unmarried, as I do. But if they cannot control themselves, they should marry, for it is better to marry than to burn with passion" (vs.8-9) – thus leaving themselves open to transgressing the Christian moral boundary against any form of extra-marital sex (Gk, *porneia*).

The word "widow" here (Gk, *chēra*) means just what it does in English; it is someone who has been married but whose husband or wife has died. The word translated "unmarried" (Gk, *agamos*) is a bit trickier, for it is a generic term that hypothetically would include persons who have never been married and/or persons who were once married but who are now either widowed or divorced; all these people would be *un-* (*a* = not [alpha-privative]) *married* (*gamos*). By virtue of the context, however, Paul appears to be using the word with specific reference to divorced persons.²

To the widows and divorcees in Corinth, Paul adds a third type of single person at verse 25. Using his formulaic phrase for introducing new topics (Gk, *peri de* = now about, cf. 7:1; 8:1; 12:1; 16:1,12) and structuring his responses to the Corinthian questions, he writes: "Now about virgins" (Gk, *peri de tōn parthenōn*). Again, the apostolic counsel is consistent. Under the circumstances in play at the time Paul wrote to Corinth, "I think that it is good for a man to remain as he is." As if to stress that this is counsel rather than command, the apostle makes it clear that anyone who chooses to marry "has not sinned" – even though, he warns, "those who marry will face many troubles in this life, and I want to spare you this" (v.28). It just wasn't an ideal time to be taking on the responsibilities of a family during the "crisis" he had mentioned.

A Summary of Paul's Teaching

There is so much more to say about related topics in 1 Corinthians 7, but that is all the exegetical time we have right now. So let me summarize what Paul has said – and show you that his counsel (for which he is confident that "I have the Spirit of God" to offer, v.40b) is consistent with Jesus' own life and teaching.

First, the obvious: *Being single must not be an obstacle to a healthy and fulfilling life, for both Jesus and Paul were single persons.* To the common-but-mistaken notion that no one can be happy without lots of sex, the one-word answer is "Jesus." To the false-and-deceptive claim that the priority for every human life is to marry and have children, Jesus' teaching is that seeking first the Kingdom of God and his righteousness is the priority for his people (Matt 6:33).

Second, *Paul declared both the single and married state a "calling" from God (1 Cor 7:17) and Jesus himself said it would be a "gift" for some but not all of his followers (Matt 19:11-12).* Whether for a lifetime or for a season of life, embrace the situation you are in today as God's calling – rather than chafe under the notion that what you are doing now is a "holding pattern" until you can get what you really want. Live your situation today to his glory and trust him to call you to some other – if he so wills. My presence at Harpeth Hills is a calling. Is it for two years or for the rest of my life? I don't know. If you are a stay-at-home mom today, that isn't going to be your lifelong calling. Children grow up. If you are single today, view that as your calling rather than a curse. Ask God to show you how to use your present situation to his glory – and don't change your life circumstance before you and God work that out. If you can't be a "whole" and "functional" man or woman, you won't be made "whole" and "functional" by becoming a wife or husband. You will more likely become codependent!

Third, *Paul said he could wish that more believers would follow the course of singleness he had chosen for the sake of serving God's kingdom.* In explaining his own choice, Paul said it gave him more freedom and flexibility for travel, teaching, and serving (especially in hard fields of missionary work!) than he could have had if responsible for a wife and children (vs.32-35; cf. 9:5). The only option some Christian parents seem to offer their children is education, marriage, and grandchildren for them. Why are we reluctant to suggest careers in mission work for our children who are interested in other languages and cultures? Bible translation for our children who excel at language studies? Working – as a single friend of mine who is a nurse practitioner chose to do – on a terribly underserved reservation for Native Americans in New Mexico?

Fourth, *if you are single or single again, establish some loving and supportive relationships with a variety of other people.* Dating apps aren't sinful. But is being single a curse from which marriage will free you? Will you find a "green pasture" in marriage? Will a wedding day really translate to "and they lived happily ever after"? A fate far sadder than anyone's situation of singleness is getting married because someone is "in love with being in love" – only to wake up to the discovery of being "unequally yoked" to someone whose heart is centered on something less than Jesus. The single-and-celibate Jesus appears to have had a marvelous friendship not only with Peter, James, and John when he was "at work" but with Mary, Martha, and Lazarus "as extended family" when he took a break in Bethany. The counter to being single isn't always marriage. It can be serious, caring, and supportive friendships.

Fifth, *sexual purity is God's calling on us at every stage and calling of our lives.* In the sex-obsessed culture of Corinth and Rome, Los Angeles and New York, Atlanta and Brentwood, the life goal of single people seems to be built around "the chase" rather than Christian chastity. A significant part of the calling of God on every Christian life is sexual purity. For the single or single-again believer, that means chastity so long as you are not married; for the married believers, that means fidelity to your one mate so long as you both live. As one writer puts it: "Despite the smooth illusions perpetrated by mass culture in the United States, sexual gratification is not a sacred right, and celibacy is not a fate worse than death" (Richard Hays). Whether any one of us is single, married, divorced, or widowed, "sexual restraint is mandatory for all, difficult for most, and extremely challenging for some" (N.T. Wright). This is another reason to be thankful for the gift of God's Holy Spirit – one of whose blessings as the fruit of his presence is self-discipline or self-control (Gal 5:22-23).

Sixth, *churches must stop discriminating against singles, be more intentional to include them in church life, and stop perpetuating the myth that single life is a sign that something is wrong that can be put right by a wedding ceremony.* It is on those of us who have the calling of marriage and children to expand our own vision of friendship and family. Family for us must be what it was for the single Jesus. Do you remember how he explained his idea of family? He waved his hand around a room filled with his disciples and said, "Here are my mother and my brothers. For whoever does the will of my Father in heaven is my brother and sister and mother" (Matt 12:48-49).

Jesus said there would be some people called to live single and celibate lives for the sake of the Kingdom of Heaven (Matt 19:9). In that very context, Peter asked him about the sacrifices he and others had made to be one of his disciples. And Jesus answered that anyone who had left houses, lands, or family for his sake "will receive a hundred times as much and will inherit eternal life" (vs.27-29). Surely the extended family he was promising to Peter is the one he had already claimed for himself back at Matthew 12:48-49. *"For whoever does the will of our Father in heaven is your brother and sister and mother."* For anyone who otherwise would be threatened by loneliness, Jesus shares his spiritual family.

One of the most notable and significant trends of the past half century in America is the rise of this country's population of singles. According to the U.S. Census Bureau, single-person households represented only 13% of all households in 1960. In 2018, that percentage had more than doubled to 28% - a total of some 35.7 million single-person households. What a resource of talented people without the family commitments to spouses and children who can serve in local churches. Work in outreach to inner-city ministries. Use vacation time for short-term mission work –

and consider multi-year stays in mission settings. We not only miss tapping into this pool of disciples but also too often devalue them and drive them away.

Conclusion

Some of you heard a sermon I preached here a couple of months ago in which I told of an Arab girl I witnessed as she stood before a Messianic Church in Jerusalem. Her father and brother had beaten her severely for becoming friends with a group of Christians at the college she was attending. They warned her there would be worse waiting if she ever saw them again and that they would kill her if she were to be baptized and cast her lot with those Christ-followers. So she stood before us sobbing. She had come to confess Jesus, be baptized, and begin her new life as his follower. "After this day," she said, "you are the only family I can have. I will never see my father, my mother, or my brother again! You – only you – can be my mothers and fathers, my sisters and brothers."

You and I must learn to see each other through just such eyes. Then we will begin to see each other more as God sees us now – and as we will live in the New Heaven and New Earth we will inhabit together.

ENDNOTES

1. In fact, he had already written one letter to Corinth about sexual immorality that we no longer have, which makes our *first* letter to Corinth Paul's *second* (cf. 1 Cor 5:9). We cannot date the former, but our 1 Corinthians was likely written in early A.D.55 – shortly before Paul's departure from Ephesus.

2. Paul uses the term "unmarried" (Gk, ἄγαμος) two other times in 1 Cor 7 of those who were previously married. At v.11, "unmarried" denotes one who was previously married but then divorced. Then, in v.34, an "unmarried" person is distinguished from "virgins" (παρθένος) who are never-married persons. We may reasonably conclude that "unmarried" in v.8 also refers to someone who has been previously married. When paired with "widows," as in v.8, it seems that Paul means to identify persons who have been married and whose wedded state ended either by divorce (the "unmarried") or by death (the "widows"). At v.34, the "unmarried" – when contrasted with "never-married" persons – likely takes both divorcees and widowed persons into account. NOTE: The use of "unmarried" in v.8 is what makes me suspect that Paul was either a widower or divorced. Could it be that the young rabbi's wife not only refused to follow him into the community of Jesus-followers but also refused to remain married to him?

SPECIAL NOTE:
This sermon was preached for the Harpeth Hills Church of Christ and is essentially unedited from that presentation.

APPENDIX B

Married to the Glory of God

"To the married I give this command (not I, but the Lord)" (1 Cor 7:10).

Introduction

In this sermon series, we are continuing to explore the nature of *faithful discipleship* for the baptized community of people who call ourselves Christians. Christ-followers. Christ-imitators. Last week, I asked you to focus with us on Paul's teaching from 1 Corinthians 7 about singleness, chastity, and the rights of persons who are single again by virtue of death or divorce. This Sunday, we stay in the same chapter to hear what the apostle says to married people.

Paul was facing the same challenge we encounter in taking the words of Jesus and applying them redemptively to the life situations of people for whom he both cared deeply and sensed spiritual responsibility as a Christian teacher. On his second missionary tour, he had planted a church in Corinth and then remained there for a year and a half to nurture it. Now, a couple of years later, he had received a letter from that church – a letter with several practical questions about navigating situations that were challenging for them. Some were doctrinal (e.g., the resurrection), and some were practical (e.g., combining the Lord's Supper with a larger meal that was underscoring radical differences in wealth and social standing in the church).

One of those thorny practical issues sounds very familiar to us. In a morally indulgent culture and with church members deeply influenced by its art, music, social life, entertainment, customs, and lifestyle, how were Christ's disciples at Corinth supposed to handle issues around sex, celibacy, marriage, divorce, and the like? Was it okay for non-married Christians to have sex outside of marriage? To live together – especially if their intention was eventually to get married to their lover? Are same-sex relationships acceptable – so long as they were committed and monogamous? What should we say about divorce? Was divorce always a bad thing? If someone should divorce, what about the church's attitude toward a second marriage?

Our Time Is Not So Different

These are still live-option questions that churches are being asked in our morally indulgent culture where our members are being influenced so powerfully by media and celebrities, reworked laws and social customs. Are the "traditional" answers still appropriate? Or are the "revisionist" voices giving us insights into God's heart and will we have missed all these centuries since the first?

Fortunately for us, Paul had the special empowerment of the Spirit of God to guide him. The Apostle to the Gentiles took the "traditional" views he had learned in a Jewish context and some quotes from Jesus he had heard through his fellow-apostles and used them to answer a variety of questions a Gentile church in a morally lax city (in a morally lax Roman Empire!) had put to him in a letter. We should study not only his answers but his general method of applying Scripture to hard questions on this subject.

His method was less to lay out general principles for Christians to apply than to address particular cases from which we are left to draw more comprehensive insights. Thus, he writes about celibacy, marriage, the disruption of marriages by death and divorce, and remarriage following death or divorce. What he says to these questions is invaluable for our instruction. He deals with a limited number of specific situations (as had to be the case since the viable permutations are practically infinite), yet he deals with enough to provide some parameters that are genuinely helpful to us.

Corinth's Questions / Paul's Answers

So, because the *ethical norms* of the Torah and the gospel are identical – since they are based on God's very nature that is the same yesterday, today, and forever – Paul sounds very "traditional" in his answers.

- Is it okay for Christians who are young and single to join the hook-up culture of Corinth? *No, for your physical body – not just your "invisible spirit" or your "immortal soul" – was bought by Christ's blood, belongs to God, and is a temple of the Holy Spirit. Sex outside marriage dishonors that temple and is a sin against both your own body and the God to whom it belongs (1 Cor 6:15-20).*

- But it's different if we're in love, right? If we intend to get married? *No, sleeping together or moving in together may be acceptable to your culture, but it is against the will of God. One-night stand or long-term engagement isn't the distinction between holy and unholy sexual relationships for Christ's people. Sex is God's gift to a man and woman* after *they are married; it is a couple's disobedience to God* before *their relationship is sanctified to God by marriage (1 Cor 6:18; 7:3-5).*

- Nobody has the right to tell me what to do, for I am "free in Christ" and am covered by his grace. I have the right to do anything I want to do! *Modern as that may sound to us, those are the exact words Paul himself was accustomed to hearing from people in his own day. His answer was that your freedom and God's grace to you are freedom from sin's bondage in order to make yourself a servant to righteousness and that the last thing grace means is that you can just go on sinning and presume on God's mercy (1 Cor 6:12-14; cf. Gal 5:13-21; Rom 6:1-4).*

- Do I have to be single and celibate, then, to be a Christ-follower? I am a feeling person and need the warmth of attachment and love. *No, celibacy is God's calling and gift to some – but not to most. If God calls you to marriage – and especially if you are attracted to someone and are being tempted consistently to have sexual relations with that man or woman – by all means get married (1 Cor 7:1-2).*

- What if I get married and my husband or wife dies? Does that marriage extend into eternity? Do I have to remain single then? *No, marriage is "until death do us part," and someone whose mate dies is free to marry whomever he or she chooses "in the Lord" – that is, any person who will respect and encourage your life as a disciple of Jesus Christ (1 Cor 7:39 NRSVue[1]).*

- What if something happens in our marriage and we get a divorce? Do I have to remain single for the rest of my life? *No, because divorce was common in the ancient world – perhaps, even, because some divorces came about because one of the partners was a Christian – the apostle explicitly says that previously married persons who are now divorced "have not sinned" if they choose to remarry (1 Cor 7:27-28[2]).*

To the Glory of God

What, then, are Paul's specific case studies related to those of us who are married? How is a woman or man expected to live so as to be "Wed to the Glory of God"? Let me take you back to the language used in last week's sermon about being "Single to the Glory of God." *The first question a Christian should ask about any element of his or her life is this: How do I use this to the glory of God?* Now, that's not "preacher talk." It was Paul's language to the Christ-followers at Corinth: "So whether you eat or drink or whatever you do, do it all for the glory of God" (1 Cor 10:31). It was his counsel to Christians at Colossae: "Whatever you do or say, do it as a representative of the Lord Jesus, giving thanks through him to God the Father" (Col 3:17 NLT). It is basic guidance about how to live as a follower of Christ – being careful to put the Kingdom of God and his righteousness first in all things (cf. Matt 6:33).

Here is the essence of what Paul says to married persons – as best I can filter it through the social-cultural settings of Brentwood or Los Angeles or London today.

Let's begin where Paul begins – with the fact that not everyone gets married. Some who do probably should not have. Single persons can be focused and resolute in a way someone who carries a degree of responsibility for a spouse and/or children simply cannot. Attention, energy, and resources can be undivided and laser-focused for someone who is single. Single is therefore neither a curse nor a punishment. It is not a disease for which marriage is the cure. And against the popular notion that nobody can be complete or happy or fulfilled without a marital partner, there are compelling counter-arguments. There are people such as Jesus and Paul, the

Wright Brothers and Queen Elizabeth I, Sir Isaac Newton and Florence Nightingale, Condoleezza Rice and . . . You get the point, right?

Most of us, however, *will* choose to marry. A high percentage of those who marry will then have children. And we want those wedded and parental states to work well for all parties. We pray for them to be full and satisfying experiences. So here is Paul's Spirit-led word to us: "To the married I give this command (not I, but the Lord): A wife must not separate from her husband. But if she does, she must remain unmarried or else be reconciled to her husband. And a husband must not divorce his wife (vs.10-11). Language could hardly be clearer. God's wants marriages to work. To last a lifetime. That is his "Plan A" for those of us who marry.

I find it particularly interesting that Paul reveals a neglected-by-moderns purpose for marriage in verses 12-16. Speaking of marriages where only one of the adult mates is a Christian, Paul concedes the special challenge it would be for some – yet encourages the believer to stay in that relationship for this critical reason: "For the unbelieving husband has been sanctified through his wife, and the unbelieving wife has been sanctified through her believing husband. Otherwise your children would be unclean, but as it is, they are holy (v.14). Don't hear him saying the Christian's faith is going to save the non-Christian members of that family, for saving faith is personal to each of us. The verb "sanctified" and the noun "holy" are from the same root and mean "set apart for God, dedicated to God." The presence of a Christian in that household is God's best hope for reaching the unbelieving mate and any children born to the couple. So, stay if you can.

Yet marriages didn't always work in the ancient world – and Paul grants that, too. "But if the unbeliever leaves, let it be so. The brother or the sister is not bound in such circumstances; God has called us to live in peace. How do you know, wife, whether you will save your husband? Or, how do you know, husband, whether you will save your wife?" (vs.15-16). Not all marriages work today, either. After an all-time high of divorce in the 1980s – right at 50% by the reckoning of some sociologists – things have moderated a bit of late. It has been more like 35% to 40%, but we wonder what the confinement and stresses of the COVID-19 pandemic may have done to push it upwards.

Paul gives his Spirit-provided "judgment" as one made "trustworthy" as an agent of God-breathed words about persons who are having to wrestle with troubled marriages: "Are you bound to a wife? Do not seek to be free. Are you free from a wife? Do not seek a wife. But if you marry, you do not sin, and if a virgin marries, she has not sinned" (vs.27-28a). This is basic counsel found throughout Scripture. If you are not married, you have the freedom – but not the obligation – to marry. Whether never married, divorced, or widowed, marriage is an option; but staying single is God's calling and gift to some. If you make the decision to marry, however, live the married state within God's will and to God's glory. Marriage, too, is a divine calling and gift.

Cultural Perspectives on Marriage

There are basically four different ways to think of marriage in our American cultural experience. And it just might help some of us navigate our marriages to do some analysis in view of these interconnected models. In each case, our question must be: How does this view of marriage align with God's will for his people?

First, historians and sociologists speak of *institutional marriage*. From the founding of America until around 1850, marriages revolved around such basics as protection from danger, food production, and basic economics. Emotional factors were in play, of course, but they were bonuses to a good marriage rather than the primary goal. People married to survive and move the human enterprise forward. Marriage was more a practical than romantic venture.

Second, for roughly a century between 1850 and 1950, the wedded state in America evolved to be what some label *companionship marriage*. As we shifted from rural to urban life, our language and literature shifted to the intimacy needs of loving and being loved, compatibility and permanence, stability for children and security as we aged. There was less concern for a "good match" in terms of land and farming or enhancing one's social station and more attention paid to personal attraction, romantic allure, and sexual passion.

Third, as the post-war 1950s melted into the countercultural 1960s, all our institutions (including but not limited to marriage) had their foundations shaken. As a result, the ideals of permanence and stability were mocked in favor of living for novelty, excess, and excitement. The familiar was always regarded as boring, and an insatiable quest for something new and titillating led an entire generation to drugs, sex, and social upheaval; this is marriage in the era of *self-expressive individuality*.

This third period is highly fluid and hard to describe. Some attempted to find self-fulfillment without serious personal commitment to another. Others sought a level of fuller self-realization in marriage – looking for a mate who would be a passionate sexual partner, financial colleague, emotional benefactor, and spiritual underpinning. The partner might even be of the opposite sex, same sex, or nonbinary, so long as she, he, or "they" (singular) met the person's need.

If the fluidity and complexity of our present situation sounds more like thinly veiled selfishness, you have seen through the veil. And you have put your intellectual finger on a key factor in the reason for the high rate of divorce that was mentioned earlier. In the words of the recent announcement of a celebrity couple whose divorce hit Twitter and worldwide news: "We no longer believe we can grow together as a couple in this next phase of our lives." Or, simply stated, this person has become an obstacle to my fullest self-actualization.

Fourth, there is *sacramental marriage*. You might prefer the term "holy matrimony" or simply "principled monogamy" – for this view of marriage isn't necessarily "religious" in nature. It involves a covenantal commitment by one man and one woman to serve one another, nurture the other's progress and fulfillment, and embrace mutual self-giving for the sake of a shared goal. This type of life isn't just to keep you from being lonely or to reproduce the species. It isn't two people competing to have their needs met. Quite the opposite, it often means giving up personal preference for some mutual end that they believe will nudge the world in a positive direction. In the case of Christians, praying for God's will to be done – not our own – and seeking first the Kingdom of God and his righteousness.

This fourth view does not negate anything positive about the first three. It values the convention of institutional marriage, delights in the intimacy and stability of companionship marriage, and grants the reality of personal fulfillment and growth that are possible in marriage. But its focus is not those things. It isn't even the children born to the original couple or the idolizing of one's mate and partner. It exists to advance God's kingdom. To sanctify and set apart all its members to Christ. Going back to a text cited at the beginning of this sermon, do you know a place more suited to its challenge than a sacramental marriage: "Whether you eat or drink or whatever you do, do it all for the glory of God"? (1 Cor 10:31). The "whatever you do" here unfolds as drying the dishes, cleaning the potties, having babies, cutting grass, paying bills, helping a neighbor, improving your child's school, welcoming the new family three houses down, and anything else that makes your home a center for blessing people.

Our 21st-century culture extols the value of all these models of marriage, it seems, except for the fourth. Its view of marriage as empowered and enriched by a moral-spiritual function that moves us outside our selfishness for the sake of something better seems lost to many – but certainly not all – these days. A sacramental marriage functions in imitation of Christ's love for his bride, the church. His love is neither a shallow *erōs* (romance, erotic desire) nor mere *philia* (friendship, mutual aid), but the one perfect example of *apapē* (unselfish, other-regarding actions). Perhaps that is why Paul speaks of marriage only to point to this fact: "This is a profound mystery – but I am talking about Christ and the church" (Eph 5:32).

For a husband and wife to love each other on Jesus' self-emptying, building-up-the-other, empowering-the-other model is to embrace the "secret of a happy marriage" that so many people say they are searching to find. Tim Keller takes that "profound mystery" line from Paul and tweaks it to invite couples who see their relationship as an "unsolvable puzzle" – or perhaps we might even say a "hopeless mess" – to rethink their relationship biblically. He offers this counsel: "If two spouses *each* say, 'I'm going to treat my self-centeredness as the main problem in the marriage,' you have the prospect of a truly great marriage."[3]

Conclusion

To embrace a nobler and higher view of what marriage is seems a necessary first step to creating relationships that function as Christians wish they would. Married, single, widowed; poor, wealthy, middle class; Black, White, Brown; Republican, Democrat, Independent; high school grad, university professor, dropout; baseball fan, opera buff, bass fisherman; business owner, truck driver, unemployed person – whoever you are and whatever your life situation, your calling is to be the Father's child, the Spirit's temple, the Son's disciple in the "place in life that the Lord assigned to [you] and to which God has called [you]" (1 Cor 7:17). If that place involves marriage, the "mystery" of unselfish regard for your mate is your beginning point for making the relationship what God and you want it to be.

Diverse as we are, we are nevertheless meant to be one. *One in Christ!* Called away from sin to embrace righteousness, we are commissioned to put the light of God on display in a dark world. Called out of ourselves for the sake of being in Christ, the transforming power of grace can reveal itself in the presence that God wills us to be for his sake in the world.

In that setting, a man and a woman are authentically wed to the glory of God.

ENDNOTES

1. In my view, the NIV mistakenly translates "but he must *belong to the Lord*." The phrase μόνον ἐν κυρίῳ (lit, only in [the] Lord) is equivalent to Paul's instruction that children are to obey their parents ἐν κυρίῳ at Ephesians 6:1. Both are prepositional phrases that describe an action, not a person. Just as children who are Christians are obligated to obey their parents so long as the parental instructions are consistent with faithful discipleship, so a widow is to take the implications of a possible marriage into account for its consistency with her prior commitment to Christ. In neither case does ἐν κυρίῳ describe the person – so that children have a right to disobey a parent who is not a Christian or a widow can only marry someone who is.

2. Again, the NRSVue is clearer here than the NIV. The NIV ("pledged" and "free from such a commitment") can be taken to refer simply to an engagement. The NRSVue translates as follows: "Are you bound to a wife? Do not seek to be free. Are you free from a wife? Do not seek a wife. But if you marry, you do not sin . . ."

3. Keller, *The Meaning of Marriage*, 64.

SPECIAL NOTE:

This document is one I helped draft for use in a congregational setting where church leaders felt the need to state their collective view on Christian sexual ethics.

APPENDIX C

Sexual Purity and the People of God

Scripture calls for God's people to live in holiness before him. "As obedient children, do not conform to the evil desires you had when you lived in ignorance. But just as he who called you is holy, so be holy in all you do; for it is written: 'Be holy, because I am holy'" (1 Pet 1:15-17).

Our culture exhibits sweeping disregard for the principles of premarital chastity, marital fidelity, homosexual behavior, gender identity, and pornography. These and related topics could justify separate detailed treatment each. The positions sketched here are the ones we expect anyone who holds a teaching or leadership role in the congregation to support, teach, and maintain in his or her lifestyle.

We believe that God has created males and females of the human race in his image. That humans are gendered means that sexual attraction and activity are natural, normal, and healthy to human personality. As with all human behaviors, Christians must seek to know and live our sexual lives within the revealed will of God in Holy Scripture. Grace and pardon must never be interpreted as license to sin by violating God's will.

Premarital Chastity. Paul emphasized that the physical bodies of Christians have been redeemed by Christ's blood, are indwelt by the Spirit, and are to be used to honor God; therefore, he said fornication is both "immoral" and a "sin against one's own body" (1 Cor 6:12-20). For the sake of their spiritual health and their future marriages, we plead with our teens and single adults to live sexually chaste lives prior to marriage.

Marital Fidelity. Marriage within the will of God is the physical, emotional, and spiritual union of one man and one woman who covenant to live in exclusive fidelity to one another. No marriage should be made without this intention, and difficulties within a marriage should be addressed with a view to avoiding divorce and healing the marital relationship (Matt 19:1-9).

Homosexual Behaviors. Both Old (Lev 18:22; 20:13) and New (Rom 1:18-32) Testaments speak with one voice that same-sex behavior is one example – along with gossip, arrogance, infidelity, failure to show mercy, and various other specific activities – of humankind's rebellion against the God in whose image they were created. Collectively, such actions are called "things that ought not to be done" (v.28). Struggles with illicit sexual attraction and desire are serious temptations. Left unchecked, these feelings become lust and/or sexual sin. We appeal for souls under our care to avoid temptations and environments that promote same-sex activity.

Gender Identity. The notion of "choosing" or "changing" one's gender is a novel postmodern curiosity without biblical precedent or warrant. While we acknowledge rare physiological events of "gender confusion" and the emotional-psychological confusion some persons experience around sexual issues, our understanding is that gender is a "given" of birth and not a "social construct" subject to one's choice. We encourage persons in spiritual chaos over these issues to seek counsel from trained and mature Christian counselors who take Scripture seriously.

Pornography. Because we are convinced that the multi-billion-dollar pornography industry is both evil in itself (for its particular exploitation of females and children) and a source of sexual temptation for anyone who consumes it, we strongly urge that Christian teens and adults, singles and marrieds avoid exposure to it. Its attraction is to stimulate the sort of lusts Scripture warns against (2 Tim 2:22). Online pornography is especially problematic to families, and we encourage parents to help protect their children from exposure to it by example, teaching, and monitoring of their screen (e.g., computer, smartphone, Facebook, etc.) usage.

This document is written to encourage Christians to embrace and live the purest of Christ-honoring lives and not with a judgmental or self-righteous spirit. We believe it is the duty of Christian leaders in every church to challenge believers to walk in the footsteps of Jesus himself (1 Pet 2:21). We make this appeal with full awareness of our own weaknesses. Grace, pardon, love, and redemption are the call of God to all of us.

With particular emphasis to the issue of sexual purity, we recall this word of mercy from Paul to Christians in a city filled with sexual vices: "And that is what some of you were. But you were washed, you were sanctified, you were justified in the name of the Lord Jesus Christ and by the Spirit of our God" (1 Cor 6:11).

Do we want people struggling with these issues to attend and be part of the life of our congregational life? Certainly. We not only warn against sexual sins but also Christian self-righteousness and judgment. We are a community of sinners saved by God's grace. We call one another to repentance. We nurture each other in faith and faithfulness. And we wait in hope for the return of the Lord Jesus Christ.

APPENDIX D

Movie Review:
"1946: The Mistranslation That Shifted Culture"

I had not heard of this movie still in pre-release, but a friend suggested that I see it in light of this book in progress. The documentary claims that "a biblical mistranslation of catastrophic proportions" occurred in the initial publication of the Revised Standard Version. That error, in turn, "has become the foundation for much of the anti-gay culture that exists today, especially in religious spaces."

Most simply, "1946: The Mistranslation That Shifted Culture" claims that the RSV's decision to translate the two Greek words *malakoi* and *arsenokoitai* in 1 Cor 6:9 and 1 Tim 1:10 with the single English term "homosexual" was a mistake that has generated negative sentiment toward gay persons.

The documentary offers evidence from correspondence with the RSV translation committee's chair, Dr. Luther Weigle, that acknowledged the mistake, promised to correct it, and did so. The original issue of the RSV in 1946 had its first revision only in 1971 – allowing, according to the film's self-described "LGBTQ female Christian, Sharon 'Rocky' Roggio," conservative Christian leaders to use these texts for 25 years "to condemn and marginalize LGBTQ+ Christians."

Further, Roggio claims, later English translations such as the NIV, NLT, NASB, and ESV uncritically reproduced the flawed concept that all same-sex intercourse is outside God's will. All the while, American society at large was influenced "to believe the idea that sexual and gender minorities must choose between their faith and their identity."[1]

My sense is that the church must bear significant responsibility for hounding and humiliating gay people – thus leading them not only to be skeptical of Christians but to avoid and despise us. We have been disrespectful in too many settings. Told too many denigrating jokes. Perpetuated ugly stereotypes. Most basically, perhaps, we have refused to distinguish same-sex *attraction* from same-sex *behaviors*. I, for one, have failed too often to acknowledge that *inclination and predisposition* (which may be genetic givens) are distinguishable from *conduct and activity.*

As you read these lines, perhaps you self-identify as heterosexual or straight. Is that the totality of your being? Does it mean you are morally chaste? Perhaps you self-identify as homosexual or gay. Is that the totality of your being? Does it mean you are morally decadent? Your sexual orientation is not a definition of your moral status before God. As N.T. Wright has said, "Sexual restraint is mandatory for all, difficult for most, extremely challenging for some. God is gracious and merciful but this never means 'so his creational standards don't really matter after all.'"[2]

In the twenty-first century, both heterosexual and homosexual are terms generally understood to describe a person's sexual orientation. If Christians use the latter term flatly and without nuance, practically all non-Christians and many Christians will hear us passing harsh judgment against someone who is same-sex oriented – even if they are being successful in refusing to act on those tendencies.

Early reviews of the film by generally liberal media critics have been effusive. Online comments from its viewers have included such comments as these: "It was so good! I learned so much." "I only hope it helps open people's eyes."

As with most opinions of most people, few of us are technical experts on the things about which we may express strong views. Thus, I may dismiss a physician's view of my salt intake or a mechanic's opinion that a certain repair needs to be made, but my opinion won't change the values in my bloodwork or make the car run when it breaks down on our vacation trip. Just so, none of the assured online comments I saw about "1946" appeared to be from experts in theology, linguistics, or logic. Could it be that they have fallen prey to the temptation all of us face to cherry pick items that affirm what we want to hear and/or justify things we have chosen already to think?

First, the idea that Scripture presents a negative view of same-sex intercourse did not originate in 1946. For 3,500 years, all sexual intercourse outside covenanted heterosexual marriage has been deemed sinful by Jewish and Christian scholars – and by the most casual readers of the Bible. Only in the last half century or so has this been challenged by some who work in the arena of New Testament scholarship. Do you really think we have discovered a truth that lay hidden for those millennia and without challenge by prophets, apostles, or Jesus himself? That only the last couple of generations of biblical scholars were perceptive enough to unearth and expose?

Second, a key element of social change since 1946 seems to lie in the confusion of the terms "homosexual" and "same-sex intercourse." I am reasonably sure the cultural vocabulary of 1946 – when the RSV was first released – did not make the sharp distinction we do today between a person's sexual orientation (i.e., natural inclination toward those of the same or opposite sex) and his or her sexual behaviors (i.e., what a person does with those feelings). By analogy, that one is heterosexual in orientation does not tell you what she is doing, but how she is disposed to act. But the original RSV choice of "homosexual" in 1946 is heard in 2023 to condemn a person's orientation and feelings – whether they originate in genetic, environmental, or combined factors – and not simply their lifestyle choices and actions.

Erotic feelings of whatever sort are not sinful in themselves. Fostered as lust and acted out in some form of illicit behavior (e.g., pornography, premarital sex, rape, adultery), one commits sin. Those same emotions and inclinations kept in check (e.g., chastity, fidelity) is virtuous behavior. To repeat for emphasis, it is the *behavior* that is praised or disapproved in Scripture. To equate our words "homosexual" or "heterosexual" *orientation* with the moral categories "evil" or "holy" is therefore a failure to distinguish very different things.

A gay person who is attracted to someone of the same sex may live with spiritual accountability and holiness, while his or her straight friend is shameless and immoral in conduct. Too many – and I must count myself among them – are sometimes careless in making a distinction between a person's orientation and practice.

Third, if the word "homosexual" were removed from all English versions of the Bible today, this *description* of forbidden sexual actions cannot be interpreted as anything other than a divine judgment against same-sex coupling: "If a man has sexual relations with a man as one does with a woman, both of them have done what is detestable. They are to be put to death; their blood will be on their own heads" (Lev 20:13; cf. 18:22). It is this language from a Hebrew holiness code that is background to Paul's protest of "shameful lusts" that lead to "shameful acts" as either men or women "exchanged natural sexual relations for unnatural ones" (Rom 1:26-27).[3]

The film implies that the negative biblical statements are about pederastic – perhaps even pedophilic – exploitation of boys or the rape of adults and not about committed and caring relationships between same-sex couples. That is not correct, however, for *consensual* sex between adults is portrayed in these texts. This seems obvious from the fact that *both* parties in the Leviticus text are subject to punishment – unlike a rapist and his victim. Sex is had with a "man" (Heb, *zakar* = male, not *na'ar* = youth, lad), thus the subject is not pederasty. And "has sexual relations with" is literally "lies with" – not "seizes" or "rapes."

Trained as he was in the Torah, this is background to Paul's sharp language about the "shameful acts" of certain people in the non-Jewish world to whom he is explaining Christian morality. Greek had words not only for rape/rapist (*biasmos/biastēs*) but also for pederasty/pederast (*paiderastia/paiderastēs*) that the literate Paul could have used instead of this more inclusive word for anal sex between males.

Fourth, "homosexual" may not, in fact, be the best way to translate *oute malakoi oute arsenokoitai* in 2023. Squeezing two nouns together – "neither X nor Y" – as if the underlying text had only one word is typically not good form. The "neither/nor" construction seems to indicate some sort of distinction. But what? *Malakoi* can mean "soft things" (such as cloth or fur) or, when used of males, in ancient Greek may indicate "effeminate." *Arsenokoitai* appears to be a word coined by Paul – who does this rather frequently in his letters – to identify males (Gk, *arsen* = male) who bed or sleep with (Gk, *koitē* = bed) other men. In other words, Paul seems to be describing roles (passive and active) and actions (penetrated and penetrator) rather than an orientation or persona.

Robin Scroggs has shown the best evidence is that *arsenokoitai* is a word coined by Paul to bring words from the Hebrew text into Greek. Scroggs argues that "the term used to describe male homosexuality is *mishkav zakur*, 'lying with a male.' *Arsenokoitēs* can then be seen as a literal translation of the Hebrew phrase."[4] Scroggs then proceeds to interpret 1 Cor 6:9-10 as referring to a "very specific form of pederasty." But what would be "specific" to a dominant older male having sex with a passive younger one? Would that not be the nature of every pederastic sex act?

A literate man with such an extensive vocabulary as Paul displays in his letters would be expected to use the "specific" Greek term cited above that points to pederasty rather than two words that point to sexual postures rather than the participants' ages. A more direct and natural reading is that Paul numbers such persons as "wrongdoers" so as to include not only pederasts but also male prostitutes, sexually abusive slaveowners, and/or persons in committed same-sex relationships.

In light of what has just been cited, it may seem strange that Scroggs proceeds to argue a case for Christian acceptance and affirmation of non-exploitative same-sex coupling. His argument goes that, since Paul was speaking of pederasty and dehumanizing same-sex acts in his letters, nothing he or the other biblical texts says can count against the "current model of the caring adult relationship of mutuality." Specifically, he claims that Paul knew nothing of such relationships because "the *only* model of male homosexuality [in biblical times] was pederasty."[5] Again, Scroggs adds that "it is certain that pederasty was the only *model* in existence in the world of this time. That proposed by twentieth-century gay liberation movements was, without question, entirely absent."[6]

Bold as the claim is, both the premise and conclusion are mistaken. Assuming that Scroggs did not have access to well-documented claims of caring, non-exploitative, and committed same-sex partnerships when he published in 1983, a 2013 publication by Harvard University Press has changed the evidential landscape. Kyle Harper, a classics professor at the University of Oklahoma, documents a wide variety of "durable forms of same-sex companionships" in the Roman Empire where "same-sex pairs openly claimed, and ritually enacted, their own conjugal rights."[7] As until the past few years in the United States, Roman law did not provide for same-sex marriage. Yet we have literature claiming both male-male and female-female "marriage" between consenting adults. In the early second century, Juvenal refers to one such event and "imagines the day is near when male-male marriage will take place publicly and be recorded in the state's registers."[8]

Far from referring only to pederasty, Paul appears to have coined a Greek word – translating a Hebrew term and all but quoting Leviticus 18 and 20 from the Septuagint[9] – that serves as a comprehensive rebuke of the full range of same-sex coital exchange. By avoiding the use of the narrower *paiderastēs* here, he encompasses pedophiles, pederasts, cult prostitutes, commercial same-sex intercourse, and the like. But it also prohibits same-sex intercourse between parties who are loving, committed, and monogamous. The prohibition includes both parties in same-sex encounters. By definition, this is homosexual behavior, but reducing two words to one is a move into *dynamic equivalence* or *functional sense* translation (e.g., NIV, NLT, CEV) that could be thought to compromise the RSV's official commitment to a *formal equivalence* or what is sometimes called a *word-for-word* methodology (e.g., KJV, NASB, ESV).

If the RSV veered from its attempt at word-for-word style – which is ultimately an impossibility in any translation process – it did not err in its statement of their meaning: *all same-sex genital intimacy is forbidden to Christians*. The original 1946 reading is therefore not a "mistaken translation" by any stretch of linguistics or logic. To say the very least, there is no way for filmmakers, scholars, or everyday Bible readers to make an affirmative case for homosexual intercourse by challenging the RSV's rendering of *arsenokoitai*.

In summary of the film's criticism, any legitimate criticism of how the term "homosexual" came into the original English RSV from the Greek New Testament is *a distinction without a difference* in terms of what is rebuked.

Fifth, the fact that same-sex intercourse is wrong does not justify the crude jokes, insulting or threatening behaviors, and violence visited against gay and lesbian persons. The best way to be sure the biblical message will never be heard by the LGBTQ+ community and gay persons within our spheres of contact is for an irate CHURCH-ey community to continue acting so sanctimoniously judgmental. Because I believe in the power of God's truth, I am forced to believe that honest and mature presentations of Scripture offered in the spirit of Christ's love can be heard.

Hatred does not serve God's holy purpose.

Pitched as an "impassioned academic crusade of the LGBTQIA+ Christian community – driven to discover the truth," I fear "1946" is instead a zealous-but-naïve attempt to negate the biblical call to repentance and purity to persons who are living in disobedience to God's will.

The church has not been very helpful across the centuries to people struggling with same-sex attraction. We still aren't doing enough. Gay women and men have been disparaged by stereotyping and arrogant judgments. Bigotry has been mainstream to far too many churches and professed Christians. The sinfulness of those behaviors does not, however, lessen the moral responsibility of chastity and self-control for LGBTQ+ persons – any more than, for example, the mistreatment of alcoholics, heterosexual offenders, or fallen church leaders has diminished the ethical duties of those maltreated souls. All of us are accountable for our behaviors. The transforming power of the Holy Spirit enables us to do what we cannot do in our natural and unredeemed state.

Christ's church is meant to be a sanctuary where repentant men and women can share with others the sexual desires they feel and still receive prayerful support within a community of acceptance, accountability, and nurture into an ever-increasing likeness to Christ. God's people must do better than many of us have done in the past.

Alarmed parents, preachers, elders, teachers, and friends of persons involved in same-sex or other illicit sexual behaviors will more nearly be heard by them if we speak respectfully, lovingly, and with accurate information. God loves all of us enough to show patient love as he calls us to repentance (cf. 2 Pet 3:9). May we learn to do so with one another.

ENDNOTES

1. Quotations are from the film's official website as accessed on Nov 27, 2022, at https://www.1946themovie.com.

2. From an interview with Jonathan Merritt, "N.T. Wright on homosexuality, science, gender," part 1, *Religion News Service*, June 3, 2014. https://religionnews.com/2014/06/03/nt-wright-homosexuality-science-gender.

3. An excellent overview of the biblical material in today's cultural context can be found in Hays, "Homosexuality," in *The Moral Vision of the New Testament*, 379-406.

4. Scroggs, *New Testament and Homosexuality*, 107-108.

5. Ibid., 130.

6. Ibid., 139.

7. Harper, *From Shame to Sin*, 36.

8. Ibid., 35.

9. David F. Wright, "Homosexuals or Prostitutes? The Meaning of *Arsenokoitai* (1 Cor. 6:9; 1 Tim. 1:10)," *Vigiliae Christianae* 38 (1984), 125-53.

SPECIAL NOTES IN CHAPTERS

Bordered quotations found throughout the chapters of this book are from the sources indicated below.

CHAPTER 1

- "Criminalizing Same-Sex Acts?" / Russell Moore, "Don't Pretend the Ugandan Homosexuality Law Is Christian," *Christianity Today* (June 1, 2023), accessed at https://www.christianitytoday.com/ct/2023/may-web-only/uganda-anti-lgbtq-ted-cruz-russell-moore-biblical-sin-crime.html.

- "Homophobia" / Rosaria Champagne Butterfield, *The Secret Thoughts of an Unlikely Convert: An English Professor's Journey into Christian Faith*, 2nd ed. (Philadelphia: Crown and Covenant, 2014), 169.

- "Love and Truth" / Tim Keller, *The Meaning of Marriage* (New York: Penguin Books, 2016), 44.

- "Why Male-Female Monogamy?" / Maggie Gallagher, "What Marriage Is For: Children Need Mothers and Fathers," *Weekly Standard* (Aug 2003): 22-25, as quoted in Lewis Vaughn, *Doing Ethics* (New York: W.W. Norton & Co., 2010), 435.

- "Changed Views of Same-Sex Marriage" / Gabriel Borelli, "About six-in-ten Americans say legalization of same-sex marriage is good for society," Pew Research Center (Nov 15, 2022), accessed at https://www.pewresearch.org/fact-tank/2022/11/15/about-six-in-ten-americans-say-legalization-of-same-sex-marriage-is-good-for-society.

- "Biblical Consistency" / Ron Sider, "Tragedy, Tradition, and Opportunity in the Homosexuality Debate," (Nov 18, 2014), accessed at https://www.christianitytoday.com/ct/2014/november-web-only/ron-sider-tragedy-tradition-and-opportunity-in-homosexualit.html.

- "The Highest Human Welfare" / John R.W. Stott, "Homosexual Marriage," *Christianity Today* (Nov 22, 1985).

- "Why 'Consent' Is Not Enough" / Christine Emba, "Consent Is Not Enough. We Need a New Sexual Ethic," *Washington Post* (Mar 17, 2022).

- "'No' to Cultural Accommodation" / Miroslav Volf, *A Public Faith: How Followers of Christ Should Serve the Common Good* (Grand Rapids: Brazos Press, 2011), 95.

- "'Feelings' Are Less Than Moral Justification" / Dallas Willard, *Knowing Christ Today: Why We Can Trust Spiritual Knowledge* (New York: HarperCollins Publishers, 2009), 82.

CHAPTER 2

- "Judge Not . . ." / Rubel Shelly, "Fax of Life" for Jan 6, 2014.

- "How Christian Values Became Bigotry" / From a speech given in 2014 by Charles J. Chaput, archbishop of Philadelphia, titled "Strangers in a Strange Land." Available in video format at https://www.firstthings.com/events/2014-erasmus-lecture.

- "Some Historical Perspective" / José Casanova, "The Secular and the Secularisms," *Social Research* 76, no.4 (2009): 1059-1060.

- "Orientation or Conduct?" / J. Glen Taylor, "The Bible and Homosexuality," *Themelios* 21, no.1 (1995): 4.
- "The Bible and Human Dignity" / Tom Holland, *Dominion: How the Christian Revolution Remade the World* (New York: Basic Books, 2019), 494.
- "A Whole Forest of Possibilities" / Jean Bethke Eishtain, "Judge Not?" *First Things* (Oct 1994): 36-40, quoted in Vaughn, *Doing Ethics*, 24.

CHAPTER 3

- "God Created Marriage . . ." / Keller, *Meaning of Marriage*, 9-10.
- "But Have We *Thought* about Sex?" / Matt Fradd, "Chastity as a Virtue," from The Institute of Faith and Learning at Baylor University" (online), 36-37, accessed at https://ifl.web.baylor.edu/sites/g/files/ecbvkj771/files/2022-11/ChastityArticleFradd.pdf.
- "Disordered Sexual Pairings" / Michael Ukleja, "Homosexuality in the Old Testament," *Bibliotheca Sacra*, 140, no. 559 (July-Sept 1983): 259.
- "Sexual Intimacy and Moral Commitment" / Vincent C. Punzo, *Reflective Naturalism* (Upper Saddle River, NJ: Macmillan, 1969), 193-200, as quoted in Stephen A. Satris, Taking Sides: Clashing Views on Moral Issues, 13th ed (New York: McGraw-Hill Co., 2012), 53-54.

CHAPTER 4

- "The Last 40 Years" / Jim Reynolds, *The Lepers Among Us: Homosexuality and the Life of the Church* (Maitland, FL: Xulon Press, 2007), 77,88.
- "The Move to 'Redefine'" / Brent Pickett, "Homosexuality," *The Stanford Encyclopedia of Philosophy* (Spring 2021 Edition), Accessed at https://plato.stanford.edu/cgi-bin/encyclopedia/archinfo.cgi?entry=homosexuality.
- "Justifying a Change of View" / Darrin W. Snyder Belousek, *Marriage, Scripture, and the Church: Theological Discernment on the Question of Same-Sex Union* (Grand Rapids: Baker Academic, 2021), 14.
- "Culture or Counter-Culture?" / "Exactly the Opposite," an interview with Philip Yancey in *Christian History Magazine* (online) #75 in 2002, accessed at https://christianhistoryinstitute.org/magazine/article/interview-exactly-the-opposite.

EXCURSUS / Our Sin Against Singles

- "The Church's Message to Singles" / Philip Turner, "Sex and the Single Life," *First Things* (May 1993): 20.
- "One God. A Variety of Gifts." / Bruce Reichenbach, "The Gift of Singleness," *The Reformed Journal* (March 1982), 5.
- "Singleness as Gift" / David Wenham, "Marriage and Singleness in Paul and Today," in *Readings in Christian Ethics, Vol 2: Issues and Applications,* ed. David K. Clark and Robert V. Rakestraw (Grand Rapids: Baker Books, 1996), 146-147.
- "Beyond 'Just Do It' and 'No'" / Turner, "Sex and the Single Life," 20.

SPECIAL NOTES INDEX

- "The Covenant of Singleness" / J. Scott Horrell, "The Covenant of Singleness: The Bible and Church History," *Voice* (June 12, 2015), accessed at https://voice.dts.edu/article/the-covenant-of-singleness-the-bible-and-church-history.

- "Loneliness" / Bret Rogers, "Singleness: Securing Undivided Devotion to the Lord," (sermon) accessed at https://www.redeemerfortworth.org/sermons/sermon/2016-11-13/singleness:-securing-undivided-devotion-to-the-lord.

- "Today's Business" / Elizabeth Elliot, *Quest for Love* (Grand Rapids: Fleming H. Revell, 1996), 215.

CHAPTER 5

- "God's Perfect Plan" / Sandra Richter, *The Epic of Eden: A Christian Entry into the Old Testament* (Downers Grove, IL: IVP Academic, 2008), 104.

- "Identity and Sexuality" / Arthur F. Glasser, *Announcing the Kingdom: The Story of God's Mission in the Bible* (Grand Rapids: Baker Academic, 2003), 35.

- "The Role of Genesis" / Nahum M. Sarna, *The JPS Torah Commentary: Genesis* (Philadelphia: Jewish Publication Society, 1989), xiv.

- "'One Flesh': More Than Emotional Tie" / Brian Neil Peterson, "Does Genesis 2 Support Same-Sex Marriage? An Evangelical Response," *Journal of the Evangelical Theological Society* (2017): 689.

- "Adam's 'Loneliness'" / Matthew Mason, "Man and Woman He Created Them: Same-Sex Desires, Gender Trouble, and Gay Marriage in the Light of John Paul II's Theology of the Body," *Bulletin of Ecclesial Theology* (2014): 39-40.

- "How Significant a Story?" / N.T. Wright, *Simply Christian: Why Christianity Makes Sense* (San Francisco: HarperCollins, 2006), 232.

- "About Gender Stereotypes" / Preston Sprinkle, *Embodied* (Colorado Springs: David C. Cook, 2021), 82-83.

- "Richard Dawkins on 'De-Gendered Language'" / Gabriel Hays, "Richard Dawkins declares there are only two sexes as matter of science: 'That's all there is to it,'" *Fox News*, Mar 21, 2023, ccessed Mar 23, 2023, at https://www.foxnews.com/media/richard-dawkins-declares-only-two-sexes-matter-science-thats-all.

CHAPTER 6

- "Old Testament Literature and Sex" / Donald Fortson and Rollin Grams, *Unchanging Witness* (Nashville: B&H Academic, 2016), 201-202.

- "The Sodom Story" / Stott, "Homosexual Marriage," *Christianity Today* (Nov 22, 1985).

- "Leviticus: The Holiness Code," / David F. Wright, "Homosexuality: The Relevance of the Bible," *Evangelical Quarterly* (1989): 292-293.

- "Would/Could God Be So Unclear"? / Alan Shieman, "Marriage Doctrine Alone Disqualifies Pro-Gay Theology," *Stand to Reason* (website). Accessed at https://www.str.org/w/marriage-doctrine-alone-disqualifies-pro-gay-theology.

- "Why Focus on the Moral Laws?" / Reynolds, *Lepers Among Us*, 146-147.

CHAPTER 7

- "Did God Really Say?" / Rubel Shelly, compiled from various sources, esp. Guy Hammond, *Gay & Christian?* (Spring, TX: Illumination Publishers, 2021), 37-38, and online data from Amazon.com and Goodreads.com.

- "The Life Experience of Jesus" / Todd Wilson, *Mere Sexuality: Rediscovering the Christian Vision of Sexuality* (Grand Rapids: Zondervan, 2017), 49-50.

- "Does Jesus' 'Silence' Mean Permission?" / Guy Hammond, *Gay & Christian?*, 84-85.

- "The Eunuchs of Matthew 19:12" / Rodney Reeves, *Matthew* (Grand Rapids: Zondervan, 2017), 376.

- "Jesus and the Created Order," Gregory Kouki and Alan Shlemon, "A Reformation the Church Doesn't Need – Part 1," *Stand to Reason* (online), June 30, 2015, accessed at https://www.str.org/w/a-reformation-the-church-doesn-t-need-part-1.

- "Demythologizing Sex" / Richard Hays, *The Moral Vision of the New Testament* (New York: HarperCollins, 1996), 390-391.

EXCURSUS / Sex(es) and Gender(s): The Other 72 Genders?

- "Biological Sex in Healthcare" / Sara Dahlen, "Biological sex is vital in healthcare," *British Medical Journal* 373 (May 24, 2021), accessed at https://www.bmj.com/content/373/bmj.n1261/rr-2.

- "*Sola Experientia*" / Christopher Yuan, "Gender Identity and Sexual Orientation," *The Gospel Coalition*, no date, accessed at https://www.thegospelcoalition.org/essay/gender-identity-and-sexual-orientation.

- "Analogy: Primary and Secondary Characteristics" / Colin Wright, "JK Rowling Is Right – Sex Is Real and It Is Not a "Spectrum," *Quillette*, June 7, 2020, accessed April 13, 2023, at https://quillette.com/2020/06/07/jk-rowling-is-right-sex-is-real-and-it-is-not-a-spectrum.

- "Loving Concern" / John Mark Hicks, "Gender Ideology: 'What Is a Woman," accessed April 14, 2023, at https://johnmarkhicks.com/2023/01/09/gender-ideology-what-is-a-woman.

CHAPTER 8

- "Religion and Ethics: Two Views" / Larry Hurtado, *Destroyer of the Gods: Early Christian Distinctiveness in the Roman World* (Waco, TX: Baylor University Press, 2016), 170-171, 188.

- "Sex: Procreation and Recreational" / Scot McKnight, *A Fellowship of Differents* (Grand Rapids: Zondervan, 2014), 124-125.

- "Roman Erotica as Status" / John R. Clarke, *Roman Sex: 100 B.C. to A.D. 250* (New York: Harry N. Abrams, 2003), 158.

- "We Are Not So Different Today!" / Magdalene J. Taylor, "Have More Sex, Please!", *New York Times* (Feb 13, 2023).

- "Sex as Roman Capitalism" / Kyle Harper, *From Shame to Sin* (Cambridge, MA: Harvard University Press, 2013), 46-47.

CHAPTER 9

- "Temporary and Age-Related?" / John Boswell, *Same-Sex Unions in Premodern Europe* (New York: Villard Books, 1994), 71-72.

- "Commitments Beyond *Paiderastia*" / Luc Brisson, "Agathon, Pausanias, and Diotima in Plato's *Symposium: Paiderastia and Philosophia*," in J.H. Lesher, Debra Nails, and Frisbee C.C. Sheffield (eds), *Plato's Symposium: Issues in Interpretation and Reception* (Cambridge, MA: Harvard University Press, 2006), 238-239.

- "Greek 'Marriage' of Same-Sex Partners" / Boswell, *Same-Sex Unions in Premodern Europe*, 10-11.

- "Lifelong Same-Sex Commitments" / Louis Crompton, *Homosexuality and Civilization* (Cambridge, MA: Harvard University Press, 2003), 57.

- "Aristotle on Nature or Nurture" / Crompton, *Homosexuality and Civilization*, 65.

- "'Enlightened' Greek Attitudes?" / Jeffrey Carnes, "Plato in the Courtroom: The Surprising Influence of the *Symposium* on Legal Theory," in J.H. Lesher, Debra Nails, and Frisbee Sheffield (eds), *Plato's Symposium: Issues in Interpretation and Reception* (Cambridge, MA: Harvard University Press, 2006), 278.

CHAPTER 10

- "The Moral Code of Rome" / Colin Ricketts, "Promiscuity in Antiquity: Sex in Ancient Rome," HistoryHit (website). Accessed at https://www.historyhit.com/the-oldest-obsession-sex-lives-in-ancient-rome/

- "Public Recognition of Same-Sex Unions" / Boswell, *Same-Sex Unions in Premodern Europe*, 80.

- "Two Modes of Male-Male Love" / Maximus of Tyre, "Oration 9," *The Philosophical Orations*, trans. M.B. Trapp (New York: Oxford University Press, 1997).

- "Same-Sex 'Orientation'" / Preston Sprinkle, "Romans 1 and Homosexuality: A Critical Review of James Brownson's Bible, Gender, Sexuality," *Bulletin for Biblical Research* 24.4 (2014): 525.

- "Impulses and Behavior Control" / Timothy Keller, *Preaching: Communicating Faith in an Age of Skepticism* (New York: Penguin Books, 2016), pp 135-136.

- "Christianity: An Alternate Attitude" / Harper, *From Shame to Sin*, 99.

EXCURSUS / The Book of Acts: A Method for "Changing the Rules"?

- "Mirrors and Inkblots" / Scot McKnight, *The Blue Parakeet* (Grand Rapids: Zondervan, 2008), 48-49.

- "Reading Human Experience" / Eve Tushnet, "Homosexuality & the Church: A Second View," *Commonweal*, June 11, 2007. Accessed at https://www.commonwealmagazine.org/print/36052.

- "Relating Scripture to Culture" / Gordon Fee and Douglas Stuart, *How to Read the Bible for All Its Worth*, 4th ed. (Grand Rapids: Zondervan, 2014), 86.

- "The Jerusalem Decision" / Belousek, *Marriage, Scripture, and the Church*, 229-230.

CHAPTER 11

- "A Classicist on Paul's Position" / Harper, *Shame to Sin*, 12.
- "Adam and the Root of False Worship" / Christopher J.H. Wright, *The Mission of God: Unlocking the Bible's Grand Narrative* (Downers Grove, IL: InterVarsity Press, 2006), 164.
- "Clarity of Language in Romans 1" / Harper, *Shame to Sin*, 95.
- "A Non-Roman Perspective" / Holland, *Dominion*, 288-289.
- "The Language of 'Exchange'" / Kevin DeYoung, *What Does the Bible Really Teach about Homosexuality?* (Wheaton: Crossway, 2015), 53.
- "Degrading of Their Bodies" (v.24)? / Frank Thielman, *Romans: Zondervan Exegetical Commentary on the New Testament* (Grand Rapids: Zondervan, 2018), 110.
- "Josephus on *para physin*" / Darrin Snyder Belousek, "Appendix E: Paul on Same-Sex Intercourse: Romans 1," Supplement to *Marriage, Scripture, and the Church: Theological Discernment on the Question of Same-Sex Union*, 94.

CHAPTER 12

- "How Best to Translate?" / Wesley Hill, *Two Views on Homosexuality, the Bible, and the Church* (Grand Rapids: Zondervan, 2016), 138-139.
- "Paul's Positive Message" / Guy Waters, "Paul's Understanding of Sexuality: μαλακοὶ and ἀρσενοκοῖται in 1 Cor 6:9, accessed at https://gospelreformation.net/pauls-understanding-of-sexuality.
- "Greek Background to *Malakos*" / Harper, *Shame to Sin*, 98.
- "Philo on Male-Male Sex" / Philo, *On the Life of Abraham,* XXVI. 133-136. *The Works of Philo: Complete and Unabridged*, trans. C.D. Yonge. Accessed at https://www.friendsofsabbath.org/Further_Research/e-books/PHILO.pdf.
- "Contrary to 'Sound Teaching'" / Hays, *Moral Vision of the NT*, 382-383.
- "Authenticity and Virtue" / N. T. Wright, *After You Believe: Why Christian Character Matters* (New York: HarperCollins, 2010), 56-57.
- "The Message of Hope in Romans" / Michael F. Bird, *Romans* (Grand Rapids: Zondervan, 2016), 69.

CHAPTER 13

- "Power to Break Free from Sin" / Douglas J. Moo, *NIV Application Commentary: Romans* (Grand Rapids: Zondervan, 2000), 259.
- "The Spirit and the Flesh" / Paul Achtemeier, *Romans* (Atlanta: John Knox Press, 1985), 132.
- "Self-Control: Empowered by the Spirit" / Christopher J.H. Wright, *Cultivating the Fruit of the Spirit: Growing in Christlikeness* (Downers Grove, IL: IVP Press, 2017), 146.
- "The Work of the Holy Spirit" / Philip D. Kenneson, *Life on the Vine: Cultivating the Fruit of the Spirit* (Downers Grove: InterVarsity Press, 1999), 225-227.

- "Self-Denial: Martyrdom *vs* Freedom" / Wesley Hill, "The Long Defeat," (online), accessed at https://www.baylor.edu/content/services/document.php/277021.pdf%20Feb%2019.

- "Cause Your Fruit to Ripen in My Life" / Wright, *Cultivating the Fruit of the Spirit*, 13.

CHAPTER 14

- "Please Don't Minimize" / Wesley Hill "The Long Defeat."

- "Gospel-Centered Support" / Christopher Yuan, "Why 'God and the Gay Christian' Is Wrong About the Bible and Same-Sex Relationships," *Christianity Today* (June 9, 2014).

- "The Loving Opposition" / Stanton L. Jones, "The Loving Opposition," *Christianity Today* (July 19, 1993), accessed at https://www.christianitytoday.com/ct/1993/july-19/loving-opposition.html.

- "Going Forward" / Ron Sider, "Tragedy, Tradition, and Opportunity in the Homosexuality Debate," (Nov 18, 2014).

- "Restoring Spiritual Friendship" / Wilson, *Mere Sexuality*, 114.

- "Faithful Witness" / Beth Felker Jones, "Radical Faithfulness." (online), accessed at https://www.baylor.edu/content/services/document.php/277023.pdf.

CHAPTER 15

- "Slavery and True Freedom" / Terence E. Fretheim, *Exodus* (Louisville, KY: John Knox Press, 1991), 20.

- "About Gender Roles" / Matthew Mason, "Man and Woman He Created Them," *Bulletin of Ecclesial Theology* 1.1 (2014): 42.

- "Gender and Language" / Abigail Favale, *The Genesis of Gender: A Christian Theory* (San Francisco: Ignatius Press, 2022), 43.

- "Where to Find Truth" / Randy Alcorn, "God's Revealed Truth Is Something We Discover, Not Invent," *Eternal Perspective Ministries* (blog), Oct 20, 2017, accessed at https://www.epm.org/blog/2017/Oct/20/gods-revealed-truth.

- "It Really Helped . . ." / Rosaria Champagne Butterfield, *The Secret Thoughts of an Unlikely Convert*, 177.

- "God Is Love" / DeYoung, *What Does the Bible Really Teach?*, 122-123.

- "Why Bother with the Old Testament?" / Christopher J.H. Wright, *Old Testament Ethics for the People of God* (Downers Grove, IL: InterVarsity, 2004), 46.

- "Faithfulness: Alternative to Procreation?" / Sean McDowell, "Book Review: Scripture, Ethics & The Possibility of Same-Sex Relationships," Nov 1, 2018, accessed at https://seanmcdowell.org/blog/book-review-scripture-ethics-the-possibility-of-same-sex-relationships.

SCRIPTURE INDEX

Genesis 91, 92, 100, 111, 245, 346, 365
  1 *91, 141, 266*
  1–2 *20, 97, 102, 104, 109, 110, 114*
  1:1 *95*
  1:20-21 *100*
  1:22 *59*
  1:26-28 *98, 126*
  1:27 *61, 95, 97, 112, 120, 158*
  1:27-28 *138, 267*
  1:28 *59, 106*
  1:31 *95*
  2 *96, 101, 146, 255, 346*
  2:7 *100,*
  2:15 *106*
  2:18 *96, 98, 105*
  2:18-24 *267*
  2:20 *112*
  2:20-24 *98*
  2:22-24 *112, 138*
  2:24 *60, 158*
  3 *107, 108, 110, 345*
  5:1 *106*
  6:19 *106*
  12:1-3 *338*
  12:3 *153*
  13:13 *129*
  15:18 *142*
  18:1-8 *128*
  18:2 *133*
  18:7 *133*
  18:20 *130*
  19 *127, 130, 134-135*
  19:1-3 *128*
  19:4 *134*
  19:4-5 *128*
  19:5 *133, 142*
  27:4,9,14 *142*
  29:14 *112*
  33:4 *112*
  38:27-30 *339*

Exodus 60, 341
  20:4 *100*
  20:12 *61*
  20:14 *60*
  21:5 *142*
  28:6-8 *364*
  30:31-38 *364*
  34:15 *142*
  39:4-5 *364*

Leviticus 135, 136, 137, 139, 146, 156, 205, 338, 359, 361, 400
  11:44-45 *52*
  15:19-33 *364*
  17-26 *60, 135, 137*
  17:10 *137*
  18 *12, 131, 146, 402*
  18:1-5 *136*
  18:6-18 *156*
  18:20 *139, 145*
  18:21 *139, 156*
  18:22 *131, 136, 139, 145, 157, 207, 283, 290, 291, 295, 394, 400*
  18:23 *139, 156*
  18:24 *139, 141*
  18:26 *140*
  19:2 *139*
  19:13 *137*
  19:18 *142, 360*
  19:19 *137*
  19:28 *137*
  20 *11, 296, 402*
  20:13 *125, 131, 136, 138, 207, 283, 291, 295, 400*
  24:19-21 *94*
  28:18 *137*

Numbers
  12:1 *339*
  15:32-36 *140*

Deuteronomy 350
  14:3-21 *137*

  22:22-29 *207*
  23:1 *161, 349*

Joshua
  2:1ff *339*

Judges
  19 *134-135*
  19:22 *142*
  19:23 *133*
  20:2 *350*

Ruth
  1:4 *339, 349*
  1:14-17 *145*

1 Samuel
  10:1 *145*
  11:1 *142*
  15:17-19,26 *144*
  17:45-47 *144*
  18 *143, 144*
  18:3 *142*
  18:16 *144*
  18:22 *144*
  20:16-17, 42 *145*
  20:30-31 *144*
  20:42 *145*
  23:16-18 *145*

2 Samuel
  1:26 *142*
  5:1 *112*
  7:1ff *145*
  11:3 *339*
  19:11-12 *112*

1 Kings
  5:1 *144*

1 Chronicles
  11:1 *112*

Psalms 20
  8:3-8 *126*
  19:1 *95, 261*

68:4-6 *327*
84:11 *116*
115 *262*
119:97 *142*
121 *315*
147:5 *21*

Proverbs
2:13-14 *362-363*
5:15-20 *356*
6:16-19 *138*
14:12 *18*
17:19 *142*

Isaiah
1:9-23 *130*
2:2-4 *339*
8:3 *82*
8:18 *82*
53 *253*
56 *350*
56:1-8 *350*
64:8 *116*
66:13 *116*

Jeremiah
10:23 *18*
11:15 *363*
16:1 *82*
17:9 *363*
23:14 *130*

Ezekiel
16:49 *130*
16:50-51 *131*
18:10-13 *137*
22:6-12 *137*
22:11 *131*
24:15-17 *83*
24:18-24 *83*
33:26 *131*
44:5-7 *137*

Daniel
1:3-7 *83*
1:21 *83*

Hosea 60
2:2 *83*

5:14 *116*
13:8 *116*

Joel
2:28 *254*
2:28-32 *252, 340*

Amos
1:6 *254*
9:11-12 *251*

Matthew 183
5:3-12 *363*
5:17-20 *20, 147, 342*
5:18-19 *155*
5:21-48 *155, 342*
5:43-48 *62*
6:24 *26*
6:33 *54, 100, 352, 379*
7:28-29 *20*
10:37-38 *54*
12:1ff *342*
12:48-49 *381*
15:17-20 *146, 152*
15:19 *147*
19 *104, 114, 159, 245*
19:1-9 *394*
19:4-5 *61, 103, 138, 157*
19:8 *108, 346*
19:9 *381*
19:10 *81, 162*
19:12 *81, 84, 158, 160, 349, 357, 379*
22:30 *85, 133, 373*
23 *117*
23:23 *162*
28:8-10 *339*
28:18 *21*
28:19 *251*

Mark
1:15 *342*
7:18-23 *360*
7:21 *147*
8:31-34 *89*
8:34-35 *19, 54*
10 *331*

10:29-30 *89, 102, 327*
12:25 *133*

Luke
2:1-7 *224*
2:36-37 *101*
4:16-21 *341*
4:18-19 *254*
6:26-27 *62*
13:34 *117*
14:26-27 *54, 89*
16:13 *26*
18:18-23 *19*
24:9-12 *339*
24:37-39 *133*
24:47 *339*

John
1:17 *11*
2:1ff *81*
3:3,5 *308, 363*
3:16 *302*
4:1ff *41*
4:39 *339*
5:1ff *342*
7:24 *40*
8 *13*
8:1-11 *12, 20*
8:34 *308, 341*
8:44 *263*
10:10 *302*
14:15 *20, 345*
14:21 *54*
16:12-13 *20*
17:17 *184*

Acts 245
2:17-21 *252, 344*
2:27 *340*
8 *349*
8:5ff *252*
8:26-40 *350*
10 *252-253, 360*
15 *163, 245-256*
15:22-29 *339*
16:37 *191*
17 *273*
17:18 *241*

17:22-34 *261*
17:30 *254*
18:11 *377*
18:26 *344*
19:21 *258*
22:25 *191*
24:25 *225*

Romans *259*
1 *17, 104, 130, 208, 258, 263, 265, 281, 295, 355*
1:11-12 *258*
1:18-32 *25, 257-279, 394*
1:26-27 *62, 138, 152, 207, 237, 400*
6:1-7 *335*
8:22-23 *313*
9:1-3 *330*
11:24 *271*
12:1-2 *263*
12:17-21 *62*
13:1-7 *11*
14:1 *277*
14:5-6 *360*
14:17 *31, 88*
15:23-26 *258*

1 Corinthians
2:3 *32*
5:1 *10, 141*
5:9-13 *8, 10, 29, 43, 141, 306*
5:3-5, *365*
6:9-11 *43, 62, 109, 147, 152, 186, 252, 281-289, 342, 395, 397, 401*
6:12-20 *393*
6:19 *314, 363*
7 *84, 162, 373-382, 383-391*
7:3-5 *72, 255, 344*
7:7 *80, 160*
7:9 *309, 330, 357*
7:12 *257*

7:17 *81, 84*
7:21 *341*
7:25-28 *101, 258*
7:26 *80*
7:32-35 *81, 356*
9:5 *330*
9:19-23 *163*
11:4 *344*
11:5-6 *297*
14:28-34 *297*
14:37 *257*
15:33 *352*

2 Corinthians
5:17 *301, 303*
7:10 *370*

Galatians *185, 318*
1:10 *141*
2:20 *27, 315, 363*
3:21 *274*
3:28 *73, 297*
4:16 *357*
5 *359*
5:6 *360*
5:13-21 *385*
5:22-24 *225, 309, 314, 363, 381*

Ephesians
2:10 *302*
2:19 *87*
3:16-19 *316, 317*
4:19 *110*
4:20-24 *110*
4:28 *24*
5:23-33 *97, 390*

Colossians *188*
1:13-14 *301*
3:5 *25, 357*
3:9-10 *266, 370*
3:17 *386*

1 Thessalonians
4:3-6 *353*
4:11-12 *159*

1 Timothy *295*
1:9-11 *289-291*
1:10 *62, 152, 397*

2 Timothy
2:22 *394*
3:16-17 *184, 251*

Titus
1:3 *155, 342*
1:8 *309*

Philemon *341*
15-17 *297*

Hebrews *152*
1:1-4 *24*
13:4 *15, 58-59, 109, 344*

James *152*
1:13-15 *353, 362*
5:16 *317, 332*

1 Peter
2:9-12 *32, 52*
2:18–3:7 *188*

2 Peter
2:6-7 *132, 134, 281*

1 John
1:1-4 *102*
4:8 *52*

Jude
6-8 *132-134*
7 *152, 281*

Revelation *185*
14:4 *190*
21:2-4 *303*

INDEX OF PERSONS & SUBJECTS

abortion, 38, 69, 192

abuse, sexual, 17, 147, 188, 206, 220n, 281, 318

Adam and Eve, 92-93, 109, 111-112, 346; sameness and differentiation, 96-100, 103, 106; more than "kinship bond," 111-112, 114, 365; meaning of Adam's "aloneness," 96-98, 103, 106,121n, 327, 407n, 410n

adam, Heb for "human," 78, 112, 122n

adultery, 6, 12, 15, 19, 20, 29, 33n, 50, 60, 62, 65, 71, 74, 75n, 94, 113, 114, 127, 130, 133, 134, 137, 138-141, 147, 155-156, 161, 187, 192, 199, 245-246, 252, 255, 278n, 289-290, 293, 351, 360, 364, 399

"affirming," terminology, 8, 334-335, 368-370

Agathon of Athens, 198, 199n, 206, 211-212, 216, 218, 221n, 222, 409n

Alcibiades, 288, 290

alone, Adam's original setting "not good," *See* loneliness

Aristophanes, 211-217, 233

androgynous/*androgynos*, 161, 212-213, 221n

Aphrodite, 27, 213, 216, 288

Aristotle, 188, 191, 202, 215, 218, 220, 223, 271, 278n, 312, 314, 341, 409n

aselgeia, 134

arsēn, 292, 400

arsenokoitēs/arsenokoitai, 43, 281-283, 289, 291-292, 294-295, 298n, 299n, 397, 400-402, 404n

Artemis, 25

Athens, 32, 65, 154, 193, 195, 198, 199n, 200n, 204, 206, 214, 220n, 224, 226, 227, 229, 241, 261, 273, 356

bathing/bathhouse, 196, 202, 226, 286

beards, *See* hair, facial

beauty, 27, 161, 165n, 170, 204, 217, 285, 290, 291

bestiality, 60, 62, 65, 74, 112, 114, 137, 139-141, 147, 157, 161, 253, 293, 360, 364

Bible
  authority of, 9, 16, 20-21, 28, 49, 148, 256
  misuse of, 10-11, 20, 386
  relation to experience, 6, 20, 161-162, 250, 256, 345

bigot/bigotry, 19, 21, Ch 2 (37-55), 94, 122n, 151, 368

Boeothian "yoke-mates", 198

Caesar, Julius, 198, 223, 231, 243n

Callicratidas, 287-288, 298n

castration, 159, 160, 273, 89, 154, 158, 160, 252, 328, 332, 356, 357, 381, 384, 385

celibacy, 18, 84, 85, 154, 158, 160, 252, 328, 381, 384-385

   not to be confused with purity, 89, 356, 357, 380, 393-395

Chrysostom, John, 19

church, Ch 14 (301-316)

   duty to teach biblical truth, 14, 23, 31, 33, 63, 72, 73, 83, 93, 116, 155, 184, 245, 259, 267, 324-325

   failure to give moral guidance, 5, 8, 13, 369

   historic view of same-sex activity, 16-17, 29, 45, 70-71, 72

   relationship to state, 9-11, 28, 30, 125-126, 140-141

silence on violence to LGBTQ+ community, 8, 11, 326, 331, 402

   support center for spiritual growth, 49, 102, 369, 381, 403

church discipline, 34n

Christian Nationalism, 8, 20, 30, 34n, 55n

Cicero, 202, 229, 231, 240, 244n

civil law and Christian ethics, 9-11, 27-29

Corinth, 8, 10-11, 29-30, 32, 43, 80, 101, 140, 198n, 199n, 226, 258, 282, 289, 295, 309, 318, 377-380, 382n, 383-386

Cybele, cult of, 165n, 198, 273

Damon and Pythias, 198

David-Jonathan relationship, 142-146

Dawkins, Richard, 118, 119

Diana, *See* Artemis

diatribe

   claim of Paul's use in Rom 1, 273-276

Dio Cassius, 231-232, 243n

Diogenes Laertius, 286, 290

disciple/discipleship, 7, 19, 20, 24, 54, 63, 77

divorce, 28-29, 34n, 41, 55n, 61, 66n, 68, 69, 78, 83, 84, 88, 90n, 100, 103, 104, 108, 114, 155, 158, 160, 187, 189n, 257, 315, 320, 324, 327, 331-332, 346, 365, 373, 376-379, 381, 382n, 384-389, 394

Dolezal, Rachel, 117-118

drunkenness, 252, 377

effeminacy, 165n, 192, 195, 202, 214, 225, 227, 234, 235, 243n, 272-273, 278n, 282, 285-286, 287, 292, 294, 400

Elagabalus, 198, 232, 243n

enkrateia/enkratēs, 225, 309-310, 312, 314, 316n

INDEX OF PERSONS & SUBJECTS

epithymia, 353
erastēs, 195, 202, 211, 216-217, 227, 288, 293, 294
erōmenos, 195, 202, 211, 214, 216-217, 227, 288, 294
Eros, god of love, 27, 51, 101, 211, 212, 215
erōs, 211, 236, 258, 286, 290, 390
Erōtes by Pseudo-Lucian, 186, 200n, 218, 286, 298n, 299n
eunuch, 81, 101, 113-114, 122n, 158, 160
Eve, 60, 92, 99, 103, 109, 111-112, 346, 365
ēzer, 98, 99, 112, 121n

fate, 239-241, 244n
feelings and morality, 33, 50, 116, 240, 249-250, 256, 326-327, 329-330, 353-356, 361, 394, 399, 405n
fluidity, sexual/gender, *See* spectrum theory of sexual identity
fornication, *See porneia*

Galba, 198, 200n, 223
Ganymede, 221n
gender, 4, 5, 44
Genesis
   "image of God" borne by both male and female, 96-98
   importance of Creation Story, 65, 74-75, Ch 5 (91-123)
   normative for male-female marriage, 20, 59-61, 92-95, 102-104
   sexual differentiation, 97, 99, 106, 111-115, 115-120
   distorted view in Gushee, 104-111
Genderbread Person, 173-174, 180n
graffiti, 188
Greek
   chart of LGBTQ+ activities, 198
   sexual ethics, 27, 58, Chs 8 & 9 (183-222)
   paiderastia, 206, 211, 217, 221n, 227, 235, 243n, 400, 409n
   same-sex "marriage", 13, 17, 58, 70, 191, 194, 197, 198, 199n, Ch 9 (201-222), 229
"Greek love," 193, 243n
gymnasium, 235, 271

Hadrian, 198, 234-236
hair
   cephalic, 179, 272-273, 285-286,

facial, 173, 179, 199, 200n, 288

heterosexuality, 193, 228, 230, 237, 352, *See also* marriage, sexual orientation

Hercules, 200n, 218

Holiness Code, 12, 45, 60, 61, 94, 131, 135, 137, 139-141, 145-148, 156, 158, 163, 206, 245, 265, 289, 295, 349, 360, 364, 400

Holland, Tom, 189

Holy Spirit, Ch 13 (301-316)
    Indwelling presence, 8, 49, 63, 249-250, 317
    role in divine revelation, 20, 141, 162, 257, 345
    source of spiritual life, 31, 88-89, 306, 370n-371n
    supplier of moral strength, 309-311, 314, 315-316, 326, 332, 367, 381, 403

Homer, 153

homophobia, 11, 12, 19, 126, 163, 368, 405n

homosexual/homosexuality
    orientation vs behavior, 4, 22, 42, 47-49, 348, 353, 399
    origin of term, 135, 209, 290-299, 347-348, 397-403
    translation issues, 282-289, 397-403
    use of term, 4, 47-49

idolatry, 25-27, 127, *See also* Ch 11 (257-279)
    ancient cultures, 249, 252, 262
    dehumanizing effect, 68
    link to sexual sin, 27, 260-268
    variety of forms, 69, 82, 101, 127, 260, 303, 308

incest, 11, 34n, 53, 60, 62, 74, 105, 114, 130, 137, 147, 156, 157, 161, 199n, 253, 255, 299n, 360, 364

ish/ishah, 20, 100, 112, 114, 122n

Jerusalem Conference, 248-250, 253, 255-256, 339

Jesus
    life as single (unmarried) person, 51, 80-82, 101, 245, 315, 377, 379-380, 381, 386
    on same-sex relationships, 20, 40, 61, 125, 147, Ch 7 (151-165), 209, 245-246, 342, 345, 360

Jews/Judaism (on same-sex relationships), 16, 21, 71-72, 74, 125, 139-140, 163, 193, 197, 266, 290, 311

judging, 367-368
    appropriate moral judgments, 29-30, 40, 54, 305-306, 394
    inappropriate judgments, 49, 304, 402

INDEX OF PERSONS & SUBJECTS

kata physin, 271, 272, 356
Kertbeny, Karl Maria, 299n
Klinefelter syndrome, 123, 171

law, *See* civil law and Christian ethics
lesbian/lesbianism, 4, 7-8, 10-13, 18, 19, 24, 27, 42, 53, 65, 66n, 70, 78, 105, 109, 126, 137-138, 140, 151, 156, 158, 186, 193, 207, 213, 215-216, 242n, 265, 268-269, 272, 278n, 287l, 291, 321, 324, 334, 345, 351, 357, 370n, 402
loneliness
   nature of Adam's, 78, 96-101, 103, 106, 121n, 327
   psychological/emotional, 96-98, 106, 114
love
   God's love, 8, 52, 53, 55, 91, 189, 263, 276, 301-302, 311, 316-317, 341, 362, 395, 403
   love and truth/repentance, Ch 1 (9-35), 341-342, 345, 369-370, 403
   love in friendship relations, 142-146, 313, 331
   love for God, 162, 261, 284, 314
   love for LGBTQ+ persons, 21, 23-25, 102, 326, 328, 333-335, 357-358
   married love, 51, 57, 59, 68-69, 105, 226, 390
   misdirected love, 50, 54-55, 101, 190, 193, 206, 211-219, 221n-222n, 227-228, 233-236, 241, 285-295, 297, 322, 363, 380, 385
Lucian of Samosata, *See* Pseudo-Lucian
Luther, Martin, 19

malakos/malakoi, 43, 195, 227, Ch 12 (281-300), 397, 400, 410n
marriage
   heterosexual, 15-16, 22, 23, 27, 29, 58-59, 65, Ch 4 (67-76), 91, 105, 109-111, 157, 161, 226, 311
   homosexual, 16, 22, 29, 42, 55, 58, 157, 208-210, 215, 228-230, 236
moichos, 15, 58, 59, 71-72, 283, cf.214
moral law
   defined by God's character/holinesss, 138, 146-148, 342
   relation to ceremonial law, 9, 135, 147, 363-365
Movie: "1946", Appendix D (397-403)
Musonius Rufus, 185, 199n

nature, *See kata physin, para physin*
Nero, 185, 198, 200n, 209, 221n, 230-232, 239, 243n, 265, 270, 281

Orestes and Pylades, 198, 200n, 218
orientation, sexual, 48, 102, 105
orientation vs activity, sexual, 48, 71, 353, 361-362, 394

paiderastēs/paiderastein, 285
para physin, 270-272, 285, 288, 355, 410n
passivity, sexual, 186, 192-193, 195, 215, 225, 227, 228, 234, 241, 243n, 266, 282-284, 286, 292, 400, 401
pathicus, See passivity, sexual
Paul
   life as single person, 51, 80-84, 90n, 101, 160, 378-380
   See Chs 11 & 12 (257-300)
Pausanias of Athens, 198, 199n, 206, 211-212, 213, 216-218, 221n, 232, 233, 238, 409n
pedophilia, 17, 52, 65, 195, 203, 237, 293, 338
penetration, sexual, 161
   anal, 13, 128, 141, 189, 182, 195, 202, 203, 227, 266, 270, 288, 299n, 338, 400
   intercrural, 227
   oral, 227, 266, 321
Peter
   ethical instruction, 31-32, 188, 190, 248-256, 375
   reference to Sodom, 132, 134, 281
Philosophy, Stanford Encyclopedia of, 299, 406
pimp, 196, 206, 296
Plato
   view of same-sex relationships, 154, 164n, 198, 199n, 200n, Ch 9 (201-222), 233, 235, 238, 239, 241, 244n, 271, 278n, 341, 348, 409n
polygamy, 20, 69, 103, 109, 253-254, 256n, 360
Pompeii, 72, 188, 198, 226
porneia, 43, 55, 71-72, 147, 245, 255-256, 293, 333, 339, 360, 378
pornos, 15, 58, 59
procreation, *See* reproduction
prostitute/prostitution, 15, 17, 21, 24, 58, 65, 73, 74, 102, 134, 139, 191, 193, 194, 196, 199n, 201, 203, 205, 208, 223, 225, 226, 237, 243n, 255, 269, 278n, 282, 283, 284, 292, 293, 294, 296, 299n, 338, 347, 360, 367, 377, 401, 402, 404n
Pseudo-Lucian, 218, 286
purity, sexual, *See* celibacy
Pylades and Orestes, 198, 218

repentance, 14, 19, 24, 63, 110, 147, 251, 330, 332, 342, 354, 357, 364, 369-370, 395, 403

INDEX OF PERSONS & SUBJECTS

reproduction, 51, 63, 97, 102-106, 111-113, 160, 186, 214-215, 272, 288, 352, 365

Roman

   chart of LGBTQ+ activities, 198

   sexual ethics, Ch 8 (183-200) & 10 (223-244)

   same-sex "marriage", 226-233

Romans, Epistle to the, 130, 152, 164n, 165n, 222n, Ch 11 (257-280), 283, 297, 307-308, 313, 323, 355, 370n, 408n, 410n

Sacred Band of Thebes, 198, 199n, 200, 218

same-sex partnerships

   known in antiquity, 43, 70, 186, 191, 194, 197-198, 199n, Ch 9 (201-222), Ch 10 (223-244), 265, 269, 296-297, 338-340, 377, 401-403

   recent shift in attitude with regard to, 19, 70, 292, 351

   recent legalization, 59, 69

Scripture, *See* Bible

self-control, 80, 81, 155, 194, 225, Ch 13 (301-316), 326, 381, 403, 410n

singles, Excursus (77-90), 101, 324, 328-329, 331, Appendix A (373-282), 406n

slaves/slavery

   connection to sexual abuse, 20, 59, 72-74, 83, Ch 8 (183-200), 205, 206, 208, 225, 237, 239, 242n, 243n, 269-270

   not approved in Scripture, 107, Ch 8 (183-200)

   not parallel to same-sex relationships, 253-254, 256n, 296, 340-342

Socrates, 199n, 211, 223, 239, 288

Sodom, 127-135, 142, 148n, 281, 287, 407n

sodomy/sodomite, 129, 282, 283, 287

spectrum theory of sexual identity, 118, 122n, 161, Excursus (167-181), 408n

Stoics/Stoicism, 194, 199n, 240-241, 291, 355

Stott, John R.W., 85, 314

stuprum, 227

Symposium, 154, 199n, 200n, 213-219, 220n, 221n, 222n, 232-233, 288, 299, 348, 409n

temptation, different from sin, 71, 353, 361-362, 394

Thebes, *See* Sacred Band of Thebes

toevah, 12, 131, 135-141, 146, 148n, 363-365

transgender, 7-8, 12, 65,107, 109, 121n, 158-161, 164n, 168, 170, 171, 174, 177, 180n, 198, 228, 232, 243n, 349-350, 377

transitioning, sexual, 122n

Uganda, Anti-Homosexuality Act 2023, 10-11, 33n, 405n

unmarried persons, *See* singles

Valerius Maximus, 198
vase painting, 165n, 200n, 219, 222n
Venus, *See* Aphrodite
virgin/virginity, 69, 85, 101, 109, 130, 170, 190, 225, 231, 233, 258, 304, 379, 382n, 388

Warren Cup, 198, 200n
"Welcoming but not affirming" language, 323, 334, 368-370
Westboro Baptist Church, 370
World Health Organization, 169

Zeus, 25, 154, 212-214, 221n

INDEX OF AUTHORS

Achtemeier, Mark, 21-22, 121n, 204, 220n, 255
Achtemeier, Paul, 303
Ainsworth, Claire, 179, 180
Alcorn, Randy, 351
Altrock, Chris, 122n
Barth, Karl, 262, 359
Belousek, Darrin W. Snyder, 72, 201, 255, 272
Bird, Michael, 297
Bird, Phyllis A., 120
Borelli, Gabriel, 19
Boswell, John, 128, 135, 139, 140, 142, 165n, 204, 210, 212, 215, 216, 219, 220n, 229, 231-236, 283-285, 293, 355
Brisson, Luc, 206
Brooten, Bernadette J., 230, 239
Brownson, James V., 204, 237
Brueggemann, Walter, 149n
Butterfield, Rosaria Champagne, 12, 354
Carnes, Jeffrey, 202, 217
Casanova, José, 44
Chaput, Charles J., 42
Clarke, John R., 190, 200n
Clement, 226
Crompton, Louis, 140, 213, 215, 217, 220n, 238
Dahlen, Sara, 170
Danylak, Barry, 77, 82, 84
Dawkins, Richard, 118, 119
Derrett, J.D.M., 33n
Dershowitz, Alan M., 34n
DeYoung, Kevin, 267, 362

Didache, 188, 336n
Dio Cassius, 231, 232
Dover, K.J., 165n
Dunn, James D.G., 289
Eishtain, Jean Bethke, 54
Elliot, Elizabeth, 89
Elsesser, Kim, 179n
Emba, Christine, 26
Fausto-Sterling, Anne, 123, 169, 171-172
Favale, Abigail, 346
Fee, Gordon, 34n, 184, 252
Fortson, Donald, 129, 278
Foucault, Michel, 168, 210, 237-238, 290, 347
Fox, Robin Lane, 196, 227
Fradd, Matt, 59
Fretheim, Terence E., 341
Gagnon, Robert A.J., 133, 281, 286
Gallagher, Maggie, 14
Gary, Sally, 369
Gibbon, Edward, 231
Glasser, Arthur F., 97
Gomes, Peter, 139
Grams, Rollin, 129
Grube, G.M.A., 221n
Gushee, David P., 16, 34, 53, 104-111, 127-130, 132, 134, 136-138, 146, 199n, 204, 223, 268-270, 283-285, 289, 293, 345
Hamilton, Adam, 17, 137, 199n, 204, 256n, 284
Hammond, Guy, 157, 408
Harper, Kyle, 183, 190, 196, 229, 241, 256n, 258, 263, 286, 401

Hays, Gabriel, 122, 407
Hays, Richard, 91, 127, 133, 154, 162, 289, 294-295, 351, 381
Hicks, John Mark, 178
Hill, Wesley, 283, 313, 320
Holland, Tom, 53, 266
Horrell, J. Scott, 85
Hubbard, Thomas K., 199n-200n, 219, 238
Hunter, James Davison, 93
Hurtado, Larry, 185
Instone-Brewer, David, 66n
Jobes, Karen H., 76n
Johnson, Luke Timothy, 161-163, Excursus (245-256)
Jones, Beth Felker, 333
Jones, Stanton L., 326
Josephus, 188, 270, 272
Justin, 311
Juvenal, 230, 233-234, 402
Keen, Karen R., 17, 111, 114, 365, 366
Keller, Tim, 14, 57, 240, 390
Kenneson, Philip D., 310
Killermann, Sam, 180n
Lewis, C.S., 28-29, 34n
Livy, 165n
Loader, William, 145-146, 205, 208, 257
Longman, Tremper, 327
Lucian/Pseudo-Lucian, 186, 200n, 218, 286-288, 298n, 299n
Martial, 233, 243
Mason, Matthew, 106, 343

Maximus (of Tyre), 198, 235
McDowell, Sean, 365
McKnight, Scot, 186, 246, 333-334
McLaren, Brian, 349
Miller, Paul D., 34n
Moo, Douglas J., 133, 278n, 302
Moore, Russell, 11
Newbigin, Lesslie, 92
Pauls, Dale, 220n
Peterson, Brian Neil, 104, 121, 131, 148
Philo, 188, 210, 284, 285, 287, 298n
Pickett, Brent, 70
Plato, 153-154, 198, 199n, 202, Ch 9 (201-222), 223, 233, 235, 238-239, 241, 278n, 3451, 348
Punzo, Vincent C., 64
Reeves, Rodney, 158
Reichenbach, Bruce, 80
Reynolds, Jim, 69, 147
Richter, Sandra, 93
Ricketts, Colin, 225
Rogers, Bret, 87
Romm, James, 199n, 200n, 219
Sacks, Jonathan, 67-68
Sarna, Nahum M., 100
Scroggs, Robin, 17, 61, 165n, 203, 205, 219-220, 223, 293, 295-296, 401
Sider, Ron, 22, 328
Smith, Mark D., 219
Sprinkle, Preston, 117, 237
Stassen, Glen H., 35n
Stone, Lawrence, 67
Stott, John R.W., 23, 133
Stuart, Douglas, 252
Stuart, Elizabeth, 66n
Suetonius, 198, 223, 231
Tacitus, 243n, 311
Taylor, J. Glen, 48
Taylor, Magdalene J., 192
Thielman, Frank, 269
Turner, Philip, 79, 83
Tushnet, Eve, 245, 250
Ukleja, Michael, 62
Vines, Matthew, 149n, 255, 324
Volf, Miroslav, 31
Wadeson, Douglas, 159
Waters, Guy, 284
Wenham, David, 81
White, Mel, 139
Willard, Dallas, 33
Wilson, Todd, 154, 331
Wright, Christopher J.H., 260, 277, 288, 306, 314, 363
Wright, Colin, 175
Wright, David F., 137, 291
Wright, N.T., 110, 295, 381, 398
Yancey, Philip, 74
Yuan, Christopher, 174, 324

ACKNOWLEDGMENTS

No book has ever been written by one person. Even if only one name is on the cover, no book has ever come from its author alone.

This book grows directly out of a conversation with some ministers, Christian educators, and church consultants in April 2022. We shared various concerns we have about church health generally and the impact of the cultural pressures being felt in churches to adopt an affirming posture toward same-sex relationships. At that meeting, Doug Peters "assigned" the task of writing a book on LGBTQ+ issues to me. It was likely more in jest than a serious charge that day.

As I became quite focused on the research and writing reflected here, Doug graciously consented to read the manuscript in process. His suggestions, corrections, and encouragements were invaluable. His background in both biblical studies and pastoral ministry are consistent with what this volume seeks to link together – loving people sincerely and taking scripture seriously.

John Mark Hicks also agreed to read the manuscript as it moved from draft to draft. A former student of mine in undergraduate days, he has long since made me his student. He thinks deeply and meticulously. He cares about people genuinely and lovingly.

Neither Doug nor John Mark should be held accountable to every position expressed here. These are my conclusions that were tested in conversation after conversation with these two faithful brothers and dear friends.

Karl Halverson and his staff at College Press – especially Angela Blethen – have supported this project without reservation.

Finally, I thank my wife – to whom this book is dedicated – for her unstinting support for everything I ever felt called to undertake in service to Christ. For six decades, she encouraged me to write. She proofread for me. She challenged fuzzy thinking and awkward grammar. She prayed for the things we generated together to bless readers. I believe this book is the one she felt the two of us were most obligated to produce.

Because she died of an aggressive cancer she had battled for two years shortly before the book's release, she saw it only in pre-publication form. It pleased her that we had completed it as our last joint writing project. My grief over her death is still so fresh that in writing this sentence tears are flowing down my cheeks and blurring my ability to read the words.

May God be honored by all that has gone into producing this book. May at least one soul be rescued from the false path some wish to justify in their revisionist readings of what Scripture has said for more than 3,000 years on this subject.

—RUBEL SHELLY

www.ingramcontent.com/pod-product-compliance
Lightning Source LLC
Chambersburg PA
CBHW080833230426
43665CB00021B/2829